Internet Intermediaries and Trade Mark Rights

Despite the apparent advantages of the internet, there is little debate that it facilitates intellectual property infringements, including infringements of trade mark rights. Infringers not only remain hidden by the anonymity the internet provides but also take advantage of its increasing reach and the associated challenges with regard to cross-border enforcement of rights. These factors, among others, have rendered the internet a growing source of counterfeit and other infringing products. It has, therefore, become necessary for right holders to shift their focus from individual infringers to internet intermediaries, such as Internet Service Providers (ISPs), hosts and navigation providers, which are responsible in numerous ways for making content promoting infringements available to internet users.

In light of these developments, this book conducts a comprehensive analysis of the liability of such intermediaries for trade mark infringements and considers the associated issues and challenges in the diverging approaches under which liability may be imposed. At present, however, neither UK trade mark law nor English common-law principles relating to accessorial liability provide a basis to hold internet intermediaries liable for trade mark infringements. As such, this book considers approaches adopted in some of the Continental European countries and the US in order to propose reforms aimed at addressing gaps in the existing legal framework. This book also examines alternative remedies, such as notice and takedown and injunctions, and discusses the associated shortcomings of each of these remedies.

Althaf Marsoof is an Assistant Professor of Law at the Nanyang Business School, Nanyang Technological University, Singapore.

Routledge Research in Intellectual Property

Available:

Well-Known Trade Marks
A Comparative Study of Japan and the EU
Hiroko Onishi

Contemporary Issues in Pharmaceutical Patent Law
Setting the Framework and Exploring Policy Options
Edited by Bryan Mercurio and Daria Kim

Intellectual Property, Finance and Corporate Governance
Janice Denoncourt

Protecting Intellectual Property in the Arabian Peninsula
The GCC States, Jordan and Yemen
David Price and Alhanoof AlDebasi

Biodiversity, Genetic Resources and Intellectual Property
Developments in Access and Benefit Sharing
Edited by Kamalesh Adhikari and Charles Lawson

Pharmaceutical Patent Protection and World Trade Law
The Unresolved Problem of Access to Medicines
Jae Sundaram

Patent Pools, Competition Law and Biotechnology
Devdatta Malshe

Copyright Law and Derivative Works
Regulating Creativity
Omri Rachum-Twaig

The Patentability of Software
Software as Mathematics
Anton Hughts

Internet Intermediaries and Trade Mark Rights

Althaf Marsoof

Routledge
Taylor & Francis Group
LONDON AND NEW YORK

First published 2019
by Routledge
2 Park Square, Milton Park, Abingdon, Oxon OX14 4RN

and by Routledge
605 Third Avenue, New York, NY 10017

First issued in paperback 2021

Routledge is an imprint of the Taylor & Francis Group, an informa business

Publisher's Note
The publisher has gone to great lengths to ensure the quality of this reprint but points out that some imperfections in the original copies may be apparent.

British Library Cataloguing-in-Publication Data
A catalogue record for this book is available from the British Library

Library of Congress Cataloging-in-Publication Data
Names: Marsoof, Althaf, author.
Title: Internet intermediaries and trade mark infringements / Althaf Marsoof.
Description: Abingdon, Oxon [UK] ; New York, NY : Routledge, 2019. | Series: Routledge research in intellectual property | Includes bibliographical references and index.
Identifiers: LCCN 2019005576 | ISBN 9780815382461 (hardback)
Subjects: LCSH: Trademark infringement. | Trademarks—Law and legislation. | Internet service providers—Law and legislation. | Intellectual property.
Classification: LCC K1568 .M37 2019 | DDC 346.04/88—dc23
LC record available at https://lccn.loc.gov/2019005576

ISBN 13: 978-1-03-224099-2 (pbk)
ISBN 13: 978-0-8153-8246-1 (hbk)

DOI: 10.4324/9781351208512

Typeset in Galliard
by Swales & Willis Ltd, Exeter, Devon, UK

Contents

Foreword by Graeme B. Dinwoodie vii
Acknowledgements ix
List of abbreviations xi

1 The internet, intermediaries and trade mark infringements 1

2 Liability under trade mark law 25

3 Accessory liability 47

4 Approaches elsewhere—across the English Channel and the Atlantic 78

5 A proposal for law reforms 104

6 Notice and takedown 131

7 Notice and takedown and its impact on legitimate third-party uses of trade marks 152

8 Injunctions against intermediaries—*legal basis* 176

9 Injunctions against intermediaries—*practical considerations* 204

Bibliography 231
Index 243

Foreword

Graeme B. Dinwoodie

The role of intermediaries whose services are used by others to commit wrongs has been at the forefront of recent public debate regarding regulation of online conduct. Once hailed as the conduits by which to deliver a transformed human existence on a global scale, many online intermediaries have become targets of legislators and commentators dissatisfied with the tenor of contemporary political debate and the potential distortion of both our politics and a fair marketplace.

The realm of intellectual property has not been immune to this debate; indeed, intellectual property has been one of the contexts in which that debate has been most vigorous. Most recently, the European Union adopted a Directive on Copyright in the Digital Single Market that would (in Article 17) impose obligations on a certain group of ISPs to implement technological measures, primarily filtering, to help prevent copyright infringement. According to the European Commission, Article 17 (originally Article 13 in the Commission's proposal) was designed to solve what it called the 'value gap', whereby it was alleged that some user-uploaded content platforms were obtaining revenue from copyright-protected content that should be going to the relevant right holders. But the core of Article 17 is in truth a reallocation of enforcement duties among right holders and intermediaries.

And, in that guise, the proposal has been described by critics in cataclysmic terms. It's going to 'kill the internet', some have charged. Others have called it an instrument for censorship. The UN Special Rapporteur for Freedom of Expression wrote to the EU saying that the proposal was inconsistent with the EU's human rights commitments. And a large group of leading internet thinkers had urged the EU to delete Article 13 from the proposal (although it has now, subject to some modifications, been renumbered and adopted by both the European Parliament and Council as Article 17). Some of the debate might seem technical, but the stakes are high.

As this public policy debate has raged over the last few years, a number of scholars have published important books addressing the topic and illuminating the public discussion. Some have focused on the liability of intermediaries generally for a wide variety of wrongs; others have sought to focus on particular regimes, such as copyright law. Trade mark law has received less focused attention.

Within the United Kingdom and the European Union, although copyright litigation has been more frequent and arguably more high-profile, some of the leading cases have involved trade marks. The Court of Justice's *eBay* decision remains a marker (if a rather vague one) in setting out the variables according to which non-liable intermediaries may remain accountable (to use Martin Husovec's dichotomy) to assist in terminating and potentially preventing infringements. Likewise, it was a trade mark case (*Cartier v Sky*) in which the Supreme Court of the United Kingdom addressed who between the intermediaries and right holders should bear the costs of the 'accountability' regime that has developed. And it is in the field of trade marks (and counterfeits) where we have seen some of the most important systems of private ordering arise, both at the firm level (such as the notice and takedown system operated by eBay) and in broader structured agreements among multiple intermediaries and brand owners (such as the Memorandum of Understanding negotiated under the superintendence of the European Commission).

Despite these developments, and notwithstanding some useful policy reports and law journal articles, trade mark law has not received the focused attention it has deserved. In this informative and eminently readable book, Althaf Marsoof helps to correct this omission. And he does so with an eye to the comparative method that is not only intellectually stimulating but practically vital. There is a reason that large American actors and non-governmental organisations have been so intimately involved in the negotiations concerning the Directive on Copyright in the Digital Single Market. Of course, Europe is a big market on its own terms, but any compromise in the European area will surely serve as a starting position for parallel debates in the United States.

Prof. Marsoof is also attentive to the distinct doctrinal and normative features of trade mark law that might require treating intermediaries facilitating trade mark infringement differently even from how they are treated in the adjacent field of copyright law. The different technological capacity to scale detection of copyright and trade mark infringements might also counsel in favour of a less horizontal approach insofar as that capacity should inform intermediary responsibility. Despite a more comprehensive horizontal harmonisation of trade mark law throughout Europe, and the existence of a unitary regime at the EU level, the Court of Justice appears more ready to address *all* facets of intermediary liability for copyright infringement at the EU level than it has been for trade mark infringement. The reconceptualisation of accessory claims as primary infringements in copyright, but not trade mark, law is the most notable example.

This attention to the particularities of trade marks—to be hugely welcomed for the reasons mentioned above—does not however prevent Prof. Marsoof from commenting in passing on broader systemic features of intellectual property law that make this puzzle harder than it might otherwise be. He thus offers insights into such matters as adjudication of foreign or multiple claims, or the increasing use of fundamental rights to shape intellectual property law. There is much to be learned here.

Graeme B. Dinwoodie
Global Professor of Intellectual Property Law
Chicago-Kent College of Law

Acknowledgements

One afternoon in March 2010, Professor Lionel Bently, addressing a small group of LLM students at the University of Cambridge, announced the ruling of the Court of Justice of the European Union (CJEU) in *Google v Louis Vuitton* [2010] ECR I-02417 and posited that it will shape the landscape of intermediary liability in the European Union (EU). I was one of the students to whom this prophetic remark was made. Not surprisingly, the CJEU's ruling was followed in subsequent cases, including the ruling in *L'Oréal v eBay* [2011] ECR I-06011. According to the CJEU, intermediaries, such as Google, do not commit trade mark infringements because they make no use of trade marks in their 'commercial communication'. Just the week before, however, we had discussed *Rescuecom v Google* 562 F.3d 123 (2009), a case where the United States Court of Appeals for the Second Circuit came to the opposite conclusion on the exact same facts. According to the US court, there was a possibility that Google could be found liable for trade mark infringements and Google did indeed make use of the trade mark in question 'in commerce'. It was these diverging judicial decisions that initially sparked my interest on the topic of internet intermediaries and their liability for trade mark infringements. At the time, little did I know that my new-found interest would be so strong that it would motivate me to give up the public office I held at Sri Lanka's Attorney General's Department and move into full-time academia.

The research that underpins this book began in the autumn of 2014, when I was welcomed into King's College London as a doctoral researcher. Five years later, I find myself penning these words at the Nanyang Technological University in Singapore, where I currently hold an academic position in law in its Business School. As my research progressed over the years, it was influenced and shaped by a multitude of factors, which include the works of legal giants, landmark cases, trends in industrial practice and technological developments, and, of course, Brexit. I trust, as a reader of this book, you will observe these influencing factors as they emerge from its text.

At this point, however, I wish to devote some space to acknowledging and showing gratitude to the human elements that have influenced my research in numerous ways. First and foremost, I am immensely grateful to Professor Tanya Aplin for accepting to become my guide and mentor at King's. The insightful and constructive comments, and invaluable guidance that I received from her throughout my research work, have been immensely helpful in refining my thinking. She was very generous with her time and provided me with instant advice, and pointed me towards useful resources, at the most crucial stages of my work. Most of all, the encouragement and support that I received through her mentorship and friendship were beyond expectations, and continue to this day. I would also like to thank Professor John Philips, whose role was no less important, in guiding my research at King's, especially in the early stages where my thoughts were muddled and less refined. I am also very grateful for the generous funding that was made available to me through the Dickson Poon Scholarship, without which my research, and subsequent book, would have remained a figment of my imagination.

I am also thankful to many individuals who kindly offered me their guidance and support during various stages of my work. In particular, I am grateful to Professor David Llewelyn, for vetting my initial ideas and playing devil's advocate towards the very end; Professors Ira Nathenson and Eric Goldman, for providing critical feedback on my research at the 4th Internet Law Work-in-Progress Symposium in 2014; Cedric Manara, for sharing his insights on notice and takedown from the industry's perspective; Ben Allgrove, for his valuable comments on blocking injunctions; and both Jaani Riordan and Christina Angelopoulos, for sharing drafts of their monographs on internet intermediary liability, even before they were published.

I am grateful to Professor Irene Calboli, who was instrumental in my appointment as a visiting researcher to the Applied Research Centre for Intellectual Assets and the Law in Asia (ARCIALA) at the Singapore Management University (SMU), where I spent several months working on my research. At ARCIALA, I was exposed to numerous talks, workshops and seminars on intermediary liability, which helped with the continued efforts in refining my work. I also wish to acknowledge Benjamin Tham, with whom I became acquainted at SMU, for being a 'critical third-eye' and whose comments tremendously helped me in refining my work even further.

Indeed, these acknowledgements will not be complete without a mention of my friends and family. Chinthaka and Ghazzali, my closest friends since childhood, have never hesitated to extend their emotional support and, importantly, kept me updated about developments back home, whether in sports, politics or entertainment. I am thankful for their companionship. I am ever so grateful to my wife, Farhana, and son, Adil, for their patience and understanding, and putting up with, at times, an annoying husband and grumpy dad. My parents, Saleem and Muneera, have always been supportive of my aspirations. I owe them endlessly for their encouragement and sacrifices, and to them I dedicate this book.

Finally, yet importantly, I extend my thanks to Professor Graeme Dinwoodie, who generously agreed to write the foreword for this book. I also owe thanks to Chloe James and her colleagues at Routledge for their exceptional editorial work.

Singapore
15 April 2019

Abbreviations

ACTA	Anti-Counterfeiting Trade Agreement, signed in October 2011 but still not in force
AG	Advocate General (of the Court of Justice of the European Union)
Brussels I Regulation (Recast)	Regulation (EU) No 1215/2012 of the European Parliament and of the Council of 12 December 2012 on Jurisdiction and the Recognition and Enforcement of Judgments in Civil and Commercial Matters (Recast) [2012] OJ L 351
CDA	Communications Decency Act 1996 (US)
CDPA	Copyright Designs and Patents Act 1988 (UK)
CJEU	Court of Justice of the European Union
Comparative Advertising Directive	Directive 2006/114/EC of the European Parliament and of the Council of 12 December 2006 Concerning Misleading and Comparative Advertising [2006] OJ L 376/21
CA	Court of Appeal of England and Wales
Chilean IP Law	Law 17.336 of 28 August 1970 on Intellectual Property
DMCA	Digital Millennium Copyright Act 1998 (US)
DNS	Domain Name Service
EAASM	European Alliance for Access to Safe Medicines
ECHR	European Convention for the Protection of Human Rights and Fundamental Freedoms 1950
E-Commerce Directive	Directive 2000/31/EC on Certain Legal Aspects of Information Society Services, in Particular Electronic Commerce, in the Internal Market [2000] OJ L 178/1
E-Commerce Regulations	Electronic Commerce (EC Directive) Regulations 2002, SI 2002/2013 (UK)
EEA	European Economic Area
Enforcement Directive	Directive 2004/48/EC of the European Parliament and of the Council of 29 April 2004 on the Enforcement of Intellectual Property Rights [2004] OJ L 157/16
EU	European Union

EU Charter	Charter of Fundamental Rights of the European Union [2000] OJ C364/01
EUIPO	EU Intellectual Property Office
Europol	European Union Agency for Law Enforcement Cooperation
gTLD	Generic Top Level Domain Name
High Court or HC	High Court of England and Wales (unless the context otherwise refers to a court of another jurisdiction)
ICANN	Internet Corporation for Assigned Names and Numbers
ICTSD	International Centre for Trade and Sustainable Development
Info-Soc Directive	Directive 2001/29/EC of the European Parliament and of the Council of 22 May 2001 on the Harmonisation of Certain Aspects of Copyright and Related Rights in the Information Society [2001] OJ L 167/10
INTA	International Trademark Association
IP address(es)	Internet Protocol address(es)
ISP(s)	Internet Service Provider(s)
Lanham Act	Lanham (Trademark) Act 1946 (US)
Liberty Study	C Ahlert, C Marsden and C Yung, How 'Liberty' Disappeared from Cyberspace: The Mystery Shopper Tests Internet Content Self-Regulation (2004) http://pcmlp.socleg.ox.ac.uk/sites/pcmlp.socleg.ox.ac.uk/files/ liberty.pdf (accessed 31 January 2019)
Multatuli Study	S Nas, The Multatuli Project: ISP Notice & Take Down (2004) www-old.bof.nl/docs/researchpaperSANE.pdf (accessed 31 January 2019)
OECD	Organisation for Economic Co-operation and Development
SSCS	Sea Shepherd Conservation Society
SSUK	Sea Shepherd UK Ltd
Technical Standards Directive	Directive (EU) 2015/1535 of the European Parliament and of the Council of 9 September 2015 Laying Down a Procedure for the Provision of Information in the Field of Technical Regulations and of Rules on Information Society Services (Codification) [2015] OJ L 241/1
TEU	Treaty on European Union (Consolidated) [2016] OJ C 202/1>
Trade Marks Directive	Directive 2008/95/EC of the European Parliament and of the Council of 22 October 2008 to Approximate the Laws of the Member States Relating to Trade Marks [2008] OJ L 299/25 (unless the context otherwise refers to a particular version of the Trade Marks Directive, in which case, the reference is prefixed by the year of the directive: e.g. 1988 Trade Marks Directive, 2008 Trade Marks Directive or 2015 Trade Marks Directive)

TRIPS	Agreement on the Trade-Related Aspects of Intellectual Property Rights
TTD	Turkish Telecommunications Directorate
UK	United Kingdom
UNCTAD	United Nations Conference on Trade and Development
Urban and Quilter Study	JM Urban and L Quilter, 'Efficient process or "chilling effects"? Takedown Notices under Section 512 of the Digital Millennium Copyright Act' (2006) 22 *Santa Clara Computer and High-Technology Law Journal* 621
URL(s)	Unified Resource Locator(s)
US	United States of America
WIPO	World Intellectual Property Organization
Withdrawal Agreement	Draft Agreement on the Withdrawal of the United Kingdom of Great Britain and Northern Ireland from the European Union and the European Atomic Energy Community, as Agreed at Negotiators' Level on 14 November 2018, TF50 (2018) 55
WTO	World Trade Organization

1 The internet, intermediaries and trade mark infringements*

The internet has transformed every aspect of human life. In the late 1990s, when it was only beginning to revolutionise the world, the United States (US) Supreme Court defined the internet as 'an international network of interconnected computers'.[1] Five years later, the High Court of Australia, the land's highest court, described the internet as 'ubiquitous, borderless, global and ambient in its nature'.[2] While both these descriptions of the internet are equally accurate, the former highlights its real state, as being a collection of interconnected devices, while the latter is a description of how the internet is perceived by its users, as being something that is omnipresent. It is clear, therefore, that the internet's very definition postulates connectivity, i.e. connectivity between devices, servers and networks all synchronised and harmonious in performing their assigned roles in transforming the internet into the repository of diverse content that it is today. Yet not all that is diverse is legal.

Online content could be unlawful at many levels. Some may offend our most fundamental moral standards and thus attract criminal liability (e.g. child pornography). Others may violate personal rights (e.g. the right to privacy and dignity) and property rights, such as intellectual property rights, thereby giving rise to civil liability, although certain aggravated forms of intellectual property infringements do also attract criminal sanctions.[3] There is no room for doubt that those who create unlawful content ought to be held liable for their actions, as they are directly involved in the commission of wrongdoing. However, this book is not concerned about such individual wrongdoers. Instead, its focus is on intermediaries that are responsible for providing access to, hosting or indexing unlawful content. In addressing the liability of such intermediaries, a conscious choice is made to consider the associated issues and challenges from a trade mark perspective.

* This book reflects the law and political landscape as at 15 April 2019.

1 *Reno v American Civil Liberties Union* 117 S. Ct. 2329 (1997) (*Reno v ACLU*), 2334 (Stevens J).

2 *Dow Jones v Gutnick* [2002] HCA 56, [80] (Gleeson CJ, McHugh, Gummow and Hayne JJ).

3 Agreement on Trade-Related Aspects of Intellectual Property Rights Agreement (TRIPS), Article 61. The text of the agreement is available in Annex 1C of the Marrakesh Agreement Establishing the World Trade Organization 1994.

Defining 'internet intermediaries'

In the 1990s there was a conception that the internet would give rise to 'disintermediation', a catchphrase that was the subject of much academic debate.[4] In essence, disintermediation means the displacement of the middleman.[5] In reality, however, the experience was quite the opposite. But for a few exceptions, the internet saw not only the replacement of traditional intermediaries with their online equivalent but also the emergence of new intermediaries that did not have a comparable offline manifestation.[6] Intermediaries that operate on the internet come in many shapes and sizes,[7] but there is one feature that is common to all of them. That is, they *facilitate* connections between internet users and online content.

Take the example of YouTube and eBay. YouTube permits users to upload audio-visual content on its platform via individual accounts or channels. eBay permits registered sellers on its platform to advertise and publish the availability of products for sale. In this manner, both YouTube and eBay act as intermediaries between internet users, who consume content published on YouTube or purchase products on eBay, and the content that makes such consumption and purchases possible. The focus of this book is on intermediaries like YouTube, which do not themselves generate any content but merely facilitate the transmission, storage or indexing of content created by third parties, i.e. 'third-party content'.

There are three types of intermediaries considered in this book, namely Internet Service Providers (ISPs), hosts and navigation providers. ISPs provide internet users with access to the internet and have been recognised as a distinct category of intermediaries.[8] In essence, ISPs act 'as the gateway through which material is uploaded or downloaded by the end-users'.[9] British Telecom, Sky and TalkTalk are typical examples of ISPs, the primary task of which is to connect devices, such as personal computers and smartphones, with one another. In the example we considered above, it would not be possible to store and share audio-visual content on YouTube, or product listings on eBay, unless internet users and the relevant platforms were connected via the internet. Thus, ISPs are an important category of intermediaries without which internet users cannot gain access to online content.

4 See e.g., R Gellman, 'Disintermediation and the Internet' (1996) 13(1) *Government Information Quarterly* 1 and JP Baily and Y Bakos, 'An Exploratory Study of the Emerging Role of Electronic Intermediaries' (1997) 1 *International Journal of Electronic Commerce* 7, 20.

5 C Ryan, 'How Disintermediation Is Changing the Rules of Marketing, Sales and Distribution' (2000) 1 *Interactive Marketing* 368.

6 D Rowland, U Kohl and A Charlesworth, *Information Technology Law* (4th edn, Routledge 2012), 70.

7 Rowland et al, above n6, 71.

8 G Sutter, 'Online Intermediaries' in C Reed and J Angel (eds), *Computer Law: The Law and Regulation of Information Technology* (6th edn, Oxford University Press 2007), 233–34. See also, Rowland et al, above n6, 72.

9 B Fitzgerald et al, *Internet and E-Commerce Law: Technology, Law and Policy* (Lawbook Co 2011), 9. See also, GS Takach, *Computer Law* (2nd edn, Irwin Law Inc 2003), 32.

Hosts provide digital storage spaces on the internet[10] and include any intermediary that stores third-party content. As such, the use of the term 'host' requires some clarification. First, some intermediaries provide hosting as a professional service to individuals and businesses. They are commonly known as web-hosts. Services such as GoDaddy, HostGator and HostPapa are typical examples of web-hosts. Second, some entities operate websites (e.g. news sites, blogs and forums), where third-party internet users are allowed to post comments and upload their content. In this scenario, two hosts are involved in hosting such third-party content, i.e. the web-host responsible for hosting the entire website and the operators of the website that exercise administrative control over the comments posted and content uploaded by third parties making use of the website. Third, some entities host their own website, along with any content generated by third-party internet users. In essence, the third type of host is a hybrid of the first and second.

Riordan, providing a useful taxonomy of intermediaries that comprise the internet, has sought to distinguish between the first and second category of hosts described above.[11] He has argued that in determining the liability of internet intermediaries, it is necessary to consider the architecture of the internet, which takes a layered structure.[12] Accordingly, Riordan has envisaged three layers, namely 'physical', 'network' and 'application' layers.[13] Within this structure, both ISPs and web-hosts form part of the network layer.[14] However, according to Riordan, websites that display content created by their visitors (which he calls 'user-created content') are situated in the application layer.[15] He has suggested that entities in the application layer are 'closest to end-users and exercise the most direct control over application content'.[16] As such, this is a factor that is likely to play a crucial role in determining the extent to which hosts ought to be held liable for infringing third-party content.

Lastly, navigation providers are entities that 'act as signposts to . . . information'.[17] Search engines and online directories are the most commonly used navigation providers today. Both search engines and directories index resources across the internet so that the 'user can either perform a keyword search for relevant sites, or consult a structured directory for sites of interest'.[18] According to Smith, online shopping malls, as well as content aggregators and customisers, are examples of navigation providers.[19] Although content aggregators and customisers could be regarded as navigation providers, it is doubtful in the case

10 GHJ Smith, *Internet Law and Regulation* (4th edn, Sweet & Maxwell 2007), 9.
11 J Riordan, *The Liability of Internet Intermediaries* (Oxford University Press 2016), 36.
12 Riordan, above n11, 37.
13 Riordan, above n11, 37.
14 Riordan, above n11, 38–39.
15 Riordan, above n11, 40.
16 Riordan, above n11, 40.
17 Smith, above n10, 14.
18 Smith, above n10, 14.
19 Smith, above n10, 14. Content aggregators and customisers are websites where users can selectively choose content they desire.

of online shopping malls. Take, for instance, eBay or Amazon. Both these intermediaries could be described as online shopping malls. Various online retailers/sellers purchase space on such platforms to list and advertise their products for sale or auction. However, in terms of functionality, what eBay and Amazon do is to allow third-party sellers/retailers to create product listings or advertisements, which are then stored and displayed on the respective platforms. Thus, these intermediaries are better categorised as hosts of third-party product listings and advertisements. Of course, internet users may also perform searches within both these platforms to find products they desire to purchase. Thus, they also incorporate functions of a navigation provider. Although this seems to blur the line between hosts and navigation providers, online shopping malls (or online marketplaces) such as eBay and Amazon are better described as hosts.

Accordingly, in this book, a reference to 'navigation provider' should be regarded as a reference to an intermediary that links internet users to content hosted at locations that are *extraneous* to that of the intermediary providing the navigation service. Search engines and online directories do precisely that. For instance, Google links users to third-party content hosted on various devices and servers across the globe, upon users performing a search on Google's search engine. However, in the case of eBay and Amazon, their search functionality links users to third-party product listings and advertisements *within* the same platform. What is distinct about navigation providers, as defined in this book, is that they merely link internet users to content, without having the capacity to exercise control over that content.[20] In contrast, in the case of online shopping malls, such as eBay or Amazon, they do exercise control over the third-party content stored on their platforms. The same is true about keyword advertising services offered by search engines (e.g. Google's AdWords). When search engines allow third parties to create and store advertisements so that they are triggered as sponsored links when a keyword search is performed, they act as hosts, and not as navigation providers. Accordingly, caution must be exercised before proceeding to categorise an online actor. One must pay close attention to the actor's conduct in relation to content, and not the general description of the services they offer.

Shifting focus—from individual infringers to intermediaries

Given the focus of this book on intermediaries, as opposed to individual infringers of trade mark rights, it is necessary to explain as to why such an approach is adopted. In this section, economic, pragmatic and moral considerations that collectively justify this approach are examined.

The law and economics literature suggests that liability for any wrongdoing must lie with the lowest cost avoider—i.e. the party that is in the best position

20 Riordan has categorised 'gateways', which include search engines, within the application layer (above n11, 44). Yet, this contradicts his position that actors operating in the application layer exercise a higher degree of control over content (above n11, 40).

to terminate or prevent the wrongdoing incurring the least cost.[21] In its recent decision in *Cartier v Sky*,[22] the English High Court has regarded internet intermediaries as the lowest cost avoiders in the deterrence of infringements that are committed on the internet:

> it is economically more efficient to require intermediaries to take action to prevent infringement occurring via their services than it is to require rightholders to take action directly against infringers.[23]

There are several reasons as to why this might be the case. First, the identity of those who create objectionable content, including content that conflicts with rights of trade mark proprietors, is often hidden by the anonymity that the internet provides, making it difficult for right holders to detect and trace individual instances of infringements, and the persons behind those infringements.[24] In contrast, intermediaries that provide access, hosting or navigation services are easily identifiable owing to their conspicuous presence. What this means is that it is less costly for right holders to target intermediaries than to utilise resources to track and monitor individual infringers, who are not only greater in number but also more difficult to trace.

Second, the internet's architecture enables intermediaries to detect and deter infringements at a lower cost. Every wrongdoer on the internet must go through some intermediary to gain access to the internet, as doing so independently is prohibitively costly. Given that internet users are heavily dependent on intermediaries, they are transformed into attractive *nodes* or *choke points*[25] at which unlawful content can be identified and removed. Since all communications go through a central node at which they can be monitored, theoretically it may be argued that internet intermediaries could detect infringing content at a lower cost.

Third, and as a matter connected with the second point, internet intermediaries exercise a certain degree of control over the content that is transmitted, hosted or indexed on their platforms. Litchman and Posner have pointed this out in the context of cyber-security:

21 See e.g. RH Kraakman, 'Gatekeepers: The Anatomy of a Third Party Enforcement Strategy' (1986) 2 *Journal of Law, Economics, and Organization* 53, 61; A Hamdani, 'Who's Liable for Cyberwrongs' (2002) 87 *Cornell Law Review* 901, 910–11; PR Goold, 'Corrective Justice and Copyright Infringement' (2014) *Vanderbilt Journal of Entertainment and Technology Law* 251, 260; and SG Gilles, 'Negligence, Strict Liability, and the Cheapest Cost-Avoider' (1992) 78 *Virginia Law Review* 1291, 1306.

22 *Cartier International AG v British Sky Broadcasting Ltd* [2015] ETMR 1 (*Cartier v Sky*).

23 *Cartier v Sky*, [251] (Arnold J).

24 D Lichtman and E Posner, 'Holding Internet Service Providers Accountable' (2006) 14 *Supreme Court Economic Review* 221, 233–34. See also, Rowland et al, above n6, 73.

25 G Dinwoodie, 'A Comparative Analysis of Secondary Liability of Online Service Providers' in G Dinwoodie (ed), *Secondary Liability of Internet Service Providers* (Springer 2017), 17.

> Service providers control the gateway through which Internet pests enter and reenter the system. As such, service providers can help to stop these pests before they spread and to identify the individuals who originate them in the first place.[26]

In essence, the control that intermediaries exercise over the content that they transmit, host or index enables them to 'detect, deter, or otherwise influence the bad acts in question',[27] placing them in a better position, in comparison to right holders, to detect and deter infringements at a lower cost.

Lastly, it may be argued that holding internet intermediaries liable is of significance given the ripple effect this would have on individual wrongdoers.[28] From a right holder's point of view, it no doubt is more efficient and effective to seek to control the activities of an intermediary, as opposed to a large number of individual wrongdoers. Since internet intermediaries provide online services, which may be used for the purposes of infringing rights, or to gain access to infringing content, dealing with them directly would empower right holders to put an end to infringements or, at least, mitigate the effects of infringing content. In effect, exercising control over intermediaries will have a ripple effect on individual instances of infringements.

In addition to the above, there are three pragmatic reasons as to why it is desirable to focus on intermediaries. First and foremost, although '[a]dvances in technology are making it increasingly possible to locate and identify bad actors online, such that online anonymity is difficult to maintain',[29] wrongdoers may be residing in jurisdictions where laws either do not seek to regulate conduct on the internet or only provide for very minimal regulation.[30] Thus, bringing legal action against infringers may not be an effective solution.

Second, even where the 'bad actor is identified but is found outside the jurisdiction, sovereign governments have developed methods for resolving disputes to permit the direct extraterritorial application of domestic law, such as rules of jurisdiction, conflict of laws, and recognition of judgments'.[31] However, the enforcement of judgments against foreign wrongdoers remains a challenge, given the territoriality of intellectual property rights,[32] the requirement to litigate in

26 Lichtman and Posner, above n24, 225.
27 Lichtman and Posner, above n24, 236.
28 Lichtman and Posner, above n24, 236.
29 HB Holland, 'Section 230 of the CDA: Internet Exceptionalism as a Statutory Construct' in B Szoka and A Marcus (eds), *The Next Digital Decade: Essays on the Future of the Internet* (TechFreedom 2011), 201.
30 Rowland et al, above n8, 73.
31 Holland, above n29, 201.
32 GB Dinwoodie, 'The Demise of Territoriality?' (2009) 57 *William and Mary Law Review* 711, 734 ('There may be international intellectual property law, but there is no such thing as an international copyright, patent, or trademark').

multiple jurisdictions[33] and the costs involved in enforcing judgments in multiple territories.[34] As such, unless, as some argue, an international framework is adopted to resolve internet-related disputes,[35] right holders are better off targeting intermediaries in their enforcement efforts.[36]

Third, and in any case, even if the individual wrongdoers are capable of being identified and are within reach of the law, they may not have sufficient assets to compensate right holders in proportion to the damage caused by their infringing conduct.[37] By contrast, this problem may not arise as much when right holders turn to internet intermediaries to seek compensation.[38]

The foregoing economic and pragmatic considerations collectively support the shift from individual infringers to intermediaries in the continuing efforts to deal with online infringements. By holding intermediaries liable for their role in making infringing content accessible and available to internet users, they become incentivised to detect and deter infringements from happening in the future.[39] However, merely because internet intermediaries are lowest cost avoiders, are easily identifiable or have deeper pockets, this does not necessarily mean that they should be required under the law to compensate aggrieved right holders or to implement technical measures to detect and deter infringements. As such, the economic and pragmatic justifications discussed above must be weighed against the following counterarguments.

First, the orthodox theory of responsibility dictates that 'a person should only be held responsible for acts to which he has contributed'.[40] Thus, in order for individuals to become legally responsible for their actions, they must have caused the harms complained of.[41] The existence of a causal link between the acts of a wrongdoer and the harm inflicted on the victim justifies the imposition of liability on the ground that those who have acted in a morally blameworthy

33 M Trimble, 'Extraterritorial Intellectual Property Enforcement in the European Union' (2011) 18 *Southwestern Journal of International Law* 101, 104:

> options for enforcing these rights will depend on whether the individual countries' conflict-of-laws provisions allow for the concentration of proceedings on infringements under the substantive laws of multiple countries, or whether right holders must enforce their rights on a country-by-country basis. Typically, no concentration of proceedings is possible when registered rights such as patents or trademarks are at issue.

34 J Bornkamm, *Intellectual Property Litigation under the Civil Law Legal System; Experience in Germany*, WIPO/ACE/2/3 (4 June 2004), 7.

35 See e.g., A Segura-Serrano, 'Internet Regulation and the Role of International Law' in A von Bogdandy and R Wolfrum (eds), *Max Plank Yearbook of United Nations Law, Volume 10* (Koninklijke Brill NV 2006), 191 and L Hamilton, 'Regulation of the Internet: An Impossible Task?' (2010) 4 *Galway Student Law Review* 33, 40.

36 Rowland et al, above n8, 73.

37 Lichtman and Posner, above n24, 234.

38 Rowland et al, above n8, 73.

39 Goold, above n21, 265.

40 PS Davies, *Accessory Liability* (Hart Publishing 2015), 13.

41 Goold, above n21, 265.

manner must be required to compensate the victim.[42] However, this approach is inconsistent with the economic and pragmatic justifications, set out above, that support the shift from individual infringers to intermediaries to enforce rights in the online space. It is true that internet intermediaries are responsible for making online content, including content with the potential of infringing someone's registered trade mark, available to internet users. However, the mere act of transmitting, hosting or indexing such content does not, without more, suggest that a particular intermediary was *legally* responsible for the commission of a specific infringement, thus acting in a morally blameworthy manner.

Second, as Litchman and Posner have argued, the 'control' that intermediaries exercise over the *gateway* through which content is transmitted on the internet enables them to detect and deter unlawful activities. However, this argument was made in a discussion concerning *internet pests*, such as worms, viruses and malicious computer code.[43] Thus, in view of being able to 'detect criminal behavior by analysing patterns of use', intermediaries are in a good position to exercise control over suspicious content and users.[44] However, this argument is context specific, and cannot be easily extended to other categories of unlawful content. Unlike in the case of internet pests, it is much more difficult to detect content that promotes an infringement of trade mark rights purely by analysing patterns. While filtering technology may be useful in flagging infringing websites or content (by highlighting suspicious patterns in online text), infringers have learnt to outsmart such technology by avoiding terms that trigger suspicion in the first place. Thus, although internet intermediaries are no doubt gateways through which content is made available to users, the detection of instances of trade mark infringement by monitoring data patterns may not be as cost-effective as in the case of detecting internet pests.

Third, as Burrell and Weatherall have suggested, 'even under the conventional economic model it may not be desirable to impose liability on a cheapest cost avoider where to do so would cause substantial interference with legitimate activity'.[45] This concern very much applies to the context of intermediaries, not only because they may not be in the best position to distinguish between legitimate and unlawful user activities[46] but also since they are private entities that face no constitutional constraints and attract little public accountability.[47] The latest debates in the copyright context, concerning some of the controversial

42 Davies, above n40, 13.

43 Litchman and Posner, above n24, 234.

44 Litchman and Posner, above n24, 236–37.

45 R Burrell and K Weatherall, 'Before the High Court–Providing Services to Copyright Infringers: *Roadshow Films Pty Ltd v iiNet Ltd*' (2011) 33 *Sydney Law Review* 801, 830. Here the authors cite the example used by Litchman and Posner (above n24, 231) that highlights the problematic outcome of holding telephone companies accountable for 'crank calls'.

46 Hamdani, above n21, 904.

47 NK Katyal, 'Criminal Law in Cyberspace' (2001) 149 *University of Pennsylvania Law Review* 1003, 1007–08.

provisions of the new European Union (EU) Directive on Copyright in the Digital Single Maket,[48] highlight the concerns of shifting the onus from right holders to intermediaries in the enforcement of copyright.[49] Those who resist the new directive have argued that obligating intermediaries to engage automated content filtering technology could significantly deter free speech and fair use,[50] and hinder cultural diversity.[51]

Although these counterarguments to some extent dilute the justifications, set out above, that support the shift towards internet intermediaries in the enforcement of rights and deterrence of infringing activity, they are not inconsistent with the proposition that liability should extend to intermediaries in certain specific and limited circumstances. Thus, for instance, where an intermediary acquires *actual knowledge* of infringements, in circumstances where it exercises *control* over the content giving rise to such infringements,[52] there is no sound basis to reject the imposition of liability on that intermediary had it failed to

48 The Directive on Copyright in the Digital Single Market was adopted by the European Parliament on 26 March 2019 and formally endorsed by the Council of the EU on 15 April 2019. Once the text of the directive is published on the Official Journal, Member States will have 24 months to transpose the new directive into their domestic legislation.

49 In 2016, the European Commission introduced its draft for a new Copyright Directive in the Digital Single Market, which was approved by the Legal Affairs Committee of the European Parliament on 20 June 2018. However, on 5 July 2018, the European Parliament voted against rubber-stamping the position of the Legal Affairs Committee, paving the way for further debate and amendments to the proposal, especially to the controversial Article 13, which dealt with the liability and obligations of a certain class of online platforms. On 12 September 2018, the European Parliament adopted its position on the copyright directive, which included amendments to Article 13. Thereafter, following closed-door trialogue negotiations between the European Parliament, Council and the Commission, the European Parliament gave its final approval to the directive on 26 March 2019. The controversial Article 13, now renumbered as Article 17, will hold 'online content-sharing service providers' liable for copyright infringement, unless they 'made, in accordance with high industry standards of professional diligence, best efforts to ensure the unavailability of specific works and other subject matter for which the rightholders have provided the service providers with the relevant and necessary information' and 'acted expeditiously, upon receiving a sufficiently substantiated notice from the rightholders, to disable access to, or to remove from, their websites the notified works or other subject matter, and made best efforts to prevent their future uploads'.

50 A Kuczerawy, 'The Power of Positive Thinking: Intermediary Liability and the Effective Enjoyment of the Right to Freedom of Expression' (2017) 8 *Journal of Intellectual Property, Information Technology and Electronic Commerce Law* 226, 235.

51 S Jacques et al, 'Automated Anti-Piracy Systems as Copyright Enforcement Mechanism: A Need to Consider Cultural Diversity' (2018) 40 *European Intellectual Property Review* 218, 229.

52 SL Dogan, 'Principled Standards vs. Boundless Discretion: A Tale of Two Approaches to Intermediary Trademark Liability Online' (2014) 37 *Columbia Journal of Law & the Arts* 503, 509–10:

> The 'reasonableness' principle seems—albeit implicitly—to be pursing a modified 'best-cost-avoider' strategy: it places responsibility for infringement detection and elimination with the party best positioned to accomplish each task. Detection falls on the intellectual property owner, who is best suited to recognize unauthorized versions of its work or trademark. Responsibility for terminating the infringement, in turn, rests on the intermediary, assuming that it has control over the means of used to infringe.

take reasonable measures to terminate or mitigate the infringements in question. Placing emphasis on the element of actual knowledge and control avoids the problems associated with high monitoring and detection costs. It also, at least theoretically, limits interferences on legitimate uses of the internet.[53]

As you read through the chapters of this book, it will become evident that intermediaries may be held legally responsible for their conduct of making infringing content available to internet users, primarily in two ways: first, by imposing *liability* on intermediaries to compensate aggrieved trade mark proprietors, and, second, by compelling intermediaries to adopt technical measures with the aim of terminating, if not mitigating, infringements, even though there is no fault on their part (*no-fault liability*). This is typically achieved through injunctive relief.

Reasons for a trade mark perspective

Since the internet comprises a wide range of unlawful content, it is necessary to state why the focus of this book is on content that promotes the infringement of trade mark rights. First, there is a need for ensuring that the key functions of a trade mark are protected in the online space, to a greater extent than in our physical world, especially given the unique interplay between these functions and the online environment. Second, the evidence suggests that the internet is a significant source of content that promotes the sale of products in violation of trade mark rights. These factors, coupled with the challenges associated with initiating legal action against individual infringers, and the advantages right holders derive in shifting their enforcement efforts towards intermediaries, collectively indicate the importance of determining the question of intermediary liability from a trade mark perspective.

The greater need for trade mark protection in the online space

Trade marks are 'signs' that are capable of distinguishing the goods or services of one undertaking from those of others.[54] Such signs may comprise 'words including personal names, letters, numerals, figurative elements and combinations of colours as well as any combination of such signs'.[55] Unconventional signs include sounds, shapes, gestures, smells and even taste. Although some of these signs, such as smells and taste cannot be represented in the form of online content, most other types of signs can be translated into their online equivalent, and so trade marks have become integrated for use on the internet through digitisation—also attracting the catchphrase 'cybermarks'.[56] Today, most

53 The impact of technical measures on legitimate activities are considered in greater detail in subsequent chapters.

54 TRIPS, art 15:1 (first sentence).

55 TRIPS, art 15:1 (second sentence).

56 DL Burk, 'Cybermarks' (2010) 91 *Minnesota Law Review* 1375.

providers of goods or services have an online presence or use online services to advertise and sell their products on the internet. Online content that consists of distinctive signs, therefore, is an important aspect of engaging in business on the internet.

The Court of Justice of the European Union (CJEU) has recognised several functions that trade marks perform, which not only include the essential function of indicating origin but also certain other functions, such as guaranteeing the quality of goods or services and those of communication, investment and advertising.[57] Historically, trade marks designated the ownership of the goods to which they were attached.[58] In later times, however, trade marks came to be used to indicate the *origin* of goods or services,[59] although in today's context, due to growth in international trade, consumers seldom know the actual origin of a product bearing a particular trade mark.[60] That said, consumers perceive trade marks as a guarantee that products bearing a particular mark originate from a single entity exercising control over the product's quality.[61] This perception is despite the possibility of products not originating from a single manufacturing plant,[62] and entities other than the registered trade mark proprietor being involved in the manufacturing, packaging and distribution of the underlying products through various licensing arrangements.[63]

The practical implication of the origin function of trade marks is that consumers expect a consistent quality to be maintained in the manufacture of a product bearing a particular mark.[64] The origin and quality assurance functions of trade marks are intricately linked.[65] As such, when invidious traders utilise well-known marks, known for their quality products, to pass off products that are unable to achieve the same standards, this would negatively affect both trade mark proprietors and consumers alike. Thus, it is crucial for the law to protect both the origin and quality assurance functions of trade marks,[66] in order to safeguard

57 Case C-487/07, *L'Oréal SA v Bellure NV* [2009] ECR I-05185, [58]. See also, W Cornish, D Llewelyn and T Aplin, *Intellectual Property: Patents, Copyright, Trade Marks and Allied Rights* (8th edn, Sweet & Maxwell 2013), 644.

58 TD Drescher, 'The Transformation and Evolution of Trademarks – From Signals to Symbols to Myth' (1992) 82 *Trademark Reporter* 301, 319.

59 For one of the earliest judicial definitions, see *Hanover Star Milling Co v Metcalf* 240 U.S. 403 (1916).

60 FI Schechter, 'Rational Basis of Trademark Protection' (1927) 40 *Harvard Law Review* 813, 815. See also, BG Paster, 'Trademarks – Their Early History' (1969) 59 *Trademark Reporter* 551, 552.

61 D Shanahan, 'The Trademark Right: Consumer Protection or Monopoly?' (1982) 72 *Trademark Reporter* 233, 239.

62 R Burrell and M Handler, *Australian Trade Mark Law* (Oxford University Press, 2010), 3.

63 Shanahan, above n61, 239.

64 Cornish et al, above n57, 646. See also, EW Hanak, III, 'The Quality Assurance Function of Trademarks' (1975) 65 *Trademark Reporter* 318.

65 Shanahan, above n61, 239–40.

66 But see FK Beier, 'Territoriality of Trade Mark Law and International Trade' (1970) 1 *International Review of Intellectual Property and Competition Law (IIC)* 48, 61 (where it is argued that the only function that the law ought to protect is a trade mark's origin function).

the interests of trade mark proprietors,[67] as well as consumers.[68] Failure to do so would lead to an inefficient marketplace.[69] Justifying the existence of trade marks from a quality assurance point of view, Economides has pointed out:

> In many markets, sellers have much better information as to the unobservable features of a commodity for sale than the buyers. This is known as information asymmetry. Unobservable features, valued by the consumer may be crucial determinants of the total value of the good. Observable features can often be imitated to the smallest detail, even though huge differences remain in the unobservable features of the product. In the absence of trademarks, faced with the choice between goods which look identical, the consumer will only by chance pick the one with the desirable unobservable qualities.[70]

It may be posited that Economides's observation has much more significance and relevance to the online context than to our physical world. This is because, when consumers are faced with having to make a purchasing decision on the internet, not even the observable features of a product (such as packaging or scent), which are normally available as points of reference in the offline context, are present to aid an internet purchase. An online consumer must rely solely on the representations made by the seller, including the trade mark under which a product is sold, and has no other means of verifying the quality of a product, let alone its origin. However, consumers who are familiar with the quality of a product bearing a particular trade mark would expect the same standard of quality to exist when making an online purchase. Thus, there is a greater need to protect the origin and quality assurance functions of trade marks in the online context than in the brick-and-mortar environment, in view of the manner in which consumers interact with, and rely on, trade marks on the internet.

In addition to the origin and quality assurance functions, trade marks also perform a communication function. It has been suggested that the most convincing argument for the protection of trade marks is their capacity to supply information to consumers.[71] Essentially, this allows consumers to have easy access to any relevant information about the underlying product, including advertising claims, community

67 The investment that goes into maintaining standards and quality in relation to products entitles trade mark proprietors to be protected against the unauthorised use of their marks in relation to third-party products (see M Stuart, 'The Function of Trade Marks and the Free Movement of Goods in the European Economic Community' (1976) 7 *International Review of Intellectual Property and Competition Law (IIC)* 27).

68 A necessary consequence of trade mark protection is the protection of consumers from being confused or misled as to the origin, and therefore the quality, of goods or services (see L Bently et al, *Intellectual Property Law* (5th edn, Oxford University Press 2018), 845). Thus, even in situations where consumers are not fully aware of the actual source of a product, they could be misled and therefore must be protected against imitations (see, to this effect, *Powell v Birmingham Vinegar Brewery Co Ltd* (1896) 2 Ch 54).

69 WM Landes and R Posner, 'Trademark Law: An Economic Perspective' (1987) 30 *Journal of Law and Economics* 265. Landes and Posner utilise economic theories to justify trade mark protection and have argued that trade marks are necessary to maintain an efficient market.

70 NS Economides, 'The Economics of Trademarks' (1988) 78 *Trademark Reporter* 523, 526.

71 Bently et al, above n68, 854.

reputation, and the individual's previous experience with that product,[72] while also enabling consumers to relate newer products with older ones through effective comparisons.[73] In this sense, trade marks have the capacity to reduce consumer search costs, which serves as a valid justification for their protection.[74]

The heavy reliance consumers place on trade marks in the online space transforms the internet into an ideal platform for crafty traders to imitate trade marks, thereby abusing their informational function, not only to misinform consumers but also to appeal to their emotions. In effect, online consumers have become easy targets of trade mark infringement. Also, the internet is a repository of information,[75] comprising tools such as search engines that enhance the flow of information in innovative ways, increasing the chances of information-overload.[76] These factors justify the protection of trade marks in the online environment to a much greater extent than in our physical world.

Another function associated with trade marks is the advertising function.[77] The communicative features of trade marks discussed above render them effective advertising tools.[78] The capacity of trade marks to distinguish products allows persuasive advertising to be directed at a single brand.[79] Accordingly, trade marks are symbols around which a business's investment in the promotion of its products is built, and that investment deserves protection even where there is no misuse of a mark leading to misrepresentations concerning origin or quality.[80] In recent times courts have recognised the advertising function of trade marks as distinct from their other functions.[81]

72 LR Bradford, 'Emotion, Dilution, and Trademark Consumer' (2008) 23 *Berkeley Technology Law Journal* 1227, 1240.

73 AK Sanders and SM Maniatis, 'A Consumer Trademark: Protection Based on Origin and Quality' (1993) 11 *European Intellectual Property Review* 406, 409.

74 Landes and Posner, above n69. See also, MP McKenna, 'A Consumer Decision-Making Theory of Trademark Law' (2012) 98 *Virginia Law Review* 67, 75–76 and W Landes and RA Posner, *The Economic Structure of Intellectual Property Law* (Harvard University Press 2003), 168.

75 *Reno v ACLU*, 2334.

76 GB Dinwoodie and MD Janis, 'Confusion Over Use: Contextualism in Trademark Law' (2007) 92 *Iowa Law Review* 1597, 1622.

77 Cornish et al, above n57, 644.

78 RS Brown, Jr, 'Advertising and the Public Interest: Legal Protection of Trade Symbols' (1948) 57 *Yale Law Journal* 1165.

79 Brown, above n78, 1187.

80 Cornish et al, above n57, 644.

81 Joined Cases C-236/08, C-237/08 and C-238/08, *Google France Sarl v Louis Vuitton Malletier SA* [2010] ECR I-02417 (*Google v Louis Vuitton*), [91]:

> Since the course of trade provides a varied offer of goods and services, the proprietor of a trade mark may have not only the objective of indicating, by means of that mark, the origin of its goods or services, but also that of using its mark for advertising purposes designed to inform and persuade consumers.

See also, *JT International SA v Commonwealth of Australia* [2012] HCA 43, [286]:

> Whilst the prime concern of the Trade Marks Act is with the capacity of a trade mark to distinguish the goods of the registered owner from those of another trader, trade marks undoubtedly perform other functions. For example, a trade mark can be an indicium of the quality of goods sold under or by reference to it and it may be accepted that distinctive marks can have a capacity to advertise, and therefore to promote, sales of products sold under or by reference to them.

Unlike traditional forms of advertising, such as television, radio and billboards, which are passive, thus only allowing one-way flow of information, the internet is an interactive medium enabling consumers to react to advertisements instantly. Take, for instance, keyword advertising (such as Google's AdWords service) or online marketplaces (such as eBay). When traders advertise the availability of products as sponsored links on a search engine or display their product listings in an online marketplace, internet users may obtain further information and reviews of relevant products, and also instantly make a purchase, with the simple click of a button. Thus, a third party's unauthorised use of a trade mark on the internet could have an instant, but negative, impact on both consumers and trade mark proprietors. Therefore, the need to protect the advertising function of trade marks is felt even more in the online environment, in comparison to the offline context.

While the translation of our physical world into a digital one has provided trade mark proprietors with an unparalleled opportunity to reach a much larger audience and consumer base, it has also resulted in right holders having to police and enforce their rights not only in the brick-and-mortar environment but also on the internet. Despite the benefits of digitisation, the ease of duplicating content on the internet, coupled with the anonymity it provides to its users, increase the prevalence of infringements. After all, duplicating an online store along with all its trade marks and other indicia takes significantly less effort than doing the same in the offline context. It is clear that the origin, quality, information and advertising functions of trade marks are not only magnified in the online context but also could easily be hijacked and abused, thereby misleading consumers.

Therefore, ensuring that the functions associated with trade marks remain unhampered is essential as a means of promoting an efficient internet marketplace, while at the same time protecting the interests of both consumers and trade mark proprietors. To a great extent, this could be achieved if the law provides right holders with a viable means of holding intermediaries liable for their role in making infringing content accessible and available to internet users.

The internet, a significant source of counterfeits

The internet poses a serious threat to trade mark proprietors, which is evident from the scale of content promoting the sale of products and services in violation of trade mark rights. Counterfeiting is the most blatant form of trade mark infringement.[82] A note attached to Article 51 of TRIPS, which deals with border measures that every World Trade Organization (WTO) member must provide, defines 'counterfeit trademark goods' as:

82 D Llewelyn, 'Statutory Damages for Use of a "Counterfeit Trade Mark" and for Copyright Infringement in Singapore: A Radical Remedy in the Law of Intellectual Property or One in Need of a Rethink?' (2016) 28 *Singapore Academy of Law Journal* 61, 66 (pointing out that the use of the term 'counterfeit' 'should be limited to (almost) exact copies that are unarguably infringements and intended to deceive').

> any goods, including packaging, bearing without authorization a trademark which is identical to the trademark validly registered in respect of such goods, or which cannot be distinguished in its essential aspects from such a trademark, and which thereby infringes the rights of the owner of the trademark in question under the law of the country of importation.[83]

According to the World Intellectual Property Organization (WIPO), the act of counterfeiting is the imitation of a product giving the impression that the product originates from the genuine manufacturer or trader.[84] Given that Article 61 of TRIPS mandates WTO members to provide for criminal punishment when persons *wilfully* engage in counterfeiting, and that some bilateral trade agreements require state parties to provide for statutory damages in cases of counterfeiting,[85] it is clear that counterfeiting is treated as a serious form of infringement

In 2005, the Organisation for Economic Co-operation and Development (OECD) estimated that international trade in counterfeits and pirated goods[86] could have been up to US$200 billion.[87] However, the OECD acknowledged that its estimate did not provide a full picture of the counterfeiting scene.[88] According to a study conducted jointly by the OECD and the EU Intellectual Property Office (EUIPO), it was estimated that trade in counterfeit products accounted for 2.5 per cent of global trade, or US$461 billion, in 2013.[89] A report commissioned by the Business Action to Stop Counterfeiting and Piracy (BASCAP) and the International Trademark Association (INTA) has projected that by 2022 the economic value of the global counterfeit trade is likely to be in the range between US$1.9 trillion and US$2.81 trillion.[90] In 2015, US law enforcement agencies confiscated counterfeit goods valued at US$1.35 billion.[91] In 2017 alone, EU customs authorities made over 57,000 detentions at the borders, consisting of 31.4 million articles, the domestic retail value of which was over €582 million.[92]

83 TRIPS, note 14.

84 WIPO, *Intellectual Property Handbook: Policy, Law and Use* Publication No 489(E) (2008), para 2.495. See also, K Weckström, 'Liability for Trademark Infringement for Internet Service Providers' (2012) 16 *Marquette Intellectual Property Law Review* 1, 3.

85 See e.g., US-Singapore Free Trade Agreement 2003, art 16.9.5.

86 The term 'pirated goods' generally refers to goods that infringe copyright.

87 OECD, *The Economic Impact of Counterfeiting and Piracy* (OECD Publishing 2008), 96.

88 OECD, above n87, 96:

> The figure does not include counterfeit and pirated products that are produced and consumed domestically, nor does it include the significant volume of pirated digital products that are being distributed via the Internet. If these items were added, the total magnitude could well be several hundred billion dollars higher.

89 OECD/EUIPO, *Trade in Counterfeit and Pirated Goods: Mapping the Economic Impact* (OECD Publishing 2016), 7.

90 Frontier Economics, *The Economic Impacts of Counterfeiting and Piracy* (2017), 56 <www.inta.org/communications/documents/2017_frontier_report.pdf> (accessed 31 January 2019).

91 A Chikada and A Gupta, 'Online brand protection' in PE Chaudhry (ed), *Handbook of Research on Counterfeiting and Illicit Trade* (Edward Elgar 2017), 343.

92 European Commission, *Report on EU customs enforcement of intellectual property rights–Results at the EU Border 2017* (Publications Office of the European Union 2018), 8.

More specifically in the United Kingdom (UK), imports of counterfeit goods accounted for £9.3 billion in 2013, representing 4 per cent of total imports.[93]

Although measuring 'the global value of counterfeit products is excruciatingly difficult',[94] the above figures suggest a real problem. This is a problem that is likely to rise given the increasing use of the internet as a medium to trade in counterfeit goods.[95] The internet 'allows a producer of counterfeit products to reach a nearly unlimited worldwide audience with his offers'.[96] Although the online counterfeit market is difficult to measure, it has been claimed that US$25 billion in counterfeit goods are traded annually over the internet.[97] Counterfeiting on the internet has brought about tremendous anxiety to luxury brand owners, as counterfeiters often target their products. Luxury brands such as Louis Vuitton, L'Oréal and Tiffany have been at the forefront in bringing legal action against those engaging in counterfeiting, as well as intermediaries that facilitate the unlawful acts of counterfeiters, to protect their economic interests.[98] In the EU, an operation initiated by Europol in 2016 resulted in the seizure of 4,780 domain names and associated online shops selling counterfeit merchandise, leading to ten arrests and the seizure of goods worth over €1.75 million.[99]

The proliferation of counterfeit goods does not entail economic considerations alone. According to Chaudhry and Zimmerman, there is a shift in trends in the counterfeiting industry where everyday products are targeted.[100] Such counterfeits

93 OECD, *Trade in Counterfeit Products and the UK Economy: Fake Goods, Real Losses* (OECD Publishing 2017), 14.

94 P Chaudhry and A Zimmerman, *Protecting Your Intellectual Property Rights* (Springer 2013), 10.

95 INTA, *Addressing the Sale of Counterfeits on the Internet* (2017), 5 <www.inta.org/Advocacy/Documents/2018/Addressing_the_Sale_of_Counterfeits_on_the_Internet_021518.pdf> (accessed 31 January 2019).

96 Chaudhry and Zimmerman, above n94, 27.

97 Chaudhry and Zimmerman, above n94, 27 (citing a special report published by *The Economist* in 2003).

98 Trade mark proprietors have filed cases against intermediaries on a number of occasions around the world. These cases include *Google v Louis Vuitton* (filed in France, with a reference to the CJEU), *L'Oréal SA v eBay Inc* [2009] ETMR 53 (*L'Oréal v eBay* (HC)) (filed in the UK, with a reference to the CJEU), *Tiffany (NJ) Inc v eBay Inc* 600 F.3d 93 (2d Cir. 2010) (filed in the US) and *Google Inc v Australian Competition and Consumer Commission* [2013] HCA 1 (filed in Australia).

99 Europol/EUIPO, 2017 Situation Report on Counterfeiting and Piracy in the European Union (June 2017), 36 <www.europol.europa.eu/sites/default/files/documents/counterfeiting_and_piracy_in_the_european_union.pdf> (accessed 31 January 2019).

100 Chaudhry and Zimmerman, above n94, 12 (these products include highly visible, high-volume, low-tech products with well-known brand names, such as toothpaste and chocolate, highly priced, high-tech products, such as computer games, CDs, DVDs, auto and airplane parts, exclusive luxury products, such as clothing, apparel and perfume, research-intensive, high-tech products, such as pharmaceuticals, chemicals and pesticides, and tobacco products, furniture, sporting goods, food and drink, and a variety of other items including educational certificates). According to the European Commission, even toys are the subject of counterfeiting, creating health and safety concerns for children (European Commission, *Too Good to Be True: The Real Price of Fake Products* MEMO/13/346 (2013) <http://europa.eu/rapid/press-release_MEMO-13-346_en.htm> (accessed 31 January 2019)).

often do not comply with the health and safety standards that genuine goods adhere to, which can result in harm to consumers, sometimes even culminating in death.[101] One of the more serious threats posed by counterfeiting arises from the sale and distribution of counterfeit medicines,[102] particularly through online pharmacies. While online pharmacies are legitimate, imposters who sell counterfeit medicines online are abundant. According to the European Alliance for Access to Safe Medicines (EAASM), intermediaries such as search engines 'are the chief method by which distributors of illegal and counterfeit medicines find customers'.[103]

It is clear that counterfeiting is not purely an economic issue that affects trade mark proprietors. It has also become a dangerous threat to consumers and, clearly, this is of significant concern for governments. Yet, it is an accepted fact that counterfeiters do not operate like normal businesses, and for the purposes of prosecution they are difficult to trace,[104] a fact which is only magnified given the relative anonymity that the internet provides. As a result, there is a need for a shift in focus from those who engage in counterfeiting to intermediaries,[105] particularly to intermediaries operating in the online space. In most instances, the only effective solution for right holders, and even governments, interested in protecting intellectual property rights and the interests of consumers is to counteract the availability of counterfeits through the relevant intermediaries responsible for making content that promotes the sale of such counterfeits accessible and available to internet users. The European Commission has acknowledged this reality in facilitating a Memorandum of Understanding between a number of major right holders, internet intermediaries and associations,[106] to promote a culture of cooperation between the stakeholders, while also publishing a watch list[107] identifying intermediaries that are not doing enough to tackle the sale of counterfeits.

101 R Smithers, 'Surge in Purchases of Counterfeit Goods', *The Guardian* (2 October 2013) <www.theguardian.com/money/2013/oct/02/counterfeit-goods-surge-uk> (accessed 31 January 2019).

102 P O'Hare, 'Revealed: Organised crime gangs flooding internet with killer fake drugs and everyday products', *Daily Record* (Glasgow, 17 September 2013) <www.dailyrecord.co.uk/news/uk-world-news/organised-crime-gangs-use-internet-2278645> (accessed 31 January 2019).

103 EAASM, *The Counterfeit Superhighway* (2008), 14 <www.eaasm.eu/cache/downloads/dqqt3sge9hwssgcgcos440g40/455_EAASM_counterfeiting%20report_020608(1).pdf> (accessed 31 January 2019).

104 WIPO, above n84, para 2.500.

105 WIPO, *Press Release of the Seventh Global Congress on Combating Counterfeiting and Piracy* PR/2013/736 (2013) <www.wipo.int/pressroom/en/articles/2013/article_0010.html> (accessed 31 January 2019).

106 European Commission, *Memorandum of Understanding on the Sale of Counterfeit Goods via the Internet* (21 June 2016) <https://ec.europa.eu/docsroom/documents/30763/attachments/1/translations/en/rendi tions/native> (accessed 31 January 2019). The Memorandum of Understanding was first signed in 2011 and revised in 2016, with more stakeholders joining in 2018.

107 European Commission, *Counterfeit and Piracy Watch List* (7 December 2018) <http://trade.ec.europa.eu/doclib/docs/2018/december/tradoc157564.pdf> (accessed 31 January 2019).

Approach and structure of the book

This book is primarily concerned about the liability of internet intermediaries for trade mark infringements under the laws applicable in the UK. At the time of writing, there were only a few notable instances where the liability of internet intermediaries had been considered under UK law,[108] or more specifically the English law. The first instance was a book by Christina Angelopoulos on *European Intermediary Liability in Copyright: A Tort-Based Analysis*,[109] in which she has dedicated space to consider the liability of intermediaries under English law. Although her work has focused on the copyright perspective, it has usefully analysed the case law on joint tortfeasance under the English common law. The second instance was Martin Husovec's book on *Injunctions against Intermediaries in the European Union*.[110] The primary focus of his book was on the regime for injunctions against intermediaries under the Info-Soc[111] and Enforcement[112] directives, in the course of which he also considers the position in England. The third, and perhaps most notable, instance was Jaani Riordan's work titled *The Liability of Internet Intermediaries*.[113] The primary purpose of his work was to provide an understanding of '*who* may be liable for internet wrongdoing and *how* rights can be enforced online'.[114] The book has adopted a broadly horizontal approach[115] covering copyright, trade marks and passing off, defamation, confidentiality and privacy, data protection and unlawful material. There were also shorter works that dealt with intermediary liability under UK law. For instance, David Llewelyn's chapter in an edited volume published in 2012,[116] in part, dealt with intermediary liability under the common law. However, the focus of his work was on the copyright context, with only a fleeting reference to a trade

108 Although the term 'UK law' is used in a general sense to indicate laws applicable in all the UK territories (i.e. England and Wales, Northern Ireland and Scotland), such as the Trade Marks Act 1994, this book also deals with English common-law principles and statutes applicable only in England and Wales, such as the Senior Courts Act 1981.

109 C Angelopoulos, *European Intermediary Liability in Copyright: A Tort-Based Analysis* (Kluwer Law International 2017).

110 M Husovec, *Injunctions Against Intermediaries in the European Union: Accountable But Not Liable?* (Cambridge University Press 2017).

111 Directive 2001/29/EC of the European Parliament and of the Council of 22 May 2001 on the harmonisation of certain aspects of copyright and related rights in the information society [2001] OJ L 167/10 (Info-Soc Directive).

112 Directive 2004/48/EC of the European Parliament and of the Council of 29 April 2004 on the Enforcement of Intellectual Property Rights [2004] OJ L 157/16 (Enforcement Directive). Although the Enforcement Directive deals with the enforcement of intellectual property rights, the Info-Soc Directive exclusively deals with the enforcement of copyright, and is therefore considered *lex specialis* vis-à-vis the Enforcement Directive.

113 Riordan, above n11.

114 Riordan, above n11, 2 (emphasis in original).

115 Riordan, above n11, 2.

116 D Llewelyn, 'Intellectual Property Liability of Consumers, Facilitators and Intermediaries: Concepts under Common Law' in C Heath and AK Sanders (eds), *Intellectual Property Liability of Consumers, Facilitators and Intermediaries* (Kluwer Law International 2012).

mark case, where the claimant sought to hold eBay liable as a joint tortfeasor.[117] More recently, Riordan's contribution to an edited volume on intermediary liability focused on blocking injunctions against intermediaries in the UK and EU.[118]

The works described above have contributed significantly to existing knowledge on intermediary liability. However, their primary focus was not on the trade mark perspective. In contrast, this book is dedicated to the question of intermediary liability *exclusively* from a trade mark point of view. It examines the role of internet intermediaries and their liability for providing access to, hosting or indexing content promoting trade mark infringements in the backdrop of existing statutory and common-law principles. In so doing, the book proposes reforms to remedy the limitations and shortcomings in the existing legal framework.

The protection of registered trade marks in the UK is governed by the Trade Marks Act 1994, which was enacted to give effect to the 1988 Trade Marks Directive.[119] Despite the obvious need to provide more enhanced protection for trade marks on the internet and the prevalence of online counterfeiting, trade mark proprietors have not been successful in pursuing infringement actions against intermediaries, even in cases where they knowingly provide services to parties engaging in trade mark infringements. The ruling of the CJEU in *Google v Louis Vuitton* has effectively ruled out any possibility of finding intermediaries providing access, hosting or navigation services liable in an action for trade mark infringement. The implications of this decision are considered in Chapter 2.

117 Llewelyn, above n116, 31–32 (where reference is made to the English High Court case of *L'Oréal v eBay* (HC) and the subsequent ruling of the CJEU in Case C-324/09, *L'Oréal SA v eBay International AG* [2011] ECR I-06011).

118 J Riordan, 'Website Blocking Injunctions under United Kingdom and European Law' in GB Dinwoodie (ed), *Secondary Liability of Internet Service Providers* (Springer 2017).

119 First Council Directive 89/104/EEC of 21 December 1988 to Approximate the Laws of the Member States Relating to Trade Marks [1989] OJ L 40/1 (1988 Trade Marks Directive). The 1988 Trade Marks Directive was repealed by Directive 2008/95/EC of the European Parliament and of the Council of 22 October 2008 to Approximate the Laws of the Member States Relating to Trade Marks [2008] OJ L 299/25 (2008 Trade Marks Directive). The 2008 Trade Marks Directive was repealed by Directive (EU) 2015/2436 of the European Parliament and of the Council of 16 December 2015 to Approximate the Laws of the Member States Relating to Trade Marks (Recast) [2015] OJ L 336/1 (2015 Trade Marks Directive), which came into force on 15 January 2019. A majority of the cases discussed in this book have applied either the 1988 or the 2008 Trade Marks Directive, both of which contain identical provisions and paragraph numbering. The infringement provisions contained in the three directives are also essentially the same, the difference being that in the 2015 Trade Marks Directive the paragraph numbering has changed. As such, in view of maintaining consistency, unless the context otherwise requires, any reference to the provisions of the 'Trade Marks Directive' should be considered a reference to the 2008 Trade Marks Directive, which in turn, where the context requires, may be considered a reference to the corresponding provisions in the 1988 Trade Marks Directive. It must also be noted that, in addition to the 2015 Trade Marks Directive, Regulation (EU) 2017/1001 of the European Parliament and of the Council of 14 June 2017 on the European Union Trade Mark [2017] OJ L 154/1 (EUTM Regulation) applies to EU trade marks (formerly community trade marks). The provisions in the EUTM Regulation relating to the scope of trade mark rights are identical to those found in the 2015 Trade Marks Directive (and its predecessors). As such, the EUTM Regulation has not been separately discussed in this book.

In view of the difficulties in holding intermediaries liable under trade mark law, right holders in the UK have had to rely on English common-law principles as an alternative. However, the common law too has not been forthcoming in providing a suitable basis for holding internet intermediaries liable for infringements committed by their users. This is so owing to the narrow confines of joint tort liability, which requires a *common design* to be established between a secondary party and the primary wrongdoer. The practical outcome of this is that internet intermediaries that provide access, hosting or navigation services remain beyond the reach of common-law liability, even in circumstances where they knowingly assist infringements on the part of their users, as was the outcome in *L'Oréal v eBay* (HC), decided by the English High Court. The implications of the common design requirement on the liability of internet intermediaries are considered in Chapter 3.

In contrast to the situation in the UK, trade mark proprietors have had better success in holding intermediaries liable for trade mark infringements in other jurisdictions. As such, in Chapter 4, approaches to intermediary liability in the US and in a select few Continental EU Member States are considered. The common themes and principles derived from this exercise are then put to use in Chapter 5 in proposing reforms to UK (and corresponding EU) trade mark law aimed at providing right holders a basis to hold internet intermediaries liable for infringements in certain limited and specified circumstances when they are at fault. The need to develop new tools within trade mark law to better deal with online infringements has already been echoed.[120]

However, it must also be acknowledged that holding internet intermediaries liable at the instance of aggrieved trade mark proprietors entails certain consequences, especially when safe harbour provisions that seek to limit such liability come into play. In the EU's context, the E-Commerce Directive[121] provides a safe harbour to intermediaries engaging in an 'information society service'. The EU safe harbour provisions 'constitute the basis for the development of notice and take down procedures'.[122] The practice of notice and takedown has become a quick and cost-effective *extrajudicial* remedy implemented mainly by intermediaries that host third-party content. This remedy allows right holders to have infringing content removed upon notifying the intermediary responsible for hosting the content in question. As such, any law reforms aimed at enabling right holders to hold intermediaries liable, leading to the award of damages, must also consider the implications of notice and takedown. Chapters 6 and 7 consider

120 Weckström, above n84, 50 ('New tools should be developed within trademark law that specifically establish the prerequisites for indirect infringement and narrowly tailor appropriate remedies').

121 Directive 2000/31/EC on Ccertain Legal Aspects of Information Society Services, in Particular Electronic Commerce, in the Internal Market [2000] OJ L 178/1 (E-Commerce Directive).

122 T Verbiest et al, *Study on the Liability of Internet Intermediaries* Markt/2006/09/E (2007), 5. See also, GB Dinwoodie, 'Secondary Liability for Online Trademark Infringement: The International Landscape' (2014) 37 *Columbia Journal of Law & the Arts* 463, 499.

the practical implications of notice and takedown and propose further reforms to ensure an effective, fair and balanced approach to this practice.

While there is utility in seeking to impose liability on intermediaries on the basis that they were somehow at fault in making infringing content accessible and available to internet users, right holders also benefit from seeking the cooperation of intermediaries in their enforcement efforts. The injunctive remedy has often been used to compel intermediaries to assist in the enforcement of rights, even in cases where no fault can be attributed to them for the underlying wrongdoings.[123] In the context of the EU, Article 11 (third sentence) of the Enforcement Directive provides the basis for injunctions against intermediaries aimed at enforcing intellectual property rights.[124] For the first time in the UK, in *Cartier v Sky*, the English High Court awarded an injunction against several ISPs compelling them to block access to websites that hosted content that infringed trade mark rights. In Chapter 8, the legal basis for the injunctive remedy is considered in detail to highlight its problematic application to the trade mark context. Chapter 9 deals with some of the practical considerations that concern the injunctive remedy, including compliance with natural justice, safeguards against abuse, circumvention and collateral damage, and costs of implementation. Both Chapters 8 and 9 contain law reform proposals that potentially could improve the efficacy and balance of the injunctive remedy.

A word about Brexit

The twenty-third of June 2016 marked a decisive day for the people of Britain, as they had to decide whether the UK should leave or remain in the EU. Of over 30 million people who voted at a referendum, 51.9 per cent voted in favour of leaving the EU, or to 'Brexit'.[125] Consequently, in March 2017, the British Prime Minister, Theresa May, officially notified the EU Council of the intention to trigger Article 50 of the Treaty on European Union (TEU), which permits an EU Member State to unilaterally withdraw from the Union.[126] This led to 29 March 2019 being declared *by default* as 'exit day', under EU law,[127] and negotiations commenced between the UK and remaining EU Member States to secure

123 *Norwich Pharmacal Co v Customs & Excise Commissioners* [1974] AC 133.

124 In respect of copyright, however, the relevant provision is art 8(3) of the Info-Soc Directive.

125 A Kirk, 'EU Referendum: The Claims that Won It for Brexit, Fact Checked' *The Telegraph* (13 March 2017) <www.telegraph.co.uk/politics/0/eu-referendum-claims-won-brexit-fact-checked> (accessed 31 January 2019).

126 Treaty on European Union (Consolidated) [2016] OJ C 202/1 (TEU)

127 TEU, art 50(3) ('The Treaties shall cease to apply to the State in question from the date of entry into force of the withdrawal agreement or, failing that, two years after the notification referred to in paragraph 2'). In the event a withdrawal agreement comes into force before 29 March 2019, the date on which such agreement comes into force will in effect be the exit day.

a 'Brexit deal' or Withdrawal Agreement.[128] Article 126 of the draft Withdrawal Agreement provides that '[t]here shall be a transition or implementation period, which shall start on the date of entry into force of this Agreement and end on 31 December 2020'. Importantly, Article 127 of the draft Withdrawal Agreement provides that '[u]nless otherwise provided in this Agreement, Union law shall be applicable to and in the United Kingdom during the transition period'. In addition, Article 4(4) provides that:

> [t]he provisions of this Agreement referring to Union law or to concepts or provisions thereof shall in their implementation and application be interpreted in conformity with the relevant case law of the Court of Justice of the European Union handed down before the end of the transition period.

On the UK side, to facilitate its withdrawal from the EU, the European Union (Withdrawal) Act 2018 (Withdrawal Act 2018) was enacted, which came into force on 26 June 2018.

Based on the draft Withdrawal Agreement, it is clear that EU law (except the ones specifically excluded under Article 127) shall continue to apply to the UK till 31 December 2020 (transition period), and may even extend till the end of 2022 (extended transition period).[129] Also, during the transition period, EU law as made applicable by the Withdrawal Agreement to the UK must be interpreted by domestic courts in conformity with relevant case law handed down by the CJEU before the end of the transition period. However, although the UK Cabinet of Ministers had approved the Withdrawal Agreement,[130] and so did the EU membership,[131] it was rejected by the UK Parliament.[132] As things stood towards the end of March 2019, this meant that unless a new withdrawal deal was negotiated, for which it was necessary to extend the Article 50 deadline,[133]

128 Draft Agreement on the Withdrawal of the United Kingdom of Great Britain and Northern Ireland from the European Union and the European Atomic Energy Community, as Agreed at Negotiators' Level on 14 November 2018, TF50 (2018) 55 (Withdrawal Agreement).

129 J Rankin, 'Brexit Transition Could Be Extended to 2022, Says Barnier' *The Guardian* (18 November 2018) <www.theguardian.com/politics/2018/nov/18/brexit-transition-could-be-extended-to-2022-says-barnier> (accessed 31 January 2019).

130 J Watts, 'Brexit deal: Theresa May's cabinet approves EU withdrawal agreement' *The Independent* (14 November 2018) <www.independent.co.uk/news/uk/politics/brexit-deal-agreed-may-cabinet-uk-eu-withdrawal-negotiation-dup-parliament-support-a8634201.html> (accessed 31 January 2019).

131 P Grafton-Green, 'Brexit Deal Approved by EU Leaders: What Happens Next and When Will Parliament Vote on It?' *The Evening Standard* (25 November 2018) <www.standard.co.uk/news/politics/brexit-news-what-lies-ahead-for-theresa-may-and-her-deal-with-the-eu-a3999501.html> (accessed 31 January 2019).

132 B Perrigo, 'Theresa May's Brexit Deal Was Crushed. What Happens Next?' *TIME* (16 January 2019) <http://time.com/5504210/theresa-may-brexit-deal-defeat> (accessed 31 January 2019).

133 C Kirkland, 'Brexit Vote Defeat: Theresa May's 'Plan B' Options Explained' *The Conversation* (14 January 2019) <https://theconversation.com/brexit-vote-defeat-theresa-mays-plan-b-options-explained-109749> (accessed 31 January 2019).

the UK was scheduled to leave the EU on WTO terms, as a result of which EU law would have no longer continued to bind the UK immediately following the default exit day (i.e. 29 March 2019).[134] Unsurprisingly, this chain of events compelled the British Prime Minister to seek an extension to the Article 50 deadline,[135] with the EU membership agreeing to a new deadline of 31 October 2019.[136]

There is yet another eventuality that must be considered: that Brexit will not happen. This is in view of the call for a fresh Brexit referendum.[137] However, even if the people of Britain change their minds and decide that the UK should remain in the EU, whether the effects of triggering Article 50 of the TEU can be legally reversed has to be considered. In this regard, the Inner House of the Court of Session in Scotland, consequent to a petition being filed seeking a declarator specifying 'whether, when and how' a notification under Article 50 of the TEU can unilaterally be revoked,[138] referred the following question to the CJEU:

> Where, in accordance with Article 50 of the TEU, a Member State has notified the European Council of its intention to withdraw from the European Union, does EU law permit that notice to be revoked unilaterally by the notifying Member State; and, if so, subject to what conditions and with what effect relative to the Member State remaining within the EU?[139]

Both the Advocate General[140] and the CJEU[141] have responded to the aforesaid question in the affirmative, which means that there is a real possibility of Brexit being derailed with the effect of the UK remaining in the EU.

134 DL Jones, 'Brexit and the Future of English Law' (2018) 49 *Victoria University of Wellington Law Review* 1, 10.

135 Initially, Theresa May sought a 'short' extension, in response to which the EU27 offered two alternatives. The first alternative was an extension till 22 May 2019 on condition that the UK Parliament vote in favour of the Withdrawal Agreement. The second alternative was an extension till 12 April 2019, in the event the Withdrawal Agreement was rejected by the Parliament. It was the latter that happened.

136 On the UK side, the European Union (Withdrawal) Act 2019 was enacted to provide the legal basis for, and deal with the practicalities of, extending the Article 50 deadline.

137 B Kentish, 'MPs Throw Weight behind Fresh Brexit Referendum as Hundreds of Thousands Prepare for Major Demonstration in London' *The Independent* (16 October 2018) <www.independent.co.uk/news/uk/politics/brexit-referendum-final-say-london-protest-eu-uk-remain-leave-peoples-vote-a8585441.html> (accessed 31 January 2019).

138 *Wightman v Secretary of State for Exiting the European Union* [2018] CSIH 62 (*Wightman v Sec of State for Exiting EU*), [3] (Lord Carloway).

139 *Wightman v Sec of State for Exiting EU*, Appendix, [8].

140 Case C-621/18, *Wightman v Secretary of State for Exiting the European Union* [2018] 3 WLR 1965 (*Wightman v Sec of State for Exiting EU* (CJEU)), Opinion of AG Sánchez-Bordona, [170].

141 *Wightman v Sec of State for Exiting EU* (CJEU), [75].

Irrespective of the uncertainty about the outcome of Brexit, which even the English judiciary has acknowledged,[142] what is clear is that EU law, as implemented and applied by domestic legislation and judicial decisions, is not going to disappear into thin air after Brexit. In this regard, it must be noted that section 2(1) of the Withdrawal Act 2018 provides that any EU-derived domestic legislation 'as it has effect in domestic law immediately before exit day, continues to have effect in domestic law on and after exit day'. In addition, domestic courts, other than the Supreme Court,[143] will be bound by pre-Brexit CJEU rulings, and domestic judicial decisions concerning the application and interpretation of EU law pronounced before exit day.[144] As a result, domestic statutes that give effect to the EU directives governing trade marks (Trade Marks Directive),[145] internet intermediaries (E-Commerce Directive) and the enforcement of intellectual property rights (Info-Soc and Enforcement directives) will continue to remain in force, until subsequently amended or repealed. Moreover, all judicial decisions that have applied and interpreted EU-derived domestic legislation, and rulings of the CJEU, will continue to bind future judges, unless subsequently overruled by the UK Supreme Court.

The upshot of all this is that EU law will continue to be of relevance to the UK during the transition period (assuming the Withdrawal Agreement comes into force), and in any case until domestic legislation and judicial decisions applying EU law are superseded by future legislation or judicial precedent. Therefore, in the following chapters of this book, especially when law reforms are proposed, the potential implications of Brexit are flagged for the benefit of the reader.

142 *W3 Ltd v Easygroup Ltd* [2016] EWHC 3304 (Ch), [37] (Master Matthews):

> I regard it as wholly speculative what the effect of Brexit is or might be. First of all, certainly high officials tell us that 'Brexit means Brexit,' but we still do not know what it means. We do not yet know whether it will actually happen at all, and if it does we do not know when it will happen. More, if it happens we have no idea what kind of Brexit it may be, what the other side of the fence will look like. Therefore, I decline to take into account anything as speculative as the effect of Brexit on this litigation.

143 Withdrawal Act 2018, section 6(4)(a). The High Court will not be bound by pre-Brexit CJEU rulings in the circumstances set out in section 6(4)(b) of the Withdrawal Act 2018.

144 Withdrawal Act 2018, section 6(3).

145 The UK Trade Marks Regulations 2018, SI 2018/825, implement the 2015 Trade Marks Directive by amending the Trade Marks Act 1994 and related secondary legislation. The Regulations came into force on 14 January 2019, resulting in the harmonisation of UK and EU trade mark law before the onset of Brexit.

2 Liability under trade mark law

Despite the significant expansion of trade mark law over the years and the much-needed protection for trade marks on the internet, it is somewhat surprising that trade mark proprietors have struggled in their attempts to hold internet intermediaries liable in an action for trade mark infringement. This is despite intermediaries playing a role in providing access to, hosting or indexing content that promotes the infringement of trade mark rights. The difficulty in imposing liability on intermediaries is brought about by the stringent 'use' requirement that must be satisfied before the unauthorised use of a trade mark by a third party can be regarded as an infringement. After all, when internet intermediaries provide their services, they do not make *any* use of trade marks in the sense required under trade mark law.

The 'use' requirement

The discussion on the 'use' requirement under trade mark law must begin with a reference to the Agreement on Trade-Related Aspects of Intellectual Property Rights (TRIPS),[1] which defines the scope of trade mark rights and has shaped trade mark protection under national and regional (e.g. EU) regimes across the world. Article 16:1 of TRIPS, which deals with *rights conferred* on the proprietor of a registered trade mark, provides:

> The owner of a registered trademark shall have the exclusive right to prevent all third parties not having the owner's consent from *using in the course of trade* identical or similar signs for goods or services which are identical or similar to those in respect of which the trademark is registered where such use would result in a likelihood of confusion.[2]

Although the phrase 'using in the course of trade' that appears in Article 16:1 of TRIPS is a key aspect of that provision in determining the scope of trade mark

1 The text of the agreement is available in Annex 1C of the Marrakesh Agreement Establishing the World Trade Organization 1994.

2 TRIPS, art 16:1 (emphasis added).

rights, it is somewhat surprising that TRIPS does not seek to define that phrase. Commentators who have provided some of the most influential interpretations of TRIPS do not seem to have placed much emphasis on this concept either. For instance, Gervais, in his commentary on TRIPS, does not consider the meaning of 'use' even in the abstract, when dealing with the scope of Article 16.[3] On the other hand, Correa states the obvious, that '[t]he exclusive rights conferred are subject to several conditions and limitations. . . . [S]uch rights only apply in relation to the use of a trademark "in the course of trade", that is, in commercial activities'.[4] Even the most elaborate comment on the 'use' requirement does not seek to properly define the exact contours of the type of use that TRIPS prohibits, and instead merely suggests that WTO members are free to provide their own domestic interpretations.[5]

In any case, for an infringement suit to be brought, it is not sufficient that a trade mark is used in the course of trade. It must also be used 'for goods or services which are identical or similar to those in respect of which the trade mark is registered'. Although these collective requirements essentially mean the use of a trade mark *as a trade mark*, i.e. to indicate the source of goods or services, the interpretative discretion conferred on WTO members in shaping their domestic laws has resulted in some countries adopting a broad definition for 'use'. For instance, under section 32(1)(a) of the Lanham Act 1946,[6] which is a federal trade mark statute in the US, the unauthorised 'use in commerce' of 'any reproduction, counterfeit, copy, or colorable imitation of a registered mark in connection with the sale, offering for sale, distribution, or advertising of *any goods or services*' that is 'likely to cause confusion, or to cause mistake, or to deceive' amounts to an infringement. This provision has, at times, captured purely *technical* and *internal* uses involving text identical or similar to trade marks on the part of some internet intermediaries.[7]

In most jurisdictions, however, the 'use' requirement has been narrowly incorporated. For instance, in the case of the EU, for a trade mark to be infringed, Article 5 of the Trade Marks Directive[8] requires that a sign, which is identical or similar to a registered mark, be used 'in the course of trade' and 'in relation to goods or services which are identical with or similar to those for which it is registered'.

3 D Gervais, *The TRIPS Agreement–Drafting History and Analysis* (3rd edn, Sweet & Maxwell 2008), 274–79.

4 CM Correa, *Trade Related Aspects of Intellectual Property Rights: A Commentary on the TRIPS Agreement* (Oxford University Press 2007), 186.

5 JH Schmidt-Pfitzner, 'Article 16–Rights Conferred' in P-T Stoll, J Busche and K Arend (eds), *WTO—Trade-Related Aspects of Intellectual Property Rights* (Martinus Nijhoff 2009), 318.

6 15 USC §1114(1)(a).

7 See e.g. *Rescuecom Corp v Google Inc* 562 F.3d 123 (2d Cir. 2009) (*Rescuecom v Google*).

8 Directive 2008/95/EC of the European Parliament and of the Council of 22 October 2008 to Approximate the Laws of the Member States Relating to Trade Marks [2008] OJ L 299/25 (Trade Marks Directive). An explanation as to why a reference is made to the 2008 Trade Marks Directive, and not the later 2015 Trade Marks Directive (Directive (EU) 2015/2436), which replaces the former, is provided in Chapter 1.

This requirement has been expressly incorporated into the Trade Marks Act 1994 applicable in the UK.[9] Given the harmonising effect of the Trade Marks Directive, it can be safely said that domestic trade mark legislation in EU member states include a similar requirement.[10] Even in other common law jurisdictions, this requirement has been incorporated, at times, with only minute differences.[11]

What is important to note is that the incorporation of the 'use' requirement into national and regional trade mark legislation has created an obstacle in relation to the enforcement of trade mark rights in the online space and, in particular, against internet intermediaries. A reference to the series of lawsuits in which the practice of keyword advertising was challenged amply demonstrates the obstacle that right holders face. It must be noted, however, that although the keyword advertising cases concerned the conduct of search engines in their capacity as *hosts*, the principles that underpin these cases are equally applicable to other types of intermediaries as well, i.e. to hosts more generally, ISPs and navigation providers.

The keyword advertising cases

Before referring to the case law in which the practice of keyword advertising was challenged, it is useful to set out how keyword advertising works. Although this form of advertising has been explained in much more detail elsewhere,[12] for the purposes of this chapter, it is described with specific reference to the AdWords service offered by Google. Google's search engine can be used to search for almost anything on the internet. Upon a search being performed, the results page is populated with two types of results, i.e. natural results and sponsored results. The natural results are a representation of the entire internet (as indexed by Google) at the time the search was performed. The entries are prioritised using Google's search algorithm, where the most relevant results that correspond to a particular search term are displayed first. In contrast, the sponsored results relate to Google's AdWords service. Under this scheme, advertisers are allowed to purchase keywords of their choice and associate advertisements with such keywords. The advertisers are solely responsible for the content of the advertisements. When an online user's search term matches a purchased keyword,

9 Trade Marks Act 1994, section 10.

10 The provisions of the Trade Marks Directive, along with some of the most influential cases interpreting them in the context of internet related infringements, are discussed later on in this chapter.

11 For instance, trade mark legislation in Singapore (Trade Marks Act 1998, section 27), Hong Kong (Trade Marks Ordinance (Chap 559), section 18) and New Zealand (Trade Marks Act 2002, section 89) have incorporated this requirement by providing that infringement occurs only where a sign is used 'in the course of trade'. In Australia, the Trade Marks Act 1995 (Cth) (section 120) incorporates this requirement in more specific terms through a 'use as a trade mark' requirement.

12 See e.g. A Tan, 'Google AdWords: Trademark Infringer or Trademark Liberalizer?' (2010) 16 *Michigan Telecommunications and Technology Law Review* 273, 475–77 and PJ Greene, 'Keyword Advertising, and Other Invisible Uses of Third Party Trade Marks in Online Advertising: A New Zealand/Australasian Perspective' (2009) 40 *Victoria University of Wellington Law Review* 106.

advertisements associated with that keyword are displayed as sponsored results. The prominence and priority afforded to these advertisements are based, among other things, on the fee advertisers pay Google.

A potential conflict between keyword advertising and existing trade mark rights arises where a keyword purchased by an advertiser is identical or similar to a registered trade mark and the advertiser in question is neither the trade mark proprietor nor someone authorised.[13] Thus, when a Google search is performed using a search term that is concurrently a trade mark and a purchased keyword, Google will display the relevant sponsored link, in addition to the natural search results. Upon clicking the sponsored link, one of several possibilities may arise. First, the user may be taken to the website of the trade mark proprietor, in the event where the proprietor is the advertiser that sponsored the link. This scenario presents no trade mark-related issue. Second, the user might be taken to a competitor's website or a website selling counterfeits. This is possible where a third party purchases a keyword from Google and displays an advertisement with the keyword being identical or similar to a trade mark.[14] Third, the user may be taken to a website providing information about, or criticising, the brand or product concerned. Such an instance could potentially be justified by exceptions to trade mark rights permitted under Article 17 of TRIPS, as incorporated into domestic and regional trade mark legislation. Lastly, the user might be taken to a website dealing with the resale of goods already placed on the market with the trade mark proprietor's consent, i.e. goods resold in the secondary market. This may result in parallel importation and could give rise to issues of infringement.[15]

A US court has succinctly explained Google's keyword advertising practice in the following way:

> For example, using Google's AdWords, Company Y, a company engaged in the business of furnace repair, can cause Google to display its advertisement and link whenever a user of Google launches a search based on the search term, 'furnace repair.' Company Y can also cause its ad and link to appear whenever a user searches for the term 'Company X,' a competitor of Company Y in the furnace repair business. Thus, whenever a searcher interested in purchasing furnace repair services from Company X launches a search of the term X (Company X's trademark), an ad and link would appear on the searcher's screen, inviting the searcher to the furnace repair services of X's competitor, Company Y. And if the searcher clicked

13 G Psaroudakis, 'In Search of the Trade Mark Functions: Keyword Advertising in European Law' (2012) 34 *European Intellectual Property Review* 33.

14 This was what gave rise to the dispute in Joined Cases C-236/08, C-237/08 and C-238/08, *Google France Sarl v Louis Vuitton Malletier SA* [2010] ECR I-02417 (*Google v Louis Vuitton*), a reference to the CJEU from France.

15 The circumstances in which online content incorporating trade marks could pose a threat to trade mark rights are considered at length in Chapter 7.

> on Company Y's link, Company Y's website would open on the searcher's screen, and the searcher might be able to order or purchase Company Y's furnace repair services.[16]

As part of the AdWords service, Google also employs a 'Keyword Planner',[17] a tool that recommends keywords to advertisers. The tool is designed to improve the effectiveness of advertising by helping advertisers identify keywords related to their area of commerce, resulting in the placement of their ads in respect of users who are most likely to be responsive. Thus, continuing the example given above, if Company Y employed Google's Keyword Planner, the tool might:

> suggest to Company Y that it purchase not only the term 'furnace repair' but also the term 'X,' its competitor's brand name and trademark, so that Y's ad would appear on the screen of a searcher who searched Company X's trademark, seeking Company X's website.[18]

Based on this description of how keyword advertising works (or at least how Google employs it), it is clear that the practice of keyword advertising may give rise to trade mark infringements. In the circumstances, given the impracticalities involved in filing individual infringement actions against the advertisers who misused keyword advertising, right holders have attempted to, instead, hold the relevant intermediaries liable under trade mark law. In this regard, although trade mark proprietors may have a better prospect of success under the US Lanham Act 1946,[19] the position under the Trade Marks Directive, which has been implemented in EU member states and is also reflective of the current law on trade marks in the UK, is quite the opposite. The cases discussed below demonstrate this fact.

16 *Rescuecom v Google*, 126 (Leval J). The CJEU has also explained how Google's AdWords service operates (*Google v Louis Vuitton*, [22]–[27]).

17 This was previously called the 'Keyword Suggestion Tool'. See <https://adwords.google.com/intl/en_sg/home/tools/keyword-planner> (accessed 31 January 2019).

18 *Rescuecom v Google*, 126 (Leval J).

19 In *Rescuecom v Google*, the US Court of Appeal (2nd Cir.) reproached the US District Court (Northern District of New York) for summarily dismissing the trade mark infringement claim against Google on the basis that Google did not make any use of Rescuecom's trade mark in commerce. Accordingly, the Court of Appeals remanded the case back to the lower court for further proceedings to consider whether Google's use in commerce of Rescuecom's mark amounted to one that is prohibited under the Lanham Act 1946 giving rise to an infringement (at pp. 130–31). This was possible in view the fairly broad definition that the Lanham Act 1946 accorded to the phrase 'use in commerce' in section 45 (15 USC §1127). Interestingly, there was some ambiguity whether the section 45 definition for 'use in commerce' applied to the context of infringements, as the definition began with the words '[t]he term "use in commerce" means the bona fide use. . .', whereas infringing use is anything but bona fide. In an appendix attached to the judgment (at pp. 140–41), the Court highlighted the difficulty associated with interpreting the 'use in commerce' requirement in relation to the infringement provisions of the Lanham Act 1946 and concluded that '[i]t would be helpful for Congress to study and clear up this ambiguity'.

Wilson v Yahoo!

One of the first trade mark infringement cases to be filed against an internet intermediary questioning the legitimacy of the practice of keyword advertising was *Wilson v Yahoo!*.[20] The claimant, who owned the 'Mr Spicy' trade mark registered for poultry and meat products, sauces, and restaurant and bar services, claimed that Yahoo! made an unauthorised use of a 'sign' in the course of trade that was identical to the claimant's trade mark in relation to identical or similar goods or services.[21] The complaint arose because when an internet user typed the term 'Mr Spicy' and performed a search on the Yahoo! search engine, sponsored links to the websites of Sainsbury's and Pricegrabber were listed among the search results.[22] Both Sainsbury's and Pricegrabber offered products that were in direct competition with the claimant's products.

In defence, Yahoo! pleaded that neither Sainsbury's nor Pricegrabber (or any other advertiser) had chosen 'Mr Spicy' as their keywords to trigger sponsored links.[23] In essence, Yahoo!'s main argument was that neither it nor its advertisers at any point used the claimant's trade mark to trigger the sponsored links. All that was selected as a keyword by Yahoo!'s advertisers was the word 'spicy', in various forms, which by itself was a generic term.[24] In the circumstances, when internet users performed a search for 'Mr Spicy', the disputed advertisements appeared as a sponsored link amidst the natural search results.[25] Yahoo! put forward an additional defence: even if 'one holds that the defendants did use the phrase "Mr Spicy" then they did not use it in respect of the goods or services for which it is registered'.[26]

Considering these defences, Morgan J concluded:

> I can put my conclusions really quite concisely, and in my own words, as follows: The trade mark in this case is not used by anyone other than the browser [or internet user] who enters the phrase 'Mr. Spicy' as a search query in the defendants' search engine. In particular, the trade mark is not used by the defendants. The response of the defendants to the use of the trade mark by the browser is not use of the trade mark by the defendants. That is enough to decide the case in the defendants' favour.[27]

Thus, since neither the advertisers nor Yahoo! used the 'Mr Spicy' trade mark but instead merely utilised a generic term ('spicy') to trigger the sponsored links on Yahoo!'s search page, there simply was no trade mark infringement. However, one might ask: what if the advertisers did select 'Mr Spicy' as the keyword to

20 *Wilson v Yahoo! UK Ltd* [2008] ETMR 33 (*Wilson v Yahoo!*).
21 *Wilson v Yahoo!*, [7] (Morgan J).
22 *Wilson v Yahoo!*, [9] (Morgan J).
23 *Wilson v Yahoo!*, [31] (Morgan J).
24 *Wilson v Yahoo!*, [31] and [55] (Morgan J).
25 *Wilson v Yahoo!*, [32] (Morgan J).
26 *Wilson v Yahoo!*, [34] (Morgan J).
27 *Wilson v Yahoo!*, [64] (Morgan J).

trigger the sponsored links hosted on Yahoo!'s system? In *Wilson v Yahoo!*, even assuming that the keyword that was selected by the respective advertisers was 'Mr Spicy', there was nothing to establish that the text appearing on the sponsored links itself, which was visible to internet users, comprised the 'Mr Spicy' trade mark. As such, the only use made of the trade mark was purely *internal* and *technical*, first at the time of keyword selection and, second, when Yahoo!'s technology operated to display the sponsored links when the search term matched the keyword. According to Morgan J, such uses of a trade mark do not amount to 'use as a trade mark', even when that concept is applied in the wider context as propounded in *Arsenal v Reed*,[28] i.e. to use of trade marks made by third parties calculated at prejudicing the various functions of a trade mark.[29]

What *Wilson v Yahoo!* establishes is that, even in circumstances where a trade mark is selected as a keyword to trigger a sponsored link, the intermediary that is responsible for providing the service and hosting the third party's advertisement cannot be held liable for infringement under section 10 of the Trade Marks Act 1994. Such an outcome is inevitable, as the requisite 'use' requirement necessary to establish an infringement claim remains unsatisfied. However, this begs the further question: what if the text of the sponsored link expressly incorporates a trade mark? Could that amount to *trade mark use* on the part of the intermediary hosting the sponsored link? This issue, among others, was explicitly dealt with by the CJEU in *Google v Louis Vuitton*, discussed below.

Google v Louis Vuitton

The ruling of the CJEU in *Google v Louis Vuitton* is of fundamental importance to this discussion, as it sets out the key principles that come into play in determining the liability of internet intermediaries under EU and national trade mark regimes. The jurisdiction of the CJEU was invoked consequent to a reference being made by the French Cour de cassation, the court of last resort in civil and criminal matters, for a preliminary ruling in three connected cases where Google was the defendant-appellant.[30] Google was originally found liable by the Tribunal de grande instance de Paris (High Court of Paris) for trade mark infringement because Google permitted its advertisers to select and use keywords that were identical or similar to registered French trade marks.[31] On appeal by Google, the Cour d'appel de Paris (Court of Appeal of Paris) affirmed the decision at first instance.[32] Google appealed against that decision to the French Cour de cassation, consequent to which a reference was made to the CJEU.[33]

28 Case C-206/01, *Arsenal Football Club plc v Mathew Reed* [2002] ECR I-10273 (*Arsenal v Reed*).

29 *Wilson v Yahoo!*, [58] and [66] (Morgan J).

30 Although Louis Vuitton was the claimant in only the first reference (C-236/08) and several other claimants were involved in the other references, the CJEU pronounced a ruling that was common to all the references.

31 For the procedural history of the case, see *Google v Louis Vuitton*, [31].

32 *Google v Louis Vuitton*, [31].

33 *Google v Louis Vuitton*, [31].

The Cour de cassation referred, among other things, the following question for CJEU's response:

> Must Art.5(1)(a) and (b) of [the Trade Marks Directive] be interpreted as meaning that a provider of a paid referencing service who makes available to advertisers keywords reproducing or imitating registered trade marks and arranges by the referencing agreement to create and favourably display, on the basis of those keywords, advertising links to sites offering infringing goods *is using those trade marks in a manner which their proprietor is entitled to prevent*?[34]

In other words, the CJEU was asked to consider whether a trade mark proprietor was entitled to prevent the use of a keyword that was identical or similar to a registered trade mark by an intermediary (such as Google) in offering keyword advertising services. This raises a further, more crucial, question as to what types of use of a trade mark made by an unauthorised third party are prohibited under the Trade Marks Directive. In this regard, reference must be made to Article 5(1) of the Trade Marks Directive, which provides:

> The registered trade mark shall confer on the proprietor exclusive rights therein. The proprietor shall be entitled to prevent all third parties not having his consent from using in the course of trade:
>
> (a) any sign which is identical with the trade mark in relation to goods or services which are identical with those for which the trade mark is registered;
> (b) any sign where, because of its identity with, or similarity to, the trade mark and the identity or similarity of the goods or services covered by the trade mark and the sign, there exists a likelihood of confusion on the part of the public; the likelihood of confusion includes the likelihood of association between the sign and the trade mark.[35]

Upon a reading of Article 5(1), it becomes clear that the reference to 'use' has a double significance. First, only third-party use of a registered trade mark made *in the course of trade* may be prohibited. Second, only third-party use of a registered trade mark *in relation to goods or services that are identical or similar to those for which the trade mark is registered* may be prohibited.

Before the CJEU delivered its ruling, it sought the opinion of the Advocate General, who explicitly highlighted the limitations of trade mark law when it was applied to intermediaries operating in the online space, such as Google.

34 *Google v Louis Vuitton*, [32] (emphasis added).

35 Articles 5(1)(a) and (b) of the 2008 and 1988 Trade Marks Directive has been reproduced, in essential form, in Articles 10(2)(a) and (b) of the 2015 Trade Marks Directive. But the opening sentence of Article 5(1) in the older directives—'The registered trade mark shall confer on the proprietor exclusive rights therein'—is now found in Article 10(1) of the 2015 directive.

The Advocate General's opinion

The Advocate General's opinion concerning the use of the claimants' trade marks by Google was formulated by considering two interrelated points. First, he opined that, when Google offers advertisers the possibility of selecting keywords, which correspond to trade marks, it does so as a commercial activity, and in the process, makes use of trade marks *in the course of trade*.[36] In view of this conclusion, the Advocate General had to consider whether Google made use of trade marks *in relation to any goods or services* for which such marks were registered. In this connection, the Advocate General observed:

> It seems evident that AdWords is not identical or similar to any of the goods or services covered by the trade marks. Accordingly, this condition is not satisfied and, in consequence, the use consisting in allowing advertisers to select in AdWords keywords which correspond to trade marks, so that ads for their sites are presented as results for searches involving those keywords, does not constitute a trade mark infringement.[37]

In essence, Google's use of keywords corresponding to trade marks amounted to use in the course of trade. However, Google did *not* make use of any trade marks in relation to any goods or services for which the claimants' marks were registered, as Google's AdWords service was not a type of service that either Louis Vuitton or any of the other claimants offered.

The Advocate General's analysis raises an important question, i.e. could Article 5(2) of the Trade Marks Directive[38] play a role in cases such as this? Unlike Article 5(1), Article 5(2) applies to marks with a reputation and allows trade mark proprietors to prohibit the unauthorised third-party use of a trade mark even in relation to goods or services that are dissimilar to those for which the mark is registered, provided that the third party's use 'without due cause takes unfair advantage of, or is detrimental to, the distinctive character or the repute of the trade mark'. This is regarded as the provision in the Trade Marks Directive that protects against the 'dilution' of trade marks (the anti-dilution provision).[39] Neither the Advocate General nor the CJEU had the opportunity of providing any guidance on the applicability of Article 5(2) to the factual matrix of *Google v Louis Vuitton*, as the French Cour de cassation did not seek guidance on this specific point. This was presumably because, when Louis Vuitton brought its claim before the French courts, it never pleaded infringement under the French provision that corresponds to Article 5(2). However, attempting to formulate an answer to this question is important, as Article 5(2)

36 *Google v Louis Vuitton*, Opinion of AG Maduro, [61].

37 *Google v Louis Vuitton*, Opinion of AG Maduro, [67].

38 Article 5(2) of the 2008 and 1988 Trade Marks Directive has been reproduced, in essential form, in Article 10(2)(c) of the 2015 Trade Marks Directive.

39 L Bently et al, *Intellectual Property Law* (5th edn, Oxford University Press 2018), 1052.

of the Trade Marks Directive may be a potential avenue to hold intermediaries offering an online service liable for infringements.

In order to address this point, reference must be made to the slightly different but related context of *cybersquatting*. Generally speaking, a 'cybersquatter'[40] or 'cyber pirate'[41] is someone who registers a domain name associated with an existing trade mark or trade name with the intention of selling counterfeit goods, imitating the brand or selling the domain name to the proprietor of the trade mark or trade name. Thus, it is clear that cybersquatting is a cause for concern to trade mark proprietors. Despite the Internet Corporation for Assigned Names and Numbers (ICANN) having devised the Uniform Domain Name Dispute Resolution Policy (UDRP), which allows domain name disputes to be resolved, there are instances when trade mark proprietors have chosen to institute a trade mark infringement action instead.

Even in this regard, the 'use' requirement imposed under trade mark law has caused difficulty in protecting the interests of trade mark proprietors vis-à-vis cybersquatters. The English Court of Appeal[42] and High Court[43] decisions in a case instituted by British Telecom and three other major UK brand owners, against a cybersquatter, demonstrate this difficulty. In this case, several well-known trade marks were incorporated into domain names and were registered by the defendants without the consent of the claimants.[44] This included, for instance, 'britishtelecom.co.uk', 'sainsburys.com', 'marksandspencer.com', '0700.net', 'macdonalds.co.uk' and 'ladbrokes.com'.[45] The aggrieved trade mark proprietors brought two simultaneous claims, i.e. for trade mark infringement (under the Trade Marks Act 1994) and passing off. At first instance, and during the subsequent appeal, the courts had no difficulty in concluding that the claim for passing off should succeed, albeit the trade mark infringement claim was less straightforward.

At first instance, it was established that none of the domain names in question were being used in relation to active websites.[46] Thus, the defendants were mere passive holders of the domain names that were identical or similar to the claimants' well-known marks. This meant that the defendants were not making any use of the claimants' marks ***in relation to goods or services which were identical with or similar to those for which the trade mark was registered***. As a result, no claim could have been brought (and in fact was not) under sections 10(1) or (2) of the Trade

40 D Lindsay, *International Domain Name Law: ICANN and the UDRP* (Hart Publishing 2007), 96–99. See also, M Servian, 'Help! Someone's Squatting on My Brand—Cybersquatting' (2013) 19 *Computer and Telecommunications Law Review* 92.

41 A Davidson, *The Law of Electronic Commerce* (Cambridge University Press 2009), 146.

42 *British Telecommunications Plc v One in a Million Ltd* [1999] FSR 1 (*BT v One in a Million*).

43 *British Telecommunications Plc v One in a Million Ltd* [1998] FSR 265 (*BT v One in a Million* (HC)).

44 *BT v One in a Million* (HC), 267–68 (Sumption J).

45 *BT v One in a Million* (HC), 268–69 (Sumption J).

46 *BT v One in a Million* (HC), 269 (Sumption J).

Marks Act 1994, which resemble Articles 5(1)(a) and (b) of the Trade Marks Directive. However, since the trade marks concerned had a reputation in the UK, the claimants pleaded infringement under section 10(3),[47] which corresponds to the anti-dilution provision of the Trade Marks Directive. Accordingly, at first instance, the Court had to first decide whether the defendants' use of the trade marks in the domain names amounted to use *in the course of trade.* The judge came to the same conclusion reached by the Advocate General, as well as the CJEU,[48] almost a decade later in *Google v Louis Vuitton*—'[u]se "in the course of trade" means use by way of business. It does not mean use as a trade mark. . .'[49] However, the observation of the judge, which immediately followed, was somewhat odd:

> The use of a trade mark in the course of the business of a *professional dealer for the purpose of making domain names more valuable and extracting money from the trade mark owner* is a use in the course of trade.[50]

Clearly, the defendants were not selling any goods. However, it appears that the judge wrongly assumed that the defendants were providing a *service.*[51] The Court of Appeal endorsed this finding. Thus, having found that injunctive relief must be granted as *threats to infringe* trade mark rights had been established,[52] Aldous LJ (with whom the other judges agreed) went on to hold that the domain names incorporating the claimants' marks 'will be used *in relation to the services provided by the registrant who trades in domain names*'.[53] This is indeed an unusual conclusion because it has the effect of equating the practice of cybersquatting to the provision of a *professional service* relating to domain names. The English High Court, in *Global Projects Management Ltd v Citigroup Inc*,[54] followed the decision in *BT v One in a Million*, despite it being criticised by academics[55] and expressly rejected by the Australian Federal Court, which had to apply the infringement provisions of the Australian Trade Marks Act 1995 (Cth) to a similar dispute.[56]

47 This provision of the Trade Marks Act 1994 corresponds to Article 5(2) of the Trade Marks Directive.

48 The CJEU's ruling in *Google v Louis Vuitton* is considered later in this chapter.

49 *BT v One in a Million* (HC), 272 (Sumption J).

50 *BT v One in a Million* (HC), 272 (Sumption J) (emphasis added).

51 The High Court's language, particularly the use of the phrase 'professional dealer', implies this.

52 *BT v One in a Million*, 25 (Aldous LJ).

53 *BT v One in a Million*, 25 (Aldous LJ) (emphasis added).

54 [2006] FSR 39.

55 See e.g. M Moore, 'Cybersquatting: Prevention Better Than Cure?' (2008) 17 *International Journal of Law and Information Technology* 220, 223.

56 *CSR Ltd v Resource Capital Australia Pty Ltd* [2003] FCA 279, an Australian case factually identical to *BT v One in a Million*. The Australian Federal Court denied the trade mark infringement claim on the basis that the defendant made no use of trade marks as required under the Australian Trade Marks Act 1995 (Cth) (Hill J at [42]). This was followed in *Sports Warehouse Inc v Fry Consulting Pty Ltd* [2010] FCA 664 and *Mantra Group Pty v Tailly Pty Ltd (No2)* [2010] FCA 291.

Although the finding that the defendants in *BT v One in a Million* were providing a service is questionable, the case suggests that section 10(3) of the Trade Marks Act 1994 may provide a basis for holding intermediaries that make use of trade marks in the course of providing an online service liable for infringement. In fact, unlike the defendants in *BT v One in a Million*, Google was providing a genuine service as an intermediary. Thus, in *Google v Louis Vuitton*, had the French Cour de cassation sought a clarification on the applicability of Article 5(2) of the Trade Marks Directive, which corresponds to section 10(3) of the Trade Marks Act 1994, to the context of an intermediary providing an online service, the Advocate General might have opined that Google did, in fact, make use of the 'Louis Vuitton' and other marks in offering its AdWords service. This, in turn, would have required the Advocate General to consider whether Google's use of those well-known marks *as keywords* took unfair advantage of, or was detrimental to, the distinctive character or repute of the trade marks in question. Accordingly, the logic in *BT v One in a Million* supports the view that the anti-dilution provision of the Trade Marks Directive, at least in respect of marks with a reputation, *may* provide a basis for right holders to prohibit the use of trade marks by intermediaries, such as Google, provided the other requirements for infringement under that provision are met.

It must be noted, however, that the subsequent ruling of the CJEU in *Google v Louis Vuitton* stands as an obstacle against the potential use of the anti-dilution provision as a basis to hold internet intermediaries liable for infringements. This is in view of the 'commercial communication' requirement that the CJEU introduced in dealing with infringement in the online space, significantly curtailing the reach of trade mark law to intermediaries providing online services.

The CJEU ruling and the 'commercial communication' requirement

In *Google v Louis Vuitton*, the CJEU commenced its analysis, just as the Advocate General did, by considering whether Google made use of any trade marks *in the course of trade*.[57] In this regard, the CJEU came to the same conclusion as the Advocate General, i.e. that Google did make use of the trade marks concerned with a view of gaining economically and that this constituted use in the course of trade.[58] It is clear, therefore, that in offering keywords for sale and hosting the sponsored links, Google was engaging in a commercial activity. However, the Court added the following qualification:

> In that regard, suffice it to note that the use, by a third party, of a sign identical with, or similar to, the proprietor's trade mark implies, at the very least, that *that third party uses the sign in its own commercial communication*.[59]

57 The CJEU observed (at [50]) that '[t]he use of a sign identical with a trade mark constitutes use in the course of trade where it occurs in the context of commercial activity with a view to economic advantage and not as a private matter'.

58 *Google v Louis Vuitton*, [53].

59 *Google v Louis Vuitton*, [56] (emphasis added).

In essence, according to the CJEU, the act of creating the technical conditions necessary for the use of a trade mark by a third party (i.e. the advertisers in this case) and being paid for that service does not mean that the party offering the service itself uses the mark in its own commercial communication.[60] This was the first time the CJEU used the phrase 'commercial communication', effectively introducing a novel concept into EU trade mark jurisprudence. Notably, the Trade Marks Directive itself does not provide the basis for the introduction of such a concept.

It is unclear as to what the CJEU meant by this phrase.[61] However, the Court's ruling suggests that the 'commercial communication' requirement was meant to be applied as a threshold factor. In this regard, a point worth considering is whether the CJEU was merely restating the 'trade mark use' requirement, which essentially has the effect of limiting an infringement action to situations concerning the unauthorised use of a trade mark to indicate the *source* of the underlying goods/services.[62] It must be noted that both the Advocate General[63] and the CJEU,[64] in dealing with the scope of trade mark rights under the Trade Marks Directive, have preferred to avoid the language of 'trade mark use', that being a concept more familiar to English courts.[65] Especially after the CJEU's ruling in *Arsenal v Reed*, the usual question posed is whether a third party's

60 *Google v Louis Vuitton*, [57].

61 Unfortunately, the recent editions of leading texts on the subject do not adequately discuss the meaning attaching to the phrase 'commercial communication'. See e.g. W Cornish, D Llewelyn and T Aplin, *Intellectual Property: Patents, Copyright, Trade Marks and Allied Rights* (8th edn, Sweet & Maxwell 2013), 759 (where the 'use' requirement is discussed in relation to infringement) and Bently et al, above n39, 1113 (where the issue of 'use' is discussed in the context of the internet). Even the more recent journal articles written in the European context have not adequately addressed this matter. See e.g. Psaroudakis, above n13, 33–34; T Bednarz, 'Keyword Advertising before the French Supreme Court and beyond – Calm at Last after Turbulent Times for Google and Its Advertising Clients?' (2011) 42 *International Review of Intellectual Property and Competition Law (IIC)* 641; C Morcom, 'Trade Marks and the Internet: Where Are We Now?' (2012) 34 *European Intellectual Property Review* 40, 41–43; and A Blythe, 'Trade Marks as Adwords: An Aid to Competition or a Potential Infringement? An Evaluation of the Law in the Light of Recent Decisions' (2015) 37 *European Intellectual Property Review* 225.

62 *R v Johnstone* [2003] UKHL 28, [13] (Lord Nicholls):

> the essence of a trade mark has always been that it is a badge of origin. It indicates trade source: a connection in the course of trade between the goods and the proprietor of the mark. That is its function. Hence the exclusive rights granted to the proprietor of a registered trade mark are limited to use of a mark likely to be taken as an indication of trade origin. Use of this character is an essential prerequisite to infringement

and *Mothercare UK Ltd v Penguin Books* [1988] RPC 113, 118 (Dillon LJ):

> it stands to reason that a Trade Marks Act would only be concerned to restrict the use of a mark as a trade mark or in a trade mark sense, and should be construed accordingly. If descriptive words are legitimately registered [as a trade mark], there is still no reason why other people should not be free to use the words in a descriptive sense, and not in any trade mark sense.

63 See e.g. *Arsenal v Reed*, Opinion of AG Colomer, [41].

64 See e.g. Case C-100/02, *Gerolsteiner Brunnen GmbH & Co v Putsch GmbH* [2004] ECR I-00691, [15].

65 See B Trimmer, 'An Increasingly Uneasy Relationship – The English Courts and the European Court of Justice in Trade Mark Disputes' (2008) 30 *European Intellectual Property Review* 87.

unauthorised use of a trade mark is *liable to affect the essential function of the trade mark*.[66] However, in *R v Johnstone*, the UK House of Lords observed that the CJEU's characterisation of the function of a trade mark in *Arsenal v Reed* was 'in terms which accord with the approach of English law', alluding that the notion of 'trade mark use' is reconcilable with the Trade Marks Directive.[67] Accordingly, 'trade mark use' after *Arsenal v Reed* simply refers to use that is calculated at affecting the *essential function of a trade mark*. Thus, in *Google v Louis Vuitton*, when the CJEU ruled that Google did *not* make use of the trade marks in question in its own commercial communication, one possibility is that the Court simply meant that Google's use was not the kind that was bound to affect the essential function of a trade mark, i.e. to indicate trade source.

The CJEU in *Hölterhoff v Freiesleben*[68] ruled that *purely descriptive* uses of trade marks made by third parties do not affect the origin function of a trade mark protected by Article 5 of the Trade Marks Directive. In this case, the disputing parties were jewellers. The claimant was the proprietor of two German marks, 'SPIRIT SUN' and 'CONTEXT CUT' for diamonds and precious stones. In July 1997, the defendant sold two garnets to a jewellery business. The garnets were identified in the delivery note and invoice simply as 'rhodolites', although it was accepted that the defendant had referred to the claimant's trade marks in the course of the pre-sale negotiations, and that the order was placed for two stones in the *Spirit Sun* cut. In the ensuing trade mark dispute, a reference was made to the CJEU by the Oberlandesgericht Düsseldorf (Higher Regional Court in Düsseldorf) on the question of whether *purely* descriptive uses of a trade mark are prohibited under Article 5(1) of the Trade Marks Directive. In response, the CJEU ruled:

> Article 5(1) of the directive is to be interpreted as meaning that the proprietor of a trade mark cannot rely on his exclusive right where a third party, in the course of commercial negotiations, reveals the origin of goods which he has produced himself and uses the sign in question solely to denote the particular characteristics of the goods he is offering for sale so that there can be no question of the trade mark used being perceived as a sign indicative of the undertaking of origin.[69]

In essence, *Hölterhoff v Freiesleben* suggests that *purely* descriptive uses of trade marks do not amount to a type of 'use' within the meaning of the Trade Marks Directive.

66 J Davis, *Intellectual Property Law* (3rd edn, Oxford University Press 2008), 220.

67 Although the CJEU has avoided the language of 'trade mark use', it has been suggested that the trade mark use doctrine has survived. See NM Dawson, 'Non-Trade Mark Use' [2012] *Intellectual Property Quarterly* 204, 226.

68 Case C-2/00, *Michael Hölterhoff v Ulrich Freiesleben* [2002] ECR I-04187 (*Hölterhoff v Freiesleben*).

69 *Hölterhoff v Freiesleben*, [17].

Again, in *Adam Opel v Autec*,[70] the CJEU had to determine the 'use' requirement in the infringement context. The claimant, a manufacturer of vehicles, discovered that its figurative German trade mark had been reproduced in the front radiator grille of a 1:24 remote-control scale model of the claimant's 'Opel Astra V8 coupé'. The toy scale model was manufactured by the defendant and marketed under the 'Cartronic' trade mark. The claimant's figurative mark was registered for both motor vehicles and toys. In the ensuing dispute, a regional German court (Landgericht Nürnberg-Fürth) made the following reference to the CJEU:

> Does the use of a trade mark registered also for 'toys' constitute *use as a trade mark* for the purposes of Article 5(1)(a) of the Trade Mark Directive if the manufacturer of a toy model car copies a real car in a reduced scale, including the trade mark of the proprietor of the trade mark as applied to the real car, and markets it?[71]

In response, the CJEU ruled:

> [T]he affixing by a third party of a sign identical to a trade mark registered for toys to scale models of vehicles *cannot* be prohibited under Article 5(1)(a) of the directive *unless it affects or is liable to affect the functions of that trade mark*.[72]

In commenting on certain explanations provided by the referring German Court, relating to the facts of the dispute, the CJEU observed:

> If, by those explanations, the referring court intended to emphasise that the relevant public does not perceive the sign identical to the Opel logo appearing on the scale models marketed by Autec as an indication that those products come from Adam Opel or an undertaking economically linked to it, it would have to conclude that the use at issue in the main proceedings does not affect the essential function of the Opel logo as a trade mark registered for toys.[73]

In essence, *Adam Opel v Autec* confirms that the Trade Marks Directive does not apply to the unauthorised third-party use of a trade mark when the relevant public does not perceive such use as indicating the origin of the third party's goods or services.

Accordingly, *non-trade mark use* is not the kind of use that comes within the meaning of Article 5 of the Trade Marks Directive. In terms of outcome, this is

70 Case C-48/05, *Adam Opel AG v Autec AG* [2007] ECR I-01017 (*Adam Opel v Autec*).
71 *Adam Opel v Autec*, [13].
72 *Adam Opel v Autec*, [22] (emphasis added).
73 *Adam Opel v Autec*, [24].

precisely what the CJEU ruled in *Google v Louis Vuitton*; that Google's use of the trade marks in question was not within the meaning of Article 5 of the Trade Marks Directive.[74] As such, when the ruling in *Google v Louis Vuitton* is taken in light of the CJEU's prior rulings in *Hölterhoff v Freiesleben* and *Adam Opel v Autec*, it may be posited that the 'commercial communication' requirement added nothing in substance, and that it was merely a restatement of the 'trade mark use' requirement.

However, there is a point that possibly dilutes the above supposition. Although in *Hölterhoff v Freiesleben*[75] and *Adam Opel v Autec*[76] the CJEU ruled that there was no 'trade mark use' in the circumstances of those cases, the Court nevertheless pointed out that those were instances where the third party did, in fact, make use of a trade mark *in the course of trade* and *in relation to goods or services.* In contrast, in *Google v Louis Vuitton*, when the CJEU introduced the 'commercial communication' requirement, it was focussing on the 'in the course of trade' aspect of Article 5(1) of the Trade Marks Directive. In fact, the Court's analysis of the 'in relation to goods or services' aspect of Article 5(1) was reserved only in respect of the advertisers.[77] More importantly, the CJEU pointed out that the role of Google had to be examined 'from an angle of rules of law other than Article 5 of [the Trade Marks Directive]', hinting that the Court regarded Google as an accessory and not an infringer at all. Given these differences between the CJEU's approach in *Google v Louis Vuitton* and the previous case law on *trade mark use*, it is more likely that the 'commercial communication' and 'trade mark use' requirement are distinct concepts. Based on the analytical framework adopted by the CJEU in respect of Article 5 of the Trade Marks Directive, as visible from the case law discussed above, it seems that the 'commercial communication' requirement is a factor that must be considered *before* engaging in an analysis about 'trade mark use'.

A second point worth considering is whether the CJEU's stance in regarding Google's use of the trade marks in question as not in its own commercial communication was because Google made no *discernible use* of the trade marks. After all, when Google provided its advertising services, its use of any trade marks in

74 *Google v Louis Vuitton*, [55]:

> Although it is clear from those factors that the referencing service provider operates 'in the course of trade' when it permits advertisers to select, as keywords, signs identical with trade marks, stores those signs and displays its clients' ads on the basis thereof, it does not follow, however, from those factors that that service provider itself 'uses' those signs within the terms of Article 5 of [the Trade Marks Directive].

75 *Hölterhoff v Freiesleben*, [14] ('It is common ground that, in such a situation, the use of the trade mark is a use in the course of trade in relation to products identical with or similar to those for which the trade mark was registered').

76 *Adam Opel v Autec*, [20] ('In that regard, it should be noted in particular that the use at issue in the main proceedings is made "in relation to goods" within the meaning of Article 5(1)(a) of the directive').

77 *Google v Louis Vuitton*, [59]:

> Consequently, the conditions relating to use 'in relation to goods or services' and to the effect on the functions of the trade mark need to be examined only in relation to the use, by the advertiser, of the sign identical with the mark.

the form of keywords was purely *internal*, *technical* and *invisible* to the internet user. A similar argument was put forward in the context of the 'trade mark use' requirement—'an internal use of the sign, which is not discernible by consumers, cannot be *a use as a trade mark*'.[78]

However, an analysis of the CJEU's ruling in *Google v Louis Vuitton* reveals that the 'commercial communication' requirement does not necessarily relate to the issue of discernibility. In addressing the conduct of the advertisers, the Court was concerned with two types of factual situations. In the first situation, the third-party advertisers had utilised the claimants' trade marks in the text of the sponsored links.[79] In doing so, the advertisers were making use of the trade marks in question in a manner that was visible to internet users. In the second situation, the advertisers made no reference to the trade marks of the claimants in the text of the sponsored links.[80] In other words, neither Google nor its advertisers made any *visible* use of the trade marks. Accordingly, if the argument that any indiscernible use of a mark cannot amount to use of that mark in a 'commercial communication' was acceptable to the CJEU, in respect of the second situation the Court should have concluded that no infringing use of any marks was being made. Instead, the CJEU ruled:

> [T]he fact that the sign used by the third party for advertising purposes *does not appear in the ad itself cannot of itself mean that that use falls outside the concept of [use] within the terms of art.5 of [the Trade Marks Directive].*[81]

Thus, although in some of the sponsored links the advertisers made no visible use of any trade marks, the Court did not disqualify such use as being not in the advertisers' own commercial communication. Accordingly, purely invisible uses of trade marks may still go on to satisfy the 'commercial communication' requirement. Under this logical construct, it cannot be stated that discernibility is a precondition for a third party's use of a trade mark to be in its own commercial communication.

This conclusion is supported by a subsequent ruling of the CJEU in *Belgian Electronic v Peelaers*,[82] a reference that concerned the Comparative Advertising Directive.[83] The Court had to interpret the term 'advertising' appearing in that directive in the context of the use of trade marks as 'metatags' that were embedded in the internal code that related to a particular website. Some search engines prioritise their natural search results based on metatags that appear in the internal

78 Psaroudakis, above n13, 33 (citation and internal quotation marks omitted) (emphasis added).

79 *Google v Louis Vuitton*, [62].

80 *Google v Louis Vuitton*, [63].

81 *Google v Louis Vuitton*, [65] (emphasis added).

82 Case C-657/11, *Belgian Electronic Sorting Technology NV v Bert Peelaers* [2013] ETMR 45 (*Belgian Electronic v Peelaers*).

83 Directive 2006/114/EC of the European Parliament and of the Council of 12 December 2006 Concerning Misleading and Comparative Advertising [2006] OJ L 376/21 (Comparative Advertising Directive).

code of websites.[84] Metatags could embed anything, but usually, keywords that are related to the content of a website are embedded so that the website would turn up among the search results when a search is performed using the embedded keyword. In short, metatags are used to indicate relevance. Just as with keyword advertising, trade mark-related issues could arise where metatags that are identical or similar to trade marks are used in a third party's website. In this regard, the CJEU observed:

> In so far as the use of metatags corresponding to the names of a competitor's goods and its trade name in the programming code of a website has, therefore, the consequence that it is suggested to the internet user who enters one of those names or that trade name as a search term that that site is related to his search, such use must be considered as a form of representation within the meaning of Article 2(1) of Directive 84/450 and Article 2(a) of Directive 2006/114.[85]

In essence, the use of trade marks as metatags in the internal code of a website, albeit not visible to internet users, amounted to a 'representation' capable of advertising goods or services.[86] By the same logic, it must be concluded that the determination as to whether a third party's use of a trade mark was in the user's own 'commercial communication' does not depend on whether the use was discernible to internet users.

At best, we can only speculate as to what the CJEU meant, in the course of delivering its ruling in *Google v Louis Vuitton*, when it said that Google did not make use of any trade marks in its own commercial communication.[87] What we know for certain is that 'commercial communication' does not mean 'trade mark use'. Nor is it a reference to discernible use. The requirement applies as a threshold factor to determine whether a right holder could prohibit a third party's use of a trade mark. Unless there is use of a trade mark in the third party's own commercial communication, there cannot be use within the meaning of Article 5 of the Trade Marks Directive or its national equivalent.

The impact of the 'commercial communication' requirement on the liability of internet intermediaries

The 'commercial communication' requirement has effectively rendered the Trade Marks Directive inapplicable to *internal*, *technical* and *invisible* uses of

84 See TP Ross, *Intellectual Property: Damages and Remedies* (Law Journal Press 2005), 6–43 and DE Bouchoux, *Intellectual Property Law* (5th edn, Cengage Learning 2018), 158.

85 *Belgian Electronic v Peelaers*, [57].

86 *Belgian Electronic v Peelaers*, [58].

87 A Blythe, 'A Useful Test for Trade Mark Use: An Analysis of Current CJEU Guidance and the Difference between Defining Use Online and Offline' (2016) *European Intellectual Property Review* 563.

trade marks on the part of intermediaries providing keyword advertising services. The CJEU has also followed the approach in *Google v Louis Vuitton* in subsequent cases. Thus, for instance, in *L'Oréal v eBay*, the threshold requirement was applied in relation to an intermediary that hosted third-party product listings in an online marketplace.[88] According to the Court:

> If a sign identical with, or similar to, the proprietor's trade mark is to be 'used', within the meaning of Art.5 of [the Trade Marks Directive], by a third party, that implies, at the very least, that that third party uses the sign in its own commercial communication. *In so far as that third party provides a service consisting in enabling its customers to display on its website, in the course of their commercial activities such as their offers for sale, signs corresponding to trade marks, it does not itself use those signs within the meaning of that EU legislation.*[89]

The 'commercial communication' requirement has also been applied by the English courts. Thus, for instance, in the course of delivering the decision of the English High Court in *OCH-Ziff v OCH Capital*,[90] Arnold J applied the 'commercial communication' requirement, albeit to a different context:[91]

> The reasoning with respect to the referencing service provider (i.e. the operator of the search engine, such as Google) is not entirely easy to follow. As I understand it, however, the Court of Justice's starting point is that it was common ground that the referencing service provider was carrying out a commercial activity with a view to economic advantage (see [53]). Nevertheless, the Court of Justice held that there was no 'use in the course of trade' by the referencing service provider (see [58]). The key step in the reasoning is at [56], where the Court holds that a referencing service provider does not itself use the sign in question because it does not use the sign 'in its own commercial communication.' It seems to me that this reasoning may be interpreted in two ways. The first is that the referencing service provider does not use the sign 'in the course of trade' because its use is 'as a private matter' even though it is 'in the context of commercial activity with a view to economic advantage'. . . . The second is that the referencing service provider does not 'use' the sign at all within the meaning of Article 5 of the Directive . . . : it simply provides the medium for the use made by the

88 Case C-324/09, *L'Oréal SA v eBay International AG* [2011] ECR I-06011 (*L'Oréal v eBay*).

89 *L'Oréal v eBay*, [102] (emphasis added).

90 *OCH-Ziff Europe Ltd v OCH Capital* [2011] Bus LR 632 (*OCH-Ziff v OCH Capital*).

91 This case did not concern the use of trade marks by an internet intermediary. Rather, the question was whether the defendant's use of a trade mark in *internal emails* was 'use' that could be prohibited by the claimant. Mr Justice Arnold held that it was not, as internal use was not use in the defendant's own commercial communication (at [66]).

> advertiser. Although in most cases it will not matter which interpretation is adopted, since the result will be the same, I consider that the second interpretation is to be preferred.[92]

It is important, however, to distinguish *Google v Louis Vuitton* and *L'Oréal v eBay* from a more recent case, *Cosmetic Warriors v Amazon*.[93] In this case, the English High Court had the opportunity to consider the 'commercial communication' requirement in relation to Amazon, an intermediary that functioned like eBay. One of the infringement claims brought by the claimant (the proprietor of the 'LUSH' trade mark) concerned the internal search engine provided by Amazon to assist users to find products listed for sale on its platform. The Court explained:

> [I]f a consumer searches for the word 'Lush' in the relevant 'department' of Amazon's UK site (e.g. 'Beauty' or 'Health and Personal Care'), the first thing to happen after the letters 'lu' are typed, is that a drop down menu appears and various options are offered such as 'lush bath bombs' or 'lush cosmetics' or 'lush hair extensions', the consumer being offered the opportunity to click on one of these options whereupon a new page will appear.[94]

The main grievance of the claimant was that the new webpage to which users were taken contained listings of similar products to those sold by the claimant under the 'LUSH' brand, but 'without any overt reference to the Lush item not being available'.[95] The products listed on the webpage comprised three categories: goods owned by Amazon, goods owned by third parties for which Amazon provides fulfilment services (e.g. dispatching, customer service and returns) and goods owned and sold by third parties.[96] The question before the judge was whether Amazon made infringing use of the 'LUSH' mark when its search tool auto-generated links incorporating the word 'lush' with various combinations such as 'bath bombs', 'cosmetics' and 'hair extensions', directing users to products that were sold by Amazon, as well as third parties. In this regard, Baldwin J observed that '[t]he facts of the present case are quite different from those in either *Google France* or *L'Oreal v eBay*',[97] and concluded:

> On the facts of this case, I do not think Amazon can escape from the conclusion that it has used the Lush sign in the course of trade in relation to the relevant goods based on the principles to be found in *Google France* and

92 *OCH-Ziff v OCH Capital*, [59]–[61] (Arnold J).
93 *Cosmetic Warriors v Amazon.co.uk Ltd* [2014] EWHC 181 (Ch) (*Cosmetic Warriors v Amazon*).
94 *Cosmetic Warriors v Amazon*, [11] (Baldwin J).
95 *Cosmetic Warriors v Amazon*, [11] (Baldwin J).
96 *Cosmetic Warriors v Amazon*, [15] (Baldwin J).
97 *Cosmetic Warriors v Amazon*, [57] (Baldwin J).

> *L'Oreal v eBay*. It has used the sign as part of a commercial communication that it is selling the goods on its website.[98]

Considering the above, when Google sold keywords that were identical to trade marks and when eBay permitted its users to display trade marks in the course of listing and selling goods without the consent of the trade mark proprietors, neither Google nor eBay used any trade mark in their own commercial communication. On the other hand, what *Cosmetic Warriors v Amazon* suggests is that the unauthorised use of a trade mark in the course of trade and in relation to goods sold by the party making use of that mark without doubt satisfies the 'commercial communication' requirement:

> Amazon had *communicated* the LUSH sign to consumers to indicate that it was selling the goods on its website, and . . . this amounted to use in the course of trade.[99]

The role of Amazon, unlike Google or eBay, was not passive and neutral. Instead, it played a more active role and was involved commercially with the underlying transactions, part of which concerned its own goods. In light of this, it would be difficult to classify Amazon as an intermediary that merely provided access to, hosted or indexed content. Thus, although *Cosmetic Warriors v Amazon* did concern an online marketplace, its role went beyond that of a true intermediary.

The upshot of all this is that the 'commercial communication' requirement will not be satisfied where trade marks are used merely in a *technical* capacity without reference to any goods or services. In fact, if *BT v One in a Million* had to be decided today, the 'commercial communication' requirement would prevent a finding that a cybersquatter's conduct comes within the prohibitions set out in Article 5 of the Trade Marks Directive (or section 10 of Trade Marks Act 1994), as the mere passive holding of a domain name comprising a trade mark would not constitute use of that trade mark in any commercial communication.

Ultimately, the requirement that a trade mark must be used in a third party's own commercial communication in order to sustain a claim for infringement

98 *Cosmetic Warriors v Amazon*, [61] (Baldwin J). Since Amazon's use of the 'LUSH' mark in the context of its search tool was in relation to the sale of goods on its website, particularly goods of its own, the conclusion that the use was in Amazon's own commercial communication was inevitable. This is patently clear from the following observations of the judge at [57]: 'Nor do I consider it necessary to distinguish for the purposes of determining liability the three separate categories of sales via the website. In relation to the third category, Amazon may just be an online market place but the items in this category are mixed up with those in the other two categories, and Amazon's involvement in the transactions of these other two categories is more than sufficient for it to be commercially involved in the offering for sale and selling; *the display on the website is part of its own commercial communication within paragraph [102] of L'Oreal v eBay*' (emphasis added).

99 D Fields and K Shaw, 'UK High Court Considers Extent to Which Retailers May Use Third-Party Trade Marks in Advertisements' (2014) 20 *Computer and Telecommunications Law Review* 113, 114 (emphasis added).

against that party, will have implications for internet intermediaries in general, and not just for search engines and online marketplaces that host third-party advertisements or product listings. Although internet intermediaries, whether ISPs, hosts or navigation providers, engage in economic activity, their conduct does not come within the parameters of the Trade Marks Directive (or the Trade Marks Act 1994), since they do not make use of any trade marks in their own commercial communication. As a result, the action for trade mark infringement does not provide a viable basis upon which internet intermediaries could be held liable for providing access to, hosting or indexing content that gives rise to trade mark infringements.

The position in the UK is unlikely to change, even after Brexit, because UK courts have always applied the 'use' requirements strictly to the online context, as cases such as *Wilson v Yahoo!* demonstrate. As such, it becomes necessary to look outside the boundaries of conventional trade mark law in order to consider approaches to holding internet intermediaries liable for their role in making infringing content accessible and available to internet users. The next chapter does precisely that, by considering the scope of accessory liability under the English common law.

3 Accessory liability

Although internet intermediaries, in a technical capacity, may become involved in the transmission, storage or indexing of content that gives rise to trade mark infringements, it is difficult to describe them as primary infringers, as they do not make *use* of any trade marks in a strict trade mark sense. Rather, these intermediaries, or at least a subclass of them, are better described as secondary parties, whose services are used by subscribing internet users to commit infringements. Even though it might be thought that the burden of imposing accessorial liability for civil wrongs, particularly for tortious conduct, is less in comparison to the criminal context, that is not necessarily the case. This is an outcome of the 'common design' requirement, that must be satisfied before a court can find a secondary party jointly liable for the acts of a primary tortfeasor. Importantly, when internet intermediaries provide their services, they do not necessarily entertain a common design with their infringing users, making it difficult to hold them liable. However, it stands to reason for the law to hold intermediaries liable, at least, in circumstances where they ***knowingly*** assist infringements.

Accessorial liability, a concept alien to trade mark law

At an international level, the Agreement on the Trade-Related Aspects of Intellectual Property Rights (TRIPS)[1] confers on trade mark proprietors the ***right*** to prohibit the unauthorised third-party use of a registered trade mark. However, TRIPS does not deal with the conduct of a secondary party that *assists* another to engage in the infringing use of a trade mark. Weatherall, commenting on the provisions of the Anti-Counterfeiting Trade Agreement (ACTA),[2] a plurilateral trade agreement that was conceived almost 15 years after TRIPS, has pointed out that

1 The text of the agreement is available in Annex 1C of the Marrakesh Agreement Establishing the World Trade Organization 1994.

2 The ACTA was signed in October 2011 by Australia, Canada, Japan, Morocco, New Zealand, Singapore, South Korea and the US. It is a multinational treaty for the purpose of establishing international standards for the enforcement of intellectual property rights. The ACTA is yet to come into force, as only Japan has ratified the treaty, whereas a total of six countries must ratify the treaty for it to come into force.

'[p]rior to the ACTA, there were very few provisions in international [intellectual property] agreements that addressed secondary liability[3] at all'.[4] Article 23(4) of the ACTA, which deals with 'Criminal Offences',[5] provides:

> With respect to the offences specified in this Article for which a Party provides criminal procedures and penalties, that Party shall ensure that criminal liability for aiding and abetting is available under its law.

If ever the ACTA comes into force, it would be the only international instrument that expressly provides for the concept of accessorial liability, albeit restricted to the context of criminal enforcement and to those who strictly 'aid' and 'abet' an intellectual property infringement. Currently, however, there is no provision available under international intellectual property law that provides for accessorial liability for trade mark infringements in the context of civil enforcement. This is perhaps why, as Weatherall has suggested, civil accessorial liability 'has been left to domestic legal developments, and varies significantly as between countries'.[6]

Similarly, in the context of the EU, although the Trade Marks Directive[7] has to a significant degree harmonised substantive trade mark law within the Member States, it contains no reference to accessorial liability.[8] Since the Trade Marks Directive does not exclude the applicability to trade marks of provisions of law relating to unfair competition, *civil liability* or consumer protection,[9] EU member states are free to apply principles of accessorial liability to the context of enforcing

3 The liability of a secondary party to a trade mark infringement has been referred to in numerous ways. Some use the phrase 'secondary' liability. For instance, in Weatherall's submission (see below n4), she makes the following observation (at p. 11) under the heading 'Secondary Liability': 'While Australia presently does recognise *accessorial liability* in IP, it is under no international obligation to do so. . .' (emphasis added). Others prefer to use 'contributory' liability. Yet the terms secondary and contributory liability attract specific meanings in certain jurisdictions (such as the US). As such, the more neutral term of 'accessory' or 'accessorial' liability (as opposed to secondary or contributory liability) has been consciously adopted in this book, and more specifically for the purposes of this chapter, to describe the liability of a secondary party who provides assistance in respect of another's infringement, in circumstances where the first mentioned party does not make use of the trade mark under consideration in an infringing manner.

4 K Weatherall, *Submission to the Joint Standing Committee on Treaties Inquiry into the Anti-Counterfeiting Trade Agreement*, Submission No 3 TT (21 November 2011), 9.

5 These offences include, for instance, wilful trade mark counterfeiting and copyright piracy on a commercial scale (Article 23(1)) and wilful importation and domestic use of labels or packaging comprising a sign identical or similar to a registered trade mark (Article 23(2)).

6 Weatherall, above n4, 9.

7 Directive 2008/95/EC of the European Parliament and of the Council of 22 October 2008 to Approximate the Laws of the Member States Relating to Trade Marks [2008] OJ L 299/25 (Trade Marks Directive). An explanation as to why a reference is made to the 2008 Trade Marks Directive and not the later 2015 Trade Marks Directive (Directive (EU) 2015/2436), which replaces the former, is provided in Chapter 1.

8 PS Davies, 'Accessory Liability: Protecting Intellectual Property Rights' [2011] *Intellectual Property Quarterly* 390 ('Accessory Liability: Protecting Intellectual Property Rights').

9 Trade Marks Directive, Recital (7) (reproduced in Recital (40) of the 2015 Trade Marks Directive).

trade mark rights, should they choose to do so.[10] In fact, in *L'Oréal v eBay* (HC),[11] the English High Court has recognised this possibility:

> [I]t is settled law that arts 5 to 7 of the Trade Marks Directive embody a complete harmonisation of the rules relating to infringement of the rights conferred by registration of a trade mark within the Community. Those rules do not, however, harmonise the law of accessory liability applicable to such infringements. Accordingly, the question of accessory liability is primarily a matter for national law.[12]

Since TRIPS allows WTO members to provide more extensive protection than what is required under the agreement,[13] some countries have introduced provisions in their domestic trade mark legislation that go beyond the scope of Article 16 of TRIPS. Section 10(5) of the UK Trade Marks Act 1994 serves as a good example, when it provides:

> A person who applies a registered trade mark to material intended to be used for labelling or packaging goods, as a business paper, or for advertising goods or services, shall be treated as a party to any use of the material which infringes the registered trade mark if when he applied the mark he knew or had reason to believe that the application of the mark was not duly authorised by the proprietor or a licensee.

While it has been suggested that section 10(5) of the Trade Marks Act 1994 provides for a form of 'contributory infringement',[14] the phrase 'secondary infringement' has also been used to describe the very same provision.[15] Thus, there is some confusion in describing the type of infringement section 10(5) refers to, albeit both 'contributory' and 'secondary' give the impression that

10 However, in view of the safe harbour afforded to internet intermediaries in terms of Articles 12–14 of Directive 2000/31/EC on Certain Legal Aspects of Information Society Services, in Particular Electronic Commerce, in the Internal Market [2000] OJ L 178/1 (E-Commerce Directive), the imposition of accessorial liability will be subject to the limitations set out therein.

11 *L'Oréal SA v eBay Inc* [2009] ETMR 53 (*L'Oréal v eBay* (HC)).

12 *L'Oréal v eBay* (HC), [344] (Arnold J). This position was confirmed by the Advocate General consequent to the English High Court's reference to the CJEU seeking guidance on the interpretation, and application, of the Trade Marks Directive to the facts of the case (Case C-324/09, *L'Oréal SA v eBay International AG* [2011] ECR I-06011 (*L'Oréal v eBay*), Opinion of AG Jääskinen, [55]).

13 TRIPS, art 1:1.

14 W Cornish, D Llewelyn and T Aplin, *Intellectual Property: Patents, Copyright, Trade Marks and Allied Rights* (8th edn, Sweet & Maxwell 2013), 757.

15 L Bently et al, *Intellectual Property Law* (5th edn, Oxford University Press 2018), 1126:

> Unlike an action for primary infringement, in which knowledge is not a relevant factor, secondary infringement under section 10(5) arises only where the person who applied the mark 'knew or had reason to believe that the application of the mark was not duly authorized by the proprietor or a licensee'.

the provision incorporates a form of liability that goes beyond the realms of Article 16 of TRIPS.

Section 10(5) of the Trade Marks Act 1994 is comparable to section 32 of the Lanham Act 1946,[16] applicable in the US. The US provision draws a distinction between two situations. While section 32(1)(a) deals with circumstances where an unauthorised third party uses in commerce a 'reproduction, counterfeit, copy, or colorable imitation of a registered mark'[17] in respect of goods or services, section 32(1)(b) deals with a slightly different scenario. The latter provision captures persons that:

> reproduce, counterfeit, copy, or colorably imitate a registered mark and apply such reproduction, counterfeit, copy, or colorable imitation to labels, signs, prints, packages, wrappers, receptacles or advertisements *intended to be used in commerce.*[18]

However, section 32(1)(b) of the Lanham Act 1946 qualifies the liability of such persons, in that there is no entitlement to seek damages 'unless the acts have been committed with *knowledge that such imitation is intended to be used to cause confusion, or to cause mistake, or to deceive*'.[19] The use of the words 'intended to be used in commerce' in section 32(1)(b) indicates that the acts envisaged therein are preparatory acts, just as in the case of section 10(5) of the Trade Marks Act 1994. Thus, liability may be imposed on persons engaging in preparatory acts (e.g. printing promotional material consisting of trade marks or printing trade marks and applying them to goods) only in circumstances where they become aware that their acts will lead to an infringement. In the context of the Lanham Act 1946, just as in relation to its UK counterpart, there is some confusion as to how this type of *knowledge-based* liability should be characterised. Academic commentaries in the US on contributory trade mark infringement have only seldom referred to section 32(1)(b) of the Lanham Act 1946.[20] Nor have the key cases against internet intermediaries that were premised on contributory infringement referred to this provision.[21] In fact, Cross has sought to draw a distinction between the type of knowledge-based liability that section 32(1)(b) creates and the species of liability described as 'contributory' liability under US trade mark law:

16 15 USC §1114.
17 15 USC §1114(1)(a).
18 15 USC §1114(1)(b) (emphasis added).
19 15 USC §1114(1)(b) (emphasis added). A trade mark proprietor may, however, seek injunctive relief without having to demonstrate knowledge. Similarly, section 32(2) of the Lanham Act 1946, 15 USC §1114(2), limits remedies to injunctive relief as against 'innocent infringers' including (1) those in the business of printing marks, (2) those providing paid advertising services and (3) domain name registrars.
20 See e.g. AS Oddi, 'Contributory Copyright Infringement: The Tort and Technological Tensions' (1989) 64 *Notre Dame Law Review* 47, 69 (the author states that contributory trade mark infringement of the 'implied concerted conduct' type is codified in section 32(1)(b) of the Lanham Act 1946).
21 See e.g. *Tiffany (NJ) Inc v eBay Inc* 600 F.3d 93 (2d Cir. 2010) (*Tiffany v eBay*).

> A contributory infringement cause of action, however, cannot be implied from the Lanham Act. . . . Because the contributory infringer used neither the mark nor any other misleading words or symbols, its acts do not fit within the relatively narrow sphere of conduct that Congress intended the Lanham Act to regulate.[22]

What may be gleaned from this distinction is that, in the US's context, the phrase 'contributory infringement' is used to identify situations where a party becomes liable for contributing to a third party's trade mark infringement, without that party itself making any use of a mark. In contrast, section 32(1)(b) of the Lanham Act 1946 (as well as section 10(5) of the Trade Marks Act 1994) captures persons who do not directly benefit from an infringement, although that party makes use of a trade mark in an infringing manner, where the infringer's mental state becomes a deciding factor.

Take the example of a commercial printer whose services are retained to print labels comprising trade marks. The commercial printer commits the act of reproducing a registered mark, which is then applied to a label that is intended for use in trade. This type of activity, if done without the consent of the trade mark proprietor and with the requisite knowledge, constitutes an act of infringement. Notably, it is only if such actors possess knowledge that the material they produce (that incorporates a reproduction of a trade mark) was intended for infringing use that the law would fault them for their actions culminating in an award of damages. Therefore, the type of conduct envisaged by section 10(5) of the Trade Marks Act 1994, and the corresponding provision in the US, cannot be described as giving rise to accessory liability. The actors, such as commercial printers, to whom these provisions apply do not *merely* assist, encourage or otherwise contribute towards an infringement but are *in fact* committing acts of infringement. Thus, describing these provisions, which impose a knowledge-based type of liability, as constituting 'secondary' or 'contributory' infringement is somewhat misleading, if those terms are used to describe a form of accessorial liability. There is nothing accessorial about the infringing acts envisaged by these provisions, as they apply to parties who are treated as having made use of a registered trade mark *in a trade mark sense*.[23]

22 JT Cross, 'Contributory Infringement and Related Theories of Secondary Liability for Trademark Infringement' (1995) 80 *Iowa Law Review* 101, 119 (citation omitted).

23 For there to be use of a trade mark within the meaning of the infringement provisions of the Trade Marks Act 1994 (and the Trade Marks Directive), there is no requirement that the third party must make use of a sign identical or similar to a registered trade mark in relation to *his own* goods or services. For instance, a commercial printer who prints and applies a trade mark on labels intended to be used in commerce, with knowledge that the trade mark is being applied without the consent of the proprietor, is treated as having used the trade mark in a trade mark sense, even though the labels are ultimately applied to goods that do not belong to the commercial printer. This view is supported by the CJEU's ruling in *L'Oréal v eBay*:

> In that regard, the words 'in relation to goods or services' do not relate solely to the goods or services of a third party which is using signs corresponding to the trade marks but may also refer to the goods or services of other persons.
>
> (at [91])

The case of internet intermediaries is noticeably different to that of commercial printers. Although there is no doubt that the conduct of internet intermediaries results in content (including those that infringe trade mark rights) being made accessible and available to internet users, their acts are not captured by the type of conduct to which section 10(5) of the Trade Marks Act 1994, or section 32(1)(b) of the Lanham Act 1946, relates. The crucial difference is that both these provisions require some form of *use* of a trade mark by the party concerned, such use being conspicuously absent in cases involving internet intermediaries. In essence, neither section 10(5) of the Trade Marks Act 1994 nor its US counterpart, which seeks to impose a form of knowledge-based liability, is capable of capturing the conduct of accessories to a trade mark infringement, including actors such as internet intermediaries which make no use of trade marks in any manner. Therefore, it is necessary to consider whether the conduct of internet intermediaries, in providing access to, hosting or indexing content that gives rise to trade mark infringements, is capable of being captured by common-law principles relating to accessorial liability.

A reference to the common law is a logical choice. First, it has long been recognised that trade marks 'are a creature of the common law'.[24] Trade marks are not a novel invention. Rather, they have been associated with craft and trade since medieval times.[25] As Schechter has pointed out:

> The repression of trademark infringement came into the common law through an action of deceit and, although it is the public rather than the owner of the trademark who is actually deceived, the common law trademark action is still deceit.[26]

Thus, although 'the right to a trade mark, after being more and more assimilated to proprietary rights, has become a statutory franchise',[27] its origins could be traced back to the common law of torts:

> Infringements of rights in such immaterial or intellectual property as trade marks, patents, copyrights and design rights are today made tortious by statute, the basic enactments being, respectively, the Trade Marks Act 1994, the Patents Acts 1949, 1977 and 2004, and the Copyright, Design and Patents Act 1988. These torts may be regarded as allied to injurious falsehood in the sense that the defendant, by infringing the claimant's trade mark, patent,

24 GB Dinwoodie, 'The Common Law and Trade Marks in an Age of Statutes' in L Bently, C Ng and G D'Agostino (eds), *The Common Law of Intellectual Property Essays in Honour of Professor David Vaver* (Hart Publishing 2010), 331 citing *The Trade-Mark Cases* 100 U.S. 81 (1879).

25 See G Ruston, 'On the Origin of Trademarks' (1955) 45 *Trademark Reporter* 127; BG Paster, 'Trademarks – Their Early History' (1969) 59 *Trademark Reporter* 551, 552; and SA Diamond, 'The Historical Development of Trademarks' (1983) 73 *Trademark Reporter* 222.

26 FI Schechter, 'Rational Basis of Trademark Protection' (1927) 40 *Harvard Law Review* 813, 819. See also Bently et al, above n15, 849.

27 PA Landon, *Pollock's Law of Torts* (15th edn, Stevens and Sons Ltd 1951), 231.

> copyright or design right is misrepresenting to third parties that he is entitled to put on the market the article, invention, writing or design which he offers, although the element of deception in the sense that the third parties are made to think that the article, invention, writing or design emanates from the claimant is not so likely to be present.[28]

In fact, even though courts of equity, as opposed to courts of law, assumed jurisdiction in trade mark cases on the basis of a claimant's 'title' to a trade mark, thus giving trade marks a proprietary flavour, over time there seemed to be a shift in the basis for trade mark protection from a property rights approach to the original basis premised on deceit.[29] Accordingly, a fall back on common-law principles, from which modern trade mark law originates, to unlock its limitations stands to reason.

Second, in view of the fact that trade mark infringements are committed by infringers with the aid of services offered by certain types of internet intermediaries, it is indeed worthwhile asking the question whether these intermediaries could be regarded as 'accessories' to trade mark infringements. It has been suggested that '[t]he common roots of both criminal and civil accessory liability can be found in the common law'.[30] Thus, this stands as a further reason as to why the common law becomes an attractive choice in exploring means by which internet intermediaries could be held liable for infringements of trade mark rights.

Although this book is concerned with approaches to holding internet intermediaries liable in civil proceedings, since TRIPS requires WTO members to make criminal remedies available against infringers, it is also useful to consider the approach to accessory liability under the principles of criminal law. Also, Davies, whose work has significantly contributed towards the law on accessories, has suggested that considering the imputation of accessorial liability under the criminal law may be a useful exercise because the criminal law is far more expansive than civil law in this regard.[31]

Accessory liability under the common law

It is the general rule that everyone is responsible for his or her actions. This principle operates in respect of both civil and criminal liability. Where an act, or omission, on the part of one individual results in a change in the status quo of another, leaving the second individual worse off, the law would generally hold the

28 H McGregor, *McGregor on Damages* (20th edn, Sweet & Maxwell 2017), 48–034.

29 Schechter, above n26, 819 and MP McKenna, 'The Normative Foundations of Trademark Law' (2007) 82 *Notre Dame Law Review* 1856 citing *Croft v Day* (1843) 49 ER 994 (Rolls Ct) and *Hogg v Kirby* (1803) 8 Ves Jun 215.

30 PS Davies, 'Accessory Liability for Assisting Torts' (2011) 70 *Cambridge Law Journal* 353 ('Accessory Liability for Assisting Torts').

31 Davies, 'Accessory Liability for Assisting Torts', above n30, 353; Davies, 'Accessory Liability: Protecting Intellectual Property Rights', above n8, 390.

first individual legally responsible. Changes in status quo may be considered under one or a combination of three distinct areas of the law: contracts, torts and crime.

However, there are instances where the law seeks to hold liable persons who did not themselves commit the acts that led to a change in status quo of a third party. A classic example that comes to mind is the liability of an employer for the acts of an employee. Such liability may be imposed due to the existence of a particular relationship that gives rise to certain obligations. Where an employee negligently causes an injury to a third party when performing an act in the course, and within the scope, of his or her employment, the employer becomes vicariously liable for the acts of the employee, even though the employer did not commit the wrongful act in question.[32] Similarly, certain acts committed by an employee, in the course and within the scope of employment, *may* result in criminal liability being imposed on the employer.[33] Here, the legal relationship between the primary wrongdoer and the employer[34] justifies the imposition of liability on the latter for the former's wrongful acts, such acts being committed within the employee's authority to act[35] and foreseeable at the time of entering into the employment contract.[36] However, the vicarious liability of an employer for an employee's wrongful act, though categorised as part of the broad species of joint liability,[37] cannot properly be described as a form of *accessory liability*.[38]

In order to establish a case of accessorial liability, it must be shown that the secondary party 'did something in relation to the primary wrong (the conduct element) and was at fault in some way (the mental element)'.[39] For instance, where someone (the secondary party) employs another (the primary wrongdoer) to commit an assault, tortious liability on the secondary party for the injuries sustained by the victim is not premised on the relationship between the primary wrongdoer and the secondary party but rather on other bases of joint tortious

32 K Horsey and E Rackley, *Tort Law* (4th edn, Oxford University Press 2015), 586.

33 Law Commission, *Assisting and Encouraging Crime: A Consultation Paper*, Consultation Paper No 131 (1993) ('*Assisting and Encouraging Crime*'), para 1.25: 'a master for instance "sells" goods even though all the physical acts involved in that operation are performed by one of his employees' (citation omitted). Thus, for instance, an employer may be held vicariously liable when an employee engaged in the act of selling adult videos to a child under the age of 18 (*Tesco Stores Ltd v Brent London Borough Council* [1993] 2 All ER 718), although no liability will be imposed on an employer for acts of an employee outside the scope of employment (*Adams v Camfoni* [1929] 1 KB 95). On the other hand, acts of an employee that amount to fraud, assault, battery or manslaughter will not give rise to criminal liability on the part of the employer solely on the ground that the employee was acting in the course of employment (see D Ormerod and K Laird, *Smith and Hogan's Criminal Law* (Oxford University Press 2015), 311–12).

34 Horsey and Rackley, above n32, 590. See also GP Fletcher, *Rethinking Criminal Law* (Oxford University Press 2000), 648.

35 C Witting, *Street on Torts* (14th edn, Oxford University Press 2015), 624.

36 D Neild, 'Vicarious Liability and the Employment Rationale' (2013) 44 *Victoria University of Wellington Law Review* 707.

37 See J Cooke, *Law of Tort* (9th edn, Pearson 2009), 492 and Witting, above n35, 661.

38 NJ McBride and R Bagshaw, *Tort Law* (5th edn, Pearson 2015), 886.

39 PS Davies, *Accessory Liability* (Hart Publishing 2015), 1 ('*Accessory Liability*').

liability, such as procurement or concerted action. Likewise, the secondary party may become criminally liable for the actions committed by the primary wrongdoer on similar bases of accessorial liability imposed under the criminal law, such as joint enterprise[40] or conspiracy.[41] In both these instances, tortious and criminal liability is imposed on the basis that the parties entertained some form of a common design, object or intention. However, this form of accessorial liability is difficult to apply to the context of internet intermediaries, as they do not share a common design, object or intent with their infringing users.

There could also be instances where a secondary party is held liable for the acts of a primary wrongdoer, in circumstances where he or she provided some form of *assistance* towards the commission of the wrong, even though the secondary party did not directly perform the wrongful act. Under the criminal law, this may be a case where the accessory 'aids' or 'abets' the primary offence.[42] In the case of some internet intermediaries, it might be argued that they provide assistance towards, or facilitate, the commission of infringement, and therefore the allocation of liability for providing assistance or facilitation must be considered. It must, however, be noted that the concept of 'aiding' and 'abetting' is familiar to the criminal law, and not to the law of torts.

The allocation of accessory liability under the law could take various forms and theoretical approaches. But the concept of accessorial liability is alien to trade mark law, compelling us to rely on common-law principles, which in turn inform the imposition of accessorial liability in relation to both tortious and criminal conduct. The next part of this chapter considers in greater detail the approaches to accessorial liability under the common law in order to assess their potential application to the context of trade mark infringements and internet intermediaries.

Joint tortfeasance

Under the common law, although there are multiple ways by which one party may be held liable for the acts of another, for the purposes of this discussion we shall examine the liability of joint tortfeasors.[43] Generally, where the 'same wrongful act is committed by two or more people, they are described as joint tortfeasors'.[44] A simple, yet more influential, definition[45] of joint tortfeasors was provided in *Clerk and Lindsell on Torts*: 'persons whose respective shares in the

40 Ormerod and Laird, above n33, 205.

41 J Horder, *Ashworth's Principles of Criminal Law* (8th edn, Oxford University Press 2016), 486.

42 Ormerod and Laird, above n33, 206.

43 Joint liability could arise in the context of employment, agency, parent and child, and subsidiary and parent company, as well as between companies and their directors. See MA Jones, AM Dugale and M Simpson (eds), *Clerk and Lindsell on Torts* (21st edn, Sweet & Maxwell 2014), 296.

44 C Elliott and F Quinn, *Tort Law* (5th edn, Pearson 2005), 315.

45 This definition, which appeared in the seventh edition of *Clerk and Lindsell on Torts*, was cited by all members of the Court of Appeal in *The Koursk* [1924] P 140, 151, 156 and 159. The latest (i.e. 21st) edition of this text continues to maintain this definition.

commission of a tort are done in furtherance of a common design'.[46] It has also been suggested that '[w]here persons with a joint purpose take "concerted action to a common end" and one of them commits a tort, they are joint tortfeasors'.[47] The crucial point is that a tort must be committed by the acts of two or more persons who shared the same 'common design', a term which has also been described as 'common end', 'common object' or 'joint or common purpose'. In essence, where two persons act in furtherance of a common design, then they are both liable for a tort committed in the course of executing that common design, even in circumstances where only one of them committed the acts that resulted in the damage or harm.

The UK Supreme Court, in *Sea Shepherd v Fish & Fish*,[48] reaffirmed the role of 'common design' in the allocation of liability between joint tortfeasors. The facts that led to the damage complained of were as follows. The claimant, Fish & Fish, operated a fish farm off Malta and, when transporting tuna in fish cages (which were below the sea's surface), the claimant's vessel came under attack by a vessel known as *Steve Irwin*, divers from which tore open the cages setting all the fish free, thus carrying out 'Operation Bluerage'. The *Steve Irwin* was under the command of one Mr Watson, an environmentalist, who formed the Sea Shepherd Conservation Society (SSCS), which became the parent of a network of Sea Shepherd entities including Sea Shepherd UK Ltd (SSUK), which had a UK presence. For the purposes of establishing jurisdiction, the cause of action arose outside the UK, and neither Mr Watson nor SSCS was domiciled in the country. Thus, at first instance, the English High Court had to determine whether it had jurisdiction to hear the case, which depended on 'whether the incident was directed and/or authorised and/or carried out by' SSUK, the only entity which had a presence within the jurisdiction.[49] The basis upon which the action was maintained was that the defendants, i.e. SSUK, SSCS and Mr Watson, were joint tortfeasors.

Mr Justice Hamblen (as he then was), dismissed the action on the basis that Mr Watson, as master of the *Steve Irwin*, acted for SSCS and not SSUK, which only held a bare legal title to the vessel that was used for Operation Bluerage. By contrast, the vessel was 'beneficially owned and operated by SSCS'.[50] On appeal, the English Court of Appeal overruled this finding, holding SSUK jointly liable with Mr Watson and SSCS.[51] On further appeal, the Supreme Court reversed the Court of Appeal's judgment. Notably, all five Supreme Court justices were unanimous on the law, although two dissented on the application of the law to the facts.[52]

46 Jones et al, above n43, 297.
47 Witting, above n35, 661.
48 *Sea Shepherd UK v Fish & Fish Ltd* [2015] UKSC 10 (*Sea Shepherd v Fish & Fish*).
49 *Sea Shepherd v Fish & Fish*, [2] (Lord Toulson).
50 *Fish & Fish Ltd v Sea Shepherd UK* [2012] EWHC 1717 (Admlty), [35] (Hamblen J).
51 *Fish & Fish Ltd v Sea Shepherd UK* [2013] EWCA Civ 544 (*Fish & Fish v Sea Shepherd*).
52 The majority comprised Lord Neuberger, Lord Kerr and Lord Toulson, whereas Lord Sumption and Lord Mance comprised the minority.

Lord Neuberger provided a succinct three-step test in order to determine whether two parties were joint tortfeasors:

> First, the defendant must have assisted the commission of an act by the primary tortfeasor; second, the assistance must have been pursuant to a common design on the part of the defendant and the primary tortfeasor that the act be committed; and, thirdly, the act must constitute a tort as against the claimant.[53]

Accordingly, *mere* assistance is insufficient to find joint liability. The Supreme Court[54] reiterated the following principle that was set out by the Court of Appeal in *Credit Lyonnais v ECGD*:[55]

> Mere assistance, even knowing assistance, does not suffice to make the 'secondary' party jointly liable as a joint tortfeasor with the primary party. What he does must go further. He must have conspired with the primary party or procured or induced his commission of the tort . . . or he must have joined in the common design pursuant to which the tort was committed.[56]

Thus, unless the assistance provided by a secondary party towards the primary wrongdoer is pursuant to a common design, there cannot be a finding of joint liability. In determining whether the secondary party acted pursuant to a common design, it is necessary to consider 'whether the person has been so involved in the commission of the tort as to make the infringing act his own'.[57] This is a question of fact to be determined on a case-by-case basis.[58] As such, it is not surprising that the Supreme Court was divided 3:2 in determining the level of SSUK's involvement in the commission of the tort.

For instance, Lord Kerr found SSUK's involvement in relation to the activities of SSCS passive and not so significant. [59] Although SSUK allowed SSCS to use its resources, it was solely the activities of SSCS that generated the funds for Operation Bluerage.[60] The finding was no different in regard to SSUK's recruitment and employment of two men to install a pump and carry out a day's work on the vessel.[61] Therefore, the ground upon which SSUK was exonerated from liability was not on the basis that it did not share a common design with

53 *Sea Shepherd v Fish & Fish*, [55] (Lord Neuberger).

54 *Sea Shepherd v Fish & Fish*, [42] (Lord Sumption).

55 *Credit Lyonnais Bank Nederland NV (now Generale Bank Nederland NV) v Export Credits Guarantee Department* [1998] 1 Lloyd's Rep 19 (*Credit Lyonnais v ECGD*).

56 *Credit Lyonnais v ECGD*, 46 (Hobhouse LJ).

57 *Sea Shepherd v Fish & Fish*, [24] (Lord Neuberger) citing *Sabaf SpA v Meneghetti SpA* [2003] RPC 264, [59] (Gibson LJ).

58 *The Koursk*, 151 (Bankes LJ).

59 *Sea Shepherd v Fish & Fish*, [84] (Lord Kerr).

60 *Sea Shepherd v Fish & Fish*, [87] (Lord Kerr).

61 *Sea Shepherd v Fish & Fish*, [89] (Lord Kerr).

Mr Watson and SSCS but rather because its acts were de minimis and therefore did not reach the threshold to be regarded as a party that was *involved* in the commission of the tort. Although both the Supreme Court and the High Court held in favour of SCUK, this was a point on which the Supreme Court disagreed with the approach at first instance. At first instance, the judge found there to be no common design on the basis that, although SSUK was fully aware that there was a possibility of a violent intervention against property (such as cutting fishing nets) that was not the purpose or object of the campaign.[62] In the Supreme Court, Lord Sumption found this to be an unrealistic distinction.[63] The use of force in the circumstances of this case was highly foreseeable. Although the majority in the Supreme Court did not find that SSUK's participation was anything more than de minimis, the judges did agree with the Court of Appeal on the matter of common design. For instance, Lord Neuberger observed that 'SSUK had sufficient knowledge that tortious acts were contemplated, indeed were intended, by SSCS'.[64] A similar approach was apparent in Lord Toulson's judgment, where, but for the finding that the contribution on the part of SSUK was de minimis, a finding of joint liability would have been inevitable, as SSUK and SSCS shared a common design.[65]

What is clear from this decision is that there could be instances where a party, although acting pursuant to a common design, does not contribute towards the commission of the tort in terms that are significant enough for a finding of liability as a joint tortfeasor. On the other hand, there could be instances where one party's assistance towards the commission of another's tort is more than de minimis, although not done in furtherance of a common design. In both these instances, the law does not impute liability on the party providing the assistance.

Given that intellectual property infringements are regarded as a species of tort,[66] right holders have, at times, invoked principles of joint liability in their attempt to hold parties with 'deeper pockets' liable for infringements. In the context of such disputes, courts have applied the principle that mere assistance, absent a common design, does not give rise to joint liability, which has significantly curtailed the ability of right holders to cast a wider net beyond those who are directly involved in the infringements. One of the earliest cases, decided almost a decade before *Credit Lyonnais v ECGD*, was *CBS v Amstrad*.[67] In this case, the claim was for copyright infringement against a manufacturer of high-speed twin tape recorders that made it possible for purchasers to engage in unlawful copying

62 *Sea Shepherd v Fish & Fish*, [47] (Lord Sumption).

63 *Sea Shepherd v Fish & Fish*, [48] (Lord Sumption).

64 *Sea Shepherd v Fish & Fish*, [67] (Lord Neuberger).

65 *Sea Shepherd v Fish & Fish*, [27] (Lord Toulson).

66 D Llewelyn, 'Assessment of Damages in Intellectual Property Cases: Some Recent Examples of "the Exercise of a Sound Imagination and the Practice of a Broad Axe"?' (2015) 27 *Singapore Academy of Law Journal* 480, 482. See also PR Goold, 'Is Copyright Infringement a Strict Liability Tort?' (2015) 30 *Berkeley Technology Law Journal* 305.

67 *CBS Songs Ltd v Amstrad Consumer Electronics Plc* [1988] AC 1013 (*CBS v Amstrad*).

of copyrighted works. In exonerating the manufacturer of the twin tape recorders from liability, Lord Templeman explained that mere assistance, or facilitation, alone does not suffice to impose joint liability.[68]

In the trade mark context, two cases are worth mentioning here, i.e. *Louis Vuitton v Toea*,[69] which was decided by the Australian Federal Court, and *L'Oréal v eBay* (HC), decided by the English High Court. While both cases concerned claims of trade mark infringement and a secondary party, only the latter concerned an internet intermediary. Nevertheless, *Louis Vuitton v Toea* is still instructive because it was decided in a common-law jurisdiction and concerned a flea market, which shared some resemblance to how eBay operates. In this case, Louis Vuitton brought an action against Toea, which was the party responsible for operating, supervising and controlling a flea market trading as 'Carrara Markets', in which certain stallholders were selling counterfeit Louis Vuitton products.[70] There were three types of stalls: permanent, long-term casual and casual.[71] In the case of permanent stalls, each stallholder was granted a licence to occupy a specific stall for a weekly fee.[72] A permanent stallholder was able to transfer his or her interest to another, and Toea received a commission of ten per cent on such sales. Long-term casual stalls were similar to permanent stalls, although the interests were non-assignable.[73] Both permanent and long-term casual stallholders were subject to a 'License to Occupy', whereas casual stalls were allocated depending on the type of product and availability of stalls, and these stallholders were subject to the 'Conditions of Renting a Stall'.[74]

On numerous occasions, Louis Vuitton's agents entered the flea market and engaged in trap purchases of counterfeit Louis Vuitton items,[75] collecting evidence of stallholders engaging in the sale of counterfeit goods. However, Louis Vuitton did not pursue legal action against such individual stallholders, and instead brought an action against the owner and manager of the flea market on the basis that they were involved in the stallholders' infringements, and therefore also committed infringements of the 'Louis Vuitton' trade mark.[76] Thus, joint liability was the central issue in this case.

Toea and its manager, Mr Rosenlund, did have overall control over the market, and had the legal capacity to exercise control. The 'License to Occupy' provided the following condition: '[t]he licensee whilst in occupation shall not carry on any illegal, offensive or hazardous trade or occupation'.[77] Moreover, Toea's website, in relation to 'Casual Stall Information', published the following policy:

68 *CBS v Amstrad*, 1057 (Lord Templeman).
69 *Louis Vuitton Malletier SA v Toea Pty Ltd* [2006] FCA 1443 (*Louis Vuitton v Toea*).
70 *Louis Vuitton v Toea*, [2] (Dowsett J).
71 *Louis Vuitton v Toea*, [5] (Dowsett J).
72 *Louis Vuitton v Toea*, [6] (Dowsett J).
73 *Louis Vuitton v Toea*, [9] (Dowsett J).
74 *Louis Vuitton v Toea*, [7]–[8] (Dowsett J).
75 *Louis Vuitton v Toea*, [19] and [102] (Dowsett J).
76 *Louis Vuitton v Toea*, [103] (Dowsett J).
77 *Louis Vuitton v Toea*, [7] (Dowsett J).

> Carrara Markets does not condone the sale of products identified as infringing Australian copyright and/or Trademark laws. It is your responsibility to ensure your products do not infringe Australian copyright and/or Trademark laws. Carrara Markets reserves the right to take immediate action to exclude products identified to us as infringing these laws.[78]

Louis Vuitton relied on the legal control that Toea and its manager had over the stalls and argued that their failure to prevent infringements notwithstanding such control was sufficient to infer 'concurrence' in the infringements.[79] In this regard, the Australian Federal Court made the following observation:

> However, the legal right to control the range of goods being sold says nothing about physical ability to prevent all infringing sales. *Had a stallholder evinced a clear and overt intention to sell counterfeit goods, then Toea may arguably have been obliged to terminate his or her right to occupy a stall or otherwise trade in that way at the Market. . . . There is no evidence that Toea or Mr Rosenlund ever had prior knowledge of a stallholder's possession of infringing goods or of his or her intention to sell such goods.*[80]

Thus, had Toea and its manager been wilfully blind, in that had they failed to take any action in circumstances where the infringements were so blatant or where they had prior knowledge of specific infringements, could this have resulted in their liability as joint tortfeasors? The answer, of course, is in the negative, which is made clear upon a reference to Scrutton LJ's definition of a joint tortfeasor in *The Koursk*: 'two persons who agree on *common action*, in the course of, and to further which, one of them commits a tort'.[81] Louis Vuitton did assert that the common action agreed upon between Toea and each stallholder was the function of their joint businesses at the Carrara Market.[82] However, the Federal Court disagreed:

> No doubt [Toea] desired that the Market be successful and took steps to achieve that aim. No doubt, too, each stallholder desired that his or her stall be successful and took steps to achieve that aim. However, that does not lead to the conclusion that [Toea] and each stallholder had agreed on common action. Aims are not actions. The term '*common action*' must surely mean '*steps to be taken*'.[83]

In essence, neither control over the tools of infringement nor knowledge of an underlying infringement are sufficient to imply a common design, purpose

78 *Louis Vuitton v Toea*, [16] (Dowsett J).
79 *Louis Vuitton v Toea*, [165] (Dowsett J).
80 *Louis Vuitton v Toea*, [138] (Dowsett J) (emphasis added).
81 *The Koursk*, 155 (Scrutton LJ) (emphasis added).
82 *Louis Vuitton v Toea*, [142] (Dowsett J).
83 *Louis Vuitton v Toea*, [152] (Dowsett J).

or object between a secondary party and a primary infringer.[84] The secondary party must have taken some positive steps in furtherance of a common design. Therefore, even in circumstances where Toea made stalls available to those that it *knew* were infringing intellectual property rights, this would not, without more, be sufficient to regard Toea, a joint tortfeasor. In the circumstances, anything short of 'inducement', 'incitement' or 'procurement' of infringement would not render a secondary party jointly liable with the primary infringer,[85] even where the secondary party provided *knowing assistance* towards the commission of the infringement in question.[86]

In *L'Oréal v eBay* (HC), the English High Court applied the 'common design' requirement to the context of an internet intermediary. In this case, L'Oréal brought an action against eBay alleging that it was jointly liable with its users who infringed L'Oréal's trade mark rights. L'Oréal submitted that eBay 'had participated in a common design to infringe [its trade marks] because [eBay] had combined with the [other defendants, who used eBay's services] to secure the doing of acts which proved to be infringements'.[87] eBay is an online marketplace, where its users can list products for sale. L'Oréal's claims related to four types of product listings. They were: counterfeit goods, parallel imports of goods placed on the market outside the European Economic Area (EEA), goods not placed on the market at all (such as tester perfumes), and products placed on the market within the EEA in circumstances that allowed L'Oréal to prevent its further commercialisation (e.g. unboxed products).[88]

Unlike in *Louis Vuitton v Toea*, the evidence revealed that eBay had played a more active role in respect of the content and sales, and also directly profited from sales that took place on the platform. For instance, eBay had:

1 assisted and encouraged sellers on the platform to actively promote their listings for sale;
2 significant control in the sale process, where every aspect was controlled by eBay's software save for the actual delivery of the goods sold;
3 played a role that was very close to that of an auctioneer, and it received a commission on every successful sale on the platform; and
4 used software to filter listings and control the content on its platform, which was often used to detect prohibited or suspicious listings.[89]

Clearly, the activities described above demonstrate a greater involvement on the part of eBay with its sellers, in contrast to the role of Toea in *Louis Vuitton v Toea*.

84 *Louis Vuitton v Toea*, [168] (Dowsett J).
85 *Credit Lyonnais v ECGD*, 46 (Hobhouse LJ).
86 See e.g. *Townsend v Haworth* (1875) 48 LJCh 770 and *Innes v Short & Beal* (1898) 15 RPC 449. Both these cases concerned the liability of a secondary party in respect of a primary actor's patent infringements.
87 *L'Oréal v eBay* (HC), [360] (Arnold J).
88 *L'Oréal v eBay* (HC), [310] (Arnold J).
89 *L'Oréal v eBay* (HC), [361] (Arnold J).

However, in relation to the infringements that arose from the listing of counterfeit goods, tester perfumes and unboxed products, the English High Court did not find eBay jointly liable with its infringing users, because neither eBay's system nor its policies favoured or encouraged its users to list those products.[90] In this regard, it has been pointed out that:

> To encourage someone can mean to make someone more likely to do something or to talk or behave in a way that gives someone confidence to do something. To favour someone can mean to give an advantage to someone or something, in an unfair way.[91]

The approach adopted by Arnold J in exonerating eBay from joint liability on the basis that it neither encouraged nor favoured its users' infringing acts has been criticised for adding a layer to the 'common design' requirement that right holders must otherwise satisfy in cases where accessorial liability is pleaded.[92]

Insofar as the infringements relating to the parallel imports were concerned, the Court did not find eBay jointly liable with its infringing users because facilitation, even with knowledge, and an intention to profit from an infringement were not sufficient to impute joint liability.[93] The specific conduct of eBay that came under scrutiny was its facility that enabled sellers to target consumers in a specific jurisdiction. In this regard, Arnold J made the following observation:

> [I]n my judgment eBay Europe do facilitate the infringement of third parties' trade marks, including L'Oréal's Trade Marks, by sellers; they do know that such infringements have occurred and are likely to continue to occur; and they profit from such infringements except where the rights owner makes a . . . complaint in sufficient time. I would add that, while it is true that the fourth to tenth defendants' trading histories are different from one another, certain common patterns and themes do emerge from the narratives set out above.[94]

Despite the above finding, Arnold J concluded: '[n]evertheless, I accept [the] submission that these factors are not enough to make eBay . . . liable as joint tortfeasors'.[95] The decision in *L'Oréal v eBay* was recently followed in *Vertical*

90 *L'Oréal v eBay* (HC), [377], [378] and [379] (Arnold J).

91 D Lievens, 'eBay's Accessory Liability for Counterfeiting–Why Joint Tort Liability Just Doesn't Cut the Mustard' (2011) 42 *International Review of Intellectual Property and Competition Law (IIC)* 506, 515 (internal quotation marks and citation omitted).

92 Lievens, above n91, 517. See also D Lievens, 'L'Oréal v. eBay – Welcomed in France, Resented in England' (2012) 43 *International Review of Intellectual Property and Competition Law (IIC)* 68, 72.

93 *L'Oréal v eBay* (HC), [382] (Arnold J).

94 *L'Oréal v eBay* (HC), [381] (Arnold J).

95 *L'Oréal v eBay* (HC), [381] (Arnold J).

Leisure v Poleplus,[96] a case involving cybersquatting and passing off. Here the Intellectual Property Enterprise Court, a specialist court within the Chancery Division of the English High Court, held that, 'in order to establish joint liability for infringement of an intellectual property right, the alleged joint tortfeasor must have done something more than having knowingly (and even profitably) facilitated the infringements'.[97]

In essence, the 'common design' requirement has significantly curtailed the ability of right holders to seek relief against secondary parties to an infringement. The outcome is that no reliance can be placed on common-law principles relating to joint liability in order to hold secondary parties, such as internet intermediaries, liable for infringements, even when they knowingly facilitate or assist the primary infringers. In fact, Davies has identified this as a problematic outcome in the broader context of civil accessorial liability and has called for the recognition of ***assistance liability***, i.e. liability for ***knowingly*** assisting a tort.[98] Since assistance liability is a concept that is familiar to the criminal law, before assessing the merits of Davies's proposition, it is useful to consider criminal accessorial liability.

Criminal accessorial liability

Although, today, principles of accessorial liability under the criminal law are found in various statutory provisions,[99] they are very much derived from the common law.[100] There are numerous ways in which a person could be found guilty of a criminal offence as an accessory. For instance, one might aid, abet, counsel or procure another's offence[101] or become involved in a joint enterprise.[102] Joint enterprise can be dismissed at once as inapplicable to the discussion at hand, as this doctrine has as its premise that the parties to such an enterprise must

96 *Vertical Leisure Limited v Poleplus Limited, Peter Bowley* [2015] EWHC 841 (IPEC) (*Vertical Leisure v Poleplus*).

97 *Vertical Leisure v Poleplus*, [35] (Hacon J).

98 Davies, 'Accessory Liability for Assisting Torts', above n30, 397.

99 See e.g. the Accessories and Abettors Act 1861 (section 8) and Magistrates' Courts Act 1980 (section 44), which deal with those who aid, abet, counsel or procure an offence, and the Serious Crimes Act 2007 (section 59). The Serious Crimes Act 2007 abolished the common-law offence of incitement, which has now been replaced by the offence of encouraging or assisting, which addresses some of the gaps found in the common law (see Law Commission, ***Inchoate Liability for Assisting and Encouraging Crime***, LAW COM No 300 (2006), para 1.16).

100 Law Commission, ***Assisting and Encouraging Crime***, above n33, para 1.1.

101 It was suggested in *Carter Patersons and Picvordr v Wessel* [1947] 1 KF3 849 (at p. 852) that section 8 of the Accessories and Abettors Act 1861 (and thus, section 44 of the Magistrates' Courts Act 1980), which incorporates this phraseology in providing for accessorial liability, is a mere declaration of the common law. See also ***Du Cros v Lambourne*** [1907] 1 KB 40, 44.

102 This is a common-law doctrine that is derived from *R v* ***Swindall and Osborne*** (1846) 2 Car & K 230.

entertain a common object, purpose or intent,[103] whereas, when intermediaries provide internet access, hosting or navigation services, they do so without sharing any common object, purpose or intent with their users.[104] In view of this, such intermediaries cannot be held jointly liable for being involved in a joint enterprise with those who commit an offence under the Trade Marks Act 1994.[105]

On the other hand, the imputation of liability on a secondary party on the basis of aiding, abetting, counselling or procuring an offence committed by the primary wrongdoer, does not require the sharing of a common object, purpose or intent between the parties, and therefore has the potential of being applied to the context of internet intermediaries. In the case of trade mark infringements, section 92 of the Trade Marks Act 1994 sets out offences, which are capable of being tried either summarily or upon indictment (an offence triable either way).[106] Accordingly, anyone who aids, abets, counsels or procures the commission of an offence under that provision may become guilty as an accessory under section 44 of the Magistrates' Courts Act 1980 or section 8 of the Accessories and Abettors Act 1861, depending on how the offence is tried. Section 92(1) of the Trade Marks Act 1994 provides that:

> A person commits an offence who with a view to gain for himself or another, or with intent to cause loss to another, and without the consent of the proprietor—
>
> (a) applies to goods or their packaging a sign identical to, or likely to be mistaken for, a registered trade mark, or
> (b) sells or lets for hire, offers or exposes for sale or hire or distributes goods which bear, or the packaging of which bears, such a sign, or
> (c) has in his possession, custody or control in the course of a business any such goods with a view to the doing of anything, by himself or another, which would be an offence under paragraph (b).[107]

Several limitations apply in respect of the operation of section 92(1). First, the acts identified in paragraphs (a), (b) and (c) of section 92(1) are offences only

103 *R v A and others* [2011] QB 841, [9]–[10] (Hughes LJ). See also S Parsons, 'Criminal Liability for the Act of Another: Accessorial Liability and the Doctrine of Joint Enterprise' (1998) 62 *Journal of Criminal Law* 352, 354. The need for a shared intention to sustain a charge of joint enterprise was made explicitly clear in the recent Supreme Court decision of *R v Jogee* [2016] UKSC 8.

104 A similar finding was reached in *L'Oréal v eBay* (HC), albeit in the context of determining joint tortious liability.

105 Trade Marks Act 1994, section 92 (sets out offences relating to the unauthorised use of trade marks).

106 Trade Marks Act 1994, section 92(6)(a).

107 Section 92(2) of the Trade Marks Act 1994 relates to persons who apply a sign identical to a registered trade mark to material *intended* to be used for packaging or labelling, business paper or advertising. Section 92(3) relates to persons who make an article specifically designed to make copies of a sign that is identical to a registered trade mark.

if the goods in relation to which those acts are committed are identical to the goods for which a trade mark is registered for, or where the trade mark has a reputation in the UK, in circumstances where the conflicting sign takes unfair advantage of, or is detrimental to, the distinctive character or repute of the registered trade mark.[108] Thus, it is only in relation to very specific acts of trade mark infringement,[109] carried out in the circumstances as specified above that criminal liability may be imposed under the Trade Marks Act 1994. Second, it cannot be argued that services provided by internet intermediaries in any way aid their users to *apply* registered trade marks on goods or packaging, without the requisite consent being obtained from the trade mark proprietors. Although section 10(4) of the Trade Marks Act 1994, which deals with infringements in the civil context, provides for a much broader base for types of conduct that could amount to an infringement, the criminal provision is limited to the unauthorised application of a mark on the goods or packaging themselves. Thus, it cannot be argued that section 92(1)(a) applies to the context of internet intermediaries, as their services do not in any way relate to the conduct proscribed by that provision. Similarly, section 92(1)(c) of the Trade Marks Act 1994 does not apply to the context of internet intermediaries, as their services do not assist their users in maintaining possession, custody or control of infringing goods.

On the other hand, it might be argued that section 92(1)(b) could apply to the online context, as that section deals more generally with the sale, exposing for sale or distribution of infringing goods bearing a registered trade mark, without the consent of the trade mark proprietor and with the intent of gaining economically or causing loss to another.[110] Since those who engage in infringements on the internet must rely on intermediaries to create, store and disseminate content promoting the sale of infringing goods, there is merit in considering whether such intermediaries aid, abet, counsel or procure the commission of an offence under section 92(1)(b) of the Trade Marks Act 1994.

It is a cardinal rule in criminal law that for any offence to be committed both the actus reus and mens rea elements relating to the offence must be satisfied.[111] Therefore, it is first necessary to investigate whether the conduct of internet intermediaries satisfy the actus reus element of aiding, abetting, procuring or counselling an offence under section 92(1)(b) of the Trade Marks Act 1994. Second, and if the actus reus element is satisfied, it would then become necessary to consider the mental element required to complete the offence. Although initially (i.e. before 1975) there was no attempt to distinguish between the different

108 Trade Marks Act 1994, section 92(4).

109 It is generally understood that, unless a case of 'civil' trade mark infringement can be established, there could be no offence under section 92 of the Trade Marks Act 1994 (see *R v Johnstone* [2003] UKHL 28 (*R v Johnstone*), [25]–[27] (Lord Nicholls)).

110 The case of *R v Georgina Ellain Pettit* [2009] EWCA Crim 2573 supports the view that section 92(1)(b) applies to the sale of counterfeit goods on the internet. In this case, the accused sold several counterfeit items on eBay.

111 Ormerod and Laird, above n33, 50.

terms used in section 8 of the Accessories and Abettors Act 1861 (which are also reflected in section 44 of the Magistrates' Courts Act 1980), in *A-G's Reference* the English Court of Appeal made the following observation:

> We approach section 8 of the Act of 1861 on the basis that the words should be given their ordinary meaning, if possible. We approach the section on the basis also that if four words are employed here, 'aid, abet, counsel or procure,' the probability is that there is a difference between each of those four words and the other three, because, if there were no such difference, then Parliament would be wasting time in using four words where two or three would do.[112]

Consequently, this means that the four terms incorporated into section 8 of the Accessories and Abettors Act 1861 (and section 44 of the Magistrates' Courts Act 1980) attract distinct meanings, and accordingly must be analysed and interpreted separately. Davies does this eloquently, beginning each analysis with a reference to the Oxford English Dictionary.[113] What Davies's analysis reveals is that the meanings attaching to 'aid', 'abet', 'counsel' and 'procure' are in many ways overlapping, and therefore extremely difficult to be treated in isolation.

The meaning of 'aid' is 'to give help, support, or assistance, or, alternatively, to be or constitute an aid to (a person or thing); to promote or encourage; to facilitate'.[114] On the other hand, while 'abet' means to 'encourage or assist',[115] 'encourage' means to 'incite, induce, instigate; in weaker sense, to recommend, advise'.[116] At once, an overlap becomes noticeable. That is, to aid someone could also mean to encourage, while at the same time abetting could also mean to provide assistance. Similarly, overlaps are noticed in respect of 'counsel', 'procure' and 'abet'. Thus, 'counsel' means to 'give or offer counsel or advice',[117] whereas 'procure' means 'to contrive or devise with care (an action or proceeding); . . . to bring (usually something harmful) upon a person, or to prevail upon, induce, persuade, get (a person) to do something'.[118] Again, providing advice to someone could result in both counselling and abetment, while procuring another's offence could also be encouraging its commission and thereby abetting that offence. Nevertheless, since the Court of Appeal in *A-G's Reference* preferred to ascribe separate meanings for each term in section 8 of the Accessories and Abettors Act 1861 (and by extension to section 44 of the Magistrates' Courts Act 1980), Davies has suggested that 'aid' and 'abet' should be given distinct meanings. Thus, 'abet' generally equates to 'encouragement',[119] whereas 'aid' equates to

112 *A-G's Reference (No 1 of 1975)* [1975] QB 773 (*A-G's Reference*), 779 (Lord Widgery CJ).
113 Davies, *Accessory Liability*, above n39, 22–31.
114 Davies, *Accessory Liability*, above n39, 22.
115 Davies, *Accessory Liability*, above n39, 24.
116 Davies, *Accessory Liability*, above n39, 24.
117 Davies, *Accessory Liability*, above n39, 27.
118 Davies, *Accessory Liability*, above n39, 29.
119 Davies, *Accessory Liability*, above n39, 24.

providing 'assistance'.[120] Similarly, Davies has suggested that '[i]f "counsel" has a meaning distinct from that of "aid", "abet" and "procure", it must be found in the concept of advice'.[121]

Virgo has also provided a useful summary of the actus reus envisaged by 'aid', 'abet', 'counsel' and 'procure':

> Essentially, procuring involves causing the substantive offence; counselling involves encouraging the crime before it is committed; abetting involves encouraging the crime at the time it is committed; and aiding involves assisting the crime before or during its commission.[122]

Based on the foregoing definitions, it is possible to rule out the applicability of 'counselling' and 'abetting' to internet intermediaries, as it cannot be argued that they encourage the commission of an offence under section 92(1)(b) of the Trade Marks Act 1994 either before or at the time of its commission. Internet intermediaries that provide access, hosting or navigation services do not encourage or provide advice to their users when they sell, expose for sale or distribute infringing goods via the internet. Nor can it be said that internet intermediaries 'procure' an offence under section 92(1)(b) of the Trade Marks Act 1994 on the part of their users.

The more crucial question is whether an internet intermediary could be regarded as having 'aided' the offence described in section 92(1)(b) of the Trade Marks Act 1994. Since aiding could take place without there being any consensus between the parties,[123] the problematic requirement of a common object, purpose or intent is avoided in this form of accessory liability. As stated above, aiding is synonymous with providing assistance, for which there is no requirement that the accessory must be present at the crime scene.[124] This means that internet intermediaries that supply services to its users across the internet, thus lacking physical proximity to the place where the primary offender operates, are still capable of being captured as accessories. Moreover, there is no requirement for a 'but for' type of causal link between the act of aiding and the commission of the primary offence. In this regard, the Law Commission has observed:

> It would appear that 'aid' likewise does not imply a causal link, *since there are many reported cases where it is arguable that the perpetrator would have gone on to commit the offence whether assisted or not.*[125]

120 Davies, *Accessory Liability*, above n39, 22.
121 Davies, *Accessory Liability*, above n39, 27.
122 G Virgo, 'Making Sense of Accessorial Liability' (2006) 6 *Archbold News* 6.
123 Ormerod and Laird, above n33, 216.
124 Ormerod and Laird, above n33, 215.
125 Law Commission, *Assisting and Encouraging Crime*, above n33, para 2.16 (citation omitted) (emphasis added).

In essence, 'aiding' entails a very broad category of conduct, provided the assistance supplied in some way actually assists the primary wrong committed.[126]

Among the three classes of intermediaries considered in this book, it is clear that ISPs that merely provide internet access do not aid wrongdoers in *committing* an offence under section 92(1)(b) of the Trade Marks Act 1994, even if they acquire knowledge of such wrongdoings taking place in their networks (e.g. through a specific notice of infringement by a right holder). Arguably, navigation providers, such as search engines, that merely index and link internet users to content are also similarly circumstanced.

In contrast, however, intermediaries that provide hosting services are exposed to the risk of getting caught up as accessories to the offence set out in section 92(1)(b) of the Trade Marks Act 1994. That is on the basis that they are capable of providing assistance to a party involved in selling, or exposing for sale, infringing goods bearing a registered trade mark. After all, hosts are directly involved in storing, and making available, the content of its subscribers. In the online context, infringing goods as described in section 92(1)(b) cannot be sold, or exposed for sale, unless the availability of such goods is made known to internet users. Therefore, where an infringer commits an offence under section 92(1)(b) of the Trade Marks Act 1994 by selling, or exposing for sale, infringing goods via the internet, it may be argued that the services supplied by the host responsible for hosting the content that promotes such sale are *utilised* for the purpose of committing the offence. The Law Commission has observed that 'assistance' extends to any conduct on the part of the accessory that, as a matter of fact, makes it easier for the primary wrongdoer to commit the offence.[127] It is evident that the services offered by hosts in allowing their subscribers to store online content on their platforms make it easier for the primary wrongdoer to commit the offence set out in section 92(1)(b) of the Trade Marks Act 1994. In the circumstances, it may be posited that hosts are capable of 'aiding' the offence of selling, or exposing for sale, infringing goods. Of course, as stated earlier, the mere fulfilment of the actus reus is insufficient to hold a secondary party liable as an accessory under criminal law, since the requisite mens rea must also be satisfied.

Consequently, it must be established that a secondary party 'intended to do the acts which he knew to be capable of assisting or encouraging the commission of the crime'.[128] While the mental element can be satisfied by establishing that the secondary party acted in order to assist the primary wrongdoer (direct intent), it is sufficient that the secondary party 'knew his acts would be virtually certain to assist' the primary wrongdoer (oblique intent).[129] A person who

126 N Cross, *Criminal Law and Criminal Justice: An Introduction* (SAGE Publications 2010), 76:

> For aiding, there is no need for D's actions to be the 'but for' cause of the main offence. But there does have to be some kind of 'causal link' between D helping and P committing the main offence . . . D is still guilty even if P does not know about, or does not want, the help that D has given.

See also Davies, *Accessory Liability*, above n39, 23.

127 Law Commission, *Assisting and Encouraging Crime*, above n33, 104.

128 Ormerod and Laird, above n33, 224.

129 Ormerod and Laird, above n33, 225.

intends to assist a trade mark infringement must act 'with the purpose of achieving something',[130] whereas hosts are indifferent to whether or not their users commit infringements. However, since an oblique intent is sufficient for a secondary party to become classified as an accessory to a crime, it is possible for a host that is put on notice about a particular infringement to become caught up as an accessory. Although, usually, assistance implies a positive act on the part of the secondary party, assistance includes facilitation.[131] Davies has suggested that '[f]acilitation might conceivably cover acts of omission: by not intervening to prevent a primary wrong, a person might facilitate its commission'.[132] Although not all omissions are deemed to facilitate a crime, in circumstances where an individual or entity had the power or right to control the actions of a primary wrongdoer and deliberately refrains from doing so, such inactivity may be regarded as having facilitated the primary wrong.[133] After all, the mens rea element of aiding another's crime is satisfied where the accessory was able to foresee or turned a blind eye towards the essential matters that constitute the crime.[134] Thus, in principle, an intermediary that hosts content at the direction of its subscribers, could become caught up as an accessory to the offence under section 92(1)(b) of the Trade Marks Act 1994, where it fails to remove content that exposes for sale infringing goods in circumstances where the host had acquired knowledge about the infringements.

The analysis of accessorial liability under the criminal law reveals that there is some scope to hold at least intermediaries that host third-party content liable for the infringing conduct of their users. Although this finding is encouraging, trade mark proprietors may still prefer to bring civil proceedings against internet intermediaries that facilitate or assist infringements. Although criminal proceedings are bound to have a deterrent effect,[135] and therefore would benefit trade mark proprietors in the long run, there are several disadvantages associated with criminal prosecutions. These include the higher burden of proof, as well as search and seizures being dependent on the willingness of local police to cooperate.[136] Also, criminal proceedings are not aimed at compensating the victims, whereas aggrieved trade mark proprietors may be more interested in seeking damages from the parties involved in committing infringements. These disadvantages may be avoided by bringing civil proceedings. Therefore, it is important for trade mark proprietors to be able to hold internet intermediaries that assist the commission of trade mark infringements liable under civil law. The next part of this chapter

130 Davies, *Accessory Liability*, above n39, 41.

131 Davies, *Accessory Liability*, above n39, 23.

132 Davies, *Accessory Liability*, above n39, 23.

133 Ormerod and Laird, above n33, 220.

134 Ormerod and Laird, above n33, 230.

135 GS Moohr, 'The Crime of Copyright Infringement: An Inquiry Based on Morality, Harm and Criminal Theory' (2003) 83 *Boston University Law Review* 731, 749.

136 G Harbottle, 'Criminal Remedies for Copyright and Performers' Rights Infringement under the Copyright, Designs and Patents Act 1988' (1994) 5 *Entertainment Law Review* 12, 14–17. Although this article was written in the copyright context, the points noted therein equally apply to other areas of intellectual property, including trade marks.

addresses the question as to whether the law ought to recognise the liability of a party for assisting another's tort, especially because trade mark infringements have a grounding in the common law of torts despite its present-day statutory flavour.

Liability for assisting a tort

For liability to be imputed on a secondary party on the basis of joint tortfeasance, the secondary party must have shared a common design, object or purpose with the primary wrongdoer. This leads to the outcome of internet intermediaries, even in circumstances when they knowingly assist the commission of a trade mark infringement on the part of their users or subscribers, escaping liability. Such an outcome is not satisfactory, and the need to hold intermediaries, such as eBay, liable for infringements in appropriate circumstances has been echoed by Arnold J in *L'Oréal v eBay* (HC):

> I confess to having considerable sympathy with the suggestion that eBay Europe could and should deal with the problem of infringement by accepting liability and insuring against it by means of a premium levied on sellers.[137]

Some academics have argued in favour of the proposition that liability for assisting another's wrong should be recognised in civil law, and particularly in the context of torts,[138] although their views have been expressly rejected by the judiciary.[139] Despite this judicial attitude, Dietrich[140] and Davies[141] have persistently argued in favour of the recognition of liability for assisting civil wrongs (or assistance liability). Davies has criticised the judicial insistence of the common design requirement by utilising the following example:

> [I]t seems as if joint tortfeasance may well not cover a person who throws a knife to another, knowing that it will be used to stab somebody else, since it could be insuperably difficult to prove either inducement or a common design.[142]

While the knife thrower in the above example will attract criminal liability for aiding the primary offender[143] engaged in the stabbing, no civil liability will ensue.

137 *L'Oréal v eBay* (HC), [370] (Arnold J).

138 See e.g. G Williams, *Joint Torts and Contributory Negligence* (Stevens & Sons Ltd 1951); PS Atiyah, *Vicarious Liability in the Law of Torts* (Butterworths 1967); P Sales, 'The Tort of Conspiracy and Civil Secondary Liability' (1990) 49 *Cambridge Law Journal* 491, 509; and JG Fleming, *Law of Torts* (8th edn, Law Book Co 1992).

139 See e.g. *Credit Lyonnais v ECGD*, 46 (Hobhouse LJ).

140 See J Dietrich, 'Accessorial Liability in the Law of Torts' (2011) 31 *Legal Studies* 231.

141 See Davies, *Accessory Liability*, above n39.

142 Davies, 'Accessory Liability: Protecting Intellectual Property Rights', above n8, 397 (internal quotation marks omitted).

143 *National Coal Board v Gamble* [1959] 1 QB 11, 23 (Devlin J).

According to Davies, this outcome represents 'a gap in the law',[144] which can be bridged by embracing the notion that all forms of participation that make a substantial contribution to the violation of a claimant's right must lead to accessory liability.[145] This would no doubt include persons who provide assistance to another in the commission of a tort. It is submitted that, if Davies's recommendation is accepted and the courts develop the common law, such that liability for assisting another's tort (or civil wrong) is recognised, this would pave the way to hold internet intermediaries, such as eBay, liable for their users' trade mark infringements in appropriate circumstances.

However, the view that assistance liability should be recognised in the civil context is not without opposition.[146] Those who oppose civil assistance liability claim that it would lead to uncertainty. For instance, McBride and Bagshaw have responded to Davies's proposition in the following terms:

> It seems that if the law were to open the door to defendants simply on the basis that they assisted someone to commit a tort, the law would soon become unacceptably uncertain and inhibit many perfectly legitimate activities. Not holding A liable in cases where he throws a knife to B, which is then used to stab C, is a price we have to pay in the interests of legal certainty and public welfare.[147]

Uncertainty is no doubt a genuine concern and, if left unaddressed, could give rise to an overly broad application of accessory liability. In fact, the scope of accessory liability in the criminal law has also recently been criticised for being too broad:

> The law of accessorial liability is an area where the need for consistency needs to be considered and, if there is to be inconsistency in the development of legal doctrine, it should operate, as with the interpretation of self-defence, so that criminal liability is more restrictive than tortious liability. The criminal law of accessorial liability in particular has much to learn from tort law, specifically as regards the need to recognise a common design as a way of restricting accessorial liability. The introduction of such a requirement into the criminal law of accessorial liability would serve to ensure that the defendant was sufficiently involved in the commission of the crime by the principal so that he can be considered to have combined with the principal to commit the crime.[148]

144 Davies, 'Accessory Liability for Assisting Torts', above n29, 380 and Davies, 'Accessory Liability: Protecting Intellectual Property Rights', above n8, 397.

145 Davies, *Accessory Liability*, above n39, 279.

146 See e.g. H Carty, 'Joint Tortfeasance and Assistance Liability' (1999) 10 *Legal Studies* 489; WVH Rogers, *Winfield & Jolowicz on Tort* (18th edn, Sweet & Maxwell 2010), 993; and McBride and Bagshaw, above n38.

147 McBride and Bagshaw, above n38, 885.

148 G Virgo, 'The Criminal Law Is Not an Island' (2015) 6 *Archbold Review* 6, 8–9.

The above critique is directed at criminal accessorial liability and does not suggest anything about civil (or tortious) accessorial liability. The critique is also not inconsistent with Davies's proposition that assistance liability should be recognised in civil law, particularly when the net is cast carefully to cover only cases of 'knowing' assistance. That is, 'only those who actually knew of–or turned a blind eye to–the fact that they were participating in a primary wrong should be susceptible to accessory liability'.[149] Notably, the knowledge standard that Davies has proposed is reflected on both sides of the Atlantic in the context of internet intermediary liability.[150]

Although Davies's proposition to some extent unifies accessorial liability in both civil and criminal law,[151] he does not in any way support an ill-considered transposition of criminal-law concepts into civil law. This is an important point to note, in light of Carty's opposition to such an approach.[152] She has taken the view that, although there are a few judicial decisions[153] and academic opinion[154] where the criminal-law language of 'aid' and 'abet' has been utilised in the context of torts, there is no justification for the introduction of criminal-law notions of accessorial liability into civil law.[155] Upon a careful consideration of Carty's thesis, it is clear that her rejection of the equivalent of criminal aiding and abetting liability in the civil law context is based on three grounds.

First, she has posited that 'assistance' and 'facilitation' are forms of conduct that may not require a causal connection with the conduct of the primary wrongdoer.[156] In precise terms, what Carty has suggested is as follows:

> With assistance liability, it is clear that causation is not a requirement: the accomplice does not have to have caused the principal's offence and merely facilitating, *that is knowing of the risk of the offence rather than intending that the offence be committed*, appears sufficient.[157]

149 Davies, 'Accessory Liability for Assisting Torts', above n29, 353. See also Davies, 'Accessory Liability: Protecting Intellectual Property Rights', above n8, 391 and Davies, *Accessory Liability*, above n39, 285.

150 See *Tiffany v eBay* (reflecting the US standard) and Article 14(1) of the E-Commerce Directive (reflecting the position in the EU). See also C Angelopoulos, *European Intermediary Liability in Copyright: A Tort-Based Analysis* (Kluwer Law International 2017), 169–70.

151 Davies, *Accessory Liability*, above n39, 216.

152 Carty, above n145. See also PW Lee, 'Accessorial Liability in Tort and Equity' (2015) 27 *Singapore Academy of Law Journal* 851, 879.

153 See e.g. *Petrie v Lamont* (1841) Car & M 93; *Barker v Braham and Norwood* (1773) 2 Wm Bl 866; *Pratt v British Medical Association* [1919] 1 KB 244.

154 In addition to the authorities cited at n138 above, Carty has cited D Cooper, *Secondary Liability for Civil Wrongs* (PhD thesis, Cambridge University 1995).

155 Carty, above n146, 503 ('It is not obvious that accessory liability should be the same in the criminal law and the civil law').

156 Dietrich (above n140, 243) has captured Carty's argument in the following terms: 'Carty . . . takes assistance and "facilitation" to mean that there is no causal connection between the acts of the accessory and the principal's decision to commit the wrong'.

157 Carty, above n146, 502 (emphasis added).

This is the position under the criminal law, as discussed in the preceding section.[158] However, the position in relation to the allocation of liability for civil wrongs, and in particular torts, is different. Some academics have suggested that a causal link is a mandatory requirement for liability (on any basis) under the law of torts. This is because the party injured cannot seek compensation from the world at large, as only the party or parties responsible for causing the injury must pay compensation[159] (insurance being an exception to this general understanding). Honoré, elaborating on the element of responsibility, has observed:

> So there must be a causal link between the defendant's conduct and the plaintiff's loss. The conduct need not be *the* cause of the harm. It is enough that it is *a* cause, and there can be more than one human cause of the harm in question, in which case both (or all) harm-doers can be responsible. The existence of the causal link is a *necessary* condition of corrective justice and of the duty to compensate in a tort action.[160]

Therefore, in the event that the 'assistance' or the 'facilitation' supplied to a primary wrongdoer lacked a causal link, there cannot be civil accessorial liability. However, in response to Carty, Dietrich has pointed out that not all instances of assistance or facilitation lack a causal link to the primary wrongdoer's conduct. According to him, there are two ways in which a secondary party's conduct may be causally connected to the wrong committed by the primary wrongdoer.[161] First, the secondary party's conduct may be a causal factor in the primary wrongdoer's decision to commit the wrong, in that the primary wrongdoer would not have committed the wrong *but for* the secondary party's actions.[162] Second, the secondary party may provide assistance to the primary wrongdoer without which the wrong could not have been committed in the way it was carried out.[163] Although Dietrich has acknowledged that the second instance attracts a much weaker form of causation,[164] he goes on to argue that a 'but for' type of causation is not necessary for the imposition of accessorial liability.[165] Rather, the causal link is supplied where the secondary party's conduct 'increases the likelihood of the commission of the tort or wrong'.[166] Thus, Dietrich's point seems to be that the absence of a 'but for' type of causation ought not to prevent the imposition of

158 See Law Commission, *Assisting and Encouraging Crime*, above n32, para 2.16.
159 JCP Goldberg and BC Zipursky, 'Tort Law and Responsibility' in J Oberdiek (ed), *Philosophical Foundations of the Law of Torts* (Oxford University Press 2014), 17.
160 T Honoré, 'The Morality of Tort Law—Questions and Answers' in DG Owen (ed), *Philosophical Foundations of Tort Law* (Oxford University Press 1997), 80.
161 Dietrich, above n140, 241.
162 Dietrich, above n140, 241.
163 Dietrich, above n140, 241.
164 Dietrich, above n140, 241.
165 Dietrich, above n140, 243 ('"But for" causation is not necessary for liability even in the core, accepted cases of liability for participation in a common design').
166 Dietrich, above n140, 243.

accessorial liability on the part of a secondary party who provides *assistance* to the primary wrongdoer in respect of the commission of the latter's wrong, so long as the requisite mental state (of *knowing* assistance) is established.[167]

Second, Carty relies on the diverging objectives of the law relating to torts and crime in objecting to assistance liability in the civil context. Despite the fact that the 'historical ties between the two bodies of law are extensive',[168] it must be kept in mind that 'criminal and civil law served related but distinct purposes, eventually leading to two distinct bodies of law'.[169] The purpose of criminal law is 'both to punish the criminal for his misconduct and to protect the public against harm by punishing conduct that causes or is likely to cause harm, as well as to deter future actors from behaving in a like manner'.[170] It has been submitted that:

> The most obvious ramification for the criminal justice system . . . is that penal measures and their use in individual sentences must be justified both on grounds of retribution and crime reduction.[171]

On the other hand, '[t]he primary purpose of the law of torts is to enable an injured party to seek redress for the harm he or she has suffered at the hands of a wrongdoer'.[172] What this essentially requires is the party injured to be compensated, i.e. to seek corrective justice,[173] although just as criminal law, the law of torts too is a mechanism by which the state seeks to discourage undesirable behaviour (entailing a deterrent effect).[174]

Thus, since criminal law is primarily concerned with retribution and deterrence, it is justifiable for those who 'aid' the commission of a crime to be held equally guilty, even if the secondary party's conduct lacked a causal link. It is clearly in the interest of security and wellbeing of society to avoid crimes,[175] and this perhaps explains why the criminal law casts a wider net to include parties that merely 'aid' a criminal act, even without intending that it be committed. In contrast, since the aim of the law of torts is to achieve corrective justice, which in turn requires the party or parties responsible for causing the harm to compensate the victim, it casts a much narrower net, although with a lesser burden of proof than in criminal cases.

167 Dietrich, above n140, 247 ('In other words, assistance by a defendant to an individual tortfeasor that identifiably (knowingly) aids in the commission of a particular tort should also generate accessorial liability').
168 NI Combs, 'Civil Aiding and Abetting Liability' (2005) 58 *Vanderbilt Law Review* 241, 250.
169 Combs, above 168, 250.
170 Combs, above 168, 251 (citation omitted).
171 D Wood, 'Retribution, Crime Reduction and the Justification for Punishment' (2002) 22 *Oxford Journal of Legal Studies* 301, 318.
172 Combs, above 168, 251.
173 EJ Weinrib, *Corrective Justice* (Oxford University Press 2012), 2.
174 Honoré, above n160, 76. See also G Williams, 'The Aims of the Law of Tort' (1951) 4 *Current Legal Problems* 137.
175 Ormerod and Laird, above n111, 5.

What Carty has suggested is that in view of the different objectives of the two bodies of law, it is not justified to import into civil law the concepts of 'aiding' and 'abetting' applied in relation to criminal conduct. In fact, in *Fish & Fish v Sea Shepherd*, the English Court of Appeal cited Carty's views with approval.[176] This was in the course of Beatson LJ's judgment when an attempt was made to determine the 'obvious policy' considerations that might have persuaded the same court in *Credit Lyonnais v ECGD*[177] in holding that accessorial liability under the common law of torts must be limited in scope in comparison to the criminal law.[178] However, none of this contradicts Davies's proposition that anyone who *knowingly* assists the commission of a civil wrong ought to be held liable. Although Davies casts a wide net as regards the types of assisting conduct, the net is narrowed down given the tighter mental element of 'knowing' assistance.[179] As such, the UK Supreme Court's concern that a person's entitlement to engage in lawful conduct may become unduly restricted unless the limitation placed on the scope of joint tortfeasance is maintained[180] could be dismissed as being inapplicable to the context of Davies's proposition. In fact, responding to the Supreme Court's concern, Davies has observed:

> This is an important point: the ambit of accessory liability should not extend too far such that it unduly restricts parties' freedom of action. However, this concern is not unique to tort law. The conduct of an accessory in every area of the law tends to be lawful when viewed in isolation (such as lending a knife later used to commit a crime, or making an offer of employment that induces a primary wrongdoer to commit a breach of an earlier contract) but only tort law insists upon a common design.[181]

Third, Carty's rejection of civil assistance liability relates to the argument put forward by both Sales[182] and Cooper[183] that a general framework for such a form of liability already exists.[184] According to Carty, the authorities relied upon in order to argue in favour of a general liability framework are from two distinct

176 *Fish & Fish v Sea Shepherd*, [44] (Beatson LJ). Other instances where courts have been reluctant to refer to criminal-law notions of accessorial liability in deciding civil disputes include *CBS v Amstrad*, 1059 (Lord Templeman) and *Credit Lyonnais Bank Nederland NV (Now known As Generale Bank Nederland NV) v Export Credits Guarantee Department* [2000] 1 AC 486, 500 (Lord Woolf MR).

177 *Credit Lyonnais v ECGD*, 46 (Hobhouse LJ).

178 *Fish & Fish v Sea Shepherd*, [44] (Beatson LJ).

179 Davies, *Accessory Liability*, above n39, 215.

180 *Sea Shepherd v Fish & Fish*, [39] (Lord Sumption).

181 PS Davies, 'Accessory Liability in Tort' (2016) 132 *Law Quarterly Review* 15, 20 (internal quotation marks omitted).

182 Sales, above n138.

183 Cooper, above n154.

184 Carty, above n146, 505.

areas of civil law.[185] Thus, Carty has rejected the idea of a general framework for civil assistance liability:

> On closer consideration . . . the two areas of the civil law relied upon do not indicate that the general framework of secondary civil liability (*if it exists*) goes beyond the participation links of the doctrine of joint tortfeasance.[186]

Carty's contention in this regard may be right. However, this does not mean that the law should not be developed in favour of recognising a framework for assistance liability in the context of civil wrongs. In any case, Carty does not oppose the recognition of a specific form of civil liability in cases where 'assistance' or 'facilitation' is an acute problem.[187] Accordingly, it must be submitted that the recognition of liability for knowingly assisting a trade mark infringement, which could no doubt help in holding internet intermediaries liable in appropriate circumstances, may be acceptable despite Carty's opposition relating to a general assistance liability framework.

There is another factor that has influenced the English courts to reject assistance liability in the context of torts. Unlike in the case of criminal law, where different degrees of culpability can be reflected in imposing sentences, joint tortfeasors are 'fully liable' for the victim's loss.[188] As a consequence, in practice, the 'deep pocket' defendants will 'often have to bear a share of the total damage quite disproportionate to that defendant's share of responsibility, an outcome which not even the theoretical right of contribution can always correct'.[189] The problem of disproportionate liability for joint torts has been recognised and addressed in some jurisdictions. For instance, in Australia, accessorial liability in relation to property damage and pure economic loss has been subject to statutory reform leading to the imposition of a more proportionate scheme of legal responsibility.[190] In the absence of such reforms, the recognition of civil assistance liability, even if restricted to knowing assistance as Davies has suggested,[191] would only result in certain parties being overburdened for the wrongful acts of others. Assuming someday the law develops to recognise assistance liability in the context of civil

185 Carty, above n146, 505:

> Though Sales asserts that there are a number of authorities and doctrines that can usefully be viewed as illustrations of this general principle, in fact this theory relies on two areas of the civil law. The first area focuses on the liability identified in *Lumley v Gye*. . . . Second, reliance for a general theory of secondary civil liability is placed on the existence in trust law of liability for those who assist in the breach of a trust.
>
> (citations omitted)

186 Carty, above n146, 506 (emphasis added).

187 Carty, above n146, 513.

188 *Fish & Fish v Sea Shepherd*, [44] (Beatson LJ).

189 C Sappideen and P Vines, *Fleming's The Law of Torts* (10th edn, Lawbook Co 2011), 303.

190 Sappideen and Vines, above n189. See also A Gurr, 'Accessory Liability and Contribution, Release and Apportionment' (2010) 34 *Melbourne University Law Review* 16.

191 Davies, *Accessory Liability*, above n39, 10.

wrongs, or specifically in relation to torts, it is important for such developments to ensure that liability is imposed on proportionate terms.

Some predictions for the future

Ultimately, subject to the possibility of legislative intervention, whether liability for providing knowing assistance must be recognised as a general means of allocating accessorial liability for civil wrongs, or more specifically in the context of torts, is a matter for the courts to decide. To date, English courts have expressly rejected the transposition of criminal-law notions of accessorial liability into the context of torts,[192] and perhaps rightly so. Nevertheless, this does not mean that a carefully crafted form of liability for 'knowing' assistance, as proposed by Davies, ought not to be recognised in the context of civil law.

Unfortunately, however, the UK Supreme Court in its recent decision in *Sea Shepherd v Fish & Fish* considered Davies's criticism about the judicial reluctance to recognise liability for knowing assistance[193] and expressly rejected it. Lord Sumption, for instance, observed: '[f]or my part, I doubt whether the criticism is justified'.[194] If liability for knowingly assisting a tort is to be formally recognised under the common law, this would require courts to depart from the common design requirement, which has always been part of the test for imposing liability on joint tortfeasors. Such a departure, however, would require a significant 'shift in approach'[195] on the part of English judges, who have been reluctant, save in exceptional cases,[196] to make developments to the common law unless they are small and incremental in nature.[197] It might be difficult to persuade a court that a finding of assistance liability, in the absence of a common design between the secondary party and the wrongdoer, amounts to a small and incremental development of the common law.

It is therefore very unlikely that liability for knowingly assisting a civil wrong, or more specifically a tort, will be recognised by the English courts any time soon. That said, unless there is a willingness to develop the common law, intermediaries operating in the online space that assist, even knowingly, the commission of wrongs, including trade mark infringements, will remain beyond the reach of liability. In the circumstances, legislative reforms will have to be explored in order to bridge the gap in the law relating to joint liability that Davies and others who share his view have identified.

192 See above n176, and accompanying text.

193 The Supreme Court specifically referred to Davies's views published in the *Cambridge Law Journal* (see above n30), which he later sets out in his monograph (see above n39).

194 *Sea Shepherd v Fish & Fish*, [39] (Lord Sumption).

195 Davies, *Accessory Liability*, above n39, 279.

196 AC Hutchinson, *Evolution and the Common Law* (Cambridge University Press 2005), 151 (citing *Rylands v Fletcher* [1865] 3 H&C 774 and *Donoghue v Stevenson* [1932] AC 562).

197 D Harvey, *Collisions in the Digital Paradigm: Law and Rule Making in the Internet Age* (Hart Publishing 2017), 167.

4 Approaches elsewhere—across the English Channel and the Atlantic

By now, it is clear that neither statutory trade mark law nor common-law approaches to civil accessorial liability are capable of providing a basis to hold internet intermediaries liable for infringements of trade mark rights, even in cases where they knowingly assist infringements on the part of their users. Waiting for the judiciary to develop the common law to fill the 'gap' in civil accessorial liability, so that the inadequacy in the current law could be addressed, is one possible choice, albeit the wait might be very long, if not forever. The choice of legislative intervention, however, will provide a surer, more expeditious and prudent approach to address the limitations of the existing legal framework.

However, before determining the nature and scope of the legislative intervention required, it is worth exploring approaches that have been developed and adopted by domestic courts in some of the EU Member States, as well as in the US, in cases instituted by trade mark proprietors against internet intermediaries. Since the Agreement on the Trade-Related Aspects of Intellectual Property Rights (TRIPS)[1] and regionally the Trade Marks Directive[2] have harmonised trade mark law to a significant degree, and the conduct of internet intermediaries gives rise to similar questions of fact and law, an analysis of these cases is useful in extracting common principles that come into play. These common principles will provide a sound basis for legislative reforms.

Cases in select EU Member States

The key EU directives

Before dealing with the case law, it is useful to set out the key EU directives that have shaped national laws in EU Member States, which have been applied by

1 The text of the agreement is available in Annex 1C of the Marrakesh Agreement Establishing the World Trade Organization 1994.

2 Directive 2008/95/EC of the European Parliament and of the Council of 22 October 2008 to Approximate the Laws of the Member States Relating to Trade Marks [2008] OJ L 299/25 (Trade Marks Directive). An explanation as to why a reference is made to the 2008 Trade Marks Directive, and not the later 2015 Trade Marks Directive (Directive (EU) 2015/2436), which replaces the former, is provided in Chapter 1.

domestic courts to disputes between trade mark proprietors and internet intermediaries. These directives are the Trade Marks Directive, the E-Commerce Directive[3] and the Enforcement Directive.[4]

The Trade Marks Directive is relevant because it is the substantive legal framework in the EU that regulates trade marks, and has been transposed into the domestic laws of the Member States. The key provisions of the Trade Marks Directive, relevant to the context of internet intermediaries, were examined in Chapters 2 and 3. The Enforcement Directive is relevant because it deals with the enforcement of intellectual property rights within the EU and contains provisions that provide for remedies against intermediaries, including those that operate in the online space. The Enforcement Directive is considered in detail in Chapters 8 and 9 when discussing injunctions. The E-Commerce Directive becomes relevant in view of the safe harbour it incorporates, which applies to the types of intermediaries considered in this book. Domestic courts in EU Member States have frequently referred to the national equivalent of the E-Commerce Directive in dealing with the liability of internet intermediaries under domestic law. Therefore, a discussion of the key provisions of the E-Commerce Directive is warranted before moving on to analyse the case law.

The E-Commerce Directive was adopted in the year 2000 with the view of promoting certainty in respect of certain principles and concepts applicable to providers of 'information society services'.[5] The type of services to which the E-Commerce Directive applies has been defined with a reference to another EU directive, the Technical Standards Directive.[6] Article 1(1)(b) of the Technical Standards Directive defines the term 'service' in the following way:

> any Information Society service, that is to say, any service normally provided for remuneration, at a distance, by electronic means and at the individual request of a recipient of services.

3 Directive 2000/31/EC on Certain Legal Aspects of Information Society Services, in Particular Electronic Commerce, in the Internal Market [2000] OJ L 178/1 (E-Commerce Directive).

4 Directive 2004/48/EC of the European Parliament and of the Council of 29 April 2004 on the Enforcement of Intellectual Property Rights [2004] OJ L 157/16 (Enforcement Directive).

5 E-Commerce Directive, Recitals (5) and (7).

6 E-Commerce Directive, art 2(a), which refers to Directive 98/34/EC of the European Parliament and of the Council of 22 June 1998 Laying Down a Procedure for the Provision of Information in the Field of Technical Standards and Regulations and of Rules on Information Society Services [1998] OJ L 204/37, as subsequently amended by Directive 98/48/EC of the European Parliament and of the Council of 20 July 1998 Amending Directive 98/34/EC Laying Down a Procedure for the Provision of Information in the Field of Technical Standards and Regulations [1998] OJ L 217/18. Both Directive 98/34/EC and Directive 98/48/EC have now been replaced by Directive (EU) 2015/1535 of the European Parliament and of the Council of 9 September 2015 Laying Down a Procedure for the Provision of Information in the Field of Technical Regulations and of Rules on Information Society Services (codification) [2015] OJ L 241/1 (Technical Standards Directive).

The services offered by ISPs, hosts and navigation providers are provided 'at a distance',[7] by 'electronic means'[8] and 'at the individual request of a recipient of services'.[9] The Technical Standards Directive, however, does not explain what 'normally provided for remuneration' means, although this plays an important role in determining the applicability of the E-Commerce Directive. For instance, some hosts and navigation providers offer services without obtaining a fee from the recipients of these services, although they are remunerated in other ways, such as advertising and sponsorships. Typical examples include social networking websites (e.g. Facebook), blogs (e.g. Blogger) and search engines (e.g. Google), which provide free web space and navigation services to their users. In the circumstances, the question arises whether remuneration must flow directly from the receiver of a service in order for an intermediary to come within the definition of an information society service.

In *MIS v Designtechnica*,[10] which was a defamation case involving Google and its search engine, the English High Court had to, among other things, determine whether Google came within the scope of the E-Commerce Directive when it provided its navigation services. Mr Justice Eady, delivering the judgment, observed '[i]t is difficult to see how the third defendant's search engine service could, in any ordinary meaning of the term, be described as "for remuneration" in circumstances where the user of the web does not pay for the service'.[11] Nevertheless, Eady J, having referred to Recital (18) of the E-Commerce Directive,[12] and *Gatley on Libel and Slander*,[13] concluded 'that search engines would be embraced'[14] by the definition of information society services. Accordingly, it is quite clear that the 'remuneration' requirement merely requires some form of economic activity

7 Technical Standards Directive, art 1(1)(b)(i) ('at a distance' refers to a service that is provided without the parties being simultaneously present).

8 Technical Standards Directive, art 1(1)(b)(ii) ('by electronic means' refers to a service that is sent initially and received at its destination by means of electronic equipment for the processing (including digital compression) and storage of data, and entirely transmitted, conveyed and received by wire, radio, optical or other electromagnetic means).

9 Technical Standards Directive, art 1(1)(b)(iii) ('at the individual request of a recipient of services' refers to a service that is provided through the transmission of data on an individual user's request).

10 *Metropolitan International Schools Ltd v Designtechnica Corp* [2009] EMLR 27 (*MIS v Designtechnica*).

11 *MIS v Designtechnica*, [82] (Eady J).

12 Recital (18) of the E-Commerce Directive provides that information society services embrace 'a wide range of economic activities which take place on-line; these activities can, in particular, consist of selling goods on-line; activities such as the delivery of goods as such or the provision of services off-line are not covered; information society services are not solely restricted to services giving rise to on-line contracting but also, in so far as they represent an economic activity, extend to services which are not remunerated by those who receive them, such as those offering on-line information or commercial communications, or those providing tools allowing for search, access and retrieval of data'.

13 P Milmo and H Rogers (eds), *Gatley on Libel and Slander* (11th edn, Sweet & Maxwell 2008), para 6.28.

14 *MIS v Designtechnica*, [84] (Eady J).

on the part of information society service providers, even if the users of these services are not the source of such remuneration.[15]

Once an intermediary qualifies as an information society service provider, the safe harbour provisions in Part 4 of the E-Commerce Directive operate to limit any liability arising from the transmission or storage of all forms of unlawful content provided that certain conditions set out therein are satisfied. In essence, the safe harbour applies in respect of actions instituted against internet intermediaries alleging the infringement of rights under any area of the law, including the law relating to trade marks. The specific conditions that must be satisfied in order to qualify for the safe harbour are laid down in Articles 12, 13 and 14 of the E-Commerce Directive.

Article 12(1) of the E-Commerce Directive applies to 'mere conduits'. Under this provision, an intermediary that engages in the 'transmission in a communication network of information provided by a recipient of the service, or the provision of access to a communication network',[16] will not be liable for information transmitted by that intermediary provided that it neither initiates nor determines the recipient of the transmission[17] and does not select or modify the information contained in the transmission.[18] It is clear that Article 12 applies to ISPs because they have no control over the nature of content that is transmitted in their networks, thus justifying their immunity from claims for damages.[19]

Article 13(1) applies to 'caching'. Accordingly, an intermediary that engages in the 'transmission in a communication network of information provided by a recipient of the service' will be excluded from liability for the 'automatic, intermediate and temporary storage of that information, performed for the sole purpose of making more efficient the information's onward transmission to other recipients of the service upon their request'.[20] For the immunity to apply, the intermediary must comply with a number of conditions, which include the obligation to expeditiously remove or to disable access to any information it has stored upon obtaining actual knowledge of the fact that the said information has been removed at its source, or access to it has been disabled, or that a court or an administrative authority has ordered its removal or disablement.[21] Some commentators have suggested that the caching exception would rarely apply in practice as 'many servers which are designed to retain third party content in a

15 See S Rawson, 'An Emerging Framework for Electronic Commerce: The E.U. Electronic Commerce Directive and Related Developments' (1999) 10 *International Company and Commercial Law Review* 171 and MTM Rennie, 'Electronic Commerce: A Review of the European Commission's Proposed Directive' (1999) 5 *Computer and Telecommunications Law Review* 93.

16 E-Commerce Directive, art 12(1).

17 E-Commerce Directive, arts 12(1)(a) and (b).

18 E-Commerce Directive, art 12(1)(c).

19 G Sutter, 'Online Intermediaries' in C Reed and J Angel (eds), *Computer Law: The Law and Regulation of Information Technology* (6th edn, Oxford University Press 2007), 242.

20 E-Commerce Directive, art 13(1).

21 E-Commerce Directive, art 13(1)(e).

cache will do so for long periods of time',[22] thus questioning whether the process could be regarded as temporary. However, in a recent ruling by the CJEU,[23] albeit in the context of interpreting Article 5(1) of the Info-Soc Directive,[24] the Court held:

> the on-screen copies and the cached copies made by an end-user in the course of viewing a website satisfy the conditions that those copies must be temporary, that they must be transient or incidental in nature and that they must constitute an integral and essential part of a technological process, as well as the conditions laid down in Article 5(5) of that directive, and that they may therefore be made without the authorisation of the copyright holders.[25]

This interpretation could similarly be applied to the context of Article 13 of the E-Commerce Directive. Thus, it would appear that, so long as the cached data is deleted automatically in time,[26] that should suffice to satisfy the condition that the caching was temporary.

Article 14(1) of the E-Commerce Directive applies to 'hosting'. Thus, an intermediary that provides a service consisting of 'the storage of information provided by a recipient of the service' will not be liable for damages resulting from 'the information stored at the request of a recipient of the service',[27] provided that two conditions are satisfied. First, the intermediary must not have had actual knowledge of the illegal activity or information and, specifically as regards any claim for damages, must not have been aware of facts or circumstances from which such illegal activity or information is apparent.[28] Second, the intermediary, upon acquiring such knowledge or awareness, must act expeditiously to remove or to disable access to the illegal activity or information.[29]

Of the three safe harbour provisions, it is Article 14(1) that has been regularly discussed, perhaps because hosts have been the subject of litigation more than other types of intermediaries. Most hosts merely provide a platform for its users to upload, store and share content, with minimal supervision and authorial control. In those circumstances, hosts act as neutral and passive actors, which creates difficulties in determining when such intermediaries become

22 Sutter, above n19, 242.

23 Case C-360/13, *Public Relations Consultants Association Ltd v Newspaper Licensing Agency Ltd* [2015] RPC 13 (*PRCA v NLA*).

24 Directive 2001/29/EC of the European Parliament and of the Council of 22 May 2001 on the Harmonisation of Certain Aspects of Copyright and Related Rights in the Information Society [2001] OJ L 167/10 (Info-Soc Directive). The Info-Soc Directive applies specifically to the context of copyright protection and enforcement in the EU.

25 *PRCA v NLA*, [63].

26 *PRCA v NLA*, [26].

27 E-Commerce Directive, art 14(1).

28 E-Commerce Directive, art 14(1)(a).

29 E-Commerce Directive, art 14(1)(b).

aware of facts or circumstances from which the illegal activity or information is apparent. Similar difficulties arise in establishing actual knowledge on the part of a host in relation to illegal activity or information residing on the host's servers.[30]

There is also some difficulty in determining whether the E-Commerce Directive's safe harbour applies to navigation providers, such as search engines. Although it was decided in *MIS v Designtechnica* that navigation providers qualify as an information society service for the purposes of the E-Commerce Directive (provided that they are remunerated in some way), there is still doubt as to whether the safe harbour provisions apply to them. This is because, upon a consideration of the functions of navigation providers, it is difficult to classify them within the parameters of Articles 12–14 of the E-Commerce Directive. In the context of search engines, the domestic implementations of the E-Commerce Directive in Spain, Portugal, Hungary, Liechtenstein and Romania treat them as hosts.[31] In contrast, under the domestic laws applicable in Austria and Bulgaria, search engines are treated as mere conduits.[32]

The English High Court in *MIS v Designtechnica* did not have to come to an affirmative finding on the status of Google's search engine under the E-Commerce Directive, in view of the Court's finding that Google was not liable for the defamation claims that were brought against it.[33] Nevertheless, Eady J made the following obiter remark: 'I think that, for the third defendant [Google] to be classified as or deemed a "host", statutory intervention would be needed'.[34] Thus, the status of navigation providers, and in particular search engines, remains uncertain in the UK. Although navigation providers qualify as information society services, it is unclear whether the safe harbour under the E-Commerce Directive extends to them, and, insofar as the UK is concerned, they will not be regarded as either hosts or mere conduits unless the E-Commerce Regulations,[35] which implement the EU directive, are amended accordingly.

In addition to the category-specific safe harbour provisions, Article 15(1) of the E-Commerce Directive provides that information society service providers to whom the directive applies cannot be subject to a general obligation to monitor the content that they transmit or store, or to actively seek facts or circumstances indicating illegal activity. However, that does not mean that

30 The aspect of 'actual knowledge' and 'awareness' is considered in greater detail in Chapter 5.

31 *MIS v Designtechnica*, [99], [101], [102], [103] and [105] (Eady J).

32 *MIS v Designtechnica*, [89] and [104] (Eady J).

33 The Court found that Google was not a common-law 'publisher' and was therefore not liable for the defamatory material. This allowed the High Court to avoid making a determination on the status of search engines under the E-Commerce Directive (*MIS v Designtechnica*, [112] (Eady J)).

34 *MIS v Designtechnica*, [112] (Eady J).

35 Electronic Commerce (EC Directive) Regulations 2002, SI 2002/2013 (E-Commerce Regulations).

the safe harbour provisions prevent a court or administrative authority from requiring an intermediary supplying an information society service to terminate or prevent an infringement, for instance through interim or permanent injunctions,[36] or to obligate such intermediaries, under domestic law, to disclose information to competent authorities in order to identify those committing illegal acts.[37]

Thus, it is clear that the safe harbour provisions of the E-Commerce Directive explicitly apply only to neutral and passive intermediaries that provide an information society service. While there is no doubt that ISPs and hosts are captured by the safe harbour provisions, the status of navigation providers remains uncertain, except that under the domestic laws of some EU Member States they are (perhaps wrongly) classified as either ISPs or hosts. In the context of the UK, the safe harbour provisions of the E-Commerce Regulations do not in any way refer to navigation providers. However, this is not a matter for concern, as navigation providers are never likely to be held liable for infringements of trade mark rights under existing laws prevailing in the UK, and the proposal for law reforms made in Chapter 5 of this book does not seek to alter this status quo.

Hosts

Trade mark infringement actions involving internet intermediaries are dominated by cases filed against hosts that provide advertising services (e.g. Google's AdWords service) and platforms that operate online marketplaces (e.g. eBay). This is not surprising as advertisements and product listings that are hosted by these platforms, at times, make use of trade marks without the consent of the relevant trade mark proprietors with the aim of promoting the sale or supply of infringing goods or services. Since the users of these platforms alone are responsible for the content that is hosted, the intermediaries providing the services play a neutral and passive role,[38] making it possible for them to rely on the hosting safe harbour enshrined in Article 14(1) of the E-Commerce Directive. However, the hosting safe harbour will not apply to intermediaries that do not comply with the conditions set out therein upon which immunity is granted.

Although there is no basis for a trade mark infringement suit to be brought against a host, where its services are used by a third party to store and share content that promotes an infringement,[39] actions filed by trade mark proprietors

36 E-Commerce Directive, arts 12(3), 13(2) and 14(3).

37 E-Commerce Directive, art 15(2).

38 It must be noted that some of the cases discussed in this chapter demonstrate that there are instances where the conduct of certain intermediaries, such as eBay, *may* go beyond merely hosting third-party content, and thus are not captured by the safe harbour.

39 See discussion in Chapter 2.

on alternative causes of action against hosts in France[40] and Germany[41] have been successful. In Belgium, trade mark proprietors have not been as successful, yet this was because the relevant host under consideration had acted in a responsible fashion making the hosting safe harbour applicable.[42] These cases are considered in detail below with a view of isolating common principles that emerge from them.

France

In 2012, the French Cour de cassation (the court of last resort in civil and criminal matters), in an action filed by Louis Vuitton, not only held that eBay was ineligible to invoke the French hosting safe harbour[43] but also found eBay liable for the trade mark infringements committed by its users.[44] This was an appeal from a decision of the Cour d'appel de Paris (Court of Appeal of Paris), which found in favour of Louis Vuitton, upholding the findings of the Tribunal de grande instance de Paris (High Court of Paris)[45] not only on a jurisdictional issue but also

40 See e.g., *eBay Inc v Louis Vuitton Moët Hennessy* Case 11-10505 (Cour de cassation of France, 3 May 2012) (*eBay v Louis Vuitton*); *SA Louis Vuitton Malletier v eBay Inc and eBay International* [2010] ETMR 10 (Tribunal de grande instance de Paris, 30 June 2008) (*Louis Vuitton v eBay* (Paris)); *Hermès International v Mme Cindy F, eBay France and eBay International AG* (Tribunal de grande instance de Troyes, 4 June 2008) (unreported) (*Hermès v eBay*); *SA L'Oréal v SA eBay* Case RG 07/11365 (Tribunal de grande instance de Paris, 13 May 2009) (*L'Oréal v eBay* (Paris)).

41 See e.g., *Internet Auction I* Case I ZR 304/01 [2005] ETMR 25 (Bundesgerichtshof, 11 March 2004) (against Ricardo, a website similar to eBay); *Internet Auction II* Case I ZR 35/04 [2007] ETMR 70 (Bundesgerichtshof, 19 April 2007) (against eBay); *Internet Auction III* Case I ZR 73/05 (Bundesgerichtshof, 30 April 2008) (unreported) (against eBay); *Coty Germany GmbH v eBay International AG (No1)* [2012] ETMR 19 (Landgericht Stuttgart, 20 December 2011) (*Coty v eBay (No1)*); *Coty Germany GmbH v eBay International AG (No2)* [2012] ETMR 20 (Landgericht Berlin, 10 January 2012) (*Coty v eBay (No2)*).

42 *Lancôme Parfums et Beauté v eBay International AG* Case A/07/06032 (Rechtbank van Koophandel Brüssel, 31 July 2008) (*Lancôme v eBay*).

43 Law No 2004-575 of 21 June 2004 Regarding Confidence in the Digital Economy (which transposes the provisions of the E-Commerce Directive).

44 The full text (in French) of the Cour de cassation's judgment in *eBay v Louis Vuitton* is available at www.legifrance.gouv.fr/affichJuriJudi.do?idTexte=JURITEXT000025808328 (accessed 31 January 2019). For a comment on the French Cour de cassation's decision in *eBay v Louis Vuitton*, see R Milchior, 'eBay Ruling is Good News for Brand Owners – but Evidentiary Burden is Increased' *World Trademark Review Daily* (23 May 2012) <www.granrut.com/IMG/pdf/WTR_20120724.pdf> (accessed 31 January 2019).

45 There were three separate actions filed by the Louis Vuitton Moët Hennessy (LVMH) group of companies in the High Court of Paris. The claimants in the three cases were Louis Vuitton Malletier (handbag and luggage section of LVMH), Christian Dior Couture (one of the group's fashion houses) and LVMH's perfume brands (Dior, Guerlain, Kenzo and Givenchy). These actions were joined in view of their similarity and the High Court of Paris ultimately ordered eBay to pay approximately €38 million in damages. See S Bailey, 'Fighting an Anonymous Enemy: The Uncertainty of Auction Sites in the Face of *Tiffany v eBay* and *LVMH v eBay*' (2009) 40 *California Western International Law Journal* 129, 147.

on the merits. On the jurisdictional issue, the Cour de cassation confirmed that the French courts were right in exercising jurisdiction as regards the infringing sales that took place on eBay's UK website ('ebay.co.uk'), as French consumers were encouraged to visit the UK website, which complemented eBay's French website ('ebay.fr').[46] However, the Court reproached the lower courts for exercising jurisdiction over infringing sales that took place on 'ebay.com', operated by eBay Inc registered in the US, on the basis that the website was not directed at French internet users.[47]

On the merits, the Cour de cassation did not disturb the findings at first instance, except for an adjustment in the quantum of damages.[48] Louis Vuitton's complaint was based on Articles 1382 and 1383 of the French Civil Code,[49] which translate as follows:

> Article 1382—Any act whatever of man, which causes damage to another, obliges the one by whose fault it occurred, to compensate it.
>
> Article 1383—Everyone is liable for the damage he causes not only by his intentional act, but also by his negligent conduct or by his imprudence.

A reading of the judgment of the High Court of Paris reveals that it found eBay directly liable for the infringements, rather than as an accessory. Such an outcome was inevitable given the choice of French tort law, as opposed to trade mark law, to buttress Louis Vuitton's claims. In essence, Louis Vuitton claimed that, despite repeated warnings to take effective measures aimed at preventing infringements,[50] eBay failed to take appropriate steps to address Louis Vuitton's concerns. The claim appears to impose a positive duty on eBay to take effective measures to tackle infringements, the failure to comply leading to a form of negligence-based liability.[51] The Court agreed, and imposed fairly extensive obligations on the part of eBay:

> Whereas indeed, eBay defaulted in its obligation of ensuring that its business does not generate any illicit actions, in this case acts of infringement, to the detriment of an economic player such as Louis Vuitton Malletier, whereas eBay also defaulted in its obligation of verifying that the sellers who

46 Milchior, above n44.

47 Milchior, above n44.

48 Although the High Court of Paris awarded approximately €38 million in damages, on appeal, this was reduced to €5.7 million by the Paris Court of Appeal. On further appeal, in view of the Cour de cassation's decision to limit its jurisdiction to infringements that took place on eBay's French and UK sites, it is likely that eBay would have had to pay a lower amount (see Milchior, above n44). There is, however, no reported account of the exact quantum of damages that eBay ultimately paid Louis Vuitton.

49 Ordinance No 2004-164 of 20 February 2004, Civil Code of France.

50 *Louis Vuitton v eBay* (Paris), [36].

51 *Louis Vuitton v eBay* (Paris), [38].

> habitually carry out numerous transactions on its sites are duly registered with the competent authorities and, in France, on the Trade and Companies Register, as well as with the social security or other organizations.[52]

The Court's ruling not only gives rise to a specific obligation on the part of eBay to perform checks with the competent authorities as regards the status of sellers on its platform but also creates a general obligation on eBay to ensure that sellers that make use of the platform do not engage in infringing activity. The imposition of such a general obligation was possible as Louis Vuitton claimed, and the Court accepted, that eBay was ineligible to benefit from the hosting safe harbour provided under the French equivalent of Article 14(1) of the E-Commerce Directive, in view of its status as a 'broker'.[53] In essence, the Court found that eBay was not a neutral and passive host.

Before the French Cour de cassation's decision, judicial approaches in France on the liability of hosts were at variance. As noted above, the decision of the High Court of Paris in *Louis Vuitton v eBay* (Paris) not only found eBay liable for failing to take action to remove infringing content but also that the French hosting safe harbour did not shield eBay from liability. In contrast, in *Hermès v eBay*,[54] although the Tribunal de grande instance de Troyes (High Court of Troyes) found eBay liable for the infringements committed by its sellers,[55] the Court stated that the hosting safe harbour did apply to a certain subset of its activities, namely when it acted as a pure host, but not to its auction-related activities.[56] As regards the issue of liability, however, both in *Hermès v eBay* and *Louis Vuitton v eBay* (Paris) the courts adopted a similar approach. That is, although eBay's sellers who committed the trade mark infringements were liable under the French Intellectual Property Code,[57] eBay's liability was on the basis of its 'failure to ensure within its means that the website was not used for illegal purposes'.[58]

52 *Louis Vuitton v eBay* (Paris), [71].

53 *Louis Vuitton v eBay* (Paris), [39]. See also, K Weckström, 'Liability for Trademark Infringement for Internet Service Providers' (2012) 16 *Marquette Intellectual Property Law Review* 1, 30.

54 The full text of the judgment (in French) is available at www.legalis.net/spip.php?page=jurisprudence-decision&id_article=2320 (accessed 31 January 2019).

55 The High Court of Troyes awarded over €20,000 in damages.

56 PV Eecke and M Truyens, *EU Study on the Legal Analysis of a Single Market for the Information Society–New Rules for a New Age?* SMART 2007/0037 (2009). In Chapter 6 of the study, which exclusively discusses the liability of internet intermediaries, the authors cite (at p. 17) *Hermès v eBay* to suggest that some courts have preferred to subdivide a single commercial service into several distinct activities, and only apply the safe harbour to some activities. See also, KM Saunders and G Berger-Walliser, 'The Liability of Online Markets for Counterfeit Goods: A Comparative Analysis of Secondary Trademark Infringement in the United States and Europe' (2011) 32 *Northwestern Journal of International Law and Business* 37, 76.

57 Law No 92-597 of 1 July 1992, Intellectual Property Code, art L713-2.

58 HC Wong, 'eBay's Liability for Counterfeits: A Transatlantic Comparison' (2010) 5 *Journal of Intellectual Property Law & Practice* 39, 41. See also, Saunders and Berger-Walliser, above n56, 80.

However, in contrast to the cases discussed above, the High Court of Paris dismissed an action brought by L'Oréal in favour of eBay.[59] The Court held that eBay had taken sufficient measures to meet its obligations to police counterfeits on its website.[60] One of the reasons that tilted the decision in favour of eBay was its 'Verified Rights Owner' or 'VeRO' programme, which allowed aggrieved right holders to inform eBay of any infringement of their rights. Accordingly, evidence of 'knowledge on the part of eBay of infringing content and a failure to remedy it'[61] would have been required for a finding of liability.

In summary, despite the variances in approaches adopted by the French courts, what is clear is that hosts, such as eBay, are under a duty to act in terms of French civil law to bring an end to an infringement upon being specifically notified about it by the right holder. Although the French courts have diverged in their views as to the extent of measures that hosts must adopt in order to discharge this duty, at the very least French law requires hosts to take reasonable steps to expeditiously remove any content causing an infringement upon acquiring actual knowledge of the infringing activity.

Germany

A similar series of cases came before the German courts, albeit reflecting a slightly different judicial attitude to that in France. Rolex, the exclusive watch manufacturer, was the first to bring actions against hosts that provided platforms for an online marketplace. While *Internet Auction I* was filed against Ricardo (a platform similar to eBay), *Internet Auction II* and *Internet Auction III* were actions filed against eBay. Under German law, liability may be imposed either for committing a tortious (or infringing) act or for participating in another's wrongful act.[62] The German courts in all three cases concluded that direct civil or criminal liability could not be imposed on hosts, such as Ricardo and eBay. It is unlikely that hosts would become caught up as infringers 'because usually . . . their users commit [the infringements]'.[63] As regards the imposition of liability for participating in another's wrongful act, since the 'participant needs to act intentionally in regard to the unlawful action of the third party',[64] it is unlikely that a host would qualify as a participant. However, where there is evidence of a gross and insistent breach, German courts have developed the concept to include instances of participation by forbearance,[65] which in effect could be perceived as liability for failing to act.

59 *L'Oréal v eBay* (Paris). The full text of the judgment (in French) is available at www.legalis.net/jurisprudences/tribunal-de-grande-instance-de-paris-3eme-chambre-3eme-section-jugement-du-13-mai-2009-2 (accessed 31 January 2019).

60 Wong, above n58, 42.

61 WIPO, *Trademarks and the Internet*, SCT/24/4 (2010), Annex 1, para 11.

62 See T Hoeren and S Yankova, 'The Liability of Internet Intermediaries – The German Perspective' (2012) 43 *International Review of Intellectual Property and Competition Law (IIC)* 501, 503.

63 Hoeren and Yankova, above n62, 503.

64 Hoeren and Yankova, above n62, 503.

65 Hoeren and Yankova, above n62, 503.

In *Internet Auction I*, the Bundesgerichtshof (Federal Court of Justice), Germany's highest court of civil and criminal jurisdiction, excluded the possibility of Ricardo being held liable either as an infringer or a participant:

> The fact that the defendant made its platform for third party auctions available to the suppliers and that offers were publicised there, by means of which the trade mark rights of the claimants were infringed, does not mean that the defendant itself committed any trade mark infringement. In the case in dispute, liability as participants in the infringement of the trade mark committed by the relevant supplier is also eliminated.[66]

Similar sentiments were expressed by the Federal Court of Justice in *Internet Action II*, paying attention to the workings of a typical host:

> The parties do not dispute that an automatic process was used to place the items of the auctioneers on the internet without the prior knowledge of the respondents. Intentional participation by the respondents is ruled out in these circumstances.[67]

Thus, in *Internet Auction I*, *II* and *III*, the German Federal Court of Justice had to impute liability on the hosts in question using a concept that is unique to German law known as liability for 'interference', also known as 'disturbance liability' (Stoererhaftung).[68] According to the Court '[a]n interferer—not necessarily being a perpetrator or participant—is someone who makes a deliberate and proximately causal contribution to an infringement of a protected interest in some way'.[69] A host is capable of being classified as an 'interferer' (or a 'disturber'). Although a court cannot order damages, a claim against an interferer could give rise to the imposition of an 'obligation to inspect'[70] that requires, in this case, the host to, apart from removing infringing content upon being notified, prevent future infringements of a similar kind. Thus, hosts become obligated to 'stop the "disturbing" of trademark owners',[71] which could in practice be achieved through the injunctive remedy. Once an injunction is in place, it serves as judicial notice to curtail similar future infringements. However, where a host fails to take action to prevent future infringements, upon being put on notice, a claim for damages may arise on the basis of the omission. Hoeren and Yankowa have suggested:

66 *Internet Auction I*, [30(aa)].

67 *Internet Auction II*, [31(2)].

68 In *Internet Auction II*, the Court observed that liability for interference is a form of vicarious liability under German law (at [37]).

69 *Internet Auction II*, [40(bb)].

70 *Internet Auction II*, [40(bb)].

71 H Hartwig, 'German Court Ruling Cracks Down on Internet Forgeries' (2004) 43 *European Lawyer* 12.

> The principles of tort by omission should be applied, if the focus of the offence lies in the omission or failure to prevent further similar infringements even after gaining specific notices regarding trademark violations.[72]

The principles laid down in the aforesaid German decisions were followed by the Landgericht Stuttgart (Stuttgart Regional Court) in *Coty v eBay (No1)*. Accordingly, once eBay was notified of an infringement, it was not only required to remove the infringing product listings but also required to prevent similar future infringements. The Court summarised the legal position as follows:

> The defendant company is not liable solely because the defendant company's customers place mark infringing offers. For the defendant company owes no general inspection duty. *This changes, however, the moment the defendant company gains knowledge of a right infringement.*[73]

Once a host is put on notice of an infringement, a duty to inspect is imposed on the host. This duty may then be discharged by using keyword filtering, a technology that can filter content through the use of 'keywords in both the offer caption and also the article descriptions'.[74] It has been suggested that the only means at the disposal of hosts, such as eBay, to identify future infringements is the use of filtering technology, which has the potential to detect suspicious content comprising text and information relating to goods sold in large quantities at relatively low prices, a classic sign of infringement.[75] However, such filters have limitations and, as such, the German courts have emphasised that intermediaries that host third-party content would not be liable in the event an infringement goes undetected owing to technical limitations in filtering technology.[76] Of course, where a host does not take reasonable measures to prevent future infringements, in violation of an injunction, it might be held liable for contributing to unauthorised use of trade marks by forbearance,[77] which gives rise to a claim for damages.[78]

In summary, the analysis of the cases discussed above suggests that under German law, as in the case of France, hosts that acquire actual knowledge of an infringement must take reasonable measures to terminate the infringement.

72 Hoeren and Yankova, above n62, 518.

73 *Coty v eBay (No1)*, [35(b)] (emphasis added). See also, *Coty v eBay (No2)*, where the Landgericht Berlin (Berlin Regional Court) ordered eBay to provide information about one of its customers that listed goods on the eBay platform that violated the claimant's trade mark rights, leading to an information injunction.

74 *Coty v eBay (No1)*, [37].

75 Hartwig, above n71, 12.

76 Hoeren and Yankova, above n62, 518 (citing *Internet Auction III*). See also, P Kutschke, 'German Federal Supreme Court: Injunctive Relief May Be Claimed against Online-Auctioneers if Vendors Offer Forgeries on the Internet Platform' (2008) 3 *IP Report* 16, 17.

77 Hoeren and Yankova, above n62, 518.

78 A Kur, 'Secondary Liability for Trademark Infringement on the Internet: The Situation in Germany and Throughout the EU' (2014) 37 *Columbia Journal of Law & the Arts* 525, 540.

Once such an obligation arises, a host's failure to take appropriate measures to remove the content causing the infringement could give rise to liability.

Belgium

eBay has also been the subject of litigation in Belgium. Thus, in *Lancôme v eBay*, Lancôme claimed that eBay displayed 'on its website various sales offers which Lancôme deemed as illegal, including advertisements of products presented as imitation, copy, reproduction or smell-alike of Lancôme products'.[79] eBay resisted the claim on the basis that it was eligible to benefit from the hosting safe harbour under the Belgian equivalent[80] of the E-Commerce Directive.[81] On the facts, the Rechtbank van Koophandel Brüssel (Brussels Commercial Court) held that eBay was a neutral and passive host, thus qualifying for the hosting safe harbour.[82] According to the Court, eBay was not liable because it had no actual knowledge of any infringing content, and upon being notified of the infringements had immediately removed the infringing content, which fully discharged eBay's obligations under the law.[83] The Court also found that eBay acted as a prudent and diligent operator in view of its 'willingness to cooperate with Lancôme in expeditiously removing infringing content'.[84]

Although the outcome of the legal action against eBay in Belgium was different from the outcomes in France and Germany, the principles that may be derived are comparable. In essence, a host could only be held liable if it failed to take prudent and diligent steps to terminate or prevent infringements, such as removing content that was infringing, in circumstances where it had gained actual knowledge of the infringements in question.

79 ASY Cheung and KKH Pun, 'Comparative Study on the Liability for Trade Mark Infringement of Online Auction Providers' (2009) 31 *European Intellectual Property Review* 559, 561.

80 In Belgium, the E-Commerce Directive was implemented by two laws of 11 March 2003: Act of 11 March 2003 with Regard to Certain Legal Aspects of Information Society Services (Wet van 11 maart 2003 betreffende bepaalde juridische aspecten van de diensten van de informatiemaatschappij), BS 17 March 2003, p12962 and Act of 11 March 2003 Relating to Certain Legal Aspects of Information Society Services as Referred to in Article 77 of the Constitution (Wet van 11 maart 2003 betreffende bepaalde juridische aspecten van de diensten van de informatiemaatschappij als bedoeld in artikel 77 van de Grondwet), BS 17 March 2003, p12963. In 2013, these laws were moved into the Belgian Code on Economic Law, in which they now sit at Chapters 1–6 of Book XII.

81 Cheung and Pun, above n79, 561.

82 Cheung and Pun, above n79, 561. According to Eecke and Truyens (above n56), the Belgian court followed the approach of the French court in *Hermès v eBay*, thus applying the hosting exception to a subdivision of eBay's activities. See also, PV Eecke, 'Online Service Providers and Liability: A Plea for a Balanced Approach' (2011) 48 *Common Market Law Review* 1455, 1471.

83 Cheung and Pun, above n79, 561. See also, SH Song, *New Challenges of Chinese Copyright Law in the Digital Age: A Comparative Copyright Analysis of ISP Liability, Fair Use and Sports Telecasts* (Kluwer Law International 2011), 16.

84 VW Johnson and LP Merritt, 'Tiffany v. eBay: A Case of Genuine Disparity in International Court Rulings on Counterfeit Products' (2008) 1 *Landslide* 22, 24.

Summary of the legal position relating to the liability of hosts

Domestic courts in France, Germany and Belgium have diverged in their views regarding the applicability of the hosting safe harbour to intermediaries that host third-party content. In France, the consensus is that a host cannot benefit from the hosting safe harbour if its conduct lacks neutrality and passivity. For instance, in *eBay v Louis Vuitton*, the French Cour de cassation approved the findings at first instance[85] that eBay cannot benefit from the hosting safe harbour because it was more than a passive and neutral host when it actively participated as a 'broker' in respect of the sale of counterfeits. In contrast, the hosting safe harbour was applied in Belgium to a certain *subset* of eBay's activities, indicating a slightly nuanced approach to the liability of hosts. On the other hand, in Germany, whether the hosting safe harbour applied to hosts was not a contentious matter for the courts, because hosts were only liable as disturbers or interferers in relation to which only injunctions applied, a remedy that the E-Commerce Directive permits notwithstanding the conditional immunity conferred by the hosting safe harbour.[86] While there might be differences in the various approaches to evaluating the conduct of a particular host, the CJEU in *L'Oréal v eBay*[87] has offered some guidance on the application of the hosting safe harbour. Thus, the fact that an intermediary merely engages in the hosting of third-party content is not in itself sufficient to conclude that the hosting safe harbour applies.[88] On the other hand, the fact that an intermediary engages in activities that go beyond the mere hosting of third-party content in itself cannot determine whether the hosting safe harbour does not apply.[89] For the purposes of the safe harbour, what matters is whether a host could be regarded as an 'intermediary' performing a *neutral* and *passive* role.[90]

However, since the immunity conferred by the hosting safe harbour is not absolute but only conditional,[91] it has been possible for hosts, such as eBay, to be held liable for hosting third-party content that infringed trade mark rights. Domestic courts in the three EU Member States considered above have been united in their approach concerning the imposition of liability on hosts, although they have differed in respect of the exact particulars, such as the nature and extent of the measures that hosts must adopt in order to prevent or terminate infringements. At the very least, however, a host's liability would depend on its failure to take reasonable measures to prevent or terminate an infringement, such as the removal of infringing content, upon being specifically notified about the infringement.

85 See *Louis Vuitton v eBay* (Paris).

86 In relation to hosts, see art 14(3) of the E-Commerce Directive.

87 Case C-324/09, *L'Oréal SA v eBay International AG* [2011] ECR I-06011 (*L'Oréal v eBay*), [111].

88 *L'Oréal v eBay*, [111].

89 *L'Oréal v eBay*, [115].

90 *L'Oréal v eBay*, [112], [113] and [116].

91 E-Commerce Directive, arts 14(1)(a) and (b).

In essence, the common principle that emerges from the cases considered above is that intermediaries that host third-party content may become liable for failing to expeditiously remove content giving rise to an infringement in circumstances where they had acquired actual knowledge of the infringement in question. Although this principle is derived from cases involving hosts that serve as online marketplaces, it may be applied more generally to all kinds of hosts.

ISPs and navigation providers

In every sense, ISPs are neutral and passive intermediaries. They play no part in the creation or storage of online content. Nor do they have the capacity to remove infringing content at the source. This is precisely why Article 12(1) of the E-Commerce Directive provides ISPs with complete immunity against any claim for damages in actions filed concerning infringements arising from content transmitted through their networks. Although ISPs are amenable to injunctions,[92] they cannot be held liable to pay damages.[93] Hence, it is not surprising that ISPs have never been the subject of an award of damages in any trade mark dispute, and it is unlikely that this will ever happen.

Similarly, navigation providers merely index and link internet users to content, without contributing in any way towards the creation or storage of such content. Like ISPs, they have no control over the content, and thus are incapable of removing any infringing content at its source. To date, navigation providers have never been involved in any trade mark litigation, in respect of their navigation functions, resulting in the award of either damages or injunctive relief.

Cases in the US

Before moving on to discuss the cases filed against internet intermediaries in the US, it is useful to set out the US legal framework on the protection and enforcement of trade marks. Substantive trade mark law in the US takes two forms. At the state level, trade marks are protected under the common law and state specific statutes. At the federal level, trade marks are protected under the Lanham Act 1946. For the purposes of this chapter, the analysis is confined to federal trade mark law because litigation instituted by trade mark proprietors against internet intermediaries have largely been based on the federal statute.

In Chapter 3, it was noted that an action under section 32 of the Lanham Act 1946[94] is incapable of holding internet intermediaries liable for trade mark

92 E-Commerce Directive, art 12(3).
93 E-Commerce Directive, art 12(1).
94 15 USC §1114.

infringements[95] either as direct infringers or accessories. It is to overcome this shortcoming that the concept of contributory infringement was devised. Contributory infringement is a judge-made doctrine[96] that has considerably extended the reach of trade mark law to capture entities that otherwise would not be affected by the liability principles under the Lanham Act 1946. The development of contributory trade mark liability and its application to internet intermediaries are considered below.

Liability for contributory trade mark infringement

In *Inwood v Ives*, the US Supreme Court established a two-part standard for contributory trade mark infringement.[97] In this case, Ives owned the patent to a drug by the name of 'cyclandelate', which was marketed under the 'CYCLOSPASMOL' trade mark in blue and red capsules. Once the patent expired, generic drug companies, including Inwood, started manufacturing and distributing the drug in competition with Ives. The generic drug manufacturers 'intentionally copied the appearance of the "CYCLOSPASMOL" capsules'.[98] They did not deal with consumers directly but instead reached consumers through intermediaries, such as pharmacists, who received the drugs in bulk.[99] The practice that gave rise to Ives's grievance was that pharmacists, regardless of whether they were dispensing 'cyclandelate' or a generic drug, removed the capsules from the container in which they came in and dispensed them to consumers in bottles owned by the pharmacists with their own labels attached.[100] This practice motivated some pharmacists to dispense generic drugs mislabelled as 'CYCLOSPASMOL', giving rise to an infringement of Ives's trade mark. Ives pursued action against the generic drug manufacturers (i.e. Inwood and the other drug companies) that supplied the drugs in bulk to pharmacists. The US Supreme Court, approving the findings

95 The only exception was *Rescuecom Corp v Google Inc* 562 F.3d 123 (2d Cir. 2009). However, this was in the specific context of Google's keyword advertising service, and therefore it was more readily argued that Google made 'use' of a registered trade mark in commerce when it recommended and sold keywords to its advertisers that reproduced, copied or imitated Rescuecom's trade mark. Yet, beyond keyword advertising, when intermediaries provide internet access, navigation and hosting services, they make no 'use' of trade marks 'in commerce'. Accordingly, insofar as the services offered by ISPs, hosts and navigation providers enable internet users to access content that promote infringements, it would not be possible to invoke the infringement provisions of the Lanham Act 1946 against such intermediaries.

96 See e.g., *Power Test Petroleum Distributors v Manhattan & Queens Fuel* 556 F. Supp. 392 (1982) (*Power Test v Manhattan & Queens Fuel*), 394 (McLaughlin J) ('the doctrine of contributory infringement has developed as a judicial gloss on the infringement provision of the Lanham Act') and *Rosetta Stone Ltd v Google Inc* 676 F.3d 144 (4th Cir. 2012) (*Rosetta Stone v Google*), 163 (Traxler J) ('Contributory infringement is a judicially created doctrine that derive[s] from the common law of torts') (internal quotation marks and citation omitted).

97 *Inwood Laboratories Inc v Ives Laboratories Inc* 456 U.S. 844 (1982) (*Inwood v Ives*).

98 *Inwood v Ives*, 847 (O'Connor J).

99 *Inwood v Ives*, 847–48 (O'Connor J).

100 *Inwood v Ives*, 848–49 (O'Connor J).

of the District Court (Eastern District of New York), held that, although Inwood was not liable for any infringement under section 32 of the Lanham Act 1946,[101] it was nevertheless liable as a contributory infringer. The Court set out the test for contributory trade mark infringement in the following terms:

> if a manufacturer or distributor intentionally induces another to infringe a trademark,[102] or if it continues to supply its product to one whom it knows or has reason to know is engaging in trademark infringement,[103] the manufacturer or distributor is contributorially responsible for any harm done as a result of the deceit.[104]

The first limb of the test contains an element of 'intention',[105] whereas the second limb incorporates a standard of 'reasonableness'.[106] It is noteworthy that when O'Connor J restated the principle in relation to the facts of *Inwood v Ives* in the paragraph that immediately followed,[107] the words 'or has reason to know' were omitted. Thus, it has been suggested that, by this omission, the judge sought to establish a standard which requires intent, as opposed to reasonableness.[108] However, subsequent cases that applied the test for contributory trade mark infringement have followed the first formulation.[109]

Although *Inwood v Ives* had an impact on manufacturers of goods and represented a conscious 'judicial attempt to hold the industry accountable for its direct and indirect actions',[110] the test for contributory trade mark infringement, as it was originally coined, had a limited application. Notably, the test did not extend to the supply of services. In order to address this limitation, it appears that the US courts subsequently extended the *Inwood v Ives* formula to circumstances that went beyond the manufacture, distribution or supply of goods. Thus, in *Hard*

101 *Inwood v Ives*, 854 (O'Connor J).

102 The first prong of the test is derived from *Warner & Co v Eli Lilly & Co* 265 U.S. 526 (1924).

103 The second prong of the test is derived from *Coca-Cola Co v Snow Crest Beverages Inc* 64 F. Supp. 980 (1946).

104 *Inwood v Ives*, 853–54 (O'Connor J) (citation omitted).

105 The phrases 'intentionally induces' and 'knows' establish the element of intent.

106 The phrase 'or has reason to know' establish the standard of reasonableness.

107 *Inwood v Ives*, 855 (O'Connor J):

> However, whether these petitioners were liable for the pharmacists' infringing acts depended upon whether, in fact, the petitioners intentionally induced the pharmacists to mislabel generic drugs or, in fact, continued to supply cyclandelate to pharmacists whom the petitioners knew were mislabeling generic drugs.

108 FS Fox, 'Contributory Trademark Infringement: The Legal Standard After *Inwood Laboratories, Inc. v. Ives Laboratories, Inc.*' (1983) 4 *University of Bridgeport Law Review* 387, 400.

109 See e.g., *David Berg & Co v Gatto Int'l Trading Co* 884 F.2d 306 (7th Cir. 1989); *Allen Organ Co v Galanti Organ Builders Inc* 798 F. Supp. 1162 (1992); *Power Test v Manhattan & Queens Fuel.*

110 DC Karl, '"Look-Alike" Capsules, Generic Drug Substitution, and the Lanham Act: The Elusive Contributory Infringement Standard of Inwood Laboratories, Inc. v. Ives Laboratories, Inc' (1982) 32 *Catholic University Law Review* 345, 369.

Rock v CSI[111] the US Court of Appeals (7th Cir.) applied *Inwood v Ives* to a case involving a flea market. The plaintiff (Hard Rock) was the owner of several trade marks for textiles, including T-shirts. The plaintiff's grievance was that stallholders were selling counterfeit Hard Rock T-shirts in two flea markets owned and operated by the defendant (CSI). After a bench trial, apart from awarding damages against the individual stallholders that committed infringements (some of them entering into settlements), the US District Court (Northern District of Illinois) also issued an injunction against CSI prohibiting it from permitting the sale of infringing merchandise.[112] CSI appealed on the basis that it ought not to be held responsible for the actions of individual stallholders that operated in the flea market.

The US Court of Appeals (7th Cir.) acknowledged the difficulty of applying *Inwood v Ives* in relation to a flea market:

> Despite this apparently definitive statement, it is not clear how the doctrine [of contributory infringement] applies to people *who do not actually manufacture or distribute the good that is ultimately palmed off as made by someone else.*[113]

While the defendant characterised its relationship with individual stallholders as one of landlord and tenant, the plaintiff argued that the defendant was better characterised as a licensor.[114] Either way, the Court observed that '[t]he common law . . . imposes the same duty on landlords and licensors that the Supreme Court has imposed on manufacturers and distributors'[115] in *Inwood v Ives*. Based on this reasoning, the Court held that the test in *Inwood v Ives* applied and observed that 'CSI may be liable for trademark violations . . . if it knew or had reason to know of them'.[116] This approach has been followed in subsequent cases.[117] It was this extension to the test for contributory infringement that has enabled its application to intermediaries operating in the online space.

Applying Inwood v Ives *to internet intermediaries*

Lockheed v NSI[118] signifies the first instance where the test for contributory infringement as formulated in *Inwood v Ives* was applied to the internet context.[119]

111 *Hard Rock Cafe Licensing Corp v Concession Services Inc* 955 F.2d 1143 (7th Cir. 1992) (*Hard Rock v CSI*).
112 *Hard Rock v CSI*, 1145 (Cudahy J).
113 *Hard Rock v CSI*, 1148–49 (Cudahy J) (emphasis added).
114 *Hard Rock v CSI*, 1149 (Cudahy J).
115 *Hard Rock v CSI*, 1149 (Cudahy J).
116 *Hard Rock v CSI*, 1149 (Cudahy J).
117 See e.g., *Fonovisa Inc v Cherry Auction Inc* 76 F.3d 259 (9th Cir. 1996) (*Fonovisa v CAI*); *Gucci America Inc v Frontline Processing Corp* 721 F.Supp.2d 228 (2010).
118 *Lockheed Martin Corp v Network Solutions Inc* 194 F.3d 980 (9th Cir. 1999) (*Lockheed v NSI*).
119 J Kessler, 'Correcting the Standard for Contributory Trademark Liability over the Internet' (2006) 39 *Columbia Journal of Law and Social Problems* 375, 387.

In this case, the defendant (NSI) was a domain name registrar entrusted with the task of registering domain names, which serve as an alternative, and user-friendly, designation for Internet Protocol addresses (IP addresses),[120] thus eliminating the need for us to remember lengthy numeric addresses in order to gain access to websites. Essentially, NSI provided an important service, enabling internet users to locate websites on the internet easily. The plaintiff (Lockheed) owned an aircraft design laboratory known as 'The Skunk Works'. NSI had registered several domain names that used variations of the words 'skunk' and 'works' at the request of numerous domain name applicants.[121] Although NSI had a domain name dispute resolution policy, Lockheed filed an action against NSI alleging contributory trade mark infringement on the part of NSI. It appears that Lockheed relied on the second prong of the test in *Inwood v Ives*, which renders a manufacturer liable 'if it continues to supply its product to one whom it knows or has reason to know is engaging in trademark infringement'. The US Court of Appeals (9th Cir.) had difficulty in directly applying this test, as NSI did not supply any product to its customers, but instead supplied a service.[122] Accordingly, it was necessary to apply the test for contributory infringement to a novel situation. In this regard, the Court observed:

> Hard Rock and Fonovisa teach us that when measuring and weighing a fact pattern in the contributory infringement context without the convenient 'product' mold dealt with in Inwood Lab., *we consider the extent of control exercised by the defendant over the third party's means of infringement.*[123]

Thus, distinguishing the conduct of a domain name registrar from that of a landlord or a licensor (as in *Hard Rock v CSI* and *Fonovisa v CAI*), the US Court of Appeals (9th Cir.) observed:

> The 'direct control and monitoring' rule established by Hard Rock and Fonovisa likewise fails to reach the instant situation. The district court correctly recognized that NSI's rote translation service does not entail the kind of direct control and monitoring required to justify an extension of the 'supplies a product' requirement. See 985 F. Supp. at 962 ('While the landlord of a flea market might reasonably be expected to monitor the merchandise sold on his premises, NSI cannot reasonably be expected to monitor the Internet'). Such a stretch would reach well beyond the contemplation of Inwood Lab. and its progeny.[124]

120 *Lockheed v NSI*, 981 (Trott J).
121 *Lockheed v NSI*, 983 (Trott J).
122 *Lockheed v NSI*, 984 (Trott J).
123 *Lockheed v NSI*, 984 (Trott J) (emphasis added).
124 *Lockheed v NSI*, 985 (Trott J). This approach was followed in *Size v Network Solutions Inc* 255 F. Supp. 2d 568 (2003).

Accordingly, *Lockheed v NSI* sets an important precedent. That is, '[d]irect control and monitoring of the instrumentality used by a third party to infringe the plaintiff's mark permits the expansion of *Inwood Lab.*'s "supplies a product" requirement for contributory infringement'.[125] Such an expansion no doubt would be relevant in determining the contributory liability of internet intermediaries that provide internet access, hosting and navigation services. Thus, where contributory liability is raised in circumstances where the 'supplies a product' requirement set out in *Inwood v Ives* cannot be satisfied, liability would depend on two factors:

1 whether the intermediary concerned exercised direct control and monitoring over the instrumentality used by a third party to infringe trade mark rights, and
2 whether the intermediary had actual or constructive knowledge[126] of any infringements.

Interestingly, in neither *Hard Rock v CSI* nor *Fonovisa v CAI* was the word 'monitoring' used, although there were references to 'control'. As such, whether there was ever a standard of 'direct control and monitoring' is questionable. In fact, the inclusion of a 'direct control and monitoring' analysis in extending the applicability of the test in *Inwood v Ives* to 'non-product' cases has been criticised.[127] Nevertheless, the test for contributory infringement, as modified by *Lockheed v NSI* for application to 'non-product' situations, has consistently (albeit with some variations) been used by US courts to hold intermediaries operating on the internet liable for their users' trade mark infringements. These cases are considered below.

Hosts

Like in the EU, a perusal of cases against internet intermediaries in the US reveals that they are concentrated around hosts that store third-party content. The key cases instituted against hosts where contributory trade mark infringement was claimed are made up of cases against typical web-hosts, online marketplaces and search engines that provided keyword advertising services.

Gucci v Hall[128] was one of the first cases that considered the contributory liability of a typical web-host. This case involved an ISP (Mindspring), which provided

125 *Lockheed v NSI*, 984 (Trott J).

126 *Lockheed v NSI*, 984 (Trott J). The second limb of the *Inwood v Ives* test adopts a standard of both actual ('knows') and constructive ('reason to know') knowledge.

127 Kessler, above n119, 378:

> This new standard also gives Internet actors an incentive to reduce the amount of control they have over material on the web. Although there is a clear need to enable contributory trademark liability to deal with Internet actors, the test for liability should not have been modified to consider extent of control or monitoring.

128 *Gucci America Inc v Hall & Associates* 135 F. Supp. 2d 409 (2001) (*Gucci v Hall*).

hosting services in addition to its internet access services. Mindspring hosted a website that offered counterfeit Gucci products. Gucci alleged both direct and contributory trade mark infringement on the part of Mindspring. Although the judgment of the US District Court (Southern District of New York) did not determine the liability of Mindspring (as it was merely deciding a motion to dismiss), it followed the reasoning in *Lockheed v NSI* and held that there was a possibility that hosts could become liable for contributory infringement.[129]

In *Roger Cleveland v Prince*, an American jury awarded a sum of over US$700,000 in damages against a web-hosting company on the basis that it had contributed to its client's trade mark infringements.[130] In this case, it was alleged that Christopher Prince directly infringed the plaintiff's trade marks, while a web-hosting company (Bright Builders) was liable for contributory infringement. The trial judge instructed the jury that the following elements must be satisfied in order to establish contributory infringement:

> (1) Christopher Prince and/or Prince Distribution, LLC directly violated Plaintiff's trademark; (2) Bright Builders continued to supply services to the infringer after it knew or had reason to know that the services were being used or would be used to infringe the mark; and (3) Bright Builders had *sufficient control* over the means of the infringing conduct to merit liability.[131]

Similarly, the US Court of Appeals (9th Cir.) in *Louis Vuitton v Akanoc*[132] followed the approach in *Gucci v Hall* when it applied the test for contributory infringement to a host, Akanoc, which provided both internet access and hosting services. The Court distinguished an ISP's role as a host from that of a domain name registrar (in *Lockheed v NSI*) and concluded:

> As the district court held, Appellants 'physically host websites on their servers and route internet traffic to and from those websites. This service is the Internet equivalent of leasing real estate.' . . . Appellants had control over the services and servers provided to the websites. Stated another way, Appellants had ***direct control over the 'master switch' that kept the websites online and available.***[133]

129 *Gucci v Hall*, 416 (Berman J) ('The Court agrees that *Lockheed Martin* does not foreclose the possibility that ISPs may be liable for contributory trademark infringement').

130 *Roger Cleveland Golf Co v Prince* No CA 2:09-2119-MBS, 2012 WL 1106775 (D.S.C. Mar. 30, 2012) (*Roger Cleveland v Prince*), *5 (Seymour J). See also, D Shaw and S Gunnarson, 'Web Hosting Industry Vulnerable to Federal Trademark Liability' (2011) 18 *Westlaw Journal* 3 ('the U.S. District Court for the District of South Carolina issued a judgment in *Roger Cleveland Golf Co. v Prince* against Bright Builders Inc. for $770,750 based on a jury verdict of trademark infringement under the Lanham Act').

131 *Roger Cleveland v Prince*, *4 (Seymour J) (emphasis added).

132 *Louis Vuitton Malletier SA v Akanoc Solutions* Inc 658 F.3d 936 (9th Cir. 2011) (*Louis Vuitton v Akanoc*).

133 *Louis Vuitton v Akanoc*, 942 (Gould J) (citation omitted and emphasis added).

The Court ultimately agreed with the lower court's finding that Akanoc was liable for contributory trade mark infringement on the basis that it had actual knowledge of the infringements taking place. Actual knowledge was imputed from takedown notices that were sent to the host seeking the removal of the infringing websites.[134] The failure on the part of Akanoc to remove the infringing sites, and thereby continuing the supply of hosting services to its infringing clients, resulted in its liability to pay US$10,500,000 in damages.

Similar cases have also been filed against an online marketplace and a search engine in their capacity as hosts of third-party content. Thus, the US Court of Appeals (2nd Cir.) in *Tiffany v eBay*,[135] applied the modified *Inwood v Ives* test to the context of eBay,[136] which in essence is a host for third-party product listings. Tiffany, a manufacturer of exclusive jewellery, alleged both direct and contributory trade mark infringement on the part of eBay.

The claim for direct trade mark infringement was on the basis that eBay violated section 32 of the Lanham Act 1946[137] when it used Tiffany's trade marks on its website and purchased sponsored links on search engines such as Yahoo! and Google.[138] The Court, however, concurred with the lower court's decision and found that any use made by eBay of Tiffany's trade marks on its website or search engines amounted to nominative fair use, as it was necessary to identify Tiffany's products being sold on eBay's platform.[139] By contrast, the argument that eBay made use of Tiffany's marks knowing that some of its sellers sold counterfeit goods was a matter for discussion under contributory infringement.[140]

Although initially eBay disputed the applicability of the test in *Inwood v Ives* to its conduct, on appeal it no longer maintained that objection. As such, the Court assumed that the test for contributory liability applied to eBay.[141] Thus, the only issue to be decided was whether eBay was liable for contributory infringement. Tiffany did not claim that eBay *induced* the sale of counterfeits. Rather, the claim was based on the second prong of the test. Thus, the case turned on whether eBay continued to supply its services to a party it knew or had reason to know was engaging in trade mark infringements.[142] Tiffany argued that, given the large number of takedown notices served on eBay, identifying product listings of infringing Tiffany products, and the complaints eBay received from buyers claiming they had purchased counterfeits 'established eBay's knowledge of the

134 *Louis Vuitton v Akanoc*, 940 (Gould J).

135 *Tiffany (NJ) Inc v eBay Inc* 600 F.3d 93 (2d Cir. 2010) (*Tiffany v eBay*).

136 This decision in *Tiffany v eBay* remains undisturbed despite an application being made to the US Supreme Court seeking a writ of certiorari against the judgment of the US Court of Appeals (2nd Cir.), which was denied (*Tiffany Inc v eBay Inc* 131 S. Ct. 647 (2010)).

137 15 USC 1114.

138 *Tiffany v eBay*, 102 (Sack J).

139 *Tiffany v eBay*, 103 (Sack J).

140 *Tiffany v eBay*, 103 (Sack J).

141 *Tiffany v eBay*, 105 (Sack J). In any case, based on a consideration of the cases that had applied *Inwood v Ives* to the context of services, it is clear that the test applied to eBay.

142 *Tiffany v eBay*, 106 (Sack J).

widespread sale of counterfeit Tiffany products on its website'.[143] However, the US Court of Appeals (2nd Cir.) concurred with the lower court's findings and exonerated eBay from liability on the following basis:

> Tiffany's demand letters . . . did not identify particular sellers who Tiffany thought were then offering or would offer counterfeit goods. . . . *And although the [notices of infringement] and buyer complaints gave eBay reason to know that certain sellers had been selling counterfeits, those sellers' listings were removed and repeat offenders were suspended from the eBay site.* Thus Tiffany failed to demonstrate that eBay was supplying its service to individuals who it knew or had reason to know were selling counterfeit Tiffany goods.[144]

In essence, what exonerated eBay from contributory liability was the immediate action it took to terminate the services it supplied to those who engaged in infringements (i.e. by taking down infringing product listings and suspending the offending accounts). This means that, when a host continues to supply its services to an infringing user, even after gaining actual knowledge, or having reason to know, of specific instances of infringement, that host could be held liable on a contributory basis, as such conduct amounts to wilful blindness towards infringing activity.[145]

In *Rosetta Stone v Google*, an attempt was made to apply the test of contributory trade mark infringement to Google in its capacity as a host providing keyword advertising services.[146] The US Court of Appeals (4th Cir.) had the opportunity to consider whether Google contributed towards its advertisers' infringements when it allowed them to use text identical to the 'Rosetta Stone' trade mark in sponsored links that were hosted by Google. It was given in evidence that:

> As documented, from September 3, 2009 through March 1, 2010, Rosetta Stone notified Google of approximately 200 instances of Sponsored Links advertising counterfeit Rosetta Stone products. Rosetta Stone contends that even after being notified of these websites, Google continued to allow Sponsored Links for other websites by these same advertisers to use the Rosetta Stone Marks as keyword triggers and in the text of their Sponsored Link advertisements.[147]

Despite this evidence, the US District Court (Eastern District of Virginia) allowed Google's motion to dismiss on the basis of the knowledge requirement laid down in *Tiffany v eBay*, according to which a finding of contributory

143 *Tiffany v eBay*, 106 (Sack J).
144 *Tiffany v eBay*, 109 (Sack J) (emphasis added).
145 *Tiffany v eBay*, 109–10 (Sack J).
146 The operation of keyword advertising is described in detail in Chapter 2.
147 *Rosetta Stone v Google*, 163 (Traxler J).

infringement is only possible on evidence of specific knowledge and not generalised knowledge.[148] On appeal, however, the US Court of Appeals (4th Cir.) vacated the District Court's summary judgment in favour of Google and concluded that 'the evidence recited by the district court is sufficient to establish a question of fact as to whether Google continued to supply its services to known infringers'.[149] The outcome of this case could only be a matter of speculation, as the parties later entered into a settlement, the terms of which remain confidential.[150] However, based on the other cases decided in this area, it is likely that Google would have been found contributorily liable for the infringements on the part of its advertisers, had the trial continued.

In summary, the cases discussed above establish that, under the modified *Inwood v Ives* formula, the liability of a host is predicated on its failure to discontinue its services to an infringing user in circumstances where it knew or had reason to know about the infringements being committed and also exercised control over the means of infringement.

ISPs and navigation providers

At the time of writing, there was no record of any trade mark litigation in the US that had been instituted against intermediaries that provide internet access (ISPs) and navigation services (e.g. search engines). The cases discussed in the preceding section involving ISPs and search engines concerned their conduct as *hosts* and not as access or navigation providers. However, if contributory infringement was claimed against an ISP or a navigation provider, concerning only their access and navigation functions, it is unlikely that such a claim would succeed. Such an outcome is inevitable because the modified *Inwood v Ives* test, which requires a contributory infringer to have *supplied a service* to the party committing the infringement, cannot be satisfied. After all, neither ISPs nor navigation providers supply a service to the party that is responsible for the creation of content that infringes trade mark rights.[151]

Summary of the position in the US

Although the Lanham Act 1946 fails to provide a satisfactory remedy to trade mark proprietors as against intermediaries that supply online services to those who

148 *Rosetta Stone v Google*, 164 (Traxler J).

149 *Rosetta Stone v Google*, 165 (Traxler J).

150 SW Orrick, 'Deciphering Rosetta Stone: Why the Least Cost Avoider Principle Unlocks the Code to Contributory Trademark Infringement in Keyword Advertising' (2013) 28 *Berkeley Technology Law Journal* 805.

151 This point is considered in detail in Chapter 8 when dealing with injunctions under Article 11 (third sentence) of the Enforcement Directive, according to which injunctions must be made available against intermediaries only in circumstances where their services are being 'used' by third parties to commit infringements.

commit trade mark infringements, this limitation has been overcome through the doctrine of contributory infringement. The cases instituted against hosts in the US reveal that liability for damages on the basis of contributory infringement arises when an intermediary continues to supply its services to an infringer even after it came to know, or had reason to know, that its services were being used to infringe trade mark rights, in circumstances where the intermediary exercised control over the means of infringement. In other words, an intermediary's liability under US law depends on its failure to act upon acquiring the requisite knowledge of an infringement in circumstances where it exercised control over the means of infringement.

Reflecting on commonalities

Unlike under the UK Trade Marks Act 1994 or the English common law, the approaches adopted in the US, and in France, Germany and Belgium, have been progressive and more favourable in terms of holding internet intermediaries, or at least a subclass of such intermediaries, liable for trade mark infringements in circumstances that justify such liability. While the specifics may differ, what is common between the approaches is the basis for holding intermediaries liable for infringements. In the US, liability of an intermediary is premised on its failure to discontinue its services to an infringing user, in circumstances where it had either actual or constructive knowledge of a specific case of infringement and exercised control over the means of infringement. In terms of the approaches adopted in the three Continental EU Member States considered in this chapter, the liability of an intermediary depends on its failure to take reasonable measures to prevent or terminate an infringement, upon acquiring either actual or constructive knowledge of a specific case of infringement. This approach is not dissimilar to the approach to contributory liability in the US, as the ability of an intermediary to take reasonable measures to prevent or terminate an infringement would arguably depend on the control it exercises over the means of infringement.

Accordingly, three common factors seem to underpin the imposition of liability on internet intermediaries. They are: the knowledge of infringements, the degree of control over the instrumentality used to commit infringements, and the failure to take reasonable measures to prevent infringements from occurring. These factors must be taken into consideration in developing a legislative response crafted to address the shortcomings in the laws currently applicable in the UK that outright prevent internet intermediaries of any class from being held liable for infringements of trade mark rights, even in circumstances where they knowingly assist infringements on the part of their users.

5 A proposal for law reforms

You may recall that Chapter 4 began with a proposition, that legislative intervention is the surer, more expeditious and prudent approach to address limitations in the UK's existing legal framework that prevent a finding of liability on the part of internet intermediaries even in circumstances where they knowingly assist trade mark infringements. In this chapter, the nature and scope of a proposal for law reforms are considered, wherein an amendment to the Trade Marks Act 1994 is proposed, aimed at expanding the scope of the infringement action to capture internet intermediaries that become sufficiently involved in infringements. In essence, the proposed reforms aim to confer aggrieved trade mark proprietors the right to claim damages against intermediaries in very specific circumstances.

The practical significance of monetary relief

Before discussing any legislative reforms, it is necessary to consider whether there is any practical value in permitting claims for damages against internet intermediaries. This is an important question in light of the possibility of seeking out injunctions against intermediaries in terms of the Enforcement Directive,[1] a trend that has become popular around the EU, as well as in the UK.[2] After all, injunctions, whether interlocutory or final, allow trade mark proprietors to enforce their rights. However, for the reasons set out below, monetary relief offers some distinct advantages.

First, it must be noted that the injunctive remedy has its limitations. While injunctive relief is both useful and effective, it applies only prospectively to prevent current and future infringements. It is incapable of dealing with the impact of past infringements, which could only be redressed through the payment of damages to the aggrieved party. Often, by the time a trade mark proprietor seeks an injunction, substantial damage has already been done. In light of this, once an intermediary is put on notice but fails to take steps to terminate the infringement, despite having had the capacity to do so, the conduct of such

1 Directive 2004/48/EC of the European Parliament and of the Council of 29 April 2004 on the Enforcement of Intellectual Property Rights [2004] OJ L 157/16 (Enforcement Directive).

2 The use of injunctions as a means of enforcing trade mark rights is considered in Chapters 8 and 9.

a non-cooperative intermediary reaches a degree of culpability justifying the award of damages.

Second, a cause of action against an intermediary would arise only in circumstances where an aggrieved trade mark proprietor has a 'right' of action. Every right has a corresponding duty,[3] whether imposed under statute or the common law. A cause of action would arise in favour of a trade mark proprietor, as against an intermediary, only if the latter had breached a duty owed to the former under the law. Thus, any law reform proposal that aims to confer on trade mark proprietors a right to seek damages against internet intermediaries must first impose a duty on the specific class of intermediaries concerned. The imposition of such a duty has a regulatory effect. Once a trade mark proprietor succeeds in a test case against an intermediary, all other intermediaries of the *same class* will become incentivised, in their own interest, to ensure compliance with the standard that must be met in order to discharge the duty imposed on them by the law. Failing to do so would expose them to the risk of litigation and liability. Arguably, this would allow trade mark proprietors to enforce their rights even without court intervention. The extrajudicial practice of 'notice and takedown'[4] provides a classic example of this.

Third, even if an injunction is obtained, there might be instances where an intermediary fails to comply with the court's order. For instance, non-compliance might occur where the terms of an injunction are not specific enough, leaving room for doubt about the exact parameters of the action required on the part of the intermediary,[5] or where the intermediary *wilfully* neglects to perform its duties specified in a court order. In such an eventuality, although the damage to the aggrieved trade mark proprietor will continue to take place, the only consequence for the non-compliant intermediary, if any, will be the penalty for contempt of court. However, none of the sanctions for contempt would benefit trade mark proprietors to redress the real damage sustained by them as a result of the non-compliance. The availability of monetary relief against internet intermediaries will help overcome this difficulty.

The proposal for law reforms

The class of intermediaries

In Chapter 1, several economic, moral and pragmatic arguments were set out in order to justify the imposition of liability on internet intermediaries for

3 See WN Hohfeld, 'Fundamental Legal Conceptions as Applied in Judicial Reasoning' (1913) 23 *Yale Law Journal* 13, 31–32.

4 Essentially, this entails the removal of alleged infringing content by intermediaries upon being notified of infringements by aggrieved right holders. The origins of notice and takedown, and its potential abuse, are considered in detail in Chapters 6 and 7.

5 SL Dogan, 'Trademark Remedies and Online Intermediaries' (2010) 14 *Lewis & Clark Law Review* 467, 487–88.

infringements of trade mark rights. However, it was emphasised that in determining the extent of liability one must be mindful about the class of intermediaries concerned, and in particular have regard to their role in relation to the creation and subsequent dissemination of infringing content. If the notion of liability could be represented in a spectrum, then one end of it will comprise *fault-based* liability giving rise to monetary remedies, which are normally available when a party has been involved in a wrongful act or omission. The other end comprises *no-fault* liability giving rise to non-monetary remedies, such as injunctions, through which a party can be compelled to assist right holders in their enforcement efforts.[6] Thus, an intermediary that is proximate to an infringing activity, in that it possesses *control* over the means of infringement, has a greater responsibility to terminate, if not mitigate, the infringement. Whereas, a less proximate intermediary that does not possess such control, and is in no way associated with the underlying infringement, attracts a much lower degree of responsibility. Intermediaries that are less proximate to the activities that result in an infringement cannot be compelled to terminate the infringement, although they may be called upon to ensure that infringing content is not made accessible to internet users. When an intermediary is said to have played a more proximate role in relation to the harm committed, thus becoming sufficiently *involved* in the wrong itself, then it would be justifiable to hold that intermediary liable to pay damages to the aggrieved party. In light of these distinctions, it is necessary to consider each of the three classes of intermediaries—ISPs, navigation providers and hosts—to determine their place in the liability spectrum.

ISPs

ISPs are mere conduits providing internet users with access to the internet, without getting involved in producing any content. They exercise neither contractual nor technical control over parties that commit trade mark infringements. The judgment of the High Court of Australia, in *Roadshow Films v iiNET*,[7] is illustrative of this point. In this case, albeit in the copyright context, the Court exonerated iiNET, an Australian ISP, from liability for copyright infringements committed by iiNET's subscribers who used the BitTorrent software to share and download copyrighted content unlawfully. The Australian High Court's decision was based on the lack of contractual and technical control on the part of iiNET over the instrumentality used to commit the infringements:

> [T]he power of iiNet as an ISP with respect to the use of facilities provided to subscribers was limited by the nature of their commercial relationship; iiNet could not control the choice of its subscribers and other users to utilise the

6 See M Husovec, *Injunctions Against Intermediaries in the European Union: Accountable but Not Liable?* (Cambridge University Press 2017), 14.

7 *Roadshow Films Pty Ltd v iiNet Ltd* [2012] HCA 16 (*Roadshow Films v iiNET*).

BitTorrent software, nor could iiNet modify the BitTorrent software or take down the appellants' films which were made available online.[8]

In the trade mark context, the role of ISPs in relation to infringements is even more remote, as it is difficult to suggest that an ISP's services are utilised to commit trade mark infringements when their subscribers access content that promotes the sale of infringing products.[9] Although ISPs contribute towards making infringing content (just as any other content) *accessible* to internet users, they do not in any way get involved in the commission of infringements. ISPs merely present internet users with content that is available at a particular given time a user gains access to the internet.

The passive and neutral role played by ISPs is also captured by the safe harbour afforded to them under Article 12(1) of the E-Commerce Directive.[10] Thus, although injunctive relief may be sought against ISPs, the Article 12(1) safe harbour shields them from all forms of monetary remedies. There is no reason to alter this status quo. Accordingly, the law reforms proposed later on in this chapter excludes ISPs from its scope.

Navigation providers

Navigation providers, such as search engines, index and provide hyperlinks to online content. Although search engines (e.g. Google) have been the subject of trade mark-related claims, that was in their capacity as hosts in connection with the practice of keyword advertising. Navigation providers in general, and search engines in particular, have not been the subject of any trade mark litigation in respect of their navigation or search functions. While this may be the case in the trade mark context, navigation providers have been held liable under the law relating to defamation and copyright, which questions their passive and neutral status. Thus, in determining the nature of any law reforms in the trade mark context, it is important to consider the scope of liability imposed on navigation providers in these other areas of the law.

In the context of defamation, search engines have never been held liable as a publisher of defamatory content in the UK. According to the English High Court in *MIS v Designtechnica*,[11] Google was a mere facilitator and not a publisher when

8 *Roadshow Films v iiNET*, [137].

9 This is a point that is extensively discussed in Chapter 8, when dealing with the question as to whether an ISP's services are utilised to commit trade mark infringements, a necessary condition prescribed under Article 11 (third sentence) of the Enforcement Directive that must be satisfied before an injunction can be awarded.

10 Directive 2000/31/EC on Certain Legal Aspects of Information Society Services, in Particular Electronic Commerce, in the Internal Market [2000] OJ L 178/1 (E-Commerce Directive).

11 *Metropolitan International Schools Ltd v Designtechnica Corp* [2009] EMLR 27 (*MIS v Designtechnica*).

it displayed as a search result a snippet of information along with a hyperlink to a third-party website containing defamatory content:

> When a snippet is thrown up on the user's screen in response to his search, it points him in the direction of an entry somewhere on the web that corresponds, to a greater or lesser extent, to the search terms he has typed in. It is for him to access or not, as he chooses. It is fundamentally important to have in mind that the third defendant has no role to play in formulating the search terms. Accordingly, it could not prevent the snippet appearing in response to the user's request unless it has taken some positive step in advance. There being no input from the third defendant, therefore, on the scenario I have so far posited, it cannot be characterised as a publisher at common law. It has not authorised or caused the snippet to appear on the user's screen in any meaningful sense. It has merely, by the provision of its search service, played the role of a facilitator.[12]

In contrast, in other jurisdictions, search engines have been found to be publishers of defamatory content. In Australia, the supreme courts of South Australia[13] and New South Wales[14] distinguished the English High Court's decision in *MIS v Designtechnica* on the basis that Google became a publisher the moment it was *notified* of the defamatory content, giving rise to potential liability in the event it failed to remove the hyperlinks pointing to the identified content. The Supreme Court of Victoria went further and held that Google could be classified as a publisher even without notice.[15] Hong Kong's Court of First Instance, which is the lower court of the High Court of Hong Kong, concluded that Google was a publisher when it automatically generated a list of autocomplete search suggestions, which turned out to be defamatory, although Google had access to the innocent dissemination defence if it was not aware of the defamatory material.[16] The High Court of New Zealand reached a similar decision.[17] In Canada, the Supreme Court of British Columbia[18] drew a distinction between hyperlinks and snippets that appear upon a search being performed in a search engine. According to the Court, in merely providing hyperlinks to third-party websites containing defamatory material, the search engine (in this case Google) was

12 *MIS v Designtechnica*, [51] (Eady J).

13 *Duffy v Google Inc* [2015] SASC 170, [209] (Blue J).

14 *Bleyer v Google Inc* [2014] NSWSC 897, [83] (McCallum J).

15 *Trkulja v Google Inc and another* (No 5) [2012] VSC 533, [30] (Beach J). See also, *Trkulja v Yahoo! Inc LLC and another* [2012] VSC 88.

16 *Dr Yeung, SauShing Albert v Google Inc* [2014] HKCFI 1404, [140] (Marlene Ng J).

17 *A v Google New Zealand Ltd* [2012] NZHC 2352, [73] (Abbott J):

> a search engine is a publisher but with access to the defence of innocent dissemination. The possibility of a defence in innocent dissemination where the defendant has not had notice of the defamatory material may be sufficient recognition of the fact that a search engine is a neutral index.

18 *Niemela v Google Inc* 2015 BCSC 1024 (*Niemela v Google*).

not acting as a publisher.[19] Similarly, in respect of snippets, the Court held that Google was a 'passive instrument and not a publisher of snippets',[20] although the Court did emphasise that it had 'not been asked in this case to consider whether Google could be a publisher of snippets and search results *after notice of defamatory content*'.[21]

The defamation cases considered above suggest that it will be possible to hold search engines, and more generally navigation providers, liable as publishers in circumstances where they knew about the defamatory content, e.g. through a notification served by the aggrieved party, and failed to take reasonable measures to disable access to such content.[22]

Navigation providers have also been the subject of litigation in the copyright context. Copyright issues arise in respect of navigation providers when they provide hyperlinks to websites that contain infringing material. The CJEU has ruled that the act of providing hyperlinks to third-party websites could amount to an act of *communication to the public*, a right exclusively reserved for copyright owners.[23] Such an approach has been made possible in view of the Court's broad interpretation of the phrase 'communication to the public' that appears in Article 3 of the Info-Soc Directive to include hyperlinking.[24] Thus, in *Svensson v Retriever Sverige*, the CJEU ruled that where hyperlinks make it possible for internet users to access copyrighted works, in circumstances where those works had been made available only to a *restricted public*,[25] then the provision of those

19 *Niemela v Google*, [60] (Fenlon J) ('Here, the URLs in the search results (identified by the plaintiff as leading to defamatory text) are hyperlinks to websites. . . . Google has not published the content of the text accessible through the URLs').

20 *Niemela v Google*, [107] (Fenlon J).

21 *Niemela v Google*, [108] (Fenlon J) (emphasis added).

22 A recent ruling of the European Court of Human Rights in *Magyar Jeti Zrt v Hungary* Case No 11257/16 (4 December 2018) suggests that imposing liability on navigation providers for providing hyperlinks to defamatory material could interfere with the freedom of speech guaranteed under Article 10 of the European Convention for the Protection of Human Rights and Fundamental Freedoms 1950. The Court observed (at [76]) that 'given the particularities of hyperlinks, the Court cannot agree with the approach of the domestic courts consisting of equating the mere posting of a hyperlink with the dissemination of the defamatory information, automatically entailing liability for the content itself. It rather considers that the issue of whether the posting of a hyperlink may, justifiably from the perspective of Article 10, give rise to such liability requires an individual assessment in each case, regard being had to a number of elements.' One of the elements that the Court considered to be relevant in the determination of liability is the knowledge factor, i.e. whether the party providing the hyperlink 'knew or could have reasonably known that the hyperlink provided access to defamatory or otherwise unlawful content' (at [81]).

23 See Directive 2001/29/EC of the European Parliament and of the Council of 22 May 2001 on the Harmonisation of Certain Aspects of Copyright and Related Rights in the Information Society [2001] OJ L 167/10 (Info-Soc Directive), art 3(1).

24 Whether the approach of the CJEU is normatively justified has been doubted in copyright scholarship. See e.g. J Koo, *The Right of Communication to the Public in EU Copyright Law* (Hart Publishing 2019).

25 For instance, where access to the copyrighted works is restricted exclusively to subscribers of the website in which those works are made available.

hyperlinks would amount to a communication of those works to a *new* public,[26] and hence an infringement.[27] The Court went on to say, however, that there will be no infringement where the works made accessible by the hyperlinks had already been freely made available to *all* internet users, in which case the hyperlinks do not make the works accessible to a *new* public.[28]

In essence, when a navigation provider hyperlinks internet users to websites that contain copyrighted works without the requisite authorisation of the right holders, then the navigation provider in question commits an infringement by communicating the copyrighted works to a *new* public. The Court's approach, however, would have been problematic to navigation providers, especially search engines, as the mere act of hyperlinking internet users to websites containing works protected by copyright was capable of being regarded as an infringement. The fact that the E-Commerce Directive makes no reference to navigation providers in its safe harbour complicates matters even further.

In subsequent cases, it appears that the CJEU has made further adjustments to its approach by introducing a knowledge requirement, which arguably is aimed at ensuring that passive and neutral navigation providers, such as search engines, are not held strictly liable under copyright law. Thus, under the current approach, where hyperlinks are provided to copyrighted works in circumstances where the party providing the hyperlinks *knew* of the infringing nature of the publication, such acts of hyperlinking will be regarded as constituting a communication of copyrighted works to the public.[29] In particular, where profit is

26 For instance, internet users having no authority to access the works on the website in which they are made available.

27 Case C-466/12, *Svensson and others v Retriever Sverige AB* [2014] 3 CMLR 4 (*Svensson v Retriever Sverige*), [31]:

> On the other hand, where a clickable link makes it possible for users of the site on which that link appears to circumvent restrictions put in place by the site on which the protected work appears in order to restrict public access to that work to the latter site's subscribers only, and the link accordingly constitutes an intervention without which those users would not be able to access the works transmitted, all those users must be deemed to be a new public, which was not taken into account by the copyright holders when they authorised the initial communication, and accordingly the holders' authorisation is required for such a communication to the public.

28 *Svensson v Retriever Sverige*, [27]–[28]:

> In those circumstances, it must be held that, where all the users of another site to whom the works at issue have been communicated by means of a clickable link could access those works directly on the site on which they were initially communicated, without the involvement of the manager of that other site, the users of the site managed by the latter must be deemed to be potential recipients of the initial communication and, therefore, as being part of the public taken into account by the copyright holders when they authorised the initial communication. Therefore, since there is no new public, the authorisation of the copyright holders is not required for a communication to the public such as that in the main proceedings.

29 Case C-160/15, *GS Media BV v Sanoma Media Netherlands BV and others* [2016] ECDR 25 (*GS Media v Sanoma Media*), [55]. This approach has been followed in subsequent CJEU cases. See e.g. Case C-527/15, *Stichting Brein v Wullems (t/a Filmspeler)* [2017] ECDR 14 (*Brein v Wullems*), [51]; Case C-610/15, *Stichting Brein v Ziggo BV* [2017] ECDR 19 (*Brein v Ziggo*), [26].

generated as a result of the hyperlinking activities, a *rebuttable* presumption is established that the party providing the hyperlinks knew of the protected nature of the works hyperlinked.[30] Accordingly, in the copyright context, navigation providers may be held liable for providing hyperlinks to copyrighted content hosted on third-party websites, in circumstances where such hyperlinking amounts to a communication of the copyrighted works to the public and the navigation provider had been notified about the websites that carry such unauthorised works.

In light of the obligations imposed on navigation providers in both the copyright and defamation contexts, it is appropriate to consider whether a similar knowledge-based form of liability should be imposed when navigation providers knowingly provide hyperlinks to websites that infringe trade mark rights. If the answer is in the affirmative, then navigation providers will have to be included within the scope of any law reforms proposed herein. However, unlike in the case of defamation and copyright infringements, when an intermediary provides hyperlinks to websites that infringe trade mark rights, such acts per se cannot be regarded as unlawful. The publication of defamatory content, when navigation providers engage in hyperlinking with the requisite knowledge, may constitute a tort in itself. Similarly, when navigation providers knowingly provide hyperlinks to copyrighted works without the consent of the right holder, their conduct may constitute an act of copyright infringement. The point is that, when navigation providers are found liable under the laws of defamation or copyright, such liability is premised on an existing basis of liability.

In contrast, when navigation providers provide hyperlinks to websites comprising content that promotes the sale of goods in violation of trade mark rights, their conduct does not constitute an infringement. Hence, any proposed basis for the liability of navigation providers for knowingly providing access to websites promoting trade mark infringements must take an accessorial form. Be that as it may, as indicated in Chapter 3, legal scholars who favour the expansion of accessorial liability for civil wrongs or torts have limited its application to cases of providing knowing *assistance*. Strictly speaking, when navigation providers, including search engines, index and provide hyperlinks to websites that infringe trade mark rights, they do not in any way *assist* the parties that engage in the actual infringements. As such, even when a navigation provider is served with notice and becomes aware of the existence of infringing content, the navigation provider's conduct of hyperlinking such content does not reach the level of culpability necessary to trigger accessorial liability.

For the reasons set out above, it is clear that navigation providers do not themselves engage in trade mark infringements. Nor do they assist third parties in committing infringements. Their involvement with the underlying infringements is no more, or no less, proximate than that of ISPs. Accordingly, navigation providers are consciously left out from the ambit of the reforms proposed herein, although injunctive remedies against them are considered in a subsequent chapter.[31]

30 See *GS Media v Sanoma Media*, [51]; *Brein v Wullems*, [49]; *Brein v Ziggo*, [34].
31 See discussion in Chapter 8.

Hosts

In contrast to ISPs and navigation providers, hosts generally exercise both contractual and technical control over persons creating content that becomes stored on their platforms or servers. In fact, unlike the other categories of intermediaries, the services offered by hosts are ***utilised*** by their users to commit infringements. After all, for content, whether infringing or otherwise, to become accessible to internet users, it must first be stored by an intermediary providing hosting services. Without hosts, the internet will be an empty space. As such, when a host's services are engaged in order to store infringing content, its involvement is much more direct and significant than that of ISPs and navigation providers. There is a causal link between the services supplied by hosts and the acts of parties committing trade mark infringements. Unlike in the case of other intermediaries, hosts are capable of removing or terminating infringements at the source. For this reason, hosts bear a greater responsibility for the creation and availability of infringing content. As such, the conduct of hosts, arguably, reaches a degree of culpability to be regarded as sufficiently involved in the commission of trade mark infringements on the part of their users. If liability for ***knowingly assisting*** a tort were ever to be recognised under the English common law, hosts might be more likely to become liable as accessories. Accordingly, a proposal to amend the law such that hosts could be made liable for trade mark infringements, leading to a monetary remedy being made available against culpable hosts, is easily justified. It is, however, necessary to carefully determine as to when such liability should arise.

Before dealing with the conduct and circumstances that should give rise to a host's liability, there is an important point that must be addressed. As noted in Chapter 1, hosts are intermediaries that store content at the request of third-party internet users. However, within that defined category of intermediaries, there could be instances where an intermediary, although acting as a host, is not sufficiently proximate to, or involved in, the underlying infringing activity. This is an important point to consider because, unless it could be established that a host was sufficiently proximate and involved in respect of a particular infringement, such a host should be excluded from liability to pay damages. The scenarios set out in Table 5.1 usefully illustrate this point.

It is important to determine whether it is justified to treat the hosts acting in all of the scenarios as reflected in Table 5.1 on equal terms. Scenarios 1 and 3 are straightforward because there is a contractual relationship between the parties generating the content and the hosts concerned. The hosts described in both these scenarios qualify as information society service providers for the purposes of the E-Commerce Directive, as they provide a service at a distance, by electronic means and for remuneration, the remuneration coming directly from the party receiving the service. They also qualify for the Article 14(1) safe harbour, because they provide an information society service 'that consists of the storage of information provided by a recipient of the service', unless it is determined that their conduct goes beyond the passivity and neutrality required to attract the safe harbour.

Table 5.1 Types of hosts and how they operate

Scenario 1	*A host provides hosting services enabling a third party's website to be hosted.* In this scenario, the host is called a 'web-host'. Here there are only two parties, namely the web-host and the party whose website is hosted.
Scenario 2	*A website allows third parties to generate and store their own content.* Etsy, a popular online marketplace focused on handmade or vintage items and supplies, as well as unique factory-manufactured items, is a suitable example. Etsy facilitates online sales by allowing third parties to list their products for sale on its website. In this scenario, there are three parties: (1) the web-host that hosts the Etsy website,[32] Fastly Inc; (2) Etsy Inc, the entity that is responsible for the Etsy website; and (3) individual sellers who list products for sale on the Etsy website. These sellers generate their own product listings, which are stored on the Etsy website, making them visible to internet users interested in purchasing products. Of the three parties described above, there are two that could be described as hosts. Fastly Inc is the web-host, essentially providing the space for the storage of *all* content relating to the Etsy website. Similarly, Etsy is also a host in respect of the content generated by subscribing sellers relating to the products listed for sale on the platform.
Scenario 3	*A host that operates in circumstances that combine scenarios 1 and 2 above.* An illustrative example of this is eBay. Thus, while eBay permits its subscribing sellers to generate and store their own content in respect of the products listed for sale on the platform, eBay's online marketplace at 'www.ebay.com' and its regional equivalents are all hosted by eBay Inc. In essence, eBay self-hosts its online marketplace together with the third-party content generated by eBay's sellers.

Scenario 2, however, is much more complex because it involves two hosts. Take the following example. Assume that a seller registered with Etsy creates a product listing to promote the sale of counterfeit goods bearing a well-known trade mark.[33] This is clearly an act of infringement on the part of Etsy's seller in terms of section 10 of the Trade Marks Act 1994. While Etsy is the more proximate host in respect of the infringing content and has direct control over the tools that facilitated the infringement, Fastly Inc could also be considered a host because it provides the web-hosting services in relation to the Etsy website, which includes the infringing product listing. However, in the event a monetary remedy is made available against both these hosts, the outcome could lead to an anomaly. This is because, on a literal reading of Article 14(1) of the E-Commerce Directive, it appears that the safe harbour applies only to one of the two hosts. In order for the safe harbour to apply, the intermediary concerned must supply

32 Etsy, located at 'www.etsy.com', is hosted by Fastly Inc, a US-based service provider.

33 According to a report published in 2015, as many as two million items (amounting to more than 5 per cent of the merchandise sold on Etsy) could have been in violation of intellectual property rights. See L Debter, 'Does Etsy Have a Problem with Fake Goods?' *Forbes* (11 May 2015) <www.forbes.com/sites/laurengensler/2015/05/11/does-etsy-have-a-problem-with-fake-goods/#4c89a17a5a88> (accessed 31 January 2019).

an information society service that consists of the storage of information *provided by* the *recipient of the service.* In the example above, it is clear that the recipient of Fastly Inc's web-hosting services is Etsy. However, strictly speaking, the infringing product listing was not *provided by* Etsy, as the *recipient* of Fastly Inc's web-hosting services. On the other hand, the seller who created the infringing product listing was not a recipient of Fastly Inc's web-hosting services but instead was a recipient of Etsy's online marketing services, an aspect of which provides for the hosting of various product listings. Thus, insofar as the infringing product listing is concerned, the safe harbour, arguably, does not apply to Fastly Inc, because the infringing material was not *information provided by a recipient* of its web-hosting services.

In the event that both hosts in scenario 2 are exposed to liability, the web-host *may* become liable to an aggrieved trade mark proprietor even if it complied with the conditions set out in Article 14(1) that normally renders the safe harbour applicable. This is an unsatisfactory and anomalous outcome because hosts that are more proximate to an infringement become eligible for the Article 14(1) safe harbour (such as Etsy in our example), whereas web-hosts, such as Fastly Inc, that merely provide the space for hosting entire websites (thus being less proximate to the infringing activity) do not. Such an outcome would also not be conducive to the normal operation of web-hosts and must be avoided. As such, if a monetary remedy is made available against web-hosts operating in scenario 2, it would become necessary to amend Article 14 of the E-Commerce Directive, and its UK equivalent implemented in Regulation 19 of the E-Commerce Regulations,[34] in order to add clarity about the applicability of the hosting safe harbour to web-hosts in this specific scenario. The only way around this is to argue that when content created by a third party (such as the seller in our example) becomes incorporated into a website (such as Etsy's website), it eventually becomes *information* provided by a *recipient of the web-hosting service.* However, interpreting Article 14(1) in this way would be stretching the language of the safe harbour beyond what might have been envisaged at the time it was drafted.

In addition, providing for a monetary remedy against web-hosts operating within the confines of scenario 2 above may result in holding such hosts liable for infringing content created by third parties with whom they have no contractual relationship. While a contractual relationship between a host and an infringing party ought not to be a prerequisite for the imposition of liability on the host, the existence of a contract provides a distinct benefit: the possibility of apportioning liability between the contracting parties in the event one of them is sued on the basis of content hosted. However, in the absence of a contract, such an internal arrangement cannot be achieved between a web-host and the third-party infringer (such as Etsy's seller in our example). Thus, in the event a web-host operating in scenario 2 is made liable for content created by a third-party infringer, the only

34 Electronic Commerce (EC Directive) Regulations 2002, SI 2002/2013 (E-Commerce Regulations).

viable option would be for the web-host to initiate legal proceedings against its own customer (i.e. operators responsible for the hosted website) in respect of content the latter never authored.[35] Thus, it may not be desirable to resolve the anomalous application of the hosting safe harbour to web-hosts in scenario 2 through contractual means.

In contrast to web-hosts, the operators responsible for websites (such as Etsy in scenario 2) not only have a contractual relationship with the users of their respective websites but also exercise direct technical control over the third-party content created by those users.[36] As such, a conscious choice is made to exclude web-hosts operating in the circumstances set out in scenario 2 from the scope of the legal reforms proposed herein. It is best to limit the remedies against such web-hosts to non-monetary remedies, such as injunctions. This approach is suitable in view of ensuring legal certainty, so that hosts, whether web-hosts or otherwise, are certain about their liability. On the other hand, when an entire website hosted by a web-host (as in scenario 1) is the subject of infringing activity or the web-host and the host of the infringing content are the same entity (as in scenario 3), it would not be improper to hold them liable for hosting infringing content in appropriate circumstances. Ultimately, the outcome of this approach is that only hosts that are most proximate and involved in respect of an infringement, in cases where they are directly responsible for providing the means for the infringing activity, would become exposed to liability. It is submitted that this is a fair outcome, given the contractual and technical control such hosts possess over the infringing third-party content.

Approach to reforming the law

It was noted in the previous chapter that hosts have been held liable for infringements of trade mark rights in both the US and in several EU Member States. As such, from the perspective of reforming the law, it would be instructive to consider the pros and cons of these varying approaches so that they could be suitably adopted.

The US approach is premised on the doctrine of contributory trade mark infringement established in *Inwood v Ives*.[37] The doctrine was initially applied to manufacturers of products, before it was extended to suppliers of services, the latter extension making it possible for the doctrine to be applied in relation to intermediaries supplying online services.[38] As such, theoretically, the doctrine could be applied indiscriminately to any intermediary operating in the online space, provided the following requirements are satisfied:

35 This is assuming that the contract between the web-host and the operators responsible for the website contains provisions that require the latter to indemnify the web-host in the event of any liability arising for content hosted.

36 J Riordan, *The Liability of Internet Intermediaries* (Oxford University Press 2016), 40.

37 *Inwood Laboratories Inc v Ives Laboratories Inc* 456 U.S. 844 (1982) (*Inwood v Ives*).

38 *Lockheed Martin Corp v Network Solutions Inc* 194 F.3d 980 (9th Cir. 1999) (*Lockheed v NSI*).

1 the intermediary concerned must have supplied a service;
2 the intermediary must have possessed direct control over the means of infringement; and
3 the intermediary must have continued to supply its service to the infringer, even after acquiring actual or constructive knowledge of the infringement.

Thus, one possible approach to reforming the law, so that hosts may be made liable for trade mark infringements, is to adopt the language of contributory infringement as formulated in *Inwood v Ives.* This approach has several advantages. First, the language used is fairly flexible in terms of the parties that may become the subject of contributory liability. Such flexibility is useful in capturing developments in technology and new ways by which trade mark rights might be infringed in the online, and even offline, contexts. Second, the contributory infringement test addresses the need to exclude ISPs and navigation providers from being exposed to liability in respect of their access and navigation functions. The first two limbs address this. Since neither ISPs nor navigation providers provide a service to actual infringers or possess any direct control over the means of infringement, these intermediaries will not ordinarily satisfy the test for contributory infringement. Third, the language of contributory infringement addresses the complexities surrounding scenario 2 (of Table 5.1) involving two hosts. Although a web-host in scenario 2 has overall control over a website it hosts, it may not have *direct control* over any 'tools' that may have been put into place by the operators responsible for managing the website that facilitate third parties to generate content that eventually become incorporated into the hosted website. Direct control in this regard is vested with the operators of the website and not the web-host. As such, adopting the language of contributory infringement would exclude web-hosts that operate within the confines of scenario 2 (of Table 5.1) from the scope of liability.

However, the US approach gives rise to some difficulty in view of its broad formulation. The general approach under the modified *Inwood v Ives* test is to hold a party liable for contributory infringement for *continuing* to supply a service to an infringer, even after having acquired actual or constructive knowledge of the infringement in question. This formulation does not lead to difficulty when an *entire* website is the subject of infringing activity. Take, for instance, a web-host in scenario 1. If the entire website is dedicated to infringing trade mark rights (e.g. a website exclusively promoting the sale of counterfeits), then, upon being notified, the web-host must discontinue its hosting services to the infringing party (i.e. the operators of the website). This would result in the entire website being taken down, effectively terminating the infringements. However, it is uncertain as to how the test of contributory infringement would apply to a situation where only certain parts of a website (and not the entire website) contain infringing material. Under the modified *Inwood v Ives* test, in order to avoid liability, if a web-host is required to discontinue its *hosting services* to an infringing user, even in circumstances where only a part of a hosted website contains the infringement, the outcome would be the removal of the *entire* website. Such an outcome could be disproportionate and unsatisfactory. The better approach might be to apply the test for contributory infringement flexibly so that a web-host's act of removing the infringing part of an otherwise legitimate website would be sufficient to avoid liability. Unfortunately, US courts have not had the opportunity of addressing this issue,[39] as cases that have come up in the US have involved either websites that have been entirely used for infringing purposes or actors such as eBay, i.e. hosts as described in scenario 3 (of Table 5.1), in relation to which this issue has little or no effect.[40]

In contrast to the US approach, the approach adopted in some of the EU Member States has been more specific in addressing the issue of liability. This is largely due to the influence of the E-Commerce Directive's safe harbour on the liability of intermediaries providing an information society service. Thus, upon an analysis of the approach in France, Germany and Belgium (considered in Chapter 4), the common premise upon which the liability of a host has been founded is on its *failure* to take reasonable measures to terminate or prevent infringements after being put on notice. In relation to hosts, the courts have taken the view that the expeditious removal of content promoting an infringement is a reasonable measure that could be adopted. In view of the specificity of the action required on the part of hosts, this approach avoids a potential issue that could arise under the US approach. That is, it would be sufficient for the host to remove only the identified infringing content, there being no legal obstacle for the host to continue to supply its hosting services in other respects. There is no requirement that the host must discontinue the supply of its hosting services per se, where it is possible for the infringement to be isolated, resulting in the removal of the infringing content alone. This approach, therefore, envisions a proportionate response.

However, despite the advantage set out above, the approach adopted in the EU Member States considered in Chapter 4 does not adequately address the concern set out earlier on in this chapter about web-hosts operating within the parameters of scenario 2 (of Table 5.1). Web-hosts in this scenario are likely to lack *direct control* over the tools used by third parties to create infringing content, which eventually becomes part of the hosted website. In view of the lack of clarity in Article 14(1) of the E-Commerce Directive, it is unclear how a web-host's liability in this specific scenario would be approached in the UK and other EU Member States. Accordingly, if the Continental approach to the liability of hosts is to be incorporated into UK law, it is important to limit its scope to hosts that have *direct control* over the means of infringement to the exclusion of web-hosts operating within the confines of scenario 2 (of Table 5.1). Notably, this problem

39 This is clear from the analysis carried out in Chapter 4 of all the US cases filed against hosts in federal courts on the basis of contributory trade mark infringement.

40 For instance, assume that a seller on eBay lists an infringing product for sale. Upon being specifically notified of the infringing listing, eBay could simply discontinue its service in respect of that listing by removing the listing and notifying the seller. This has no effect on other legitimate product listings displayed at the request of this particular seller or others. In fact, this was precisely what exonerated eBay from liability in *Tiffany (NJ) Inc v eBay Inc* 600 F.3d 93 (2d Cir. 2010).

is avoided under the standard for contributory trade mark liability, applicable in the US, in view of the 'direct control' requirement that it incorporates.

It seems that the approaches to the liability of hosts adopted in the US and in EU Member States have their own merits, as well as shortcomings. Accordingly, as opposed to strictly incorporating either of the two approaches into UK law, it would be prudent to adapt and consolidate them, so that the concerns set out in this chapter are also addressed in proposing the reforms. The next part of this chapter is devoted to setting out the key ingredients of a possible statutory provision providing for a monetary remedy against culpable hosts, and the most suitable place for its incorporation within the existing statutory framework in the UK. Possible reforms at EU level are also considered towards the end.

Implementation and key features of the proposed statutory provision

Any statutory provision aiming to provide trade mark proprietors with a right to claim monetary relief against hosts must first impose a 'duty' on hosts, which if breached would give rise to a cause of action. Whether the breach of a statutory duty automatically permits a claim for damages is an important question that needs to be addressed in determining the method of implementing the proposed reforms. Under the common law, a breach of a statutory duty is regarded as a separate species of tort.[41] Thus, it might be thought that, just as with any other tort, a claim premised on a breach of statutory duty would give rise to a cause of action. However, the correct position is that a breach of statutory duty does not automatically entitle the party harmed to file a civil action. Before an action for breach of statutory duty is allowed, a court 'must be satisfied that the legislature intended, when drafting the legislative provision in question, to create an entitlement to damages at common law for its breach'.[42]

In some instances, the parliamentary intent is made explicitly clear that any form of civil action is excluded.[43] In other cases, a statute may provide that a scheme of compensation set out therein is exhaustive, and no other liability may be imposed.[44] However, when a statute imposing a duty is silent on remedies for its breach, whether an action under the common law for breach of statutory duty lies is more difficult to ascertain. In this regard, Witting has observed:

> Only rarely does Parliament expressly declare that any breach of the statute should, or should not, be actionable in tort. On the other hand, since the

41 See e.g. C Witting, *Street on Torts* (14th edn, Oxford University Press 2015), 499; MA Jones, *Textbook on Torts* (8th edn, Oxford University Press 2002), 447; S Deaking, A Johnston and B Markesinis, *Markesinis and Deakin's Tort Law* (7th edn, Oxford University Press 2007), 294; and K Horsey and E Rackley, *Tort Law* (4th edn, Oxford University Press 2015), 382.

42 M Fordham, 'Breach of Statutory Duty–A Diminishing Tort' (1996) *Singapore Journal of Legal Studies* 362, 364 citing inter alia *Cutler v Wandsworth Stadium Ltd* [1949] AC 398.

43 See e.g. Safety of Sports Grounds Act 1975, section 13 and Guard Dogs Act 1975, section 5(2).

44 See e.g. Nuclear Installations Act 1965, section 12(1)(b).

courts may now refer to Hansard in interpreting statutes, parliamentary intention may sometimes be discerned from a study of the parliamentary debates.[45]

Thus, in view of ensuring certainty, the proposed statutory provision imposing a duty on hosts must also ensure that it explicitly sets out a remedy in the event the duty is breached. Only then will it be possible to ensure that trade mark proprietors are able to bring a monetary claim against hosts in appropriate circumstances. There are two ways in which this could be achieved. One way is for the provision imposing the duty to expressly provide for a claim for breach of that duty.[46] The other is to include the duty within a pre-existing framework of remedies.

In view of the simplicity involved, the second alternative may be preferred for the purposes of implementing the law reforms proposed in this chapter. In this regard, reference must be made to the Trade Marks Act 1994, not only because the proposal for law reforms concerns the interests of trade mark proprietors but also because the statute already contains a comprehensive framework of remedies in relation to the infringement of trade mark rights, within which any reforms could be couched. Therefore, incorporating a provision enabling trade mark proprietors to bring a monetary claim against hosts as an extension to the existing framework of the trade mark infringement action is possibly the simplest, and most effective, mode of implementing these reforms.[47] When trade mark rights are infringed, the right holder may file an action for infringement, in which a claim for damages could be incorporated.[48] As such, this existing framework may suitably be extended to allow right holders to bring a monetary claim (or claim for damages) against hosts in appropriate circumstances. To achieve this outcome, the scope of section 10 of the Trade Marks Act 1994 requires expansion.

Section 10(5) of the Trade Marks Act 1994 was considered in Chapter 3 in connection with the discussion on whether the statute's infringement provisions provide for a form of accessorial liability. The conclusion reached was that it did not, although section 10(5) does apply to parties that make use of trade marks *intended* to be used in trade, thus capturing acts that eventually lead to infringement. For section 10(5) to apply, the party concerned must have made *use* of a trade mark without the consent of its proprietor. However, insofar as internet intermediaries (and hosts in particular) are concerned, they make no *use* of trade marks in any sense taking them outside the scope of section 10(5). As such, what is required is for a provision to be inserted into section 10 of the Trade Marks Act 1994 that has the effect of expanding the scope of the infringement action beyond section 10(5).

45 Witting, above n41, 501 (citations omitted).

46 See e.g. Local Government Act 1988, section 17 and Trade Union and Labour Relations (Consolidation) Act 1992, section 145.

47 Trade Marks Act 1994, section 10.

48 Trade Marks Act 1994, section 14. Notably, section 14(2) provides that '[i]n an action for infringement all such relief by way of damages, injunctions, accounts or otherwise is available to him as is available in respect of the infringement of any other property right'.

Such a provision must include the following key features that take into account the concerns and considerations set out earlier on in this chapter:

1 The provision must target intermediaries that engage in the hosting of third-party content, i.e. content generated by the users of its service. This does not mean that the intermediary must exclusively be dealing with the hosting of content, but rather hosting could be an aspect of its services.
2 However, the provision must exclude from its scope intermediaries that engage in other forms of information society services, as well as hosts whose activities come within the confines of scenario 2 (of Table 5.1) above. In particular, the provision must apply only to hosts identified in scenarios 1 and 3 (of Table 5.1).
3 The provision must provide for the liability of hosts in circumstances where they host third-party content that infringes a trade mark. This means that the third party to whom the host supplies its service must have used a trade mark in a manner that is prohibited by subsections (1) to (3) of section 10 of the Trade Marks Act 1994.
4 Such liability should only arise when a host fails to remove the content giving rise to an infringement after having acquired *actual knowledge* of the infringement.
5 The provision must provide that actual knowledge of an infringement is capable of being imputed on a host *only* when an aggrieved right holder serves on the host a notice of infringement containing sufficient particulars from which the identity of the complaining party, location of the alleged infringing content and details of the infringement could be easily determined.
6 The provision must be consistent with the E-Commerce Regulations, which transposes the E-Commerce Directive into UK law.

A possible draft of a provision that may be inserted immediately after section 10(5) of the Trade Marks Act 1994 is provided below. For ease of reference, the draft provision is referred to as 'section 10(5A)'.

Section 10–Infringement of registered trade marks

(5A) (a) A service provider that supplies a service consisting of the storage (or hosting) of content provided by the recipient of the service infringes a registered trade mark if the service provider, having acquired actual knowledge of an infringement as specified in section 10(1) to (3), fails to expeditiously remove the content causing, or giving rise to, the infringement.

(b) For the avoidance of any doubt

(i) liability under paragraph (a) of this subsection only extends to service providers supplying a service consisting of the storage (or hosting) of information provided by the recipient of the service, and does not extend to other service providers supplying information society services.

(ii) for liability to arise under paragraph (a) of this subsection, it is not necessary for the service provider to have supplied a service that exclusively consists of the storage (or hosting) of content provided by the recipient of the service.

(iii) where two or more service providers are involved, liability in terms of paragraph (a) of this subsection will only extend to the service provider that was directly responsible for the storage of the content causing, or giving rise to, the infringement.

Explanation 1. Where W, a web-host, supplies A with web-hosting services enabling A's website to be hosted, but A in his website allows third parties to upload and store their own content (thus A too acting as a host), only A (and not W) can be held liable under paragraph (a) of this subsection, provided the conditions for liability set out therein are met.

Explanation 2. Where W and A are one and the same entity, then liability may be imposed on that person on the basis of paragraph (a) of this subsection.

(c) No service provider shall be imputed with actual knowledge for the purposes of paragraph (a) of this subsection, unless a notice containing the details stipulated in Regulation 22(b)(i)–(iii) of the Electronic Commerce (EC Directive) Regulations 2002 is served on that service provider.[49]

(d) The terms 'service provider', 'recipient of the service' and 'information society services' appearing in this subsection takes the same meaning attached to those terms in Regulation 2 of the Electronic Commerce (EC Directive) Regulations 2002.

The draft provision set out above addresses the key concerns raised earlier on in this chapter in the following ways. First, section 10(5A)(b)(i) ensures that ISPs and navigation providers are expressly excluded from the scope of liability. Therefore, monetary relief, by virtue of a trade mark infringement action, is only made available against hosts. Second, the clarification provided in section 10(5A)(b)(ii) ensures that the scope of section 10(5A)(a) is sufficiently broad enough to encompass intermediaries that engage in hosting merely as an aspect of its wider range of services. Third, web-hosts operating within the confines of scenario 2 (of Table 5.1) are excluded from liability (as per *Explanation 1* in section 10(5A)

49 The details set out in Regulation 22(b)(i)–(iii) of the E-Commerce Regulations are as follows: (i) the full name and address of the sender of the notice, (ii) details of the location of the information in question and (iii) details of the unlawful nature of the activity or information in question.

(b)(iii)), whereas hosts operating in scenarios 1 and 3 (of Table 5.1) fall within the scope of section 10(5A)(a) (as per *Explanation 2* in section 10(5A)(b)(iii)). Thus, only hosts that are most proximate to the infringing content will fall within the scope of the liability provision. Fourth, section 10(5A)(a) does not require a host to discontinue the supply of its hosting services to an infringing customer in order to avoid liability. It is sufficient for the host to remove the infringing content expeditiously. Such an approach ensures a more proportionate response, especially in cases where the content giving rise to the infringement is within a larger website that is otherwise legitimate.

The following additional points are also worth noting. First, the proposed section 10(5A)(a) not only mirrors the safe harbour in Article 14(1) of the E-Commerce Directive (and Regulation 19 of the UK E-Commerce Regulations) but also avoids some of the uncertainties surrounding the safe harbour. Any domestic statutory provision imposing liability on hosts must mirror the safe harbour, as imposing liability *beyond* those limitations would render the domestic provision non-compliant with the E-Commerce Directive. In the context of the UK, although Brexit will eventually render such compliance non-obligatory, given that domestic laws and regulations that implement EU law, including the E-Commerce Regulations, will continue to remain in force even after Brexit until subsequently repealed or amended, it becomes necessary to consider the hosting safe harbour in crafting a provision imposing liability on hosts.

Under Article 14(1) of the E-Commerce Directive, a host could only be held criminally liable if it failed to remove illegal content having obtained *actual knowledge* of the illegality. However, it would be permissible for EU Member States to impose civil liability (resulting in the award of damages) on hosts that fail to remove illegal content having acquired either *actual knowledge* or *awareness of the facts or circumstances from which such illegality is apparent.* The latter standard of knowledge implies a form of constructive knowledge,[50] or 'red flag' standard as popularly known in connection with the US copyright safe harbour.[51] In essence, hosts may be exposed to civil liability upon a lower standard of knowledge. In interpreting the standard of constructive knowledge,

50 See L Edwards, 'Articles 12–15 ECD: ISP Liability' in L Edwards (ed), *The New Legal Framework for E-Commerce in Europe* (Hart Publishing 2005), 114 and C Angelopoulos, *European Intermediary Liability in Copyright: A Tort-Based Analysis* (Kluwer Law International 2017), 421. The knowledge based on 'awareness' is comparable to the 'reason to know' aspect of the test for contributory trade mark infringement as set out in *Inwood v Ives.* This was made clear by the US Court of Appeals (9th Cir.) in *Lockheed v NSI*, when the Court observed that '[c]ontributory infringement occurs when the defendant either intentionally induces a third party to infringe the plaintiff's mark or supplies a product to a third party with actual or *constructive knowledge* that the product is being used to infringe the service mark' (emphasis added).

51 The US's copyright safe harbour was introduced by Title II of the Digital Millennium Copyright Act 1998 (DMCA) (codified at 17 USC §512).

Angelopoulos has argued in favour of an adjusted test, which she has described in the following terms:

> It is therefore probably more accurate to speak of an adjustment of the objective test to meet the needs of intermediary liability: a hybrid subjective/objective standard, wherein the objectivity is assured through the word 'apparent', while some subjectivity is allowed through by reference to the intermediary's individual 'awareness'.[52]

Nevertheless, there is uncertainty about what constructive (or red flag) knowledge entails, particularly in relation to the conduct of hosts. When the CJEU ruled in *L'Oréal v eBay* that the exemption in Article 14(1) will be denied to a host that became 'aware of facts or circumstances on the basis of which a ***diligent economic operator should have identified the illegality in question***',[53] the CJEU perhaps increased, rather than reduced, the uncertainty surrounding the matter of 'awareness'.[54] Arguably, adopting a standard of knowledge premised on 'awareness' is capable of imputing liability on hosts even in the absence of a sufficiently precise and adequately substantiated notice of infringement being served on them.[55] This approach would leave hosts to deal with uncertainty about whether they have acquired a sufficient degree of knowledge of an infringement compelling premature action on their part to avoid liability.[56] Such an outcome would be inconsistent with the need to maintain a healthy balance between the rights of

52 Angelopoulos, above n50, 421. Notably, the subjective/objective standard proposed by Angelopoulos in the context of the E-Commerce Directive, seems to reflect the red flag standard under the US's DMCA safe harbour. See Senate Report No 105-190 on the Digital Millennium Copyright Act, 105th Congress, 2nd Session (1998), 44:

> In determining whether the service provider was aware of a 'red flag,' the subjective awareness of the service provider of the facts or circumstances in question must be determined. However, in deciding whether those facts or circumstances constitute a 'red flag'—in other words, whether infringing activity would have been apparent to a reasonable person operating under the same or similar circumstances—an objective standard should be used.

53 Case C-324/09, *L'Oréal SA v eBay International AG* [2011] ECR I-06011 (*L'Oréal v eBay*), [120] (emphasis added).

54 See S Khan, 'The Potential Impact on Host Intermediaries of Defamatory Remarks Posted following L'Oreal v eBay' (2012) 18 *Computer and Telecommunications Law Review* 204, 207.

55 *L'Oréal v eBay*, [122]. This seems to be the case even under the US's DMCA safe harbour (see *Capitol Records Inc v MP3Tunes LLC* 2013 WL 1987225).

56 In fact, the adoption of a red flag or constructive knowledge standard has been criticised for its lack of certainty. See e.g. B Brown, 'Fortifying the Safe Harbors: Reevaluating the DMCA in a Web 2.0 World' (2008) 23 *Berkeley Technology Law Journal* 437, 457–58; M Peguera, 'The DMCA Safe Harbour and Their European Counterparts: A Comparative Analysis of Some Common Problems' (2009) 32 *Columbia Journal of Law & the Arts* 481, 489; L Chang, 'The Red Flag Test For Apparent Knowledge Under the DMCA §512(c) Safe Harbor' (2010) 28 *Cardozo Arts & Entertainment Law Journal* 195, 219–20; and H Fisher, 'Danger in the DMCA Safe Harbors: The Need to Narrow What Constitutes Red Flag Knowledge' (2015) 49 *University of Richmond Law Review* 643, 664.

trade mark proprietors and the interests of other stakeholders, including internet intermediaries and online users.[57] Therefore, the choice to avoid the language of 'awareness' and instead adopt 'actual knowledge' as a standard to determine the liability of hosts for trade mark infringements is justified and stands to reason.[58] In fact, as noted in Chapter 3, Davies's proposal for the recognition of liability for assisting civil wrongs requires a standard of *actual knowledge* on the part of the secondary party, as '[r]equiring actual knowledge ensures that the freedom of action of those who are not in a proximate relationship with the claimant is not unduly hampered'.[59] There is no reason to depart from that approach in imposing liability on hosts.

The aim of achieving certainty is further advanced in the proposed section 10(5A) by narrowing the means by which actual knowledge may become imputed. Accordingly, only a notice of infringement complying with standards set out in the E-Commerce Regulations is capable of imputing actual knowledge of an infringement on a host. Regulation 22 of the E-Commerce Regulations provides that in determining whether a service provider possessed actual knowledge 'a court shall take into account all matters which appear to it in the particular circumstances to be relevant and, among other things, shall have regard to' any notice served on the service provider concerned.[60] It appears that notice is not a prerequisite for actual knowledge to be imputed, although it is one of the best indicators of actual knowledge. However, by discarding other possible means by which actual knowledge might be imputed and limiting such imputation only

57 The national implementation of the Article 14(1) safe harbour in some EU Member States has expressly avoided the language of 'awareness'. Thus, by negative implication, hosts in those member states can only be held liable upon the acquisition of 'actual knowledge'. See e.g. Act No 458/2002 on Provision of Information Society Services, section 15 (Finland) and Law No 34/2002 of 11 July 2002 on Information Society Services and Electronic Commerce, art 16 (Spain). For a more detailed analysis of the Spanish knowledge standard, see M Peguera, '"I Just Know that I (Actually) Know Nothing": Actual Knowledge and Other Problems in ISP Liability Case Law in Spain' (2008) 30 *European Intellectual Property Review* 280 and M Peguera, 'Internet Service Providers' Liability in Spain: Recent Caw Law and Future Perspectives' (2010) 1 *Journal of Intellectual Property, Information Technology and Electronic Commerce Law* 151.

58 Of course, constructive knowledge or constructive notice is a well-established standard for the imputation of knowledge under the law and has been widely used in a range of contexts. For instance, in the context of contracts and undue influence (*Barclays Bank plc v O'Brien and another* [1994] 1 AC 180), employment and disability (*Donelien v Liberata UK Ltd* [2018] EWCA Civ 129), title to property (*Patman v Harland* (1881) 17 Ch D 353) and limitation of actions (*Adams v Bracknell Forest BC* [2004] ELR 459), constructive knowledge has been used as a standard to impute knowledge of relevant facts and circumstances on parties to disputes. However, this does not necessarily mean that constructive knowledge is an appropriate standard for the online context. Given the fact that most internet intermediaries have automated the functions that facilitate the hosting and sharing of content, the vast volume of content generated by internet users and the complexities involved in determining trade mark infringements (a point considered in Chapter 7), it is submitted that actual knowledge of infringements (as opposed to mere constructive knowledge) is the better prerequisite for the imposition of liability on hosts.

59 PS Davies, *Accessory Liability* (Hart Publishing 2015), 283.

60 E-Commerce Regulations, reg 22(a).

to circumstances in which a service provider has been served with a notice of infringement incorporating the information set out in Regulation 22(b)(i)–(iii) of the E-Commerce Regulations, the proposed section 10(5A) improves on the aspect of certainty. Accordingly, under the proposed approach, for a notice to confer actual knowledge on the part of a host, it *must* at the very least contain the full name and address of the sender,[61] details identifying the location of the content in question[62] and details of the unlawful nature of the activity arising from the content in question.[63] This approach is not inconsistent with the E-Commerce Directive, which provides in Recital (46) that the Directive does not affect the 'possibility of establishing specific requirements which must be fulfilled expeditiously prior to the removal or disabling of information'. In essence, the proposed section 10(5A) does precisely that by setting out *specific requirements* that must be fulfilled *before* the removal of alleged infringing content becomes obligatory in order for a host to benefit from the hosting safe harbour.

Second, a point must be made about the neutrality of hosts, as this is connected with the aspect of 'knowledge'. In *L'Oréal v eBay*, the CJEU ruled that the mere fact that a host 'stores offers for sale on its server, sets the terms of its service, is remunerated for that service and provides general information to its customers'[64] does not render the Article 14(1) safe harbour inapplicable. However, the Court went on to provide the following qualification:

> Where, by contrast, the operator has provided assistance which entails, in particular, *optimising the presentation of the offers for sale in question or promoting those offers, it must be considered not to have taken a neutral position between the customer-seller concerned and potential buyers but to have played an active role of such a kind as to give it knowledge of, or control over, the data relating to those offers for sale.* It cannot then rely, in the case of those data, on the exemption from liability referred to in [the E-Commerce Directive].[65]

What might be gleaned from the CJEU's language is that neutrality plays an important role in determining whether a host should be made liable for the storage of unlawful content on its platform or servers. A lack of neutrality can be inferred from a host's knowledge of, or control over, the unlawful content. However, the CJEU's approach must not be accepted without proper scrutiny. Simply because a host, such as eBay, optimises third-party content in order to make content more presentable, that does not necessarily mean that the host lacks neutrality. The CJEU's reasoning suggests that by engaging in optimisation, the host plays an *active role* of such a kind to clothe it with knowledge of the content on its platform or servers.

61 E-Commerce Regulations, reg 22(b)(i).
62 E-Commerce Regulations, reg 22(b)(ii).
63 E-Commerce Regulations, reg 22(b)(iii).
64 *L'Oréal v eBay*, [115].
65 *L'Oréal v eBay*, [116] (emphasis added).

However, in most instances optimisation takes place automatically, without human intervention, and in those circumstances it is difficult to suggest that a host would have acquired knowledge of any unlawful content.[66] Furthermore, adopting the approach of the CJEU would create uncertainty on the part of hosts. For instance, it is unclear as to what types of conduct is capable of displacing neutrality. Such uncertainties, which are likely to deter technological and business innovation, are avoided in the proposed section 10(5A), which imputes actual knowledge of infringements on hosts *only* upon them being served with a notice of infringement. In essence, the burden is placed squarely on trade mark proprietors to be vigilant about infringements, an outcome that is perfectly reasonable and balanced.

Third, the proposed section 10(5A)(a) requires hosts to *remove* infringing content to avoid liability. It does not adopt the expression of 'disable access', which is found in Article 14(1)(a) of the E-Commerce Directive.[67] It is unclear whether removal and disabling access mean the same thing. In cases in which the E-Commerce Directive[68] or the E-Commerce Regulations,[69] applicable in the UK, have been discussed, these terms have been used together without being distinguished from one another. However, from a technical standpoint, removal and disabling access require different actions. Removal is concerned with the actual infringing content, requiring the content to be removed at its source. Disabling access, however, entails a broader range of measures. Thus, e.g. where a navigation provider (such as a search engine) removes a hyperlink to infringing content, the result is the disabling of access to, and not the removal of, the infringing content. Similarly, when an ISP blocks access to infringing content, the result is that access to that content is disabled. Since the usage of 'remove' and 'disable access' without their scope being properly defined could lead to terminological confusion, the phrase 'disable access' has been consciously omitted in formulating section 10(5A). Accordingly, what a host is required to do, in order to avoid liability, is to *remove* infringing content at its source.

The consistency of the proposed reforms with EU law

It is important to consider whether the proposed section 10(5A) will run counter to the EU-wide approximation of trade mark law, which the Trade Marks

66 A Kur, 'Secondary Liability for Trademark Infringement on the Internet: The Situation in Germany and Throughout the EU' (2014) 37 *Columbia Journal of Law and Arts* 525, 531–32.

67 The UK E-Commerce Regulations also adopt the language of 'disable access' in Regulation 19(a)(ii).

68 See e.g. *L'Oréal v eBay*; Joined Cases C-236/08, C-237/08 and C-238/08, *Google France Sarl v Louis Vuitton Malletier SA* [2010] ECR I-02417; Case C-291/13, *Sotiris Papasavvas v O Fileleftheros Dimosia Etaireia Ltd and others* [2015] 1 CMLR 24.

69 See e.g. *MIS v Designtechnica*; *CG v Facebook Ireland Ltd and another* [2015] NIQB 11; *Mosley v Google Inc* [2015] EMLR 11.

Directive[70] has achieved. Thanks to Brexit, insofar as the UK is concerned, this might be a purely academic enquiry. It is, however, a point worth considering in view of the possible transition period, and in any case from the point of view of other EU Member States that might wish to adopt a similar approach in their respective domestic trade mark legislation.

Recital (10) of the Trade Marks Directive provides that '[i]t is fundamental, in order to facilitate the free movement of goods and services, to ensure that registered trade marks enjoy the same protection under the legal systems of all the Member States'. It has been suggested that 'the [Trade Marks Directive] does not provide for any protection that is more extensive than described in the compulsory protection articles to be implemented'.[71] Thus, the ultimate question is whether the proposed section 10(5A) could be regarded as an instance of providing more extensive trade mark protection in comparison to the protection afforded in other EU Member States.

In this regard, it must be noted that the scope of trade mark protection is determined by Article 5 of the Trade Marks Directive, which sets out in specific terms the instances in which a trade mark proprietor could prohibit the unauthorised use of a registered trade mark by a third party. Notably, Article 5 is limited to circumstances where third parties make *use* of a registered trade mark without the requisite consent of the right holder. However, as was pointed out in Chapter 2, internet intermediaries generally do not make use of trade marks in their operations in the sense required by Article 5. The outcome of the proposed section 10(5A) is that a new party (i.e. hosts) may become caught up for trade mark infringements even in cases where they do not themselves make use of any trade marks. By entitling trade mark proprietors to bring infringement proceedings against a party that did not make use of their marks, it might appear that the proposed section 10(5A) adds to the 'rights' conferred on trade mark proprietors, thus providing for more extensive protection than what might be conferred in the other EU Member States. However, this is not the case.

It is important to recall that the Trade Marks Directive requires the same level of trade mark protection to be granted throughout all the EU Member States 'in order to facilitate the free movement of goods and services'.[72] Thus, it is only if the proposed section 10(5A) impedes the free movement of goods or services that it would run afoul of the Trade Marks Directive's efforts of approximating

70 Directive 2008/95/EC of the European Parliament and of the Council of 22 October 2008 to Approximate the Laws of the Member States Relating to Trade Marks [2008] OJ L 299/25 (Trade Marks Directive). An explanation as to why a reference is made to the 2008 Trade Marks Directive, and not the later 2015 Trade Marks Directive (Directive (EU) 2015/2436), which replaces the former, is provided in Chapter 1.

71 TC Jehoram, C van Nispen and T Huydecoper, *European Trademark Law* (Kluwer Law International 2010), 24.

72 E-Commerce Directive, Recital (10). It must be noted, however, that the corresponding recital (Recital (10)) in the 2015 Trade Marks Directive, which replaces the 2008 Directive, does not contain this part, although the new Directive still maintains the necessity for the same level of trade mark protection across all EU Member States.

trade mark law. In this regard, section 10(5A) does not create a new species of infringement. In fact, the liability of a host under the proposed provision is dependent on the commission of an infringement on the part of the host's subscriber. Nothing in the proposed section 10(5A) adds to the usual circumstances in which a trade mark proprietor is entitled to prohibit the use of a trade mark by an unauthorised party. Take, for example, an unauthorised third party who makes use of a trade mark in relation to online content aimed at the promotion and sale of counterfeit goods. When such infringing content is stored in the platform or servers of a particular host, whose services were used by the unauthorised third party, the infringement in question comes squarely within the parameters of Article 5 of the Trade Marks Directive.

It is clearly justified for a trade mark proprietor to prevent the movement of counterfeit goods. The only addition that the proposed section 10(5A) makes is to the parties against whom an infringement action may be brought. Thus, in addition to being able to bring an infringement action against the unauthorised third party that incorporated the trade mark into online content, a right holder by virtue of the proposed section 10(5A) would also be in a position to bring an action against the host that stored the content, in circumstances where it failed to remove the infringing content after being put on notice. Considered this way, it is clear that the proposed section 10(5A) does not in any way add to the 'rights' conferred on trade mark proprietors in terms of Article 5 of the Trade Marks Directive. Rather, it merely facilitates a trade mark infringement action to be brought against an additional party, i.e. a host, in circumstances where content provided by a recipient of the hosting services gives rise to an infringement as set out in Article 5 of the Trade Marks Directive.[73]

Moreover, there is nothing in the Trade Marks Directive that precludes EU Member States from applying 'provisions of law . . . other than trade mark law, such as provisions relating to . . . civil liability. . .'[74] to the sphere of trade mark protection. Thus, just as much as there is no bar in applying English common law principles, such as joint tortfeasance, in determining the liability of intermediaries for infringements committed by their subscribing users,[75] courts in other EU Member States have applied similar domestic legal principles outside the sphere of trade mark law, in order to determine the liability of intermediaries.[76] Arguably, the proposed section 10(5A) represents the codification of a form of civil accessorial liability, which would result in the application of a provision of law relating to the civil liability to the context of trade mark protection. Simply because liability is imposed on hosts under the infringement provisions of the

73 This is achieved through paragraph (a) of the proposed section 10(5A) by making liability of a host dependent on the commission of an infringement (as specified in subsections (1) to (3) of section 10) by a recipient of its hosting services.

74 Trade Marks Directive, Recital (7). This recital has been reproduced at Recital (40) in the 2015 Trade Marks Directive.

75 See discussion in Chapter 3.

76 See discussion in Chapter 4, where domestic cases in France, Germany and Belgium have been considered.

Trade Marks Act 1994, it does not follow that the provision adds to the 'rights' conferred on trade mark proprietors. The proposed provision merely makes use of the action for trade mark infringement as a vessel to impose liability on hosts. Since the Trade Marks Directive does not seek to achieve an approximation of procedural law or accessorial liability, the method adopted in framing section 10(5A) does not run counter to the directive.

Although the proposed section 10(5A) is consistent with EU law, it may still be useful to incorporate a similar provision in the Trade Marks Directive. On the one hand, although the E-Commerce Directive (through Articles 12–15) seeks to achieve a level of harmonisation as regards the liability of internet intermediaries, there is uncertainty as to when the safe harbour applies to hosts, which seems to depend on the individualistic perception of whether a host is a 'neutral' and 'passive' service provider. On the other hand, since the matter of accessorial liability has been left out from the scope of the Trade Marks Directive, the liability of hosts under the domestic laws applicable to them in EU Member States has resulted in varying standards of liability being applied. Although some common features can be derived from these varying approaches, some inconsistencies exist which are worth setting aside in view of achieving greater certainty. The proposed section 10(5A), while drawing on the most common features capable of being derived from the varying domestic approaches, seeks to achieve certainty in several respects: (1) the types of internet intermediaries against which liability may be imposed, (2) when actual knowledge of an infringement can be imputed and (3) the precise steps that must be taken to avoid liability. As such, introducing a provision into the Trade Marks Directive that replicates the proposed section 10(5A) will provide the advantage of unifying the various domestic approaches as to a host's liability in the trade mark context.

Foreseeable consequences of the proposed reforms

Since the proposed section 10(5A) seeks to achieve the goal of providing trade mark proprietors with a legal basis to bring a claim for damages against hosts in appropriate circumstances, if brought into force, the said provision would entail certain consequences that warrant attention. The effect of the proposed section 10(5A) is that it imposes a *duty* on hosts to remove infringing content when they acquire actual knowledge of an infringement, actual knowledge being imputed only upon the service of a notice of infringement. In essence, what this gives rise to is the practice of 'notice and takedown', which is an extrajudicial means of regulating online content.

It has been suggested that the hosting safe harbour afforded under Article 14(1) of the E-Commerce Directive is the motivation behind the practice of notice and takedown.[77] However, this perception is incomplete. Certainly, the

77 See Verbiest T, G Spindler, GM Riccio and A Ven der Perre, *Study on the Liability of Internet Intermediaries* Markt/2006/09/E (2007), 5 and GB Dinwoodie, 'Secondary Liability for Online Trademark Infringement: The International Landscape' (2014) 37 *Columbia Journal of Law and Arts* 463, 499.

safe harbour does play a role in incentivising notice and takedown. However, unless hosts are capable of being held liable in terms of the underlying law, in circumstances where they fail to remove infringing content upon being put on notice, it is less likely that they would give effect to the practice of notice and takedown. This is because only if there is a real threat of liability would hosts react in ways that minimise their risk of becoming exposed to liability. Thus, the real motivation for the practice of notice and takedown on the part of hosts is the *threat* of liability under the underlying law, whereas the promise of conditional immunity conferred by the hosting safe harbour merely adds to such motivation.

Because the proposed section 10(5A) requires hosts to expeditiously remove any infringing content upon acquiring actual knowledge of infringing activity, it is easy to see how the said provision would motivate hosts to implement some form of notice and takedown mechanism. Accordingly, while the proposed section 10(5A) is a useful provision to incorporate, attention must also be placed on the impact of the practice of notice and takedown, in particular on whether such practice could be abused by right holders curtailing both legitimate uses of, and online speech relating to, trade marks. Only then can further reforms be proposed to counteract possible abuses of the practice of notice and takedown, which would be crucial in maintaining a healthy balance between the competing interests.

6 Notice and takedown

Obligating internet intermediaries to remove infringing content upon being notified of its existence, coupled with the promise of conditional immunity, which safe harbours provide, for the expeditious removal of such content, are motivations behind the practice of notice and takedown. Since notice and takedown is an extrajudicial practice, there is potential for it to be abused by right holders, thereby curtailing legitimate uses of trade marks and online speech. In view of this, it is necessary to consider how notice and takedown operates in practice in order to propose further legal reforms aimed at ensuring a healthy balance between the enforcement of trade mark rights and protection of competing interests.

It may seem somewhat odd, in view of this book's trade mark focus, for this chapter to deal with the practice of notice and takedown in the copyright context. Yet this is inevitable because it was the safe harbour introduced by the Digital Millennium Copyright Act 1998 (DMCA)[1] enacted in the US that for the first time gave some legal force and structure to the practice of notice and takedown. As such, scholarship on notice and takedown in the intellectual property context is very much dominated by discourses in the field of copyright. A consideration of these discourses is important in assessing how notice and takedown practices might be operating in the field of trade marks.

The DMCA safe harbour—a legislative response to promote online innovation and speech

The enactment of section 512 of the DMCA[2] two decades ago, commonly referred to as the DMCA safe harbour or simply DMCA 512, could be regarded as a significant milestone in US copyright history. Before the DMCA was enacted, courts in the US had adopted a very aggressive approach towards internet intermediaries as a result of which they were held liable for copyright infringements

1 Title II of the DMCA, i.e. the Online Copyright Infringement Liability Limitation Act, introduced a safe harbour for internet intermediaries that shielded them from copyright liability provided they met certain conditions set out therein.

2 17 USC §512.

on the part of their users even when they had no knowledge of the infringements or did take steps to remove infringing content upon notice. The bulletin board cases that came up in the first half of the 1990s amply illustrate this trend. Bulletin boards were the first forums the internet saw, allowing users to upload and download content. They were intermediaries that provided a platform where users could store and share content, in many ways resembling a modern-day host.

One of the earliest cases to be filed against a bulletin board was *Playboy v Frena*,[3] which came up before the US District Court (Middle District of Florida). Frena operated an internet bulletin board service, which in effect acted as a host for third-party content. The users of the bulletin board service had unlawfully uploaded images in which Playboy Enterprises Inc (PEI) owned the copyright, making the images accessible to, and downloadable by, other users who logged into the service.[4] In effect, PEI's exclusive right to distribute copies of, and display, the copyrighted images to the public[5] was infringed as a result of the acts of the bulletin board's users. It was also in evidence that, upon becoming aware of the infringing images, Frena took immediate steps to remove those images from the service.[6] However, the Court found Frena directly liable for copyright infringement, although Frena had only hosted, and not uploaded, the infringing material in question.[7] In essence, even though Frena through his bulletin board was acting as an intermediary, providing only the technical functions of a host that facilitated subscribers to upload, distribute and display content, the Court felt it fit to find Frena and his bulletin board liable for copyright infringement on the basis that they were primary infringers.[8]

However, the decision in *Playboy v Frena* was doubted in subsequent cases. Thus, in *RTC v Netcom*,[9] which unsurprisingly also concerned a bulletin board service, the US District Court (Northern District of California) had to consider the liability of a party who provided the technical facilities that enabled certain infringing material to be uploaded onto a bulletin board. Commenting on *Playboy v Frena*, the Court observed that it was:

3 *Playboy Enterprises Inc v Frena* 839 F. Supp. 1552 (1993) (*Playboy v Frena*).

4 *Playboy v Frena*, 1554 (Schlesinger J).

5 This is a right conferred on copyright owners under US copyright law, 17 USC §106.

6 *Playboy v Frena*, 1554 (Schlesinger J). In this case, Frena acquired knowledge of the infringing images only upon summons being served. Prior to the service of summons, Frena had no knowledge of the infringements. This was not a case where the aggrieved copyright owner had notified the intermediary about the infringements.

7 *Playboy v Frena*, 1556 (Schlesinger J) ('There is no dispute that Defendant Frena supplied a product containing unauthorized copies of a copyrighted work. It does not matter that Defendant Frena claims he did not make the copies itself').

8 *Playboy v Frena*, 1559 (Schlesinger J):

> There is irrefutable evidence of direct copyright infringement in this case. It does not matter that Defendant Frena may have been unaware of the copyright infringement. Intent to infringe is not needed to find copyright infringement. Intent or knowledge is not an element of infringement, and thus even an innocent infringer is liable for infringement.

9 *Religious Technology Center v Netcom On-line Communication Services Inc* 907 F. Supp. 1361 (1995) (*RTC v Netcom*).

> not entirely convinced that the mere possession of a digital copy on a [bulletin board] that is accessible to some members of the public constitutes direct infringement by the [bulletin board] operator. . . . Only the subscriber should be liable for causing the distribution of plaintiffs' work, as the contributing actions of the [bulletin board service] provider are automatic and indiscriminate.[10]

However, the Court left open the possibility of contributory infringement.[11] Similarly, in *Sega v Maphia*,[12] the US District Court (Northern District of California) held that a bulletin board service dedicated to sharing video games, including games in which Sega owned the copyright, did not attract direct copyright liability,[13] but instead was contributorily liable[14] for infringements on the part of the users.[15] The approach adopted in *RTC v Netcom* and *Sega v Maphia*, in treating bulletin boards as contributory (rather than direct) infringers, has been subsequently applied to other types of intermediaries such as hosts,[16] including typical web-hosts.[17]

Accordingly, although US courts avoided imposing direct copyright liability on internet intermediaries, the general trend was an expansion of the reach of copyright liability through the vessel of contributory infringement. This trend gave rise to debate on how the liability of online actors should be handled, as intermediaries, in particular, were crucial to the development of the internet.

10 *RTC v Netcom*, 1372 (Whyte J).

11 *RTC v Netcom*, 1373 (Whyte J) ('Netcom is not free from liability just because it did not directly infringe plaintiffs' works; it may still be liable as a contributory infringer').

12 *Sega Enterprises Ltd v Maphia* 948 F. Supp. 923 (1996) (*Sega v Maphia*).

13 *Sega v Maphia*, 932 (Wilken J):

> Sega has not shown that Sherman himself uploaded or downloaded the files, or directly caused such uploading or downloading to occur. The most Sega has shown is that Sherman operated his [bulletin board service], that he knew infringing activity was occurring, and that he solicited others to upload games. However, whether Sherman knew his [bulletin board service] users were infringing on Sega's copyright, or encouraged them to do so, has no bearing on whether Sherman directly caused the copying to occur.

14 *Sega v Maphia*, 932 (Wilken J):

> Just because Sherman is not liable for direct infringement, however, does not mean that he is free from liability. Although the Copyright Act does not expressly impose liability on anyone other than direct infringers, courts have long recognized that in certain circumstances, liability for contributory infringement will be imposed.

15 Interestingly, the same judge granted a preliminary injunction against Maphia, during the initial proceedings, on the basis that Maphia had engaged in direct copyright infringement. See *Sega Enterprises Ltd v Maphia* 857 F. Supp. 679 (1994), 686 (Wilken J) ('Sega has established a *prima facie* case of direct copyright infringement'). It appears that Wilken J may have been influenced by the decision in *Playboy v Frena* in granting the preliminary injunction (in 1994) on the basis that Maphia engaged in direct (as well as contributory) copyright infringement, although subsequently when delivering the summary judgment (in 1996) a clear indication was made following *RTC v Netcom* that no direct copyright liability could be imposed on a bulletin board.

16 See e.g. *Perfect 10 Inc v Amazon.com Inc* 508 F.3d 1146 (9th Cir. 2007); *UMG Recordings Inc v Veoh Networks Inc* 667 F.3d 1022, 1041 (9th Cir. 2011).

17 See e.g. *Marobie-FL Inc v National Ass'n of Fire Equipment Distributors* 983 F. Supp. 1167 (1997).

It has been suggested that the willingness of US courts to 'expand the reach of contributory . . . liability in copyright law has led to congressional involvement to *limit* secondary liability'.[18]

In fact, outside the sphere of intellectual property law, section 230 of the Communications Decency Act 1996 was enacted to provide complete immunity to internet intermediaries from civil liability arising out of content originating from third-party users.[19] Despite being criticised for conferring too much immunity to internet intermediaries,[20] section 230 has been hailed as the 'saviour of free speech'.[21] However, the section 230 safe harbour did not seek to 'limit or expand any law pertaining to intellectual property',[22] which meant that it did not address the concerns of intermediaries as regards their liability under intellectual property law.

It was against this backdrop that the US Congress decided to enact section 512 of the DMCA, in terms of which internet intermediaries are afforded conditional immunity from copyright liability. At the time the DMCA was enacted, it was seen as a worthy compromise[23] that balanced the interests of copyright owners and authors or publishers of online content. More importantly, as the Senate Report on the DMCA illustrates, the DMCA was regarded as a crucial legislative intervention to preserve innovation on the internet:

> At the same time, without clarification of their liability, service providers may hesitate to make the necessary investment in the expansion of the

18 M Bartholomew and J Tehranian, 'The Secret Life of Legal Doctrine: The Divergent Evolution of Secondary Liability in Trademark and Copyright Law' (2006) 21 *Berkeley Technology Law Journal* 1363, 1407.

19 47 USC §230(c)(1) ('No provider or user of an interactive computer service shall be treated as the publisher or speaker of any information provided by another information content provider').

20 HB Holland, 'Section 230 of the CDA: Internet Exceptionalism as a Statutory Construct' in B Szoka and A Marcus (eds), *The Next Digital Decade: Essays on the Future of the Internet* (TechFreedom, 2011), 199:

> Even where the online entity is alleged to be aware of the illegal acts of their users, and to be either actively facilitating those illegal acts or refusing to stop them, the intermediary retains Section 230 immunity. . . . Established norms, as expressed through the mechanisms of tort law, are neutralized by Section 230 and its judicial interpretations.

21 See e.g. DS Ardia, 'Free Speech Savior or Shield for Scoundrels: An Empirical Study of Intermediary Immunity under Section 230 of the Communications Decency Act' (2010) 43 *Loyola of Los Angeles Law Review* 373.

22 47 USC §230(e)(2).

23 It was generally felt that conferring conditional immunity to internet intermediaries was a better compromise than offering complete immunity. See BA Lehman, *Intellectual Property and the National Information Infrastructure: The Report of the Working Group on Intellectual Property Rights* (Information Infrastructure Task Force 1995), 123:

> Exempting or reducing the liability of service providers prematurely would choke development, of marketplace tools that could be used to lessen their risk of liability and the risk to copyright owners, including insuring against harm caused by their customers, shifting responsibility for infringement to the infringing subscriber through indemnification and warranty agreements, licensing (including collective license agreements), educating their subscribers about infringement and using technological protections, such as tracking mechanisms.

> speed and capacity of the Internet. In the ordinary course of their operations service providers must engage in all kinds of acts that expose them to potential copyright infringement liability. For example, service providers must make innumerable electronic copies by simply transmitting information over the Internet. Certain electronic copies are made to speed up the delivery of information to users. Other electronic copies are made in order to host World Wide Web sites. Many service providers engage in directing users to sites in response to inquiries by users or they volunteer sites that users may find attractive. Some of these sites might contain infringing material. In short, by limiting the liability of service providers, the DMCA ensures that the efficiency of the Internet will continue to improve and that the variety and quality of services on the Internet will continue to expand.[24]

The argument follows that, by providing a safe harbour to internet intermediaries, technology will flourish enabling greater freedom of speech on the internet. However, despite these optimistic undertones, the manner in which the DMCA safe harbour operates may be proof of the contrary, i.e. that the DMCA stifles both innovation and freedom of speech. The next part of this chapter considers how the DMCA safe harbour has given rise to the practice of notice and takedown, as well as the criticisms that surround this practice.

DMCA and the practice of notice and takedown

The DMCA safe harbour applies to four categories of activities that intermediaries engage in, namely, the provision of internet access,[25] system caching,[26] hosting[27] and navigation (i.e. indexing and hyperlinking).[28] It must be noted that section 512 of the DMCA shares similarities with its counterpart in the EU, i.e. Articles 12–15 of the E-Commerce Directive,[29] although certain notable differences do exist. Therefore, some of the observations made concerning the DMCA safe harbour apply to the context of the EU, as well as to the UK, at least until domestic law that implements the E-Commerce Directive is replaced or modified post-Brexit.[30]

24 Senate Report 105–190 on the Digital Millennium Copyright Act, 105th Congress, 2nd Session (1998) (Senate Report on the DMCA), 8.
25 17 USC §512(a).
26 17 USC §512(b).
27 17 USC §512(c).
28 17 USC §512(d).
29 Directive 2000/31/EC on Certain Legal Aspects of Information Society Services, in Particular Electronic Commerce, in the Internal Market [2000] OJ L 178/1 (E-Commerce Directive).
30 The Electronic Commerce (EC Directive) Regulations 2002, SI 2002/2013, transposes the EU safe harbour into UK law.

ISPs and system caching

As in the case of Article 12(1) of the E-Commerce Directive, the DMCA provides complete immunity to ISPs, provided that (1) the transmission carrying any infringing content is initiated by a third party, (2) the carrying of content is an automatic technical process, (3) the recipients of the content are not selected by the service provider, (4) the transient storage of content does not allow access to anyone other than the anticipated recipients and is not maintained for a period longer than what is reasonably necessary for the transmission, routing or provision of connections, and (5) the service provider does not modify the content in the course of providing the service.[31] This aspect of the safe harbour is uncontroversial and does not lead to any notice and takedown practices. Essentially, this is because the DMCA does not impose any positive obligation, such as the removal of infringing content, for ISPs to claim eligibility to the safe harbour. The safe harbour applies automatically to all neutral and passive ISPs that satisfy the conditions stated above.

Just as with Article 13(1) of the E-Commerce Directive, the DMCA provides conditional immunity to intermediaries that engage in system caching. Caching increases the efficiency of internet transmissions.[32] Thus, when content is made available by a third party, to be transmitted via an ISP's system or network and the storage of third-party content for caching is done automatically through a technical process,[33] then a service provider that is required to cache content is provided immunity from liability on the fulfilment of certain conditions.[34] These conditions include the implementation of notice and takedown whereby copyright owners may inform service providers of the availability of cached infringing content, upon which the service provider must expeditiously remove, or disable access to, such content, provided that the notice also includes a confirmation that either the content has been removed at its source or a competent court has ordered its removal.[35] This type of notice and takedown is not controversial as the notice received by the service provider only needs to be acted upon when the infringing content has been removed at its source by the host, or after a court has independently determined that the content is infringing. This means that, by the time an intermediary reacts to a notice received under this limb of the DMCA safe harbour, the content has already been removed at the source making caching redundant, or a court has already made a determination about the legality or otherwise of the content in question.

Hosts and navigation providers

Hosts perform a crucial, yet more controversial, role in connecting content with internet users. Unlike the provision of internet access (which merely connects

31 17 USC §512(a) (1)–(5).
32 See Senate Report on the DMCA, above n24, 42.
33 17 USC §512(b)(1)(A)–(C).
34 17 USC §512(b)(2)(A)–(E).
35 17 USC §512(b)(2)(E).

users to the internet) and caching (which is an automatic technical process invisible to internet users), hosts play a more significant and direct role in making online content available to internet users. It is for this reason that copyright owners, and indeed proprietors of other intellectual property rights, contend that hosts should play a greater role in keeping the internet free from infringing material. This attitude is visible in the way the DMCA safe harbour is structured.

For the hosting safe harbour to apply, a host must fulfil certain prescribed conditions. First, a host must not possess actual knowledge[36] of an infringement, and in the absence of actual knowledge, must not have been aware of any facts or circumstances[37] from which such infringement is apparent. Second, upon acquiring actual knowledge or awareness of the infringement, in particular, through a notice of infringement,[38] a host must take steps to remove the infringing content expeditiously.[39] Third, a host must not derive any direct financial benefit from the infringing activity in circumstances where the host has the right and ability to control such infringing activity.[40]

The DMCA's approach in relation to navigation providers, or 'information location tools' as they are referred to in the DMCA, diverges from that of the E-Commerce Directive, in that the former expressly deals with the conduct of this class of intermediaries. Accordingly, the rules applicable to hosts apply to navigation providers with only one change: it would suffice for the navigation provider to remove hyperlinks to infringing content or websites, upon receiving a notice of infringement, or otherwise gaining knowledge or awareness of the infringement.[41]

However, unlike the removal of cached content, the practice of notice and takedown adopted by hosts and navigation providers requires the removal of alleged infringing content, or hyperlinks to such content, based on information provided in a notice of infringement[42] served by a copyright owner. This requires the host or navigation provider to determine the validity of the copyright owner's claim, which determination has to be made in a manner that would facilitate the intermediary to *expeditiously* remove or disable access to such content, a condition that needs to be fulfilled in order to benefit from the safe harbour. It is this aspect of the practice of notice and takedown that is most controversial. After all, the safe harbour calls upon a private intermediary to remove or disable access to alleged infringing content based *solely* on a claim made by a copyright owner, the very individual seeking the takedown. Although the party whose interests are

36 17 USC §512(c)(1)(A)(i).

37 17 USC §512(c)(1)(A)(ii).

38 17 USC §512(c)(1)(C).

39 17 USC §512(c)(1)(A)(iii). This aspect of the DMCA safe harbour is identical to the safe harbour afforded to hosts by Article 14(1) of the E-Commerce Directive.

40 17 USC §512(c)(1)(B).

41 17 USC §512(d). The Senate Report on the DMCA (above n24) has provided an explanation on how notice and takedown operates in respect of navigation providers (at p. 48).

42 The elements of an effective notice of infringement are set out in section 512(c)(3) of the DMCA.

affected by the removal of content has the opportunity to file a counter-notice, this can only be done *after* the intermediary has executed the takedown.[43]

While this extrajudicial remedy is useful in order to keep pace with the speed and spread of the internet, the procedural fairness, transparency and accountability of the practice have been called into question. Although it is contended that the DMCA safe harbour was introduced to ensure the growth of the internet, by shielding intermediaries against liability, the notice and takedown aspect of the safe harbour may, in fact, be constraining the free flow of information, the very purpose for which the internet was built and continues to develop. The potential impact of notice and takedown practices on the dissemination of *legitimate* content on the internet has been set out in the following terms:

> [W]hile a notice-and-takedown system is one way to prevent intermediaries from actively engaging in or encouraging unlawful behaviour on their services, it is subject to abuse by both State and private actors. Users who are notified by the service provider that their content has been flagged as unlawful often have little recourse or few resources to challenge the takedown. Moreover, given that intermediaries may still be held financially or in some cases criminally liable if they do not remove content upon receipt of notification by users regarding unlawful content, they are inclined to err on the side of safety by over-censoring potentially illegal content. Lack of transparency in the intermediaries' decision-making process also often obscures discriminatory practices or political pressure affecting the companies' decisions.[44]

Although such assertions are made against the practice of notice and takedown, very few researchers have focussed on gathering empirical evidence to verify these claims. The few empirical studies conducted in the past provide some useful insights into the potential abuse of notice and takedown. These studies are considered below.

The abuse of notice and takedown—the empirical evidence

The Liberty Study, conducted by researchers at the Oxford Centre for Socio-Legal Studies,[45] and the Multatuli Study, initiated by Bits of Freedom, a non-profit organisation based in Amsterdam,[46] as well as individual academics such as Jenifer

43 17 USC §512(g)(2)(B) and (C).

44 FL Rue, *Report of the Special Rapporteur on the Promotion and Protection of the Right to Freedom of Opinion and Expression* A/HRC/17/27 (2011), para 42 (citations omitted).

45 See C Ahlert, C Marsden and C Yung, *How 'Liberty' Disappeared from Cyberspace: The Mystery Shopper Tests Internet Content Self-Regulation* (2004) <http://pcmlp.socleg.ox.ac.uk/sites/pcmlp.socleg.ox.ac.uk/files/liberty.pdf> (accessed 31 January 2019).

46 See S Nas, *The Multatuli Project: ISP Notice & Take Down* (2004) <www-old.bof.nl/docs/researchpaper SANE.pdf> (accessed 31 January 2019).

Urban and Laura Quilter (the Urban–Quilter Study),[47] have investigated the practical application of notice and takedown. The objective of these studies was to determine whether the practice of notice and takedown is abused by right holders leading to the suppression of online speech and legitimate online activity.

The Liberty Study

The primary objective of the Liberty Study 'was to gather data to illustrate the reality of [notice and takedown]. In particular . . . to see how easily [notice and takedown] can be abused, beyond theoretical speculations.'[48] In other words, what this study proposed to do was to provide validation for the criticisms levelled against the practice of notice and takedown.

In order to achieve the objective described above, the researchers picked two ISPs, one operating in the US and the other operating in the UK, which in addition to providing internet access also provided hosting services. The researchers, utilising the hosting services offered by the two ISPs, posted material where the copyright term had indisputably expired in both the US and the UK (copyright-expired material) on websites hosted by the respective ISPs. Thus, while the DMCA safe harbour applied to the US-based ISP, Article 14(1) of the E-Commerce Directive applied to the ISP operating in the UK. Once the copyright-expired material was uploaded, the researchers posed as copyright owners and filed a false complaint with the respective ISPs to assess their reactions and recorded the reaction timelines as well. If notice and takedown practices were functioning effectively, the copyright-expired material uploaded by the researchers ought not to have been removed by the ISPs.

Insofar as the US-based ISP was concerned, the sequence of events was as follows. In early August 2003, the copyright-expired material was posted on a website made available by the ISP to its users enabling them to publish content. This was followed by three notices of infringement being sent to the ISP between 30 August and 2 September falsely alleging copyright infringement. On 8 September, the ISP responded by seeking further information required to form a valid complaint under section 512 of the DMCA. On 17 September, the researchers received a response from the ISP stating that the website would only be removed if the complainant provides, under penalty of perjury, accurate information sufficient to constitute a valid notice of infringement. At that point, correspondence was discontinued.[49] The researchers concluded that the study had shown that the US-based ISP followed the procedure laid down in the DMCA with precision and did not act before it had received a notice of

47 See JM Urban and L Quilter, 'Efficient Process or "Chilling Effects"? Takedown Notices under Section 512 of the Digital Millennium Copyright Act' (2006) 22 *Santa Clara Computer and High-Technology Law Journal* 621.

48 Ahlert et al, above n45, 17.

49 Ahlert et al, above n45, 19.

infringement that was sufficiently detailed and complied with the requirements for such notices set out in the DMCA.

In contrast, the response of the ISP operating in the UK was far less cautious. The copyright-expired material was uploaded onto a free website hosted by the ISP on 9 November 2003. Subsequently, on 14 November, a notice of infringement was sent to the ISP by the researchers posing as the complainant. A day later, the copyright-expired material was removed by the ISP without there being any further correspondence between the ISP and the researchers.[50]

In sum, based on identical factual scenarios, while the US-based ISP refused to remove the copyright-expired material that it hosted without the notice of infringement being compliant with the DMCA's requirements, the UK-based ISP removed the copyright-expired material without verifying the validity of the claim. Since the E-Commerce Directive (as implemented in the UK), arguably, shaped the reaction of the UK-based ISP, it may be reasonable to suggest that ISPs operating in other EU member states might react the same way. Accordingly, the researchers concluded that 'the ISP in the UK, and probably likewise in other member states, has a high propensity to remove a website without careful examination of the content'.[51]

It must be noted, however, that the E-Commerce Directive differs from the DMCA safe harbour in an important way. That is, the E-Commerce Directive does not provide a structured approach to notice and takedown as in the case of the DMCA safe harbour. Although Articles 12(1) and 13(1) of the E-Commerce Directive, dealing with typical ISPs and system caching, to some extent resemble sections 512(a) and (b) of the DMCA, respectively, Article 14(1), which applies to hosts, varies significantly from the corresponding provision in the DMCA (i.e. section 512 (c)). Accordingly, although both the US and EU safe harbours require hosts to remove infringing content upon acquiring actual knowledge or awareness of an infringement, the E-Commerce Directive does not expressly provide for a formalised system for notice and takedown, such as prescribing the mandatory requirements that a notice of infringement must comply with before a host becomes obligated to act.[52] It is perhaps the absence of such specific guidelines in the case of the E-Commerce Directive that has led to notice and takedown being practised in the manner demonstrated by the Liberty Study. This finding is further corroborated by the Multatuli Study carried out in the Netherlands.

The Multatuli Study

The Multatuli Study was limited to investigating the notice and takedown practices of ten Dutch ISPs, in their capacity as hosts. As in the Liberty Study,

50 Ahlert et al, above n45, 24.

51 Ahlert et al, above n45, 26.

52 See JM Moreno, 'Publisher or Technical Provider? Monitoring as Editorial Control and the "Safe Harbor" of Art.14 E-Commerce Directive' (2013) 49 *Jura Falconis* 663, 671. A more comprehensive analysis of the E-Commerce Directive and its provisions was provided in Chapter 4.

copyright-expired material was deliberately published on websites hosted by these ISPs. The work in question, which was uploaded onto the websites provided by the ISPs, was authored in 1871 by Eduard Douwes Dekker, better known by his pen name, Multatuli. To add some reality to the context of the experiment, the copyright-expired material was posted under the name of Johan de Ruyter, who had a copyright dispute with Dekker over some other work in 1860.[53] Once the copyright-expired material was uploaded, the researchers began the experiment by sending a notice of infringement to the ISPs under the name 'E.D. Dekkers society', which posed as the copyright owner. Even though seven of the ten ISPs removed the copyright-expired material without questioning the validity of the notice of infringement sent to them, their responses varied in terms of timing.[54] The results are summarised in the table below.

Amongst the three ISPs that did not remove the copyright-expired material, one ignored the complaint (Freeler), whereas the other two did respond (UPC and XS4ALL).[55] UPC responded by stating that it did not proceed to remove the alleged infringing material because the complainant's identity was not verified to the satisfaction of the service provider.[56] XS4ALL was the only service provider that had actually taken time to consider the nature of the material posted on the website to find that copyright in fact did not subsist in the work.[57]

Table 6.1 A timeline of the Multatuli Study

Name of ISP/host	*Response time for content removal*	*Additional comments (as set out in the Multatuli Study)*
Yourhosting	3 hours	The service provider took all the arguments in the notice of infringement for granted, and reported verbally to its subscriber over the phone that the infringement was 'a fact'. In its email it said, '[w]e are obliged to do this after we have been notified of an alleged criminal act'. Surprisingly, it also added '[n]ormally we only take materials off-line if we receive a written notification with proof, but in this case we have made an exception'.
Tiscali	24 hours	The website was replaced with a notice referring to the service's general terms and conditions. This was so even though Tiscali normally gave subscribers 48 hours to remove alleged unlawful content. Tiscali never forwarded the details of the notice of infringement to its subscriber.

(continued)

53 Nas, above n46, see text under heading 'The Takedown Test'.
54 Nas, above n46, see discussion under 'The Results'.
55 Nas, above n46, see discussion under 'The Results'.
56 Nas, above n46, see discussion under 'The Results'.
57 Nas, above n46, see discussion under 'The Results'.

Table 6.1 (continued)

Name of ISP/host	*Response time for content removal*	*Additional comments (as set out in the Multatuli Study)*
iFast	48 hours (within 24 hours from receiving a second complaint)	The service provider upon receiving the notice of infringement forwarded the subscriber's contact details to the complainant, requesting the complainant to contact the subscriber directly. The subscriber was thus contacted directly although iFast was copied into the correspondence. Thereafter, upon a subsequent notice of infringement threatening legal action, the material was promptly removed.
Planet Internet Demon	48 hours from receiving the questionnaire (which was sent after the letter of complaint)	Once the notice of infringement was received at the service provider's general abuse email address, the complainant in return was asked to complete a questionnaire, which sought more accurate information about the infringement. When the questionnaire was returned with identical information made available in the original notice, both service providers removed the material without further questioning. It appears that the service providers did not even consider the information provided in the questionnaire before taking steps to remove the alleged infringing material.
LaDot	3 days	The service provider notified the subscriber about the notice of infringement and required the subscriber to provide evidence that the copyright-expired material was published with permission, and that failure to do so would result in the material being removed within 28 hours. The service provider also took steps to inform the complainant that it would not be in a position to determine a copyright dispute in the event the subscriber furnishes sufficient proof that the material was published with the necessary permission, and in that event, it would be advisable for the complainant to take appropriate legal action. Ultimately, the website containing the copyright-expired material was removed (it is unclear, however, whether the team of researchers responded to the service provider by providing evidence of the status of the copyright-expired material).
Wanadoo	10 days	Although this service provider acted fast to warn the subscriber about the notice of infringement and gave 24 hours to remove the alleged infringing content, adding that the subscriber 'had without permission placed a text' on the website, the service provider failed to remove the material in question. Only after a second notice of infringement was sent (ten days later) did the service provider remove the copyright-expired material. The subscriber never received the full notice of infringement.

Thus, based on these findings it was concluded that '[i]t only takes a Hotmail account to bring a website down, and freedom of speech stands no chance in front of the cowboy-style private ISP justice'.[58] These results demonstrate that notice and takedown practices of EU-based intermediaries could easily be abused, with the lack of sufficient procedural guidance in the E-Commerce Directive only making the situation worse. In contrast, the DMCA safe harbour, which provides a more detailed and structured procedure that needs to be followed in the implementation of notice and takedown practices, may increase consistency and reduce potential abuse, as demonstrated by the Liberty Study.

The Urban–Quilter Study

The study carried out by Urban and Quilter was specific to the operation of the DMCA's safe harbour in which takedown notices received by Google and other self-reported notices in the period between January 2002 and August 2004 were analysed. Of the 876 notices considered, 734 were notices of infringement received by Google (the Google notices), and the remaining 142 were self-reported notices, i.e. from individuals who had received a notice of infringement most likely from their service provider.[59] These notices were retrieved from the Chilling Effects database (now known as the Lumen database), which maintains a database of notices received by internet intermediaries and individuals.[60]

Given the size of the dataset used and the different limbs of the DMCA under which notices could be served, the statistical data generated by this study was complex. Mostert and Schwimmer, however, have provided a useful summary of the findings of the Urban–Quilter Study: 9 per cent of all notices were statutorily insufficient (defective),[61] 30 per cent presented obvious questions better suited for resolution in a court of law and 57 per cent of the notices were filed against competitors.[62] According to Urban and Quilter these findings 'comprise a rather negative snapshot of the ways in which the § 512 process is being used, and reveal little benefit to some of the constituencies it was intended to support'.[63]

58 Nas, above n46, see discussion under 'Conclusion'.

59 Urban and Quilter, above n47, 641. Urban and Quilter have pointed out that the self-reported notice may be skewed 'towards the substantively flawed; it seems plausible that individuals who have a strong defense (or at least believe there is a strong defense) are more likely to submit their notices to the Chilling Effects database' (at p. 462).

60 See www.chillingeffects.org (accessed 31 January 2019) or https://lumendatabase.org (accessed 31 January 2019).

61 These notices did not comply with the requirements set out in the DMCA, 17 USC §512(c)(3)(A)(i)–(vi).

62 FW Mostert and MB Schwimmer, 'Notice and Takedown for Trademarks' (2011) 101 *Trademark Reporter* 249, 259–60.

63 Urban and Quilter, above n47, 623.

While the above figures arguably suggest that notice and takedown may be utilised in a vexatious and frivolous manner, that alone cannot be taken to suggest that the practice in itself is flawed. In fact, caution must be exercised before adopting the findings of the Urban–Quilter Study.[64] To begin with, approximately 83 per cent of the notices considered in the study were Google notices, i.e. notices received by Google from right holders aggrieved by content either hosted or indexed by Google. However, simply because Google followed the practice of voluntarily sending all notices it received to the Chilling Effects database, that does not necessarily mean that the content to which those notices related had *in fact* been removed by Google. While the database records the receipt of notices of infringement by participating intermediaries, it does not provide more information in relation to whether the notices resulted in an actual takedown. In other words, nothing in the Urban–Quilter Study, insofar as the Google notices are concerned, indicated with certainty whether Google, as an intermediary, resorted to removing content that was legitimate or non-infringing. If the evidence did indicate such a practice on the part of Google, however, that would be a reason for significant concern.

In contrast, the self-reported notices, albeit smaller in number, might have presented a better sample to determine whether intermediaries practised notice and takedown in a manner that raised concerns for the protection of free speech and fair use on the internet. The DMCA requires service providers to forward notices of infringement received by them to the relevant subscriber responsible for creating and uploading the alleged infringing content immediately after its removal.[65] This means that, by the time a person self-reported a notice of infringement to the Chilling Effects database, the service provider responsible for hosting the content would have already removed the content to which the notice related.[66]

One of the key problems revealed by the Urban–Quilter Study is that of right holders adopting the practice of sending notices of infringement even where there was a significant likelihood for a finding of no infringement. In this regard, the study concluded that there were questions relating to the underlying copyright claim, 'including fair use defenses, other substantive defenses, very thin copyright, or non-copyrightable subject matter', in 31 per cent of *all section 512(c) and (d)*

64 Urban and Quilter themselves admit that they have approached the dataset used for their research with caution (Urban and Quilter, above n47, 642–43). See also Mostert and Schwimmer, above n62, 278.

65 17 USC §512(g)(2)(A).

66 This is assuming that the self-reported notices considered in the study had been submitted to the Chilling Effects database by individuals who had received them from their respective service providers. After all, notices that were submitted to the database could have also been cease and desist letters that were sent by right holders directly to the party responsible for the content giving rise to an alleged infringement. Unfortunately, Urban and Quilter (above n47) do not provide any clarity in this regard, and merely indicate that the self-reported notices are submitted to the database 'usually by recipients' (at p. 641).

notices,[67] which included both Google and self-reported notices.[68] This is no doubt a significant percentage, almost a third of the total dataset. However, this figure does not distinguish between the Google and self-reported notices, even though this distinction is crucial for the reasons stated above. Once that distinction is made, however, it was observed that 209 Google notices had at least one substantive flaw in the underlying copyright claim, while 43 self-reported notices came under this category.[69] Thus, assuming that none of the Google notices resulted in a takedown of content, while also assuming that all the self-reported notices did result in takedowns, approximately *5 per cent of the total notices considered in the study* would have resulted in takedowns despite the underlying claims having issues.[70] On the other hand, assuming that all Google notices did result in content being removed, while maintaining the same assumption for the self-reported notices, then approximately *29 per cent, i.e. 252 of the 876 notices considered in the study*,[71] would have resulted in takedowns despite there being issues with the underlying copyright claim. Therefore, the percentage of notices that resulted in actual takedowns despite there being issues with the underlying copyright claim can be anywhere between 5 per cent and 29 per cent, *when the entire dataset is considered*. This is a fairly large uncertainty, and therefore too much reliance cannot be placed on this study to determine the extent to which the practice of notice and takedown leads to erroneous takedowns of lawful content.

There are further issues with the study. Since the Urban–Quilter Study relied on data from the Chilling Effects database, the researchers were not able to document instances where counter-notices had been filed resulting in access to content being restored. Under the DMCA safe harbour, once an intermediary removes alleged infringing content and forwards the notice of infringement to the party aggrieved by the takedown, that party has the opportunity of filing a counter-notice consequent to which the content taken down must be restored by the intermediary in not fewer than ten but no more than 14 business days.[72]

67 Of the 876 notices considered in the Urban–Quilter Study, notices categorised under section 512(a) and multiple sections of the DMCA amounted to fewer than 100. There were no notices under section 512(b). All remaining notices were under sections 512(c) and (d) (Urban and Quilter, above n47, 642 (Fig.1)). Unfortunately, neither Fig.1 nor anything else stated in the publication reporting the study sheds any light on the actual number of the section 512(c) and (d) notices considered.

68 Urban and Quilter, above n47, 667.

69 Urban and Quilter, above n47, 667.

70 This calculation is based on the assumption that *all* of the self-reported notices with issues, i.e. 43 of the 876 notices considered in the study, amounting to approximately 5 per cent of *all* notices, would have resulted in content being removed. By the time an individual self-reported a notice to the Chilling Effects database, it is likely that the intermediary or service provider concerned had already removed the content in question. Of course, this assumption is subject to the limitation set out in n66 above.

71 This calculation is made by adding the number of Google and self-reported notices with at least one substantive flaw (i.e. 209 and 43 respectively, adding up to 252). As a percentage of the *total* notices considered in the study (i.e. 876), notices with at least one substantive flaw amounted to approximately 29 per cent.

72 17 USC §512(g)(2)(B) and (C).

Unfortunately, the dataset considered in the Urban–Quilter Study does not include counter-notices and therefore does not account for any content that may have been restored consequent to a counter-notice. In these circumstances, where content may have been taken down in cases where the underlying claim had issues, any action on the part of the intermediary restoring access to that content would have remedied any difficulty arising from an erroneous takedown. This is an important factor that must be considered if a more accurate perception of the practice of notice and takedown is to be provided.[73]

Academic commentaries on the abuse of notice and takedown

The Urban–Quilter Study considered a limited dataset. Since the Chilling Effects/Luman database is built on data submitted through the *voluntary* participation of intermediaries and individuals, the database may not present a holistic account of how notice and takedown is practised, as only a limited number of the vast amounts of notices of infringement may be getting reported. Nevertheless, the database does provide a useful insight.

Commentators who have criticised the DMCA often begin with accounts of real-life examples where content had been removed without justification, demonstrating that takedowns do take place notwithstanding genuine issues with the underlying copyright claim. The removal of a YouTube video of students protesting for a free Tibet[74] and the removal of several video clips from the YouTube channel associated with the 2008 John McCain US presidential election campaign[75] are two notable examples. Relying on these recorded incidents of legitimate content being removed and the findings of the Urban–Quilter Study, Seltzer[76] and Wilson[77] have suggested that the practice of notice and takedown

73 A similar critique was made against both the Liberty and Multatuli studies, suggesting that an assessment of how intermediaries deal with counter-notices is required before a study is able to represent 'the true situation' about notice and takedown. See T Moore and R Clayton, 'The Impact of Incentives on Notice and Takedown' in E Johnson (ed), *Managing Information Risk and the Economics of Security* (Springer 2008), 203.

74 See B Wilson, 'Notice, Takedown, and the Good Faith Standard: How to Protect Internet Users from Bad-Faith Removal of Web Content' (2009) 29 *Saint Louis University Public Law Review* 613, 615 (in this example, the sender of the notice of infringement was the International Olympic Committee (IOC), although theYouTube video had no connection with any material associated with the Beijing Olympics or the IOC).

75 W Seltzer, 'Free Speech Unmoored in Copyright's Safe Harbor: Chilling Effects of the DMCA on the First Amendment' (2010) 24 *Harvard Journal of Law & Technology* 171, 173 (in this example, several US news companies served notices of infringement on YouTube claiming that their copyright had been infringed, although the videos merely used snippets of TV programmes on which political issues were discussed, a classic example of fair use). See also J Adler, 'The Public's Burden in a Digital Age: Pressures on Intermediaries and the Privatization of Internet Censorship' (2011) 20 *Journal of Law and Policy* 231, 247.

76 Seltzer, above n75, 173.

77 Wilson, above n74, 615.

hinders, rather than promotes, free speech. Adler makes the same claim, albeit her work did not cite the Urban–Quilter Study.[78] Having noted that '[f]ederal law, through copyright and the DMCA, is responsible for this restriction on Internet speech',[79] Seltzer provided the following explanation regarding the DMCA's incentive structure:

> While the DMCA does not force service providers to avail themselves of its harbor, it does shape their risk assessment. As a result, almost all service providers take advantage of the safe harbor, even in cases where objectively no harbor appears necessary. The DMCA is at least partially to blame for this inclination on the part of service providers to take advantage of the safe harbor.[80]

In essence, the threat of liability under copyright law, coupled with the promise of conditional immunity under the DMCA, has reshaped the manner in which intermediaries assess risk, their conduct with respect to the practice of notice and takedown being motivated by the desire to avoid litigation and liability under the law. Under such an incentive structure, intermediaries are likely to err in favour of caution, with the possibility of legitimate content being removed without proper investigation.

The potential for erroneous takedowns is likely to be much greater in areas where complex legal principles, such as fair use in the copyright context,[81] have to be applied in order to determine the legality or otherwise of content. This raises an important point. That is, just as much as the law applicable *to* intermediaries in determining their liability, the body of law applied *by* intermediaries in determining the legality of content residing on their platforms influences the practice of notice and takedown. Take the example of child pornography, which is outlawed in most jurisdictions. Under US federal law, for instance, 'child pornography' is defined as 'any visual depiction of a minor[82] engaging in sexually explicit conduct',[83] where 'sexually explicit conduct' is defined as 'sexual intercourse, bestiality, masturbation, sadistic or masochistic abuse or lascivious exhibition of the genitals or pubic area of any person'.[84] Thus, where an intermediary is required to determine whether content relating to child pornography resides on its platform, the law lays down a precise definition of the outlawed content, enabling its removal without much difficulty.[85]

78 Adler, above n75, 247.
79 Seltzer, above n75, 175.
80 Seltzer, above n75, 193.
81 Adler, above n75, 247.
82 18 USC §2256(1).
83 18 USC §2256(8).
84 18 USC §2256(2)(A).
85 The general immunity afforded to internet intermediaries under section 230 of the Communications Decency Act 1996 (47 USC §230) for the transmission of unlawful content originating from third parties does not extend to liability under criminal law.

In contrast, where an intermediary is required to determine whether content residing on its platform infringes someone's copyright, a multitude of factors will have to be considered by the intermediary. These factors include relatively straightforward matters such as the ownership and subsistence of copyright, as well as highly subjective and context-specific questions about substantial copying and the application of the fair use defence. For instance, in determining fair use, the law requires an assessment of the following factors: (1) the purpose and character of the use, (2) whether the use was for a non-commercial or educational purpose, (3) the nature of the work, (4) the amount and substantiality of copying, and (5) the effect of such use on the potential market for or value of the work.[86] Accordingly, it is not too difficult to see how determining the legality of content under copyright law could be a much more complex exercise than under laws outlawing child pornography. Thus, notice and takedown may work better for certain areas of the law, while not in others. Generally, the practice of notice and takedown is more pragmatic where the distinction between what is legal and not is intelligible and is clearly codified under the law.[87]

The criticisms against notice and takedown must be assessed against several other provisions of the DMCA safe harbour. First, the counter-notice and restoration mechanism under the DMCA must be considered. Although an intermediary is not generally liable for taking down content in *good faith* pursuant to a notice of infringement,[88] such protection is only available if it complies with section 512(g)(2) of the DMCA,[89] which provides that the intermediary must forward the takedown notice to the relevant subscriber after the removal of the impugned content. Thereafter, the subscriber has the option of serving a counter-notice, upon which the content must be restored in not fewer than ten and no more than 14 business days. Even so, critics have suggested that a lay-off period of almost two weeks is far too long and does not provide much assurance for the protection of free speech. Take, for instance, the removal of political speech from YouTube associated with the 2008 McCain US presidential election campaign. The videos that were removed by YouTube remained offline for over a week. In such circumstances, the counter-notice and restoration mechanism may have been of no use at all, because 'the public begins to concentrate on elections only in the weeks immediately before they are held'.[90] Thus, despite the assurances of a possible restoration of content, often content stays offline at times when its presence would have made the most impact, thus legitimising the concerns posited by free speech advocates.

86 17 USC §107.

87 The benefits of codifying content or conduct into legitimate and illegitimate zones could not only benefit internet intermediaries, but also the more traditional actors in the offline world, such as libraries. See e.g. E Hudson, 'Implementing Fair Use in Copyright Law: Lessons from Australia' (2013) 25 *Intellectual Property Journal* 201. Even the media industry employs a code to categorise content in order to advise viewers—broadcasting codes of the Australia Communications and Media Authority and UK's Ofcom are examples.

88 17 USC §512(g)(1).

89 17 USC §512(g)(2).

90 Seltzer, above n75, 173 (citation omitted).

Second, a consideration of section 512(f) of the DMCA, which provides that any person who ***knowingly materially misrepresents*** facts in a notice of infringement or counter-notice may be held liable for ***any damages, including costs and attorneys' fees***, incurred by the party aggrieved by such misrepresentation, is warranted.[91] Although this is a provision that aims to safeguard intermediaries and their subscribers against the abusive conduct of copyright owners, critics have suggested that the safeguard is limited.[92] To begin with, an intermediary misdirected to remove content is less likely to file an action against the party misrepresenting. For one thing, the removal of content is unlikely to cause any damage to the intermediary, save to its reputation as a service provider. For another, the cost of litigating is likely to disincentivise any legal action by the intermediary. The burden falls squarely on the subscriber, whose content was taken down without a legal basis, to pursue necessary legal action.[93] It appears, however, that the evidentiary burden of establishing that a notice of infringement was served in bad faith is difficult to discharge,[94] because it requires the aggrieved party to establish a negative, i.e. that the party seeking the removal of content had *not* formed a *subjective* good-faith belief when serving the notice on the intermediary. Moreover, the phrase 'any damage' in section 512(f) has been interpreted narrowly,[95] significantly limiting the utility of the safeguard.[96]

Despite these criticisms, however, the empirical evidence, as supplied by the Liberty and Multatuli studies, suggests that the DMCA safe harbour provides for a more cautious and better-regulated approach vis-à-vis the approach adopted under the EU E-Commerce Directive. The laxity in the practice of notice and

91 17 USC §512(f).

92 Seltzer, above n75, 224.

93 Cases where section 512(f) of the DMCA (17 USC §512(f)) was successfully invoked are few. See e.g. *Online Policy Group v Diebold Inc* 337 F. Supp. 2d 1195 (2004); *Lenz v Universal Music Corp*, 572 F. Supp. 2d 1150 (2008).

94 It appears that establishing that a party knowingly made a material misrepresentation is a fairly heightened burden. See e.g. *Rossi v Motion Picture Association of America* 391 F.3d 1000 (9th Cir. 2004); *Dudnikov v MGA Entertainment* 410 F.Supp.2d 1010 (2005); *Lenz v Universal Music Corp* 815 F.3d 1145, 1154 (2016) (Tallman J):

> To be clear, if a copyright holder ignores or neglects our unequivocal holding that it must consider fair use before sending a takedown notification, it is liable for damages under § 512(f). *If, however, a copyright holder forms a subjective good faith belief the allegedly infringing material does not constitute fair use, we are in no position to dispute the copyright holder's belief even if we would have reached the opposite conclusion.*
>
> (emphasis added)

Wilson (above n74, 617) has argued that 'the proper standard for sending a takedown notification is for copyright owners to conduct an initial review of the website sufficient to form a good-faith belief' and that 'courts should allocate the burden of proving the copyright owner's good-faith belief on the copyright owner, not on the Internet user').

95 *Lenz v Universal Music Corp* No C 07–3783 JF, 2010 WL 702466 (N.D.Cal. Feb. 25, 2010), *10–11 (Fogel J).

96 I Rubenstrunk, 'The Throw Down Over Takedowns: An Analysis of the *Lenz* Interpretation of 17 U.S.C. §512(F)' (2011) 10 *John Marshall Review of Intellectual Property Law* 792, 802–03.

takedown adopted by EU-based intermediaries may be explained in view of this difference. Notably, provisions that provide for a counter-notice and restoration mechanism and for the liability of parties that misrepresent facts are conspicuously absent in the E-Commerce Directive.

Implications for the trade mark context

It may be posited that two factors have motivated, if not influenced, the practice of notice and takedown. The first is the *threat* of liability under the substantive law applicable *to* internet intermediaries. The second factor is the *promise* of immunity afforded by safe harbours that obligate intermediaries to remove, or disable access to, unlawful content upon notice. In the UK, as well as in the other EU member states, the national implementation of the E-Commerce Directive satisfies the second factor by providing part of the incentive for the practice of notice and takedown, i.e. the promise of immunity. However, insofar as the UK is concerned, unlike in the copyright context, internet intermediaries do not face a real threat of liability either under statutory trade mark law[97] or the common-law principles on accessorial liability.[98] However, if the proposal made in Chapter 5 to expand the scope of the trade mark infringement action is given legal effect, this would provide the necessary incentive for the practice of notice and takedown in the trade mark context.

While the threat of liability and promise of immunity combine to provide the impetus for the practice of notice and takedown, these factors alone do not sufficiently explain why the practice is implemented without adequate investigation as to the legitimacy of the underlying claims that seek the removal of alleged infringing content. In turn, it would be reasonable to posit that the laxity in the manner in which notice and takedown is implemented would lead to the extrajudicial remedy being abused by right holders. Whether it is abusive conduct or simply overzealous enforcement of intellectual property rights on the part of right holders, albeit with a genuine belief of entitlement to do so, the ultimate consequence of the removal of content, without a thorough investigation, is the suppression of competing interests, including free speech.

There is also a third factor that potentially influences the outcome of notice and takedown, i.e. the complexity in the law applied *by* intermediaries in determining the legality of the content identified by a notice of infringement. As was noted earlier, determining the legitimacy of a notice of infringement in the copyright context could entail a complex exercise. Arguably, extending the practice of notice and takedown to the trade mark context involves the same, if not greater, difficulties. Writing about notice and takedown for trade marks, Mostert and Schwimmer have opined:

97 See discussions in Chapter 2.
98 See discussions in Chapter 3.

> While we have reservations as to the results of the Urban-Quilter study . . . its findings should be treated at least as anecdotal evidence suggesting the existence of a significant problem.[99]

In light of this, it becomes necessary to consider how notice and takedown might be operating in the trade mark context before proposing any further legal reforms so that the negative effects of the practice could be suitably addressed and counterbalanced.

99 Mostert and Schwimmer, above n62, 278.

7 Notice and takedown and its impact on legitimate third-party uses of trade marks

The law, through the threat of liability and the promise of immunity, incentivises intermediaries hosting third-party content to practice notice and takedown. Insofar as the UK is concerned, this means that the liability framework proposed in Chapter 5 and the hosting safe harbour under the E-Commerce Regulations,[1] which transpose the E-Commerce Directive into UK law,[2] are bound to provide similar incentives in the trade mark context. The academic commentaries and empirical studies considered in Chapter 6 suggest that the practice of notice and takedown is prone to abuse. This claim is likely to hold true similarly in the trade mark context, particularly in view of the difficulties intermediaries are bound to face in determining the legality of content identified as infringing trade mark rights. As such, unless sufficient safeguards aimed at countering the abuse of notice and takedown are provided under the law, this extrajudicial practice will hinder legitimate third-party uses of trade marks on the internet.

The complex issue of 'use' on the internet

Trade mark rights are strictly territorial in nature.[3] Therefore, if anyone is to benefit from trade mark protection in a given territory, it is imperative that the trade mark in relation to which protection is sought is first registered in that territory. Although well-known marks may be regarded as an exception to this rule,[4] in

1 Electronic Commerce (EC Directive) Regulations 2002, SI 2002/2013, reg 19.

2 Directive 2000/31/EC on Certain Legal Aspects of Information Society Services, in Particular Electronic Commerce, in the Internal Market [2000] OJ L 178/1 (E-Commerce Directive).

3 See F-K Beier, 'Territoriality of Trade Mark Law and International Trade' (1970) 1 *International Review of Intellectual Property and Competition Law (IIC)* 48.

4 Article 6*bis* of the Paris Convention for the Protection of Industrial Property, read with Article 16:2 of the Agreement on the Trade Related Aspects of Intellectual Property Rights (TRIPS), prohibits the registration or use of a sign which constitutes a reproduction, imitation or translation of a well-known mark in circumstances where such registration or use is liable to cause confusion. For such protection to be granted, there is no requirement for the well-known mark to have been registered in the country in which enforcement is sought. In the UK, section 56 of the Trade Marks Act 1994 provides protection to well-known marks, even if they are not registered in the UK, against unauthorised third-party use that is likely to cause confusion.

the UK,[5] as well as in any EU Member State,[6] well-known marks, or marks with a *reputation*, are granted protection against *dilution* only if they are registered in the territory where protection is sought.[7]

In essence, assuming that an intermediary providing hosting services is served with a notice alleging a trade mark infringement, it must first consider whether the party serving the notice has a registered trade mark in the jurisdiction where enforcement is sought. This determination is reasonably straightforward, as proof of registration and ownership of a trade mark in any given jurisdiction may easily be established through a certification of registration issued by the relevant competent authority.

There is, however, a second and more complex question that an intermediary must determine. That is, whether the content (e.g. a website or other online material) identified by the notice of infringement gives rise to *use* of the trade mark in question within the jurisdiction where enforcement is sought. In the offline context, this is taken for granted, as it is always the case that use of a mark takes place within the borders of a given territory. Even though the types of infringing uses listed in Article 5(3) of the Trade Marks Directive (or section 10(4) of the UK Trade Marks Act 1994) are not controversial,[8] that list is not exhaustive.[9] In *Google v Louis Vuitton*,[10] the CJEU ruled that novel uses made of trade marks on the internet are capable of being captured as infringing uses.[11] However, in view of the cross-border reach of the internet, the question of use becomes complex to determine where a trade mark is used by incorporation into online content.

5 Trade Marks Act 1994, section 10(3).

6 Directive 2008/95/EC of the European Parliament and of the Council of 22 October 2008 to Approximate the Laws of the Member States Relating to Trade Marks [2008] OJ L 299/25 (Trade Marks Directive), art 5(3). An explanation as to why a reference is made to the 2008 Trade Marks Directive, and not the later 2015 Trade Marks Directive (Directive (EU) 2015/2436), which replaces the former, is provided in Chapter 1.

7 Article 16:3 of TRIPS, which requires the grant *more expansive protection* (i.e. protection against dilution) to well-known marks, has been interpreted to mean that a well-known mark must be registered within the territory in which such expansive protection is sought. See CM Correa, *Trade Related Aspects of Intellectual Property Rights: A Commentary on the TRIPS Agreement* (Oxford University Press 2007), 192 and JH Schmidt-Pfitzner, 'Article 16–Rights Conferred' in P-T Stoll, J Busche and K Arend (eds), *WTO—Trade-Related Aspects of Intellectual Property Rights* (Martinus Nijhoff 2009), 326.

8 The types of infringing uses listed include (1) the use of a sign (that is identical or similar to a registered trade mark) for the purposes of affixing it to goods or packaging, (2) offering goods for sale, placing them on the market or stocking them for those purposes under the sign, or offering or supplying services under that sign, (3) the importation or exportation of goods under the sign or (4) the use of the sign on business papers or in advertising.

9 See Case C-206/01, *Arsenal Football Club plc v Mathew Reed* [2002] ECR I-10273 (*Arsenal v Reed*), [38]; Case C-48/05, *Adam Opel AG v Autec AG* [2007] ECR I-01017, [16].

10 Joined Cases C-236/08, C-237/08 and C-238/08, *Google France Sarl v Louis Vuitton Malletier SA* [2010] ECR I-02417 (*Google v Louis Vuitton*).

11 *Google v Louis Vuitton*, [65].

When a trade mark is used on a website, it must be determined whether the website is *targeted* at consumers in the jurisdiction where enforcement is sought. If that is the case, then there is use within the jurisdiction concerned.[12] However, it is not essential for any goods or services to be sold via the website in question, although the mere fact that a website is accessible in a particular jurisdiction is insufficient to fulfil the use requirement.[13] For instance, in *Euromarket Designs Inc v Peters*,[14] even though a website was accessible to internet users in the UK, it was held that the website was used simply to advertise a store located in Ireland, and thus was *not* directed or targeted at UK consumers.

Factors that may suggest that a website or online material promoting goods or services is being directed at consumers in a particular jurisdiction include, but are not limited to, the language of the website or content,[15] the currency used to indicate prices and product manuals being made available in a particular language.[16] The domain name of the website which incorporates the infringing material may also be an important factor for consideration. For instance, according to the CJEU in *L'Oréal v eBay*, the eBay platform in which the alleged infringing goods were listed for sale, 'ebay.co.uk', was 'in the absence of any evidence to the contrary . . . targeted at consumers in the territory covered by the national and Community trade marks relied on'.[17] That said, in a case bearing similar facts to *L'Oréal v eBay*, the French Cour de cassation determined that 'ebay.co.uk' was targeted at French consumers, as it was *complementary* to 'ebay.fr', although it was not the case with 'ebay.com'.[18] The approach of the Cour de cassation, however, seems to contradict the approach of the CJEU in *L'Oréal v eBay*. This is particularly because, unlike in the case of a country-code top-level domain name (e.g. '.co.uk' or '.fr'), a generic top-level domain name (e.g. '.com') could be either targeted at the world at large or a particular region or country, a matter that must necessarily be determined having examined the actual contents of the landing website.

12 See e.g. *1-800 Flowers Inc v Phonenames Ltd* [2000] FSR 697; *Easygroup Ltd v Easy Fly Express Ltd* [2018] EWHC 3155 (Ch) (*Easy Group v Easy Fly*), [10].

13 Case C-324/09, *L'Oréal SA v eBay International AG* [2011] ECR I-06011 (*L'Oréal v eBay*), [64]. See also *Merck KGaA v Merck Sharp & Dohme Corp* [2017] EWCA Civ 1834, [168].

14 [2000] ETMR 1025.

15 Of course, merely because a website is in English, that does not necessarily mean that it targets any particular jurisdiction, including the UK, as English is widely spoken around the world. See *Easy Group v Easy Fly*, [18].

16 *KK Sony Computer Entertainment and another v Pacific Game Technology (Holding) Ltd* [2006] EWHC 2509 (Pat) (*Sony v Pacific Games*), [24].

17 *L'Oréal v eBay*, [66].

18 *eBay Inc v Louis Vuitton Moët Hennessy* Case 11-10505 (Cour de cassation of France, 3 May 2012). The full text (in French) of the Cour de cassation's judgment is available at www.legifrance.gouv.fr/affichJuriJudi.do?idTexte=JURITEXT000025808328 (accessed 31 January 2019). For a comment on the French Cour de cassation's decision, see R Milchior, 'eBay Ruling is Good News for Brand Owners – but Evidentiary Burden is Increased' *World Trademark Review Daily* (23 May 2012) <www.granrut.com/IMG/pdf/WTR_20120724.pdf> (accessed 31 January 2019).

What this demonstrates is that the determination as to whether a website or online content incorporating a trade mark amounts to *use* of that trade mark in the jurisdiction where enforcement is sought could be a difficult one to make. The inquiry potentially entails the application of complex, and at times conflicting, legal principles to an equally complicated set of facts. However, unless an intermediary that is served with a notice of infringement is able to make this determination accurately, a website or online content incorporating a trade mark may be removed even without there being an actual use of the trade mark in question within the territory in which enforcement is sought. It is submitted that this is a problem that is rather acute in the absence of provisions in the E-Commerce Directive, or the UK E-Commerce Regulations, that facilitate counter-notice and restorations procedures and penalise misrepresentations.

The contextual and complex nature of 'use'

Third-party use and competition

Third parties may use trade marks in numerous contexts, some being legitimate, others constituting unauthorised acts of infringement. When intermediaries receive notices alleging a trade mark infringement, it is imperative that they distinguish legitimate third-party uses of trade marks from uses that are infringing. Failure to do so would result in legitimate websites and content being removed or those that are infringing remaining accessible. In an illuminating practitioner's essay, Brege and Ovies have attempted to codify the distinct situations in which intermediaries are likely to be served with notices of infringement.[19] They make the argument that such a codification would make the task of an intermediary in assessing the merits of a notice of infringement easier. They identify four distinct categories of notices of infringement: clear-cut cases, context-specific cases, trade mark bullying and frivolous assertions. These categories are considered in detail below.

Frivolous assertions

The category identified as 'frivolous assertions' is straightforward and concerns 'assertions by those holding no trademark rights whatsoever'.[20] In the absence of any trade mark rights on the part of the party claiming infringement, the normative outcome ought to be a finding of no infringement. Therefore, where an intermediary is served with a frivolous notice, the notice and takedown process must 'establish an easy path to enable the purported infringer to successfully counter

19 JR Brege and KA Ovies, 'Taking Down Trademark Bullying: Sketching the Contours of a Trademark Notice and Takedown Statute' (2012) 2 *Wake Forest Journal of Business and Intellectual Property Law* 391.

20 Brege and Ovies, above n19, 400.

and defend against infringement allegations',[21] in effect ensuring that the content is *not* subject to a takedown and, if removed, access to it is restored expeditiously. Brege and Ovies utilise the fictional example of Apple Inc's Facebook page being taken down after a frivolous notice of infringement was sent to Facebook by one of Apple's dissatisfied customers.[22] Such an outcome is unwarranted, as the lack of trade mark rights on the part of the party serving the notice could have been easily ascertained by requiring the notifier to establish his or her rights, e.g. by furnishing a copy of the certificate of trade mark registration. Providing for an effective counter-notice and restoration mechanism and imposing liability on parties who misrepresent facts in notices of infringement may prove useful in deterring frivolous claims such as this.[23] However, since neither the E-Commerce Directive nor the UK E-Commerce Regulations contain a provision that provides for a counter-notice and restoration mechanism, or penalises perjury and misrepresentations, frivolous notices could nevertheless stifle legitimate online activities unless intermediaries adopt a cautious approach in ensuring that notices of infringement originate from parties who, in fact, have trade mark rights.

Be that as it may, the category representing frivolous claims is the least controversial, in that, when an intermediary is served with a notice of infringement that does not indicate the subsistence of any trade mark rights on the part of the asserter, a decision of *no infringement* is easily reached.

Context-specific cases

This category 'corresponds to the difficult, context-specific cases where the normative result is unclear and would warrant further analysis or court resolution'.[24] Responding to a notice of infringement under this category would require an intermediary to consider 'unclear case law, variations between not only the marks, but also the associated goods and services, and distinctions between uses',[25] significantly complicating the process and analysis that precedes the outcome of a notice. Notices of infringement under this category may concern one of three possibilities: claims where a confusion analysis is required,[26] dilution claims and

21 Brege and Ovies, above n19, 400.

22 Brege and Ovies, above n19, 393 ('Joe Smith, upset about buying an iPhone 4S for full price on the eve of the launch of the iPhone 5, frivolously and falsely notifies Facebook that Apple's Facebook page is infringing his non-existent trademarks. . .'). Although this example is fictional, it is based on a real-life incident. See B Sams, *Neowin's Facebook Page Taken Offline–We're Back! (Again)* (20 April 2011) <www.neowin.net/news/neowin039sfacebook-page-taken-offline-by-bogus-complaint> (accessed 31.12.2018).

23 Brege and Ovies, above n19, 405.

24 Brege and Ovies, above n19, 400.

25 Brege and Ovies, above n19, 400.

26 Brege and Ovies, above n19, 393

> (Small Business 1 ('SB1'), which holds a service mark registration for GREEN in connection with services described as 'garden design,' competes with Small Business 2 ('SB2'), which holds a trademark registration for GREENBOX in connection with goods described as 'raised garden planters.' SB1 notifies SB2's ISP that SB2's use of GREENBOX infringes upon SB1's service mark.

claims involving unregistered (or common-law) trade marks. What Brege and Ovies have posited is that, unlike in the other categories identified by them, the context-specific category represents an area where the ultimate normative outcome cannot be easily predicted. As such, they recommend that courts of law are better placed to determine such context-specific claims.[27]

In essence, the logic of Brege and Ovies suggests that, apart from this context-specific category of claims, notices of infringement falling under any other category identified by them are capable of being resolved through a notice and takedown process, without any need for judicial intervention. However, save for the category of frivolous claims (considered above), reaching a definitive normative outcome in respect of the other categories may not be as straightforward as one might imagine.

Clear-cut cases

In the category of clear-cut cases of trade mark infringement, the normative outcome ought to be a finding of infringement. In such instances, any notice and takedown process 'should establish an easy path to enable the potential asserter to curtail infringing activity'.[28] Clear-cut cases of infringement include circumstances of counterfeiting,[29] as well as other clear cases of trade mark infringement.[30] In relation to 'context-specific' cases (considered above), Brege and Ovies have defined 'unclear basis' to mean instances where an assessment of a likelihood of confusion has to be made.[31] This means that a 'clear-cut' case implies instances where a determination as to infringement can be made without the party serving notice having to establish a likelihood of confusion. Such an instance is informally known as the 'double identity' scenario, i.e. where the competing marks and goods or services are identical. Accordingly, where a notice of infringement concerns a third party's unauthorised use of a sign that is identical to a registered trade mark, and such use is made in relation to goods or services that are identical to those for which the trade mark is registered, the notice and takedown process should lead to the expeditious removal of the content promoting the infringement.[32] However, as is demonstrated below, not all cases of *alleged* counterfeiting or 'double identity' warrant the removal of content.

First, let us consider the suggestion that cases of counterfeiting must lead to the normative outcome of infringement. This is no doubt the right outcome. In the event that products advertised and sold under a trade mark on a website do not originate from the trade mark proprietor or a licensee, the outcome is a clear-cut case of infringement. However, the problem lies in the difficulty intermediaries

27 Brege and Ovies, above n19, 405.
28 Brege and Ovies, above n19, 400.
29 Brege and Ovies, above n19, 393 ('Oakley notices that counterfeit sunglasses bearing the OAKLEY logo are being sold by an eBay reseller').
30 Brege and Ovies, above n19, 400.
31 Brege and Ovies, above n19, 399.
32 Brege and Ovies, above n19, 400.

are bound to face in having to determine the merits of notices alleging an incidence of counterfeiting, a difficulty that is not so prevalent in the offline context. For instance, when TRIPS mandates all WTO members to provide for border measures to deal with the importation of counterfeits, right holders must satisfy the relevant competent authority with *adequate* evidence before any questionable goods can be seized and taken out of circulation.[33] Often, the evidence is supplied by inspecting the questionable goods and comparing them with genuine ones,[34] an opportunity that is not available to internet intermediaries in determining the merits of notices of infringement.

In the circumstances, unless a notice of infringement is sufficiently corroborated, e.g. through trap purchases, it would be unreasonable to expect an intermediary to determine the merits of the underlying claim with unimpeachable accuracy. In the absence of independent and credible evidence, it is quite possible that the operators of a website identified in a notice of infringement are resellers of genuine products bearing the trade mark, a scenario where the normative outcome of 'no infringement' should be reached, subject of course to the rules on exhaustion of rights.[35] Thus, in the event that an intermediary erroneously takes down a website or content of a third party promoting the resale of genuine goods placed on the market by the trade mark proprietor or a licensee, the removal of the website or content would impede competition. Such an outcome is problematic in view of the conspicuous absence of a provision in the E-Commerce Directive, and its UK equivalent, that provides for counter-notice and restoration procedures.

Second, the case of double identity must be considered. Article 16:1 (second sentence) of TRIPS provides that '[i]n case of the use of an identical sign for identical goods or services, a likelihood of confusion shall be presumed'. This presumption has been implemented in regional and national legislation.[36] In double identity cases, a claimant is not required to establish a likelihood of confusion.[37] Of course, this does not mean that the presumption as to confusion cannot be rebutted in some cases.[38] It has been suggested:

> In consequence, the 'double identity' of sign and product leads to a **shifting of the burden of proof** in favour of the trademark owner and on account of the third party. In turn, third parties are not *per se* barred from using identical signs for identical goods as they might refute the presumption of likely confusion by furnishing evidence to the contrary.[39]

33 See TRIPS, art 52.

34 See TRIPS, art 57.

35 The complexity that the rules on exhaustion adds to the task of an intermediary in determining the merits of a notice of infringement is considered under the next subheading.

36 See e.g. Trade Marks Directive, art 5(1)(a) and Trade Marks Act 1994, section 10(1)(a).

37 See e.g. Case C-291/00, *LTJ Diffusion SA v Sadas Vertbaudet SA* [2003] ECR I-02799, Opinion of AG Jacobs, [39]. The CJEU followed the Advocate General's approach, albeit tacitly (see CJEU judgment at [48]–[49]).

38 Correa, above n6, 187.

39 Schmidt-Pfitzner, above n6, 319 (emphasis in original).

Although establishing a case of double identity is generally sufficient for a finding of infringement, this may not always be the case. For instance, the trade mark infringement cases that concerned keyword advertising aptly demonstrate this fact. Thus, in *Google v Louis Vuitton*, although the CJEU's analysis concerned Article 5(1)(a) of the Trade Marks Directive (the double identity provision), the Court ruled that a trade mark proprietor may prevent the unauthorised use of a mark in connection with a keyword advertisement *only* where an average internet user is unable, or finds it difficult, to determine the source of the advertised goods or services.[40] In effect, this incorporates a confusion styled analysis into a double identity scenario.[41] Therefore, when internet intermediaries are called upon to remove alleged infringing content, consequent to a notice of infringement, even in a typical double identity scenario, they may be required to perform a confusion analysis, which significantly increases the difficulty in arriving at an accurate outcome.

Moreover, in the EU's context, the CJEU has expanded the scope of trade mark protection beyond its core origin function. In *Arsenal v Reed*, the CJEU concluded that a trade mark proprietor is entitled to prohibit a third party's use of a mark in a double identity scenario, where the use complained of jeopardises its origin function.[42] In effect, this prohibits all forms of third-party use that is liable to cause confusion. However, in subsequent cases, when interpreting the double identity provision of the Trade Marks Directive (Article 5(1)(a)), the CJEU has ruled that a trade mark proprietor may prevent a third party's use of a trade mark even in circumstances where there is no confusion, provided that one of the secondary functions of a trade mark (i.e. the quality, advertising, communication or investment functions) is affected.[43] Thus, in a double identity scenario, for

40 *Google v Louis Vuitton*, [99] (a trade mark proprietor is entitled to prevent the use of a keyword identical to a registered trade mark 'in the case where that ad does not enable an average internet user, or enables that user only with difficulty, to ascertain whether the goods or services referred to therein originate from the proprietor of the trade mark or an undertaking economically connected to it or, on the contrary, originate from a third party').

41 This approach has been followed in subsequent cases involving keyword advertising. See e.g. *Interflora Inc v Marks and Spencer Plc* [2012] ETMR 1 (*Interflora v Marks and Spencer*); *Victoria Plum Limited v Victorian Plumbing* Ltd [2016] EWHC 2911 (Ch).

42 *Arsenal v Reed*, [60].

43 See e.g. *Google v Louis Vuitton*, [78]–[79]:

> The protection conferred by Article 5(1)(a) . . . is, in this regard, more extensive than that provided for in the respective paragraphs (1)(b) of those articles, the application of which requires that there be a likelihood of confusion. . . . It is apparent from the case-law cited above that in the situation envisaged in Article 5(1)(a) . . . in which a third party uses a sign identical with a trade mark in relation to goods or services which are identical with those for which that mark is registered, the proprietor of the mark is entitled to prohibit that use if it is liable to have an adverse effect on one of the functions of the mark, whether that be the function of indicating origin or one of the other functions.

See also Case C-487/07, *L'Oréal v Bellure NV* [2009] ECR I-05185, [65] (*L'Oréal v Bellure*); *Interflora v Marks and Spencer*, [66].

instance, where a sign identical to a registered trade mark was used in a comparison list,[44] it is possible that such use could be prohibited even where there is no confusion amongst consumers, provided that one of the secondary functions of the trade mark is jeopardised. This renders the task of an intermediary, on whom a notice of infringement has been served, more difficult because an assessment beyond the confusion analysis is required to arrive at the right outcome even in a classic double identity situation.

What is clear from this discussion is that the task of an intermediary that is called upon to determine the legality of third-party content under trade mark law, even in cases where a notice of infringement has alleged counterfeiting or double identity, is not straightforward, as portrayed by Brege and Ovies in their codified approach. Be that as it may, unless an accurate determination could be made concerning such notices of infringement, content that is legitimate may be removed, whittling down competition, and, similarly, it is equally possible for infringing content to remain online promoting unfair competition. The absence of a provision in the E-Commerce Directive (and UK E-Commerce Regulations) that provides for a counter-notice and restoration mechanism, or one that penalises misrepresentations and perjury in notices of infringement, simply aggravates the problem.

Trade mark bullying

The category identified as 'trade mark bullying' concerns the assertion of trade mark rights in circumstances where a third party has made legitimate use of a registered trade mark. Brege and Ovies cite the example of a reseller of genuine products bearing a trade mark in the secondary market[45] to conclude that any claim made in such a scenario must lead to the normative outcome of no infringement.[46] Accordingly, it is submitted that notice and takedown procedures 'should establish an easy path to enable the purported infringer to successfully counter and defend against infringement allegations'.[47] However, just as with clear-cut cases of infringement, it becomes clear that an intermediary's task of accurately determining the merits of a notice alleging infringement on the part of a legitimate third-party user of a trade mark is not as straightforward as one might imagine.

First, the third-party use of trade marks for descriptive purposes must be considered. Article 17 of TRIPS permits WTO members to impose limited exceptions

44 *L'Oréal v Bellure*, [62].

45 Brege and Ovies, above n19, 393:

> High Fashion Designer ('HFD') notices that a high number of its handbags bearing its trademarks are being legitimately resold in the secondary market by resellers. HFD, in order to curtail such resale and augment direct sales, notifies eBay, and eBay, applying its policies, shuts down each reseller's site.

46 Brege and Ovies, above n19, 400.

47 Brege and Ovies, above n19, 400.

to trade mark rights,[48] provided that such limitations take into account the rights of trade mark proprietors and the legitimate interests of third parties. This affords some flexibility to WTO members to enact legislation that promotes national policies and objectives, which include the promotion of competition.[49] Article 17 of TRIPS itself provides an example of a mechanism that seeks to promote competition: the 'fair use of descriptive terms'. One may argue that the entitlement to make 'fair use of descriptive terms' need not be expressly provided because trade mark protection is only granted for trade marks that are distinctive and therefore anyone could use descriptive terms without any interference from right holders.[50] An obvious instance to which this exception applies is to trade marks that had *acquired* distinctiveness through use. Although trade mark protection must only be granted when a sign is distinctive,[51] even descriptive signs may be registered provided they have acquired distinctiveness after continuous and wide usage.[52] Thus, the 'fair use of descriptive terms' exception seeks to ensure that descriptive marks are capable of being used by third parties even though such marks attract trade mark protection.

On the other hand, since Article 17 of TRIPS refers to 'fair use of descriptive terms' and not 'descriptive marks', even in cases of highly distinctive marks, the exception enables third-party use, provided it is for the sole purpose of describing goods or services.[53] Article 6 of the Trade Marks Directive, and in the UK section 11 of the Trade Marks Act 1994, incorporates a number of important limitations that allow a third party to use a registered trade mark. For instance, third parties may use a registered trade mark, without the proprietor's consent, to describe the underlying products[54] or the intended purpose of the goods or services,[55] provided that such use is 'in accordance with honest practices in industrial or commercial matters'. Thus, it is not uncommon that third parties use trade marks for descriptive purposes, and, when an internet intermediary is served with a notice of infringement, this is an important matter that must be considered.

In *BMW v Deenik*, a case that involved the sale of second-hand BMWs and the supply of vehicle repair services, the CJEU pointed out that the use of a trade mark by a third party to indicate the intended purpose of a product, in particular

48 A WTO Panel, in *Canada–Patent Protection on Pharmaceutical Products* WT/DS114/R, explained (at [7.30]–[7.31]) that a 'limited exception' must be 'a narrow exception–one which makes only a small diminution of the rights in question'. This was followed in *EC–Protection of Trademarks and Geographical Indications* WT/DS174/R, [7.650].

49 TRIPS, art 8:2.

50 NP de Carvalho, *The TRIPS Regime of Trademarks and Designs* (Kluwer Law International 2006), 298.

51 TRIPS, art 15:1 (first sentence).

52 TRIPS, art 15:1 (third sentence).

53 de Carvalho, above n50, 299.

54 Trade Marks Directive, art 6(1)(b) (this provision has been reproduced, in essential form, in art 14(1)(b) of the 2015 Trade Marks Directive). See also Trade Marks Act 1994, section 11(2)(b).

55 Trade Marks Directive, art 6(1)(c) (this provision has been reproduced, in essential form, in art 14(1)(c) of the 2015 Trade Marks Directive). See also Trade Marks Act 1994, section 11(2)(c).

as accessories or spare parts, cannot be prohibited by a trade mark proprietor, provided that the use is *necessary* to indicate that purpose and is in accordance with *honest practices*.[56] The third party's use of a mark would be contrary to honest practices where that party disregards the 'duty to act fairly in relation to the legitimate interests of the trade mark owner'.[57] This would be the case where the mark is used to create an impression that a commercial connection exists between the third party and the trade mark proprietor, for instance that the third party is affiliated to the trade mark proprietor's distribution network or that some special relationship exists between the two.[58] Accordingly, although the normative outcome in descriptive use cases is no doubt a conclusion of no infringement and ought not to alter the status quo of any online content, arriving at an accurate determination requires the application of complex legal principles to context-specific facts. However, unless an intermediary responsible for hosting content is capable of accurately determining whether a third party's use of a mark was *necessary* for a descriptive purpose and whether the use made complies with *honest practices*, it is possible that legitimate content might be removed stifling fair competition. Of course, the converse is equally possible.

Second, the case of 'legitimate resellers' must be considered. As pointed out earlier on in this chapter, trade mark rights are territorial in nature. This, coupled with the doctrine of exhaustion of intellectual property rights, enables the legitimate use of trade marks by third parties in circumstances where they deal with genuine goods that had already been placed on the market with the consent of the trade mark proprietor. Trade mark rights are conventionally exhausted after the *first sale* of legitimately marketed goods.[59] TRIPS leaves it open to WTO members to determine appropriate rules on exhaustion,[60] providing members 'considerable room for manoeuvre in implementing exhaustion policies'.[61] Accordingly, WTO members may choose to implement a system of national, regional or international exhaustion in their domestic law.

The consequence of adopting a policy of national exhaustion is that once goods are placed on the domestic market with the trade mark proprietor's consent, trade mark rights in respect of those specific goods become extinguished. In essence, trade mark proprietors lose the ability to control the further commercialisation of goods already placed on the domestic market with their consent. Thus, a benefit of the exhaustion doctrine is that it ensures that third parties could deal

56 Case C-63/97, *Bayerische Motorenwerke AG v Deenik* [1999] ECR I-00905, [58] (*BMW v Deenik*). See also Case C-288/03, *Gillette Co v LA-Laboratories Ltd Oy* [2005] ECR I-02337, [24]–[39].

57 *BMW v Deenik*, [61].

58 *BMW v Deenik*, [64].

59 M Blakeney, *Trade Related Aspects of Intellectual Property Rights: A Concise Guide to the TRIPS Agreement* (Sweet & Maxwell 1996), 59. The doctrine of exhaustion is known in the US as the first sale doctrine.

60 TRIPS, art 6.

61 Correa, above n6, 78–79.

with second-hand goods without having to obtain the consent of the trade mark proprietors under whose authority those goods were originally placed on the domestic market. The unrestricted sale of second-hand goods improves competition by providing consumers with a wider choice in relation to their purchases without their choice being restricted only to brand new goods.

In contrast, where a policy of international or regional exhaustion is applied, the parallel importation of goods becomes possible without the interference from trade mark proprietors.[62] Parallel importation occurs when goods are purchased in one country and resold in another in competition with the distribution system preferred by the manufacturer of those goods.[63] The parallel importation of goods between national markets is made possible due to the price differences between markets.[64] In this regard, Correa has made the following observation:

> The recognition of the principles of *international* exhaustion in the TRIPS Agreement may be seen as a logical reflection of the globalization of the economy. It may help to ensure the competitiveness of local companies, which may be jeopardized if they were bound to buy inputs for their production exclusively from a local distributor that charges higher prices than in foreign markets. Likewise, the consumer should not be denied the right to buy legitimate products from foreign sources at lower prices, except where imported products present substantial differences in the quality or other essential features with respect to those locally available.[65]

Therefore, at least in jurisdictions that adopt a scheme of regional or international exhaustion of intellectual property rights, the use of trade marks by third parties in relation to parallel imports is another instance where third-party use of trade marks may be justified.[66] Just as descriptive use, rules on exhaustion are an important mechanism by which the monopolistic effects of trade mark rights are minimised by ensuring the free flow of goods within and across national borders.

It is in this context that legitimate resellers have come to use the internet as a platform to promote the sale of parallel imports. Some websites are dedicated to the sale of parallel imports, for instance 'www.parallelimported.co.nz'. Similarly, online marketplaces such as eBay have also become a popular source

62 In the EU's context, Article 7(1) of the Trade Marks Directive (reproduced in Article 15(1) of the 2015 Trade Marks Directive) implements a scheme of regional exhaustion. See also Trade Marks Act 1994, section 12(1).

63 T Hays, 'The Free Movement (or Not) of Trademark Protected Goods in Europe' in GB Dinwoodie and MD Janis (eds), *Trademark Law and Theory: A Handbook of Contemporary Research* (Edward Elgar 2008), 205.

64 Hays, above n63, 217.

65 Correa, above n6, 79 (emphasis in original).

66 See T Mylly, 'A Silhouette of Fortress Europe? International Exhaustion of Trade Mark Rights in the EU' (2000) 7 *Maastricht Journal of European and Comparative Law* 51, 53 and E Powell and C Turner, '"Fortress Europe": International Exhaustion of Trademark Rights and the EC – The Retailer's Perspective' (2002) 30 *International Business Lawyer* 3.

for second-hand goods, as well as parallel imports, which has resulted in these intermediaries becoming entangled in highly contested trade mark litigation. Thus, in *L'Oréal SA v eBay Inc*,[67] one of the claims brought against eBay before the English High Court was that goods that had been placed exclusively in markets outside the EEA[68] were being resold in the UK by third-party eBay sellers in violation of L'Oréal's trade mark rights.[69] This means that in territories where national or regional exhaustion regimes apply, trade mark proprietors have a legitimate basis for serving notices of infringement on intermediaries whose services are used in promoting the sale of goods originating from outside the territory concerned.

There could be further complications. Exhaustion rules are subject to certain exceptions. Usually, where the condition of the goods bearing a trade mark is altered or impaired after being placed on the market, trade mark proprietors may still have a legitimate interest in preventing the further commercialisation of goods the condition of which has been altered.[70] As in the case of determining whether a mark is being used for descriptive purposes, determining whether the condition of goods has been altered or impaired, in the context of exhaustion of rights, requires the application of complex legal principles to equally complex factual considerations. Thus, where the condition of the goods themselves is altered,[71] the goods are de-packaged,[72] repackaged[73] or advertised in a manner that detracts from the values of the brand,[74] trade mark proprietors *may* have a legitimate interest in preventing the resale of such goods notwithstanding the rules on exhaustion.

67 [2009] ETMR 53.

68 Both the 1988 Trade Marks Directive and its codified 2008 version, in Article 7(1), provide for the exhaustion of trade mark rights within the European Community. The 2015 recast Trade Marks Directive provides for an EU-wide exhaustion regime in Article 15(1). This has been extended to the EEA by virtue of the Agreement on the European Economic Area, which came into force on 1 January 1994. See I Calboli, 'Trademark Exhaustion in the European Union: Community-Wide or International? The Saga Continues' (2002) 6 *Marquette Intellectual Property Law Review* 47, 50.

69 Such a claim was possible because the EU adopts a scheme of regional exhaustion, and not international exhaustion. See Case C-355/96, *Silhouette International Schmied GmbH & Co KG v Hartlauer Handelsgesellschaft mbH* [1998] ECR I-04799. For an authority on exhaustion in the online context, see *Sony v Pacific Games*. In this case, Sony succeeded before the English High Court in preventing its Play Station consoles placed exclusively in the Japanese market from being resold in the EEA via the website of a Hong Kong-based company.

70 Trade Marks Directive, art 7(2) (reproduced in Article 15(2) of the 2015 Trade Marks Directive). See also Trade Marks Act 1994, section 12(2).

71 Case C-46/10, *Viking Gas A/S v Kosan Gas A/S* [2011] ECR I-06161.

72 *L'Oréal v eBay*, [83].

73 Joined cases C-427/93, 429/93 and 436/93, *Bristol-Myers Squibb v Paranova A/S* [1996] ECR I-03457.

74 Case C-337/95, *Christian Dior SA v Evora BV* [1997] ECR I-06013, followed in Joined Cases C-414/99, C-415/99 and C416/99, *Zino Davidoff SA v A & G Imports Ltd* [2001] ECR I-08691.

Thus, where parallel imports are concerned, whether or not a reseller is making a *legitimate* use of a trade mark depends on a multitude of factors that require meticulous deliberation. In these circumstances, although the normative outcome in relation to claims against legitimate resellers must be one of no infringement (as suggested by Brege and Ovies), determining the merits of such claims necessitates a complex exercise involving both questions of law and fact. This complex exercise demanded of intermediaries could possibly impinge on competition in the online space. The threat to competition is amplified in view of the lack of a provision in the E-Commerce Directive (and its UK equivalent) that provides for a counter-notice and restoration mechanism, and safeguards against misrepresentations and perjury on the part of right holders.

Third-party use and free speech rights

Parties defending trade mark infringement claims have often resorted to provisions in international[75] and regional[76] instruments, as well as constitutions,[77] which protect the freedom of expression. The increasing resort to free speech doctrine may be explained in terms of the expanding significance of trade marks in modern commercial and cultural expression. Although trade marks are a badge of origin, in view of the investment made by trade mark proprietors in building their reputation and image, a wide range of meanings and connotations become attached to trade marks. This phenomenon was expressly recognised by a US court in the following terms:

> The problem arises when trademarks transcend their identifying purpose. Some trademarks enter our public discourse and become an integral part of our vocabulary. How else do you say that something's 'the Rolls Royce of its class'? What else is a quick fix, but a Band-Aid? Does the average consumer know to ask for aspirin as 'acetyl salicylic acid'? . . . Trademarks often fill in gaps in our vocabulary and add a contemporary flavor to our expressions. Once imbued with such expressive value, the trademark becomes a word in our language and assumes a role outside the bounds of trademark law.[78]

When a trade mark becomes associated with a wider range of meanings and connotations, that increases the likelihood of third parties having a legitimate interest in making use of the mark. For instance, trade marks may be used by third parties not only to comment on the trade mark itself, the products bearing the mark or

75 See e.g. Universal Declaration on Human Rights 1948, art 19.

76 See e.g. European Convention for the Protection of Human Rights and Fundamental Freedoms 1950 (ECHR), art 10(1) and Charter of Fundamental Rights of the European Union [2000] OJ C364/01 (EU Charter), art 11.

77 See e.g. US Constitution, First Amendment.

78 *Mattel Inc v MCA Records Inc* 296 F.3d 894, 900 (9th Cir. 2002) (Kozinski J).

the trade mark proprietor but also in socially useful expressions, such as parody and satire, and also in comparative advertising.[79] However, given that trade mark rights by their very nature provide exclusivity in the use of varying categories of distinctive signs in commerce, these private rights may 'collide with the free speech rights of others'.[80] Commenting on the US context, the friction between exclusive rights over signs and the freedom of third parties to use those signs in their expression was succinctly set out in the following terms: 'Trademark laws restrict and punish the use of language. For this reason, some trademark laws conflict with the First Amendment right of free expression.'[81]

Despite such criticism, the law relating to trade marks incorporates important inbuilt safeguards that seek to protect the interests of free speech.[82] First, Article 16:1 of TRIPS only confers trade mark proprietors the right to proscribe third-party uses of trade marks *in the course of trade*. This is an important limitation to the scope of trade mark rights, in that *non-commercial* third-party uses of trade marks cannot be prohibited by right holders. Second, not all third-party uses of trade marks, even if made in the context of some economic activity, will amount to trade mark infringement. Only uses that are capable of *affecting* the functions of a trade mark are capable of being prohibited.[83] Third, the limitations imposed on the scope of trade mark rights in relation to descriptive use,[84] comparative advertising[85] and parallel importation,[86] ensure that third parties having a legitimate interest in using registered marks in *commercial speech* are able to do so without any interference from right holders.

79 IS Fhima, 'Trade Marks and Free Speech' (2013) 44 *International Review of Intellectual Property and Competition Law (IIC)* 293, 293–94.

80 *Yankee Publishing Inc v News Am Publishing Inc* 809 F. Supp. 267, 275–76 (1992) (Leval J).

81 LP Ramsey, 'Increasing First Amendment Scrutiny of Trademark Law' (2008) 61 *Southern Methodist University Law Review* 381, 458.

82 PN Leval, 'Trademark: Champion of Free Speech' (2004) 27 *Columbia Journal of Law and Arts* 187, 191 ('the law of trademark contains ingredients designed to protect free speech values').

83 See PL Loughlan, 'Protecting Culturally Significant Uses of Trade Marks (Without a First Amendment)' (2000) 22 *European Intellectual Property Review* 328.

84 In *Electrocoin Automatics Ltd v Coinworld Ltd* [2005] ETMR 31, referring to the provision in the Trade Marks Directive permitting 'descriptive use', the judge observed (at [106]) that 'the Directive ensures that the rights conferred by registration operate with due regard for freedom of expression'.

85 Article 4 of Directive 2006/114/EC of the European Parliament and of the Council of 12 December 2006 Concerning Misleading and Comparative Advertising [2006] OJ L 376/21 (Comparative Advertising Directive) sets out eight conditions that must be met before a comparative advertisement could be regarded as permitted under the law. These conditions were previously contained in Article 3a(1) of Directive 84/450/EEC, as amended by Directive 97/55/EC. An analysis of the CJEU's rulings in Case C-533/06, *O2 Holdings Ltd v Hutchison 3G Ltd* [2008] ECR I-04231 and *L'Oréal v Bellure* reveal that, if all of the conditions concerning a comparative advertisement as set out in the Comparative Advertisement Directive are met, a trade mark proprietor cannot prevent the use of a registered trade mark in a comparative advertisement.

86 The rules on exhaustion enshrined in the Trade Marks Directive maintain a fair balance between the rights of trade mark proprietors and the rights of third parties to use trade marks in respect of parallel imports. See *Levi Strauss & Co v Tesco Stores Ltd* [2002] ETMR 95.

Similar to the inbuilt safeguards in trade mark law, which seek to protect the right of expression, limitations to the right of expression also seek to balance other competing rights, including trade mark rights. Both the ECHR and the EU Charter maintain such a balance. For instance, Article 10(2) of the ECHR limits the guarantee of free expression to the extent needed to 'protect the rights of others'. Moreover, Article 1 of the First Protocol to the ECHR, titled 'protection of property', provides that '[e]very natural or legal person is entitled to the peaceful enjoyment of his possessions'. While there is no doubt that trade mark rights fall within the category of 'rights' the protection of which could restrict the right of expression under the qualification in Article 10(2) of the ECHR, the European Court of Human Rights confirmed that a trade mark must be considered a 'possession' within the meaning of Article 1 of the First Protocol.[87] Accordingly, the property rights that arise from the registration of trade marks, which are regarded as possessions, cannot be deprived 'except in the public interest and subject to the conditions provided for by law and by the general principles of international law'.[88]

Similarly, while the EU Charter recognises the right to expression, it also recognises the right to property,[89] which expressly includes intellectual property.[90] When Article 52(1) of the EU Charter provides that limitations to any right recognised therein could only be made 'if they are necessary and genuinely meet objectives of general interest recognised by the Union or the need to protect the rights and freedoms of others', it seeks to maintain a balance between competing rights and interests. Therefore, in determining whether Article 10 of the ECHR and Article 11 of the EU Charter protect a third party's right of expression that incorporates a trade mark, it becomes necessary to ensure that trade mark rights are unaffected by such use.

In effect, when the exclusive rights conferred by a registered trade mark is kept within their legitimate boundaries, i.e. only prohibiting third-party uses of trade marks that are inconsistent with these exclusive rights, the outcome would not be detrimental to the guarantee on free speech. Considered this way, legitimate speech and trade mark rights are compatible and can coexist. That said, determining when the third-party use of a trade mark should be permitted in light of competing free speech interests is not straightforward. Although political, artistic and expressive speech tends to attract a greater degree of protection, commercial speech is not protected to the same degree.[91] This corresponds perfectly with

87 *Anheuser-Busch Inc v Portugal* (2007) 45 EHRR 36, [72] ('In the light of the aforementioned decisions, the Grand Chamber agrees with the [trial] Chamber's conclusion that Article 1 of Protocol No. 1 is applicable to intellectual property as such').

88 ECHR, First Protocol, art 1.

89 EU Charter, art 17(1).

90 EU Charter, art 17(2).

91 See CR Munro, 'The Value of Commercial Speech' (2003) 62 *Cambridge Law Journal* 134; DA Farber, 'Commercial Speech and the First Amendment Theory' (1979) 74 *Northwestern University Law Review* 372; and R Caddell, 'Freedom of Commercial Speech and the UK Courts' (2005) 64 *Cambridge Law Journal* 274. See also *Casado Coca v Spain* (1994) 18 EHRR 1; *Jacubowski v Germany* (1994) 19 EHRR 64; *R v Secretary of State for Health* [2004] EWHC 2493 (Admin).

the scope of trade mark protection. This is because, although any third-party use made of trade marks that is not in the course of trade ought to be permitted (such use corresponding with political, artistic or expressive speech), the same cannot be said about the use of trade marks made in the course of trade (such use corresponding with commercial speech). The difficulty lies, however, with borderline cases where a third party's use of a trade mark is both in the course of trade and political, artistic or expressive at the same time, such use of trade marks corresponding with instances of *mixed speech*.[92]

The use of trade marks for the purpose of parody illustrates this difficulty. Although the use of trade marks by parodists in a purely non-commercial setting is less likely to give rise to any difficulty,[93] the vast majority of parodying takes place in relation to some form of economic activity, giving rise to increased scrutiny under trade mark law.[94] Since parodying could generate negative sentiments concerning the parodied subject, it is common for infringement or dilution claims to be brought on the basis that a third party's use of a trade mark in a parody is likely to cause confusion or that it dilutes the mark's distinctiveness or reputation. However, determining when a parody infringes a registered trade mark is a complex exercise, especially in view of its expressive value. Two cases from the US usefully illustrate this point. Thus, although it was held that the use of 'Chewy Vuitton' for dog toys neither infringed nor diluted the famous 'Louis Vuitton' trade mark,[95] the use of 'Buttwiper', similarly for dog toys, parodying the famous 'Budweiser' mark for beer, created a sufficient degree of confusion (albeit no dilution was established).[96] Ultimately, even disputes involving the *expressive* use of trade marks turn on the question of consumer confusion, and if not on whether the third party's use is bound to dilute the distinctiveness or reputation of a registered trade mark. These are difficult questions to answer.

In essence, balancing free speech interests and the rights of trade mark proprietors, especially in cases of mixed speech, is an exercise that requires careful judgment. The only uncontroversial instance is where an internet intermediary is served with a notice of infringement identifying the unauthorised use of a trade mark in a purely *non-commercial* setting. The normative outcome in such a circumstance is a finding of no infringement, and the associated content should remain online. In contrast, when a notice of infringement relates to either commercial or mixed speech, determining the normative outcome is far more difficult. However, unless intermediaries are capable of accurately determining the merits

92 L Bently et al, *Intellectual Property Law* (5th edn, Oxford University Press 2018), 1165. See also MA Naser, 'Trademarks and Freedom of Expression' (2009) 40 *International Review of Intellectual Property and Competition Law (IIC)* 188, 193.

93 PD Curren, 'Diluting the Commercial Speech Doctrine: "Noncommercial Use" and the Federal Trademark Dilution Act' (2004) 71 *University of Chicago Law Review* 1077, 1082.

94 M Senftleben, 'Overprotection and Protection Overlaps in Intellectual Property Law – The Need for Horizontal Fair Use Defences' in A Kurr and V Mizaras (eds), *The Structure of Intellectual Property Law: Can One Size Fit All?* (Edward Elgar 2011), 178.

95 *Louis Vuitton Malletier SA v Haute Diggity Dog LLC* 507 F.3d 252 (4th Cir. 2007).

96 *Anheuser-Busch Inc v VIP Products LLC* 666 F.Supp.2d 974 (2008).

of notices alleging the infringing use of trade marks in expressive speech, content that otherwise attracts free speech guarantees may be subject to removal as a result of the notice and takedown process. The absence of proper safeguards in the E-Commerce Directive, and its implementation in the UK, to deal with the abuse of notice and takedown is arguably a huge blow to the right of expression.

Balancing the scales—incorporating safeguards

When intermediaries become obligated under the law to expeditiously remove infringing material upon notice, and if not face liability, they are more likely to be motivated to 'act first and ask questions later'. This is not problematic if the distinction between what is legal and what is not is as clear as day. However, as the discussion hitherto patently reveals, there are significant challenges in determining disputes involving a trade mark infringement. At times, even well-experienced judges assisted by well-trained counsel turn to expert testimony and survey evidence in determining difficult questions, such as the likelihood of confusion.[97] The notice and takedown process expects private-sector intermediaries to expeditiously determine similar questions without any such assistance and, at times, even without an in-house legal team. Generally, determining the merits of a notice alleging the unauthorised third-party use of a trade mark is far from straightforward save for cases involving frivolous claims. Therefore, it is not surprising that intermediaries are likely to err on the side of caution in order to avoid potential liability, giving rise to a risk of legitimate third-party uses of trade marks being curtailed. Despite this shortcoming, however, the solution is not one that leads to the abandonment of notice and takedown. Notice and takedown provides a useful remedy to aggrieved trade mark proprietors against infringements in the online space. What is necessary is to formulate effective safeguards, at the content removal and post-removal stages, against abusive and erroneous takedowns.

Before moving onto a discussion on safeguards against the abuse of notice and takedown, it is necessary to consider whether the E-Commerce Directive permits EU Member States to introduce procedural and other safeguards at the domestic level in connection with the practice of notice and takedown as envisaged by Article 14(1). Although Brexit will eventually render such an enquiry unnecessary insofar as the UK is concerned, there is still utility in considering this point given the possible transition period and the continued relevance of EU law in the UK, as well as from the point of view of other EU Member States.

The E-Commerce Directive provides EU Member States considerable freedom in regulating notice and takedown. Recital (46) provides that the directive does not affect the possibility for Member States to establish 'specific requirements which must be fulfilled expeditiously prior to the removal or disabling of information'. This part of Recital (46) concerns the *pre-removal* stage. This means

97 J Gilson, 'Experts in Trademark Cases' (1982) 8 *Litigation* 40.

that any domestic law concerning the liability of hosts may determine *when* a host becomes obligated to remove infringing content in order to avoid liability. This is precisely what is aimed to be achieved through the proposed legislative amendment to the Trade Marks Act 1994, as set out in Chapter 5, according to which *actual notice-based knowledge* of an infringement is required before an intermediary becomes obligated to remove any content that it hosts.

However, the question arises whether the E-Commerce Directive permits individual Member States to regulate *post-removal* procedures. In this regard, reference must be made to another part of Recital (46), which provides that 'the removal or disabling of access has to be undertaken in the observance of the principle of freedom of expression and of procedures established for this purpose at national level'. As was noted earlier in this chapter, the abuse of notice and takedown has the potential of negatively impacting online speech, commercial or otherwise. Thus, procedural safeguards aimed at counteracting abusive notice and takedown practices could be regarded as necessary for preserving the freedom of expression. Given that Recital (46) expressly provides that removal of content must be done in compliance with procedures set up at national level to protect free speech, this could arguably include any post-removal safeguards. After all, this part of Recital (46) is not limited to matters *prior to* the removal of content.

In addition, Article 14(3) of the E-Commerce Directive, which sets out that nothing contained in Article 14 affects the possibility for Member States to establish 'procedures governing the removal or disabling of access to information', provides support for post-removal safeguards at national level. Unlike the reference in Recital (46) to specific requirements *prior to* the removal of content, Article 14(3) refers to the establishment of procedures *governing* the removal of content. Arguably, the phrase 'governing the removal' is reasonably broad enough to include both removal and post-removal procedures. If such an interpretation is afforded to Article 14(3), the incorporation of post-removal procedural and other safeguards will not be inconsistent with the E-Commerce Directive. In any case, in the event safeguards against abuse are introduced into the text of the E-Commerce Directive itself, any controversy concerning the compatibility of the directive with safeguards that may be introduced under domestic law will be set aside, in addition to ensuring that the safeguards are uniformly applied in all EU Member States. A few of the key safeguards are considered below.

Counter-notice and restoration

The first safeguard for consideration is the counter-notice and restoration mechanism. This safeguard is already available under the US's copyright safe harbour, i.e. the Digital Millennium Copyright Act 1998 (DMCA).[98] Despite the criticisms levelled against the DMCA, it cannot be doubted that this mechanism is

98 Title II of the DMCA, i.e. the Online Copyright Infringement Liability Limitation Act, introduced a safe harbour (codified at 17 USC §512) for internet intermediaries that shield them from copyright liability provided that they meet certain conditions set out therein.

useful in safeguarding the interests of creators and authors of legitimate online content. Under the DMCA, once an intermediary that hosts third-party content receives a notice of infringement, and that host decides to remove the alleged infringing content, it becomes obligatory for the host to notify the subscriber whose interests are affected by the takedown.[99] Thereafter, in the event the host receives a counter-notice claiming that the content was removed as a result of a mistake or misidentification of the material,[100] the host must restore access to the content,[101] after forwarding the counter-notice to the right holder who served the initial notice of infringement.[102] Failure to do so, except in circumstances where the intermediary receives a further notice from the right holder to the effect that legal action has been *instituted* 'seeking a court order to restrain the subscriber from engaging in infringing activity',[103] exposes the intermediary to a possible claim for damages by the aggrieved subscriber.[104] In effect, the counter-notice and restoration mechanism works to counteract the harshness of the ex parte and extrajudicial removal of content. At the same time, when the intermediary forwards the counter-notice to the right holder, that would enable the right holder to initiate necessary legal action against the party responsible for the alleged infringing content.

There is, however, a point to note about timing. The DMCA requires hosts to restore content in not fewer than ten and no more than 14 business days following receipt of a counter-notice.[105] When analysing the provisions of the DMCA in Chapter 6, criticisms against the period prescribed for content restoration were considered, which revealed that legitimate content may be kept offline in circumstances where its availability would have been most crucial.[106] This is no different in the trade mark context. The removal of legitimate content promoting the sale of goods on the internet could result in a large loss of sales unless the content is restored expeditiously. Thus, this raises an important question as regards the time period within which restoration of content should take place. In fact, Levin, in her proposal for a DMCA-like system for the trade mark context, has recommended that the ten- to 14-day period in the DMCA should be shortened,[107] although she does not specify a suitable shorter time period.[108]

99 17 USC §512(g)(2)(A).
100 17 USC §512(g)(3)(B).
101 17 USC §512(g)(2)(C).
102 17 USC §512(g)(2)(B).
103 17 USC §512(g)(2)(C).
104 17 USC §512(g)(1), read with §512(g)(2). It must be noted, however, that any litigation between an intermediary and its subscriber is likely to be governed by contract, often such contracts containing broad exclusion clauses.
105 17 USC §512(g)(2)(C).
106 See the discussion in Chapter 6 under the subheading 'Academic commentaries on the abuse of notice and takedown'.
107 EK Levin, 'A Safe Harbor for Trademark: Reevaluating Secondary Trademark Liability After Tiffany v. eBay' (2009) 24 *Berkeley Technology Law Journal* 491, 525–26.
108 Brege and Ovies, above n19, 405.

On the one hand, stipulating an excessively long time period for the restoration of legitimate content will be detrimental to the interests of competition and free speech. On the other hand, in view of the sheer volume of notices and counter-notices, allowing for an excessively short period for restoration could be detrimental to the interests of intermediaries practising notice and takedown. Thus, determining the most optimal period for content restoration requires a delicate balance. In this regard, it is noteworthy that the DMCA compels the restoration of content only after ten business days from the date of a counter-notice. Although the Senate Report on the DMCA[109] does not indicate why a ten-day waiting period was introduced, this is presumably to enable the party initiating the notice and takedown process to concurrently file an appropriate legal action (e.g. seeking injunctive relief) against the subscriber engaged in the infringing activity. Under the DMCA, unless an intermediary is notified within ten business days following the receipt of a counter-notice that an action has been filed against the alleged infringer, the intermediary must restore content no later than a period of 14 business days following receipt of the counter-notice. In cases where a right holder has a prima facie case, and the restoration of content would cause irremediable harm, an ex parte injunction 'without notice' may be obtained almost immediately.[110]

In the circumstances, Levin's proposal to reduce the ten-day waiting period before the restoration of content stands to reason. A possible compromise worth considering might be a three-day (i.e. business or working days) waiting period for restoration. This arguably would allow sufficient time for the right holder to obtain an injunction, or if not *at the very least initiate* legal proceedings, against the subscriber. Unless an intermediary hears from the right holder regarding the initiation of legal proceedings within the three-day window, it must *immediately* restore access to the content originally removed.

Subject to the above modification regarding timing, it is worth introducing a provision that provides for a counter-notice and restoration mechanism into the E-Commerce Directive and the UK E-Commerce Regulations. The introduction of such a provision will help counteract the abuse of the notice and takedown by right holders and erroneous takedowns by intermediaries.

Misrepresentations

The second safeguard worth considering aims to deal with misrepresentations made in notices of infringement and counter-notices. In the context

109 Senate Report 105–190 on the Digital Millennium Copyright Act, 105th Congress, 2nd Session (1998), 50.

110 Civil Procedure Rules 1998, Rule 25.3 read with Practice Direction 25A (Interim Injunctions), para 4.1.

of the DMCA, both notices and counter-notices must contain a statement that the assertions contained therein are made in *good faith*.[111] The DMCA not only requires notices and counter-notices to be made under penalty of perjury[112] but also provides that any person who ***knowingly*** makes a ***material misrepresentation*** in a notice or counter-notice shall be liable to pay damages to the party aggrieved by that misrepresentation.[113] The E-Commerce Directive does not contain equivalent provisions. Despite calls for the inclusion of this safeguard (as well as other safeguards such as the counter-notice and restoration mechanism) during the drafting phase,[114] the E-Commerce Directive eventually did not contain any of these safeguards. Although the effectiveness of the safeguard against misrepresentations has been doubted in the US context,[115] it is still useful in mitigating the abusive effects of notice and takedown.[116]

As such, it is worth introducing a similar safeguard in the EU and UK safe harbours. For instance, a new provision could be introduced that criminalises the making of a false statement in a notice of infringement or counter-notice, in addition to providing for liability in damages to any person who suffers losses as a result of a false statement.

Good faith takedowns

The third safeguard relates to the general immunity afforded to intermediaries in respect of *good faith* takedowns. Although Article 14(1) of the E-Commerce Directive ensures that hosts are 'not liable for . . . information stored at the request of a recipient of the service', it does not confer immunity from any liability that might arise for taking down content. On the other hand, the DMCA confers such immunity to hosts in conjunction with the

111 17 USC §512(c)(3)(A)(v) ('A statement that the complaining party has a good faith belief that use of the material in the manner complained of is not authorized by the copyright owner, its agent, or the law') and §512(g)(3)(C) ('A statement under penalty of perjury that the subscriber has a good faith belief that the material was removed or disabled as a result of mistake or misidentification of the material to be removed or disabled').

112 17 USC §512(c)(3)(A)(vi) and §512(g)(3)(C).

113 17 USC §512(f).

114 Electronic Frontier Foundation, *Submission on the Consultation on the EU E-Commerce Directive* (2010) <www.eff.org/files/filenode/international/effeuecommercedirectiveconsultationresponse.pdf> (accessed 31 January 2019).

115 See the discussion in Chapter 6 under 'Academic commentaries on the abuse of notice and takedown'.

116 GB Dinwoodie, 'A Comparative Analysis of the Secondary Liability of Online Service Providers' in GB Dinwoodie (ed), *Secondary Liability of Internet Service Providers* (Springer 2017), 42–43.

provision that mandates counter-notice and restoration procedures. Thus, in the event content removed from a host's server or platform turns out to be non-infringing, that host will nevertheless be shielded from any ensuing claim for damages at the instance of the aggrieved subscriber.[117] This is an important safeguard from the point of view of intermediaries that host third-party content.

There are, however, two important limitations as regards the general immunity conferred on hosts, which are aimed at safeguarding the interests of subscribers. First, as stated before, the immunity will not apply when a host fails to comply with the requisite counter-notice and restoration procedures.[118] The interaction between general immunity and the provision mandating counter-notice and restoration plays an important role in safeguarding the interests of subscribers. Second, it will be open for an aggrieved subscriber to displace good faith on the part of a host, in which event the immunity will be lifted and a claim for damages may be brought. Again, this works as an important safeguard in favour of subscribers, as hosts, at least theoretically, will be incentivised to employ some form of due diligence before exercising their discretion to either remove or retain content identified as infringing in a notice of infringement.

A point that must be noted, however, is that in nearly all situations the relationship between hosts and subscribers is governed by contract and such contracts often contain wide exclusion clauses. In light of this, the utility of the safeguard against bad faith removal and non-compliance with the counter-notification requirement, at least insofar as subscribers are concerned, is questionable. Accordingly, before adopting this safeguard, some adjustments are required. An approach that might be worth considering is to expressly set out that the immunity provision shall override any liability exclusion clause in contracts between hosts and subscribers to the extent it conflicts with the operation of the immunity provision. In other words, intermediaries that provide hosting services should not be allowed to contract out of any statutory provision specifically setting out the conditions upon which they are to be shielded from liability for taking down non-infringing content. This will ensure that aggrieved subscribers retain the right of instituting legal action against hosts that act in bad faith or fail to comply with the counter-notice and restoration procedures.

Some further reflections

The three safeguards set out above are crucial in counteracting the abusive use of notice and takedown by right holders, as well as the possibility of erroneous takedowns by intermediaries. In particular, the 'counter-notice and restoration' mechanism is an absolute necessity given the increased automation of the notice

117 17USC §512(g)(1).
118 17USC §512(g)(2).

and takedown process.[119] That said, there are other avenues to further finetune the practice of notice and takedown.

For instance, a more stringent notice requirement that explicitly requires right holders to provide externally verifiable evidence of a prima facie case, such as evidence gathered through trap purchases, and to verify the contents of the notice, such as documentary evidence of trade mark registration to establish ownership, could significantly reduce the frivolous and abusive use of notice and takedown.[120] In addition, there is a sound argument against the removal of content *prior to* any response from the alleged infringer, except in cases of counterfeiting[121] or default on the part of the subscriber.[122]

Insofar as the UK is concerned, it would be imperative to include these safeguards in the E-Commerce Regulations, and any subsequent legislative instrument that might replace it post-Brexit. Only then will the reforms proposed in Chapter 5, which widen the reach of trade mark liability to capture intermediaries engaged in the hosting of third-party content, will provide the basis for an effective, fair and transparent practice of notice and takedown in the trade mark context. It is also hoped that this book will inspire EU legislators to amend the E-Commerce Directive so that these safeguards could be introduced at the EU-level, an amendment that is long overdue.

119 In the recent times, intermediaries are increasingly using technology to detect and takedown infringing content on a voluntary basis. Soon this could even become obligatory under the law, as developments in the copyright context suggest (see e.g. Article 17 of the Directive on Copyright in the Digital Single Market, which was recently adopted by the European Parliament and endorsed by the Council on 15 April 2019). However, some have raised concerns about automated or algorithmic enforcement. See e.g. M Perel and N Elkin-Koren, 'Accountability in Algorithmic Copyright Enforcement' (2016) 19 *Stanford Technology Law Review* 473, 532:

> The automation of online copyright enforcement—algorithmic applications of the statutory Notice and Takedown regime, and especially algorithmic systems that are capable of blocking allegedly infringing content ex ante—raises serious challenges to the basic notions standing at the heart of accountable enforcement regimes: transparency, due process and public oversight

JM Urban, J Karaganis and BL Schofield, *Notice and Takedown in Everyday Practice* (Berkeley Law/American Assembly 2016), 8:

> Faced with large-scale infringement, large corporations now use automated 'bots' to search for copyright violations and generate millions of automated 'takedown' notices to OSPs. While this allows some copyright owners to police their copyrights on today's Internet, relying on machines to make decisions about sometimes-nuanced copyright law raises questions about the effect on expression;

and Z Carpou, 'Robots, Pirates, and the Rise of the Automated Takedown Regime: Using the DMCA to Fight Piracy and Protect End-Users' (2016) 39 *Columbia Journal of Law & the Arts* 551, 555:

> This Note argues that automated notice-and-takedown processes are in fact the most efficient means available to deal with the high volume of infringing content in the digital world, but that the counter-notification procedure needs to be strengthened to provide more protection to noninfringing users in the event that their content is removed.

120 F Mostert and MB Schwimmer, 'Notice and Takedown for Trademarks' (2011) 101 *Trademark Reporter* 249, 274–78.

121 Brege and Ovies, above n19, 403–04.

122 Mostert and Schwimmer, above n120, 277 (a default is the absence of a response on the part of the alleged infringer or the failure to remedy a faulty response when prompted. The alleged infringer will be in default unless the response contains verifiable information pertaining to the party's legal identity, telephone number and street address).

8 Injunctions against intermediaries—*legal basis*

The injunctive remedy is a useful means of holding internet intermediaries legally responsible for their role in providing access to, hosting or indexing content that infringes trade mark rights. Although the availability of monetary relief, as postulated in Chapter 5, in conjunction with the safeguards recommended in Chapter 7, is of practical value in the fight against infringements, you may recall that the proposed remedy is specifically targeted at hosts, to the exclusion of other categories of intermediaries. Nevertheless, that does not mean that such intermediaries have no part to play in addressing trade mark infringements taking place in the online space, albeit a more nuanced approach is required in holding them legally responsible in situations that warrant positive action on their part. To that end, injunctions have so far played an important role in compelling ISPs to adopt technical measures to block access to infringing websites. In the future, it is also possible that injunctions prescribing technical measures will be awarded against navigation providers and even hosts.

The legal basis for injunctions against intermediaries

The legal basis for injunctions against 'intermediaries' in the intellectual property context is derived from Article 8(3) of the Info-Soc Directive[1] and Article 11 (third sentence) of the Enforcement Directive.[2] Injunctions, as contemplated by

1 Directive 2001/29/EC of the European Parliament and of the Council of 22 May 2001 on the Harmonisation of Certain Aspects of Copyright and Related Rights in the Information Society [2001] OJ L 167/10 (Info-Soc Directive).

2 Directive 2004/48/EC of the European Parliament and of the Council of 29 April 2004 on the Enforcement of Intellectual Property Rights [2004] OJ L 157/16 (Enforcement Directive). It must be noted that Article 8(3) of the Info-Soc Directive deals exclusively with the enforcement of copyright and is therefore considered *lex specialis* vis-à-vis Article 11 (third sentence) of the Enforcement Directive. In this regard, Recital (23) of the Enforcement Directive provides that '[a]s far as infringements of copyright and related rights are concerned, a comprehensive level of harmonisation is already provided for in Directive 2001/29/EC. Article 8(3) of Directive 2001/29/EC should therefore not be affected by this Directive.' Moreover, Article 11 (third sentence) of the Enforcement Directive applies 'without prejudice to Article 8(3) of Directive 2001/29/EC'.

the two EU directives, may be directed at all types of internet intermediaries, as well as at intermediaries operating in the offline context. Thus, the viability of this remedy as a means of protecting trade mark rights becomes immediately apparent. Injunctions could be, and in fact have been, directed at ISPs to block access to websites containing infringing content, an approach that has gained popularity in some EU Member States,[3] as well as in the UK, also giving rise to the catchphrase 'blocking injunction'.

Although courts in the UK enjoy fairly broad powers to award injunctions[4] or interdicts as they are called in Scotland,[5] EU law has been greatly influential in shaping the operation of the remedy as a means of enforcing intellectual property rights. As such, it is not surprising that in dealing with the legal basis for injunctions against intermediaries, courts in the UK have referred to the corresponding EU directives that set out the framework for such injunctions. For instance, Article 11 (third sentence) of the Enforcement Directive played a pivotal role in determining the legal basis for the blocking injunction awarded in *Cartier v Sky*,[6] the first case in the UK, if not in the EU (and perhaps the entire world), in which ISPs were compelled to block access to websites that infringed trade mark rights. However, there appears to be a *gap* or *disconnect* between the legal basis for injunctions under Article 11 (third sentence) and the blocking injunction awarded against the ISPs in *Cartier v Sky*. Much of this chapter concerns this gap between the legal basis and execution.

Notably, the gap described above is unique to the trade mark context and is brought about by the mandatory reference to EU legal principles in determining the legal basis for injunctions under domestic law. As such, one might posit that Brexit will have the natural side effect of 'bridging the gap', so to speak, rendering any discussion about it purely academic. However, in view of the possible post-Brexit transition period, and the continued relevance of EU legal principles to the UK, at least to the extent that they have been already implemented in domestic law, the discussion undertaken in this chapter is of value in setting out

3 To date, injunctions against ISPs have been awarded in Austria, Belgium, Denmark, Finland, France, Greece, Ireland, Italy and the Netherlands. However, this approach has not been favoured by the courts in Germany and Spain, or in Norway among the EEA states. See P Savola, 'Proportionality of Website Blocking: Internet Connectivity Providers as Copyright Enforcers' (2014) 36 *Journal of Intellectual Property, Information Technology and Electronic Commerce Law* 116, 120 for a useful tabulated (but slightly outdated) summary of these cases. For a more recent account of these cases, see J Riordan, *The Liability of Internet Intermediaries* (Oxford University Press 2016), 508–35.

4 In England and Wales, section 37 of the Senior Courts Act 1981 provides that the 'High Court may by order (whether interlocutory or final) grant an injunction . . . in all cases in which it appears to the court to be just and convenient to do so'. Similarly, in Northern Ireland, section 91(1)(b) of the Judicature (Northern Ireland) Act 1978 empowers the High Court of Northern Ireland to award injunctions 'in any case where it appears to the court to be just and convenient to do so'.

5 In Scotland, injunctions are called interdicts and the Court of Sessions is empowered to grant such interdicts on a permanent and interim basis. See Court of Sessions Act 1988, section 47 (which deals with interim interdicts).

6 *Cartier International AG v British Sky Broadcasting Ltd* [2015] ETMR 1 (*Cartier v Sky*).

how the legal basis for injunctions should be viewed in the future. In any case, insofar as the remaining EU Member States are concerned, it is worth addressing the gap between the legal basis for injunctions against intermediaries and their execution in the trade mark context with a possible amendment at the EU level.

Injunctions against ISPs—the 'blocking injunction'

This part of the chapter maps out the development of the injunctive remedy against ISPs in the copyright context, and then considers the recent, albeit problematic, extension of the remedy to the context of enforcing trade marks. The copyright context is considered first for two reasons. Chronologically, the copyright cases precede the trade mark cases, and therefore it is useful to refer to the injunctive remedy in the copyright context in order to set out the principles that come into play in determining when an injunction could be awarded against an ISP. Also, the central argument set out in this part, which seeks to highlight the 'legal basis/execution' gap concerning the injunctive remedy, is derived from the difference between the ways in which copyright and trade mark infringements take place on the internet. As such, it is necessary to refer to the copyright context first.

The copyright context

In the EU, it was in the copyright context that injunctions were first used to mitigate the effects of infringements occurring on the internet. Typically, an injunction is directed at an ISP or several ISPs operating within an EU Member State compelling the ISP or ISPs to block access to websites containing content that infringes copyright. The possibility of obtaining such blocking injunctions is explicitly laid down in Article 8(3) of the Info-Soc Directive, which obligates EU Member States to ensure that aggrieved copyright owners are permitted to seek injunctions against 'intermediaries' whose services are used by third parties to commit infringements of copyright or related rights.[7] Although Article 8(3) does not contain an explicit reference to the internet as such, there seems to be a particular focus on the 'digital environment'.[8] The award of injunctions against ISPs is not contrary to the limitation of liability provisions in the E-Commerce

7 Notably, in the UK , in view of section 37 of the Senior Courts Act 1981, it would have been possible for an injunction such as the one contemplated by Article 8(3) of the Info-Soc Directive to have been obtained even before the directive came into force.

8 Recital (59) of the Info-Soc Directive, which supplies the rationale for Article 8(3), provides that '[i]n the digital environment, in particular, the services of intermediaries may increasingly be used by third parties for infringing activities'. As such, there seems to be a particular focus on the digital environment. See R Arnold, 'Who Is an Intermediary for the Purposes of Article 11 of the Enforcement Directive?' Speech made at the 1st iCLIC Conference (2015) <https://youtu.be/tpeUyOzI_iw> (accessed 31 January 2019).

Directive.[9] Even though a claim for damages does not lie against ISPs,[10] it does not mean that they are exempt from being the subject of an injunction, provided that the injunction is aimed at *terminating* or *preventing* an infringement.[11]

When Article 8(3) was implemented in the UK, through an amendment to the Copyright Designs and Patents Act 1988 (CDPA), no reference was made to the phrase 'intermediaries'. Instead, section 97A(1) of the CDPA confers the English High Court (and, in Scotland, the Court of Session) the power to award an injunction against a 'service provider', where that service provider has actual knowledge of another person using its services to infringe copyright.[12] Section 97A(3) of the CDPA provides that the term 'service provider' takes the same meaning given to it by Regulation 2 of the E-Commerce Regulations.[13] Accordingly, a 'service provider' means any 'information society service' provider, which includes ISPs. Thus, in the UK, injunctions taken out pursuant to section 97A of the CDPA are limited only to internet intermediaries,[14] and this has been utilised to enjoin ISPs from time to time.

The ambit of section 97A(1) is quite broad because an injunction may be granted where a service provider has actual knowledge of 'another person' using its services to infringe copyright. This not only includes parties with whom the service provider has a contractual relationship, for instance, subscribers of an ISP's services but also potentially any third party, which could include foreign operators responsible for websites that host or index infringing content.

It is also noteworthy that injunctions pursuant to section 97A(1) of the CDPA are available only against service providers that have *actual knowledge* 'of another person using their service to infringe copyright',[15] even though this requirement

9 Directive 2000/31/EC on Certain Legal Aspects of Information Society Services, in Particular Electronic Commerce, in the Internal Market [2000] OJ L 178/1 (E-Commerce Directive).

10 E-Commerce Directive, art 12(1).

11 E-Commerce Directive, art 12(3), which expressly permits judicial or administrative measures requiring service providers to terminate or prevent infringements.

12 In respect of performers' rights, section 191JA of the CDPA provides a similar remedy.

13 Electronic Commerce (EC Directive) Regulations 2002, SI 2002/2013 (E-Commerce Regulations).

14 Arguably, however, in terms of the broader powers conferred on the High Court under section 37 of the Senior Courts Act 1981, it is still possible to obtain injunctions against 'intermediaries' irrespective of whether they are information society service providers, or operate in the online or offline environments.

15 In *Twentieth Century Fox Film Corp v British Telecommunications Plc* [2011] EWHC 1981 (Ch) (*Twentieth C Fox v BT*), the following observation was made by Arnold J regarding the knowledge requirement (at [148]): 'I consider that what must be shown is that the service provider has actual knowledge of one or more persons using its service to infringe copyright. The more information the service provider has about the infringing activity, the more likely it is that the service provider will have actual knowledge. Thus it may well be relevant to consider whether or to what extent the service provider has knowledge of particular copyright works (or at least classes of copyright works) being involved, of particular restricted acts (or at least types of restricted act) being committed and of particular persons (or at least groups of persons) committing those acts; ***but it is not essential to prove actual knowledge of a specific infringement of a specific copyright work by a specific individual***' (emphasis added).

is not contained in Article 8(3) of the Info-Soc Directive. It appears that the inclusion of this requirement was possible because Recital (59) of the Info-Soc Directive provides that 'conditions and modalities relating to such injunctions should be left to the national law of Member States'.[16] Although actual knowledge is capable of being imputed upon a notice being served on the service provider, containing, among other things, the details of the infringement in question,[17] such notice is merely a means of imputing actual knowledge.[18] It is unclear as to why it was decided to impose such a requirement. Particularly in the case of ISPs, unlike hosts, the supply of knowledge is not capable of sustaining a claim for damages in view of the general immunity afforded to them under the EU safe harbour.[19] Perhaps the only reasonable explanation, therefore, for the existence of such a knowledge requirement is that it allows a service provider to investigate a right holder's claim.[20] However, in the case of ISPs, even in relation to a credible notice of infringement, it is unlikely that the service provider will take any positive steps to address the interests of the right holder, in the absence of a court order.[21]

In the UK, copyright owners have sought blocking injunctions in terms of section 97A of the CDPA in a number of instances. *Twentieth C Fox v BT* was the first in a series of cases where a copyright-related blocking injunction was issued. This was a sequel to an earlier dispute between the well-known film production company (Twentieth Century Fox) and Newzbin Ltd, where the latter maintained a website located at 'www.newzbin.com' that promoted large-scale copyright infringements.[22] Upon the English High Court issuing an injunction

16 T Headdon, 'Beyond Liability: On the Availability and Scope of Injunctions against Online Intermediaries after L'Oréal v eBay' (2012) 34 *European Intellectual Property Review* 137, 141.

17 CDPA, sections 97A(2)(a) and (b).

18 CDPA, section 97A(2) ('In determining whether a service provider has actual knowledge for the purpose of this section, a court shall take into account all matters which appear to it in the particular circumstances to be relevant'). See also *Twentieth Century Fox Film Corp v Newzbin Ltd* [2010] EWHC 608 (Ch) (*Twentieth C Fox v Newzbin*), [135] (Kitchin J):

> I do not accept that service of such a notice is a precondition of a finding that a service provider has actual knowledge of another person using its service to infringe copyright. Such is evident from the section which says that this is simply one of the matters to which the court must have regard.

19 This is clear upon a reading of Article 12(1) of the E-Commerce Directive.

20 This was Arnold J's explanation in *Twentieth C Fox v BT* at [141].

21 Unlike in the case of hosts, which are afforded immunity in terms of Article 14(1) of the E-Commerce Directive on the condition that they remove infringing material upon acquiring actual knowledge or awareness of an infringement, ISPs are granted unconditional immunity under Article 12(1) so long as they fulfil the criteria of neutrality. In essence, ISPs are unlikely to have any motivation to voluntarily adopt technical measures to block access to infringing content, even in circumstances where right holders put them on notice.

22 *Twentieth C Fox v Newzbin*, [126] (Kitchin J):

> The defendant is liable to the claimants for infringement of their copyrights because it has authorised the copying of the claimants' films; has procured and engaged with its premium members in a common design to copy the claimants' films; and has communicated the claimants' films to the public.

Newzbin provided its users with access to a large index on its website through which they were able to download copyrighted films, television programmes and other copyrighted works fragmented and stored in a large number of servers (known as Usenet servers) located around the world.

against Newzbin Ltd to cease operations at its website,[23] an unknown third party subsequently restored the website from an offshore location. This made it difficult for Twentieth Century Fox to seek redress against that unknown party. Thus, adopting a different strategy, Twentieth Century Fox filed an action against British Telecom, an ISP operating in the UK, seeking an injunction pursuant to section 97A of the CDPA to compel the defendant to block access to the infringing website. The Court issued a blocking injunction, resulting in British Telecom subscribers being prevented from accessing the infringing website in question. In essence, a section 97A injunction was used to mitigate the impact of copyright infringements within the UK, even where an infringing website was operating from an unknown offshore location.

Following *Twentieth C Fox v BT*, copyright-related blocking injunctions were issued in several cases including *Dramatico v Sky*,[24] *EMI Records v Sky*,[25] *Football Association v Sky*[26] and *Paramount Entertainment v Sky*,[27] consequent to which a number of infringing websites were blocked.

The trade mark context

While blocking injunctions have been mainly granted in respect of claims in relation to copyright infringements, it was only in 2014 that such an injunction was issued in the trade mark context. In *Cartier v Sky*, a blocking injunction was issued against the five major ISPs in the UK, compelling them to block access to certain identified websites that promoted the sale of counterfeit goods.[28] Unlike in the copyright context, however, there is no statutory counterpart to section 97A of the CDPA that provides a legal basis for blocking injunctions in the field of trade marks.[29] Accordingly, in *Cartier v Sky*, a two-tiered approach was adopted to determine the English High Court's jurisdiction.

Mr Justice Arnold began the jurisdictional analysis by considering the scope of section 37(1) of the Senior Courts Act 1981 on a purely domestic interpretation. While the power vested in the High Court to grant injunctions is confirmed by,

23 On 14 April 2010, Kitchin J (as he then was) granted an injunction restraining Newzbin from infringing copyright in films and television programmes in relation to which the claimant had rights. The injunction also required that Newzbin ensures that neither its website nor any of the services it provides are used by its subscribers to commit infringements. The orders were summarised by Arnold J in *Twentieth C Fox v BT* at [43].

24 *Dramatico Entertainment Ltd v British Sky Broadcasting Ltd* [2012] EWHC 268 (Ch) (*Dramatico v Sky*).

25 *EMI Records Ltd v British Sky Broadcasting Ltd* [2013] EWHC 379 (Ch) (*EMI Records v Sky*).

26 *Football Association Premier League Ltd v British Sky Broadcasting Ltd* [2013] EWHC 2058 (Ch) (*Football Association v Sky*).

27 *Paramount Home Entertainment International Ltd v British Sky Broadcasting Ltd* [2013] EWHC 3479 (Ch) (*Paramount Entertainment v Sky*).

28 Following *Cartier v Sky*, the English High Court has ordered further blocking measures on two separate occasions essentially in favour of the same applicants. See *Cartier International AG v British Sky Broadcasting Ltd* [2014] EWHC 3915 (Ch); *Cartier International Ltd v British Telecommunications Plc* [2016] EWHC 339 (Ch).

29 *Cartier v Sky*, [5] (Arnold J).

albeit not derived from, section 37(1),[30] the Court held that the said provision reflected an ***unlimited*** jurisdiction or power to grant injunctions.[31] By analogy, Arnold J relied on the following principle established in *Norwich Pharmacal Co v Customs & Excise Commissioners*:

> If a man has in his possession or control goods the dissemination of which, whether in the way of trade or, possibly, merely by way of gifts (see *Upmann v Forester*, 24 Ch.D. 231) will infringe another's patent or trade mark, he becomes, as soon as he is aware of this fact, subject to a duty, an equitable duty, not to allow those goods to pass out of his possession or control at any rate in circumstances in which the proprietor of the patent or mark might be injured by infringement ensuing. . . . This duty is one which will, if necessary, be enforced in equity by way of injunction.[32]

Building on this logic, Arnold J observed:

> [I]t is not a long step from this to conclude that, once an ISP becomes aware that its services are being used by third parties to infringe an intellectual property right, then it becomes subject to a duty to take proportionate measures to prevent or reduce such infringements even though it is not itself liable for infringement.[33]

In addition, given the novel ways in which the High Court's jurisdiction under section 37(1) of the Senior Courts Act 1981 had been previously exercised, Arnold J was satisfied that the Court had the requisite jurisdiction to issue a blocking injunction against the ISPs as requested in *Cartier v Sky*.[34] Accordingly, the judge concluded that, on a purely domestic interpretation of section 37(1) of the Senior Courts Act 1981, the English High Court had jurisdiction to award the injunctions sought by the applicants and that 'there is a principled basis for it to do so'.[35]

Alternatively, even assuming that the High Court did not have the jurisdiction to award the injunction applied for on a purely domestic interpretation of section 37(1) of the Senior Courts Act 1981, the Court held that section 37(1)

30 *Cartier v Sky*, [99] (Arnold J) citing *Fourie v Le Roux* [2007] UKHL 1, [25] (Lord Scott of Foscote):

> The power of a judge sitting in the High Court to grant an injunction against a party to proceedings properly served is confirmed by, but does not derive from, section 37 of the Supreme Court Act 1981 and its statutory predecessors.

31 *Cartier v Sky*, [101] (Arnold J) citing *Broadmoor Special Hospital Authority v Robinson* [2000] QB 775, [20] (Lord Woolf MR). See also Riordan, above n3, 498.

32 [1974] AC 133, 145–46 (Buckley LJ).

33 *Cartier v Sky*, [106] (Arnold J).

34 *Cartier v Sky*, [107] (Arnold J).

35 *Cartier v Sky*, [111] (Arnold J).

'can and should be construed' in accordance with Article 11 (third sentence) of the Enforcement Directive,[36] in light of the principle that establishes a requirement to interpret national laws in line with provisions of EU law (known as the *Marleasing* principle).[37] Under this approach, Arnold J had to consider the threshold conditions set out in Article 11 (third sentence) before determining whether an injunction could be granted. Notably, it seems that these threshold conditions would have applied even if the High Court exercised its jurisdiction on a *purely domestic* interpretation of section 37(1).[38]

Article 11 (third sentence) of the Enforcement Directive provides that:

> Member States shall also ensure that rightholders are in a position to apply for an injunction against intermediaries whose services are used by a third party to infringe an intellectual property right.

Given the similarity that the third sentence of Article 11 shares with Article 8(3) of the Info-Soc Directive, which has been implemented in the UK through section 97A of the CDPA, the threshold conditions that typically must be satisfied in a section 97A application must similarly be satisfied in the trade mark context.[39] Accordingly, in *Cartier v Sky*, Arnold J concluded that the defendant ISPs were intermediaries[40] and that their services were being used[41] by the operators of the infringing websites to commit trade mark infringements.[42] The Court also concluded that the defendant ISPs had actual knowledge that their services were being used by third parties to commit infringements.[43] As such, it was justifiable for a blocking injunction to be issued in the circumstance of the case.

However, although there was no doubt that ISPs were 'intermediaries' for the purposes of Article 11 (third sentence) and that the websites sought to be blocked were clearly promoting trade mark infringements, Arnold J's analysis regarding the other two threshold conditions is somewhat controversial.

36 *Cartier v Sky*, [132] (Arnold J).

37 Case C-106/89, *Marleasing SA v La Comercial Internacional de Alimentacion SA* [1990] I-04135.

38 *Cartier v Sky*, [140] (Arnold J):

> Parliament has not laid down any threshold conditions for the exercise of the High Court's jurisdiction to grant an injunction against an intermediary on the basis that its services have been used to infringe other intellectual property rights. Having regard to the analysis of section 37(1) of the 1981 Act above, this might be thought to lead to the conclusion that the Court's discretion is entirely unfettered. In my judgment, however, it is clear from the judgments of the CJEU in *L'Oréal v eBay* and other cases that this is not correct. On the contrary, the Court must exercise its power under section 37(1) consistently with the provisions of the Enforcement Directive, and in particular Article 3 and the third sentence of Article 11, and with other applicable provisions of EU law, and in particular Articles 12 to 15 of the E-Commerce Directive.

39 *Cartier v Sky*, [139]–[141] (Arnold J).

40 *Cartier v Sky*, [142] (Arnold J).

41 *Cartier v Sky*, [155] (Arnold J).

42 *Cartier v Sky*, [146] (Arnold J).

43 *Cartier v Sky*, [157] (Arnold J).

The actual knowledge requirement

Insofar as the knowledge requirement is concerned, it must be noted that Article 11 (third sentence) of the Enforcement Directive does not impose such a requirement, just as in the case of Article 8(3) of the Info-Soc Directive. Since the UK Government did not choose to specifically transpose Article 11 (third sentence) of the Enforcement Directive into UK law, on the basis that section 37(1) of the Senior Courts Act 1981 already provided for injunctions as contemplated by the directive,[44] there was nothing in the domestic context that required the knowledge factor to be considered as a threshold condition for blocking injunctions in the trade mark context. The mere fact that section 97A(1) of the CDPA contained a knowledge requirement does not necessarily mean that ipso facto such an additional requirement is similarly required in the context of other intellectual property rights. However, Arnold J saw it fit to read the knowledge requirement into the trade mark context, in view of the concern that the failure to do so would amount to the imposition of a general monitoring obligation on the part of ISPs contrary to Article 15 of the E-Commerce Directive.[45]

However, it is unclear as to how this conclusion was reached. Since ISPs are afforded immunity from claims for damages pursuant to Article 12(1) of the E-Commerce Directive, or its national equivalent, the acquisition of knowledge of an underlying infringement would not render an ISP liable for damages. In view of the safe harbour conferred on ISPs, there is no reason to believe that the introduction of a knowledge requirement is necessary to ensure against the imposition of a general monitoring obligation on the part of ISPs. In any case, since ISPs do not become obligated to block access to infringing websites unless a court orders to do so,[46] the knowledge requirement seems redundant. Moreover, Arnold J's own conclusion that an ISP may be supplied with knowledge, in addition to being notified by right holders, 'as a result of being served with . . . evidence in support of the . . . application [seeking a blocking injunction]'[47] seems to support this view.

For the foregoing reasons, it is doubtful that the knowledge requirement serves any practical purpose in the context of trade mark-related blocking injunctions. As such, a reference to the CJEU might have been useful in order to seek a clarification as to whether there was a need for the imposition of a knowledge requirement in circumstances where the implementing EU Member State had decided to introduce such a requirement in legislation implementing Article 8(3) of the Info-Soc Directive, but decided not to enact specific legislation transposing Article 11 (third sentence) of the Enforcement Directive.

44 *Cartier v Sky*, [116] (Arnold J).

45 *Cartier v Sky*, [141] (Arnold J) ('If ISPs could be required to block websites without having actual knowledge of infringing activity, that would be tantamount to a general obligation to monitor').

46 This is the case even under section 97A of the CDPA.

47 *Cartier v Sky*, [157] (Arnold J).

The requirement that the ISPs' services must have been used by third parties to commit infringements

Mr Justice Arnold's reasoning in *Cartier v Sky* on whether the operators responsible for the infringing websites *used* the ISPs' services to infringe trade mark rights warrants a detailed analysis. To begin with, none of the defendant ISPs had any contractual relationship with the operators of the websites in question, thus lacking contractual control over them. Nor did the ISPs have any technical control over the infringing websites. It is quite evident that the role of ISPs vis-à-vis intermediaries that host third-party content, including websites, is far removed from the conduct of the actual infringers. Thus, Arnold J's conclusion that the operators responsible for the infringing websites used the ISPs' services to infringe trade mark rights is questionable.

The approach adopted by Arnold J in reaching that conclusion was influenced by EU case law. Reliance was placed on two cases, which were both references from the Oberster Gerichtshof (Supreme Court of Austria) to the CJEU raising questions in the copyright context. Thus, in *LSG v Tele2*,[48] the claimant, which represented the interests of music producers and artists, applied for a court order against Tele2, an Austrian ISP, seeking information of its subscribers in order to file an action against those who engaged in copyright infringement by using file-sharing software. It was in this context that the CJEU was called upon to rule on the question as to whether ISPs were 'intermediaries', which the CJEU answered in the affirmative.[49]

However, in *Cartier v Sky*, there was no dispute that the defendant ISPs were intermediaries. The question that had to be decided was whether the operators responsible for the infringing websites *used* the services of the ISPs to infringe trade mark rights. As such, the CJEU's ruling in *LSG v Tele2* could not have been directly relevant in answering that specific question, albeit the following observation the Court made may have been persuasive:

> Access providers who merely enable clients to access the Internet, even without offering other services or exercising any control, whether *de iure* or *de facto*, over the services which users make use of, provide a service capable of being used by a third party to infringe a copyright or related right, inasmuch as those access providers supply the user with the connection enabling him to infringe such rights.[50]

In any case, *LSG v Tele2* concerned the use of file-sharing software on the part of a subclass of Tele2's subscribers to commit copyright infringements.[51]

48 Case C-557/07, *LSG-Gesellschaft zur Wahrnehmung von Leistungsschutzrechten GmbH v Tele2 Tele communication GmbH* [2009] ECR I-01227 (*LSG v Tele2*).

49 *LSG v Tele2*, [46].

50 *LSG v Tele2*, [43] (emphasis in original).

51 *LSG v Tele2*, [17].

Thus, the finding that the ISP's services were, in fact, being used to infringe copyright was easily reached, as some of Tele2's subscribers themselves were engaging in unlawful file sharing.

The second case relied upon by Arnold J was *UPC Telekabel v Constantin Film*,[52] which was more relevant to the question that was being considered. In this case, the claimants were the owners of copyright in films which were being made available to the public without the claimants' consent on a website located at 'www.kino.to'. The claimants applied to an Austrian court seeking an order compelling Telekabel, an ISP, to block access to 'www.kino.to'. On appeal, the Oberster Gerichtshof made a reference to the CJEU on the question whether 'a person who makes protected subject matter available on the internet without the rightholder's consent . . . is *using the services of the access providers*'.[53] The CJEU ruled as follows:

> Accordingly, given that the internet service provider is an inevitable actor in any transmission of an infringement over the internet between one of its customers and a third party, since, in granting access to the network, it makes that transmission possible, it must be held that an internet service provider, such as that at issue in the main proceedings, *which allows its customers to access protected subject-matter made available to the public on the internet by a third party is an intermediary whose services are used to infringe a copyright*.[54]

In *Cartier v Sky*, Arnold J extended the CJEU's reasoning to the context of trade marks:

> [T]he operators of the Target Websites are infringing the Trade Marks by placing on the internet advertisements and offers for sale which are targeted at UK consumers. The ISPs have an *essential role in these infringements*, since it is via the ISPs' services that the advertisements and offers for sale are communicated to 95% of broadband users in the UK.[55]

However, Arnold J's approach is not without problems, particularly in view of the differences in the way copyright and trade mark infringements are committed in the online space and the role of ISPs in respect to such infringements. In order to articulate this point, it is first necessary to consider the role of ISPs in relation to copyright infringements.

In *UPC Telekabel v Constantin Film*, the underlying claim concerned the claimants' right of communication to the public in respect of works in which they owned copyright.[56] Copyright infringement in that context was dependent upon

52 Case C-314/12, *UPC Telekabel Wien GmbH v Constantin Film Verleih GmbH* [2014] ECDR 12 (*UPC Telekabel v Constantin Film*).

53 *UPC Telekabel v Constantin Film*, [23] (emphasis added).

54 *UPC Telekabel v Constantin Film*, [32] (emphasis added).

55 *Cartier v Sky*, [155] (Arnold J) (emphasis added).

56 Info-Soc Directive, art 3(1).

copyrighted material being made available to the public without the consent of the right holders, which was only possible if internet users had access to the website containing the infringing content. Thus, by streaming the films in which copyright subsisted via 'www.kino.to', an exclusive right vested in the claimants was infringed. It was against this backdrop that Telekabel provided its subscribers, no doubt constituting part of the public, access to 'www.kino.to', thereby making the copyrighted material available to the public. Thus, it was possible for the CJEU to conclude that the ISP's access services were quintessential for the infringement to occur:

> [G]iven that the internet service provider is an inevitable actor in any transmission of an infringement over the internet between one of its customers and a third party, since, in granting access to the network, it makes that transmission possible . . . it must be held that an internet service provider, such as that at issue in the main proceedings, *which allows its customers to access protected subject-matter made available to the public on the internet by a third party is an intermediary whose services are used to infringe a copyright or related right* within the meaning of Article 8(3) [of the Info-Soc Directive].[57]

Similarly, in *Brein v Ziggo*, the claimant's principal request was for an order compelling two Dutch ISPs, namely Ziggo and XS4ALL, to block access to 'The Pirate Bay' website 'in order to prevent the services of those internet access providers from being used to infringe the copyright and related rights of the rightholders'.[58] Consequently, the Hoge Raad der Nederlanden (Supreme Court of the Netherlands) sought a clarification from the CJEU as to whether the concept of 'communication to the public', within the meaning of Article 3(1) of the Info-Soc Directive, should be interpreted as covering the acts of an online platform that allowed its users to locate copyrighted works and share them in the context of a peer-to-peer network.[59] In providing an affirmative response, the CJEU ruled:

> Furthermore, as is apparent from Article 3(1) of [the Info-Soc Directive], in order for there to be an 'act of communication', it is sufficient, in particular, that a work is made available to a public in such a way that the *persons comprising that public may access it*, from wherever and whenever they individually choose, *irrespective of whether they avail themselves of that opportunity.*[60]

Accordingly, based on the CJEU's rulings in *UPC Telekabel v Constantin Film* and *Brein v Ziggo*, it is clear that a breach of the right of communication to the

57 *UPC Telekabel v Constantin Film*, [32] (emphasis added).
58 Case C-610/15, *Stichting Brein v Ziggo BV* [2017] ECDR 19 (*Brein v Ziggo*), [13].
59 *Brein v Ziggo*, [18].
60 *Brein v Ziggo*, [31] (emphasis added).

public is established when persons comprising the public had the *possibility* of gaining access to copyrighted works without the consent of the right holders. To that end, ISPs complete, and are essential to, the act of communicating works to the public, i.e. without there being access, there can be no communication of works to the public to begin with.

The question as to whether the services of an ISP were being utilised to engage in copyright infringements was also raised in *EMI Records v UPC*,[61] an Irish case, where an order was sought to block 'The Pirate Bay' website located at 'www.priratebay.org'. Mr Justice Charleton observed in this regard:

> I ask myself the question, whether internet facilities such as those sold by UPC [an ISP] *are being used to infringe the copyright in works owned by the recording company. In the present, though intermittent, sense they are. Each time someone downloads a work from other peer-to-peer users, the facilities of UPC are then being used to infringe the copyright owned by the recording company.*[62]

What *EMI Records v UPC* establishes is that the users of an ISP's access services commit copyright infringements each time they gain access to, and download or stream, copyrighted works via an infringing website. In other words, while making copyrighted works available to the public at a website, such as 'The Pirate Bay', without the consent of the right holders, is an infringement by the website's operators, each time an ISP's subscriber gains access to such a website and downloads or streams copyrighted works the subscriber commits a separate and independent act of infringement.

The threshold condition under Article 8(3) of the Info-Soc Directive (which mirrors the third sentence of Article 11 of the Enforcement Directive) is that 'third parties' must have used an intermediary's services to commit an infringement. Such third parties include the operators of an infringing website at which copyrighted works are unlawfully made available to the public, as well as the individual subscribers of an ISP who gain access to such protected works. As such, in the copyright context, the threshold condition that an ISP's services must have been utilised by third parties to commit infringements is easily established for the grant of blocking injunctions pursuant to Article 8(3) of the Info-Soc Directive.

In contrast to the copyright context, however, trade mark infringements take place in a vastly different manner. An infringement of a trade mark generally occurs from the moment an unauthorised third party makes *use* of that mark in the course of trade and in relation to identical or similar goods or services for which the mark is registered, provided of course such use is either presumed or

61 *EMI Records (Ireland) Ltd v UPC Communications Ireland Ltd* [2010] IEHC 377 (*EMI Records v UPC*).

62 *EMI Records v UPC*, [99] (Charleton J) (emphasis added).

is likely to cause confusion.[63] In the online context, and given the territoriality of trade mark rights, it may also be necessary to establish that such infringing use took place within the territory in which enforcement is sought. Subject to that requirement, the mere unauthorised use of a registered trade mark in online promotional material (e.g. a paid advertisement on Google or product listing on eBay) would suffice to constitute an infringement. Unlike in the case of a copyright owner's exclusive right of communication to the public, the infringement of trade mark rights does not depend on whether content incorporating a trade mark is *communicated* to, or is *accessible* by, the public, although arguably only then would it have a noticeable impact. After all, it is a well-established principle that in order to sustain an action for trade mark infringement what is required is only a *likelihood* of confusion.[64] The absence of actual confusion is not fatal to an infringement action. Thus, when infringers utilise registered trade marks in their websites or other online material, that alone could prima facie constitute an act of infringement.

As such, in the trade mark context, the role played by ISPs in providing internet access to their subscribers in no way relates to the infringing acts of the operators of a website targeted for blocking. There is neither a contractual nor a technical link between the ISPs, against whom a blocking injunction is sought, and the operators responsible for the website that is targeted by the injunction. More importantly, it cannot be concluded that an internet user who purchases an infringing article via a website infringes trade mark rights, as such a purchaser is often a victim, and not a perpetrator, of a trade mark infringement.[65] Thus, unlike in the copyright context, it cannot be easily concluded that the operators responsible for websites promoting the sale of infringing goods, or internet users

63 Directive 2008/95/EC of the European Parliament and of the Council of 22 October 2008 to Approximate the Laws of the Member States Relating to Trade Marks [2008] OJ L 299/25 (Trade Marks Directive). An explanation as to why a reference is made to the 2008 Trade Marks Directive, and not the later 2015 Trade Marks Directive (Directive (EU) 2015/2436), which replaces the former, is provided in Chapter 1.

64 See e.g. *Comic Enterprises Ltd v Twentieth Century Fox Film Corporation* [2016] EWCA Civ 41; *Interflora Inc v Marks and Spencer Plc* [2013] EWHC 1291 (Ch).

65 It must be noted that section 10(4)(c) of the Trade Marks Act 1994 provides that for the purposes of section 10, a person *uses* a sign if he 'imports or exports goods under the sign'. Thus, when a person purchases an infringing article for his or her own consumption or use from a *foreign* website, that might eventually result in the *importation* of that article, assuming that the article originated from outside the country of purchase. However, the purchaser of an infringing article does not infringe any trade mark rights, as he or she does not make use of a sign in the course of trade, which the CJEU has defined as use that 'occurs in the context of commercial activity with a view to economic advantage and not as a private matter' (Joined Cases C-236/08, C-237/08 and C-238/08, *Google France Sarl v Louis Vuitton Malletier SA* [2010] ECR I-02417, [50]). As such, it would appear that *Nike International Ltd v Bateman* [2010] EWPCC 010, where an innocent purchaser of a *single* pair of counterfeit Nike shoes purchased over the internet was found to have infringed Nike's trade mark rights, was decided wrongly. After all, trade mark law exists to, among other things, protect consumers. Of course, where an infringing article is imported for the purposes of resale, that would amount to an act of infringement on the part of the person importing, as the importation is done in the course of trade.

who gain access to such websites, make use of the internet access services offered by ISPs to commit trade mark infringements. As such, contrary to what Arnold J held in *Cartier v Sky*, in the trade mark context, the threshold condition that an ISP's services must have been *utilised* by third parties to commit infringements is difficult to establish for the grant of blocking injunctions pursuant to Article 11 (third sentence) of the Enforcement Directive.

However, it has been suggested that, 'even where customers of a provider might not infringe rights themselves when using the website, website blocking injunctions can still be issued against the provider, *as long as its services are used to channel users to infringing websites*'.[66] This observation was made citing the Advocate General's opinion[67] and the CJEU's ruling[68] in *UPC Telekabel v Constantin Film*, in relation to which Recital (59) of the Info-Soc Directive played a central role.[69]

Recital (59) provides in relevant part as follows:

> [W]ithout prejudice to any other sanctions and remedies available, rightholders should have the possibility of applying for an injunction against an intermediary *who carries a third party's infringement of a protected work or other subject-matter in a network*.[70]

On the basis of Recital (59), the CJEU in *UPC Telekabel v Constantin Film* came to the conclusion that:

> Article 8(3) of [the Info-Soc Directive] must be interpreted as meaning that a person who makes protected subject-matter available to the public on a

66 M Husovec, *Injunctions Against Intermediaries in the European Union: Accountable but Not Liable?* (Cambridge University Press 2017), 91 (emphasis added). See also M Husovec and M Peguera, 'Much Ado about Little–Privately Litigated Internet Disconnection Injunctions' (2015) 46(1) *International Review of Intellectual Property and Competition Law (IIC)* 10, 13 ('It suffices that the services are capable of serving as a communication channel for the infringements').

67 *UPC Telekabel v Constantin Film*, Opinion of AG Villalón, [51]:

> intermediaries are regarded by Directive 2001/29 as the best possible addressees of measures to terminate copyright infringements, primarily because they carry data 'in a network'. The wording makes it clear that this does not necessarily mean the first transmission of the data in a network, but also the further carrying in the network. This is even more clearly expressed in the English and Spanish versions of the directive: 'who carries a third party's infringement of a protected work . . . in a network'.

68 *UPC Telekabel v Constantin Film*, [32]:

> Accordingly, given that the internet service provider is an inevitable actor in any transmission of an infringement over the internet between one of its customers and a third party, since, in granting access to the network, it makes that transmission possible . . . it must be held that an internet service provider, such as that at issue in the main proceedings, which allows its customers to access protected subject-matter made available to the public on the internet by a third party is an intermediary whose services are used to infringe a copyright or related right within the meaning of Article 8(3) of Directive 2001/29.

69 *UPC Telekabel v Constantin Film*, Opinion of AG Villalón, [51]; *UPC Telekabel v Constantin Film* [30].

70 Info-Soc Directive, Recital (59) (third sentence) (emphasis added).

> website without the agreement of the rightholder . . . is using the services of the internet service provider *of the persons accessing that subject-matter*, which must be regarded as an intermediary within the meaning of Article 8(3).[71]

Thus, it was the broad language used in Recital (59) of the Info-Soc Directive, which provides the rationale for injunctions against intermediaries in the copyright context, that allowed the CJEU to overcome the narrowness of Article 8(3).

However, in stark contrast to Recital (59) of the Info-Soc Directive, Recital (23) of the Enforcement Directive, applicable to the trade mark context, merely provides that injunctions must be made available 'against an intermediary whose services are being used by a third party to infringe the rightholder's industrial property right'. This is precisely what is replicated in the third sentence of Article 11. Thus, insofar as the Enforcement Directive is concerned, it is not sufficient that the ISP concerned merely carries a third party's infringement in a network. An ISP's services must have been *used* to commit the infringement, which is much narrower language when compared to the language used in the Info-Soc Directive in the same respect. As such, the conclusion reached by the CJEU in *UPC Telekabel v Constantin Film*, which interpreted the Info-Soc Directive in the context of copyright infringements, cannot be applied to the trade mark context to which the Enforcement Directive applies.[72]

71 *UPC Telekabel v Constantin Film*, [40] (emphasis added).

72 Husovec (above n66 at p. 92) has argued that this line of argument is 'less convincing', citing two CJEU cases. First, reference is made to the CJEU's ruling in Case C-494/15, *Tommy Hilfiger Licensing LLC v Delta Center a.s.* [2017] ETMR 5. This case concerned the sale of counterfeits by traders in a marketplace in relation to which an injunction was sought against Delta Center, the party responsible for subletting stalls to such traders. The question before the CJEU was whether an entity such as Delta Centre could be regarded as 'an intermediary whose services are being used by a third party to infringe an intellectual property right' within the meaning of the third sentence of Article 11 of the Enforcement Directive. In response, the Court ruled that

> an operator which provides to third parties a service relating to the letting or subletting of pitches in a marketplace, thanks to which they have access to that marketplace and offer for sale in that marketplace counterfeit branded products, must be classified as an 'intermediary whose services are being used by a third party to infringe an intellectual property right' within the meaning of that provision.

However, unlike in the case of ISPs, there is no debate that the services of actors such as Delta Center are *used* by the traders in offering counterfeits. In that sense, Delta Center is akin to actors such as eBay, i.e. hosts of third-party content, in relation to which the threshold condition is easily satisfied (see discussion under '*Injunctions against hosts*' below). Second, reference is made to Advocate General Szpunar's opinion in *Brein v Ziggo* at [56] where he opined that Article 8(3) of the Info-Soc Directive and Article 11(third sentence) of the Enforcement Directive 'are similar in content'. Again, there is no debate about the similarity between the two provisions. But whether the threshold conditions set out therein have been met is a factual inquiry that takes into account the type of intermediary concerned and the role of the intermediary in relation to the infringements in question. As such, even in respect of the same class of intermediaries (such as ISPs), the fact that the threshold conditions set out in Article 8(3) of the Info-Soc Directive are met, in the context of copyright infringements, does not necessarily inform a determination under Article 11 (third sentence) of the Enforcement Directive in respect of trade mark infringements.

There is a further argument that supports this point of view, in relation to which reference must be made to the E-Commerce Directive. Although the remedies available against ISPs are limited under Article 12(1) of that directive, Article 12(3) provides that '[t]his Article shall not affect the possibility for a court or administrative authority, in accordance with Member States' legal systems, of requiring the service provider to terminate or prevent an infringement'. Clearly, injunctions are envisaged by this provision. Notably, however, an injunction issued against an ISP must *terminate* or *prevent* an infringement. A blocking injunction in the copyright context achieves precisely that by ensuring that an ISP's own subscribers do not gain *access* to websites containing content in violation of copyright. Without the possibility of access, the ISP's subscribers are prevented from downloading or streaming copyrighted content, thus effectively terminating and preventing infringements that arise from the reproduction of copyrighted works. Similarly, without access to such websites, copyrighted works cannot be communicated to the ISP's subscribers, effectively terminating and preventing any violation of the right of communication to the public. In essence, a blocking injunction in the copyright context not only terminates existing infringements but also prevents future infringements from occurring.

However, the same cannot be said as regards the trade mark context. Blocking access to infringing websites does not in any way terminate or prevent trade mark infringements *as such*. This is because the existence of a trade mark infringement is independent of the conduct of the subscribers of an ISP whose services are used to gain access to the infringing websites. When an ISP blocks access to a website that is the source of trade mark infringements, it merely prevents internet users in the country in which the ISP operates from gaining access to the source of infringements. This is not the same as terminating or preventing an infringement, which in this context could only be done if the infringing content is removed at its very source. Therefore, since the blocking injunction issued against ISPs in the trade mark context by no means terminates or prevents infringements from occurring, it cannot be a permitted remedy envisaged by Article 12(3) of the E-Commerce Directive. If this is true, it might even be the case that blocking injunctions cannot be issued against ISPs in the trade mark context, in view of the general immunity that Article 12(1) of the E-Commerce Directive otherwise provides.

There is support for this proposition in the Advocate General's opinion in *L'Oréal v eBay*[73] when guidance from the CJEU was sought for the first time on the scope of Article 11 of the Enforcement Directive:

> [T]here may be cases, especially in the internet environment, where the infringement is obvious but the infringer is not identified. It is known that a third party is using the services of an intermediary to infringe an intellectual property right but the true identity of that infringer remains unknown.

73 Case C-324/09, *L'Oréal SA v eBay International AG* [2011] ECR I-06011 (*L'Oréal v eBay*).

> In such cases the legal protection of the rightsholder may require that an injunction can be obtained against the intermediary whose identity is known and who thus can be brought to a court and *who is able to prevent continuation of the infringement.*[74]

The Advocate General's language above suggests that the very basis for obtaining an injunction under Article 11 (third sentence) against an intermediary is so that the continuation of an infringement may be prevented. In other words, an intermediary's *capacity* to prevent or terminate an infringement is a good indication that its services are being used for the commission of the infringement. However, unlike in the copyright context, it is difficult to suggest that the move to block access to a website promoting a trade mark infringement operates to terminate or prevent the continuation of the infringement as such.

There is, however, an additional consequential point that needs to be addressed, which arises from the CJEU's ruling in *L'Oréal v eBay*. One of the questions referred to the CJEU was:

> whether, for the proprietor of a trade mark registered in a Member State of the EU or of a Community trade mark to be able to prevent, under the rules set out in Article 5 of [the Trade Marks Directive] . . . the offer for sale, on an online marketplace, of goods bearing that trade mark which have not previously been put on the market in the EEA or, in the case of a Community trade mark, in the EU, it is sufficient that the offer for sale is targeted at consumers located in the territory covered by the trade mark.[75]

In short, where both the conduct of an infringer and the infringing goods originate outside the EU, in circumstances where the website incorporating the trade mark in question *targets* consumers in a particular EU Member State, the key issue was whether a trade mark infringement was being committed within the territory of that state, or, in the case of a Community trade mark, within the EU. The CJEU's response was in the affirmative.[76] Although this conclusion was reached in the context of product listings in an online marketplace, it is submitted that it could also be more generally extended to other websites that incorporate trade marks, for instance in advertising the availability of goods or services. In essence, even where a trade mark is unlawfully incorporated into the contents of a website originating in a non-EU state, if the website is 'targeted' at consumers in one or more EU Member States, that would give rise to infringing use of a trade mark within the meaning of Article 5 of the Trade Marks Directive. Thus, in those circumstances, whether there is a trade mark infringement within

74 *L'Oréal v eBay*, Opinion of AG Jääskinen, [179] (emphasis added). See also M Husovec, 'Injunctions against Innocent Third Parties: The Case of Website Blocking' (2012) 4 *Journal of Intellectual Property, Information Technology and Electronic Commerce Law* 116, 118.

75 *L'Oréal v eBay*, [58].

76 *L'Oréal v eBay*, [67].

a particular EU Member State is dependent on the infringing website or content being *targeted* at consumers in that particular Member State, irrespective of where the website or content is hosted or where the infringers reside.

However, it should be noted that the fact that an infringing website or its content targets the consumers of an EU Member State does not necessarily imply that the ISPs operating in that jurisdiction are being used for the commission of the trade mark infringements. Nor can it be said that the ISPs play an 'essential role' (adopting Arnold J's language)[77] in the infringement. This is because, ISPs in a particular EU Member State enable internet users to access *any* website hosted on the internet, irrespective of whether it is targeted at consumers in that jurisdiction. ISPs do not and are unable to draw a distinction between websites targeting consumers in the jurisdiction within which they operate and other websites. In fact, the English High Court has held that, merely because a website is accessible from within a particular jurisdiction, that per se does not suggest that the website is being targeted at users of that jurisdiction.[78] Therefore, it is difficult to suggest that ISPs in a particular jurisdiction play an 'essential role' in the commission of trade mark infringements even where an infringing website hosted overseas targets consumers in that jurisdiction.

In the circumstances, there appears to be a gap between the legal basis for injunctions as set out in Article 11 (third sentence) of the Enforcement Directive and the blocking injunction awarded in *Cartier v Sky*, which was directed at ISPs that merely provided access to infringing websites, without their services being used by the infringers in any sense. Thus, the CJEU's guidance could have been sought on the specific question of whether the operators of a website, in committing trade mark infringements, make use of the internet access services of ISPs operating within the jurisdiction in which a blocking injunction is sought for the purposes of satisfying the threshold condition in Article 11 (third sentence).

Although Arnold J's approach of relying on authorities in the copyright context to support the basis for blocking injunctions in the field of trade marks is questionable, it does not mean that the outcome in *Cartier v Sky*, i.e. the defendant ISPs being required to block access to infringing websites, was unwarranted. While justifying blocking injunctions in the trade mark context is difficult on the basis of Article 11 (third sentence) of the Enforcement Directive, the broader scope of section 37(1) of the Senior Courts Act 1981 provides a better basis for such injunctions. In discussing the High Court's section 37(1) jurisdiction, Arnold J observed that:

> [O]nce an ISP becomes aware that its services are being used by third parties to infringe an intellectual property right, then it becomes subject to a duty to take proportionate measures to prevent or reduce such infringements even though it is not itself liable for infringement.[79]

77 *Cartier v Sky*, [155] (Arnold J).

78 *Euromarket Designs Inc v Peters* [2000] ETMR 1025.

79 *Cartier v Sky*, [106] (Arnold J) (referring to the principle established in *Norwich Pharmacal Co v Customs & Excise Commissioners*).

Extending that logic further, it might be argued that, once an ISP becomes aware that its services are being used by third parties *to access* websites that infringe an intellectual property right, then it becomes subject to a duty to adopt proportionate measures to disable access to such infringing websites. That equitable duty alone provides a sound basis for right holders to seek out a blocking injunction in terms of section 37(1) of the Senior Courts Act 1981. In fact, this approach better justifies the introduction of the knowledge requirement even for trade mark-related blocking injunctions, as opposed to the reasoning offered by Arnold J in *Cartier v Sky*, which was premised on the concern that the failure to impose a knowledge requirement would tantamount to the imposition of a general monitoring obligation on ISPs.[80]

However, upon an appeal being preferred by the ISPs against the first instance decision in *Cartier v Sky*, the English Court of Appeal endorsed Arnold J's analysis of the threshold conditions,[81] and made it clear that the High Court's jurisdiction pursuant to section 37(1) must be exercised subject to EU law principles, which includes those set out in Article 11 (third sentence) of the Enforcement Directive.[82] Accordingly, the Court of Appeal's decision that Article 11 (third sentence) of the Enforcement Directive provides 'a principled basis for extending the practice of the court in relation to the grant of injunctions [under section 37(1)] to encompass . . . ISPs'[83] has significantly narrowed the scope of the High Court's jurisdiction under section 37(1) by the introduction of the various threshold conditions that must be typically satisfied before an injunction can be granted against an intermediary. The end result is that the legal basis for blocking injunctions in the field of trade marks remains problematic for the reasons set out above.

It may be posited, however, that Brexit might have the effect of 'bridging the gap' between the legal basis for injunctions against intermediaries and the execution of such injunctions in the trade mark context. In *Cartier v BT*,[84] consequent to a final appeal being lodged by one of the ISPs in *Cartier v Sky* (namely, British Telecom), the UK Supreme Court hinted at this possibility when Lord Sumption made the following obiter[85] remark:

> I therefore agree with the view expressed by Briggs LJ in his dissenting judgment in the Court of Appeal that the website blocking order made in

80 *Cartier v Sky*, [141] (Arnold J).

81 *Cartier International AG v British Sky Broadcasting Ltd* [2016] ETMR 43 (*Cartier v Sky (CA)*), [99] (Kitchin LJ).

82 *Cartier v Sky* (CA), [56] (Kitchin LJ).

83 *Cartier v Sky* (CA), [65] (Kitchin LJ).

84 *Cartier International AG v British Telecommunications Plc* [2018] UKSC 28 (*Cartier v BT*).

85 Although the legal basis for blocking injunctions was heavily contested before the High Court and Court of Appeal, it was no longer under discussion before the Supreme Court. See *Cartier v BT*, [5] (Lord Sumption):

> There was a major issue in the courts below about the jurisdiction of the court to make such an injunction under the general power conferred on the court by section 37(1) of the Senior Courts Act 1981. There were also issues about some of the criteria for granting them. The Court of Appeal upheld the decision of Arnold J on these points, and they are no longer in issue.

> this case could have been made quite apart from the power derived from European law, on ordinary principles of equity.[86]

Lord Sumption was referring to the following observation of Briggs LJ (as he then was):

> In the case of the UK, the courts of England and Wales had jurisdiction for the grant of injunctions conferred in the most general terms, now to be found in section 37(1) of the Senior Courts Act 1981, but in substance reflecting an originally unfettered jurisdiction exercised by the Court of Chancery on equitable principles.[87]

This means that in a post-Brexit Britain, there is a possibility that the High Court's jurisdiction under section 37(1) may be exercised in respect of the grant of blocking injunctions in the field of trade marks without reference to any of the threshold conditions imposed under EU law. This would, in effect, bridge the gap between legal basis and execution as discussed in this chapter. Insofar as the remaining EU Member States are concerned, the problematic application of Article 11 (third sentence) of the Enforcement Directive to trade mark-related blocking injunctions could only be set aside through an amendment to the directive, which explicitly lays down the possibility of obtaining injunctions against intermediaries that merely provide *access to* infringing content.

Injunctions against navigation providers

Although the Enforcement Directive (or the Info-Soc Directive) does not define the term 'intermediaries', it is not difficult to see how that term extends to navigation providers, in particular search engines. Nevertheless, it is necessary to consider whether Article 11 (third sentence) of the Enforcement Directive provides a proper legal basis for injunctions against navigation providers in the trade mark context, particularly in view of its relevance to the exercise of the High Court's jurisdiction under section 37(1) of the Senior Courts Act 1981. As explained earlier, for an injunction to be made available against *any* intermediary under the third sentence of Article 11, that intermediary's services must have been *used* by a third party to commit an infringement of intellectual property rights. Therefore, it becomes important to consider whether persons who engage in trade mark infringements, such as the operators of websites promoting the sale of infringing goods, make use of the services of navigation providers in committing the infringements.

In this regard, it must be pointed out that navigation providers are no different from ISPs, in that they merely index and provide hyperlinks to third-party content.

86 *Cartier v BT*, [15] (Lord Sumption).
87 *Cartier v Sky* (CA), [200] (Briggs LJ).

Just as ISPs, navigation providers, possess no contractual or technical control over the content that they link and the creators of such content. Nor do they exercise any such control over internet users who utilise their services. In the circumstances, it must be concluded, for the same reasons that applied in the context of ISPs, that the services of navigation providers are not utilised by third parties to commit trade mark infringements. Accordingly, one of the threshold conditions that must be satisfied before an injunction could be awarded on the basis of Article 11 (third sentence) of the Enforcement Directive is difficult to satisfy in relation to navigation providers. Since the English High Court's jurisdiction pursuant to section 37(1) must be exercised subject to principles of EU law, which include the threshold conditions set out in Article 11 (third sentence) of the Enforcement Directive, it must be concluded that there is currently no legal basis upon which injunctions could be awarded against navigation providers to enforce trade mark rights.

Insofar as the UK is concerned, it would be interesting to see how things unfold after Brexit, in particular whether the English High Court will be willing to exercise its jurisdiction to award injunctions under section 37(1) of the Senior Courts Act 1981, unencumbered by restrictions under EU law. For EU Member States that have directly adopted Article 11 (third sentence) of the Enforcement Directive, it is only an amendment at the EU level, specifically permitting the grant of injunctions against intermediaries providing *access to* infringing material, that could provide a *proper* legal basis for injunctions against navigation providers in the trade mark context.

It is also important to consider the types of technical measures that an injunction against a navigation provider might prescribe. Just as blocking injunctions are used to compel ISPs to adopt technical measures to block access to infringing websites, injunctions awarded against navigation providers could compel them to remove any hyperlinks to such websites. In other words, injunctions against navigation providers will take a 'notice and de-link' format. Targeting navigation providers, particularly search engines, in this manner could be useful in today's context, as internet users almost always utilise navigation providers to find the content they desire.[88] More importantly, even though content could be blocked effectively by obtaining blocking injunctions against all ISPs operating within a particular jurisdiction, cached copies of the blocked content may still be available in the indexes of search engines.[89] Thus, unless injunctions are also obtained

88 Although the removal of a hyperlink does not in any way result in the infringing content being taken down at its source, it does nevertheless prevent users from gaining access to the content via the navigation provider's search or index page. The possibility of utilising injunctions against navigation providers in order to compel them to de-link infringing material is supported by the CJEU's right to be forgotten ruling in Case C-131/12, *Google Spain SL v Agencia Española de Protección de Datos (AEPD)* [2014] ECR I-1227 where the Court held that in certain circumstances a search engine may be compelled to remove hyperlinks to personal data appearing among the search engine's search results.

89 GHJ Smith, *Internet Law and Regulation* (4th edn, Sweet & Maxwell 2007), 77.

against the search engines operating within that jurisdiction, internet users may still have access to cached versions of the blocked content.[90]

Injunctions against hosts

It must be noted that the proper legal basis for injunctions against ISPs, and potentially navigation providers, is not on the ground that they are *infringers* of intellectual property rights. Rather, it is on the basis that they are 'intermediaries' providing *access* to infringing content created by third parties.[91] This is an important observation in light of the amendment proposed to the Trade Marks Act 1994 in Chapter 5, which seeks to provide for monetary relief against hosts in certain defined circumstances on the basis that they are infringers. Thus, in the event the proposed legal reforms do come into force, it is submitted that this would have an impact on the legal basis for injunctions against an *infringing* host, as it is difficult to categorise a host as an intermediary and infringer at the same time.

Hosts as intermediaries

Presently in the UK, there is no basis, either under statute or the common law, by which hosts could be made liable for their role in hosting, even knowingly, content that infringes trade mark rights. As such, it is important to consider the possibility of seeking injunctive relief against hosts pursuant to Article 11 (third sentence) of the Enforcement Directive, as presently made relevant to the English High Court's jurisdiction under section 37(1) of the Senior Courts Act 1981.

As explained before, trade mark infringements in the online context occur when a third party incorporates a trade mark into content that advertises or promotes the sale of goods or services originating from someone other than the trade mark proprietor. However, although content incorporating a trade mark may be created using computers or similar devices, they do not come into existence in the online space unless they are hosted and made available to internet users. Without hosts, content cannot exist on the internet. Therefore, unlike in the case of ISPs or navigation providers that merely provide access to, or index and hyperlink,

90 The prevalence of *cached* infringing material is arguably a bigger problem in the copyright context, where infringement lies in the consumption of content. As such, it might be important for right holders to not only block access to infringing websites but also to ensure that cached versions of those sites remain inaccessible. Cached online material promoting trade mark infringements are unlikely to give rise to much concern. For instance, although internet users may be able to access cached versions of a website promoting trade mark infringements, it is unlikely that they will be able to conclude transactions on such cached websites.

91 The discussion in the previous parts of this chapter reveals that the correct basis for the grant of injunctions against ISPs and navigation providers in the trade mark context is on the ground that they provide *access to* infringing websites and not on the current approach of requiring that their services be *used* by third parties to commit intellectual property infringements.

online content, hosts facilitate the very existence of content. Moreover, in view of the technical control that hosts possess over the content they host, it is clear that hosts are capable of terminating and preventing infringements of trade mark rights, as they are able to simply remove the content in question. In fact, this is why it was argued in Chapter 5 that any monetary remedy available to trade mark proprietors must be confined to hosts (to the exclusion of ISPs and navigation providers), in view of their capacity to prevent and terminate infringements. Since Article 14(3) of the E-Commerce Directive expressly provides that a court or administrative authority may require an intermediary that hosts third-party content to terminate or prevent an infringement,[92] it would be permissible for an injunction to be awarded directing a host to remove content giving rise to a trade mark infringement, irrespective of whether the host is otherwise afforded immunity under Article 14(1). The argument was made, in the course of discussing the legal basis for blocking injunctions, that an intermediary's capacity to prevent or terminate infringements is a good indication that its services are being *utilised* to commit such infringements.

It must be noted that although a host's contractual and technical control over the infringing content (and the party responsible for it) was considered an important factor in determining its liability for trade mark infringements,[93] the aspect of contractual control is immaterial in relation to a host's liability in respect of injunctions. This is because, as noted earlier, under Article 11 (third sentence) of the Enforcement Directive, as well as Article 8(3) of the Info-Soc Directive, EU Member States must provide for injunctions against intermediaries whose services are used by third parties to commit infringements. As such, whether a third party that created the infringing content had a contractual relationship with a host is irrelevant. What matters is whether the third party made *use* of the intermediary's services, which, as argued in this chapter, is easily established where a host has technical control over the infringing content concerned, irrespective of whether a contractual relationship exists. As such, the technical capacity that hosts possess to terminate or prevent an infringement signifies that Article 11 (third sentence) provides a proper legal basis for injunctions against hosts even in the trade mark context.

Hosts as infringers

The law reforms proposed in Chapter 5 contemplate the imposition of liability on hosts in the specific circumstance that they *fail* to remove content giving rise to a trade mark infringement upon being put on notice. It was proposed that liability should be imposed by treating such *non-compliant* hosts as infringers under the Trade Marks Act 1994, thus affording aggrieved trade mark proprietors

92 Article 14(3) of the Enforcement Directive provides that '[t]his Article shall not affect the possibility for a court or administrative authority, in accordance with Member States' legal systems, of requiring the service provider to terminate or prevent an infringement'.

93 See discussion in Chapter 5.

the entitlement to claim damages. Arguably, in most cases, the proposed monetary remedy, coupled with the hosting safe harbour, will provide the necessary incentive for the practice of notice and takedown.[94] However, there might be instances where hosts do fail to take down infringing content. Although in such a situation the reforms proposed in Chapter 5 will entitle right holders to institute an action for infringement, resulting in the award of damages, the aggrieved party may find better utility in seeking out an injunction compelling the host to remove the infringing content and keep it off the internet.[95] After all, damages are awarded in respect of past conduct, whereas injunctions dictate present and future conduct.

A consequence of treating a host as an infringer (and not an intermediary) is that trade mark proprietors become entitled to the remedies set out in section 14 of the Trade Marks Act 1994, which include 'all such relief by way of damages, injunctions, accounts or otherwise'.[96] In typical trade mark infringement suits, right holders seek both interim and permanent injunctions, in addition to monetary relief. Interim injunctions are useful in ensuring that any infringing activity is halted pending a final determination by the court.[97] In the event that a court finds that the claim for infringement should succeed, then a permanent injunction may be awarded. Such an injunction is typically of the type envisaged by Article 11 (first sentence) of the Enforcement Directive.

As such, it appears that Article 11 of the Enforcement Directive provides a valid legal basis for the grant of injunctions against hosts regardless of whether they are classified as intermediaries or infringers. More specifically in the UK, injunctions compelling a host to remove content that gives rise to a trade mark infringement may be awarded under section 37(1) of the Senior Courts Act 1981. In the event that the legal reforms proposed in Chapter 5 are adopted, trade mark proprietors could then rely on section 14(2) of the Trade Marks Act 1994 to compel a host to remove infringing content on an interim and permanent basis.

94 See discussion in Chapters 6 and 7.

95 D Llewelyn, 'Assessment of Damages in Intellectual Property Cases: Some Recent Examples of "the Exercise of a Sound Imagination and the Practice of a Broad Axe"?' (2015) 27 *Singapore Academy of Law Journal* 480, 481:

> Somewhat surprisingly for legal rights that, in the common law world at least, are in the main about money, or money's worth in the sense of securing a competitive advantage, cases on the assessment of damages for infringement of intellectual property rights are relatively few and far between outside of the US. The principal reasons for this are, first, that once a defendant has been found by a court to infringe, an out of court settlement is usually cheaper and quicker, for both plaintiff and defendant, than proceeding to the separate inquiry as to damages that the procedural rules dictate in most cases (although, as explained below, this is changing); and second, that the most important remedy for many successful plaintiffs is the injunction restraining further infringement rather than the often expensive and protracted process of obtaining an award of damages that then has to be enforced.

96 Trade Marks Act 1994, section 14(2).

97 In the context of the UK, the principles upon which interim injunctions are granted were laid down in *American Cyanamid Co v Ethicon Ltd* [1975] AC 396.

Possible reforms at the EU level

The discussion in the preceding parts of this chapter identified the difficulty in extending Article 11 (third sentence) of the Enforcement Directive as the legal basis for injunctions in the field of trade marks, at least to the extent that it applies to ISPs and navigation providers. In this final part, a proposal to amend Article 11 is explored as a means of providing a more holistic legal basis for injunctions against intermediaries that operate in the online space. Whether the Enforcement Directive is amended, as proposed below, is unlikely to raise much concern for the UK, as consequent to Brexit both legislators and the courts are likely to have the freedom to depart from problematic EU provisions. On the other hand, insofar as the remaining EU Member States are concerned, an amendment to the language of Article 11 would be beneficial, especially in respect of those Member States that have directly implemented Article 11 in their domestic law. Such a step would be crucial in ensuring that there is EU-wide uniformity in the enforcement of trade mark rights, a factor that is important not only to trade mark proprietors who may have interests in multiple EU Member States but also from the point of view of the intermediaries that are called upon to assist in the enforcement process.

The inspiration for a possible amendment may be drawn from two distant jurisdictions, namely Singapore[98] and Australia,[99] where a regime for blocking injunctions was introduced in the copyright context. In Singapore, the High Court may make an order requiring a 'network service provider', which term encapsulates ISPs, to take reasonable steps to disable access to a flagrantly infringing online location where the court is satisfied that 'the services of the network service provider have been or ***are being used to access an online location***, which is the subject of the application, to commit or facilitate infringement of copyright in that material'.[100] Thus, unlike in the context of the EU, for the grant of an injunction, there is no requirement that the ISP's services must have been used to commit the infringements in question. It is sufficient that the ISP merely provides access to an infringing website, the accessing of which leads to the commission or the facilitation of a copyright infringement.

In the Australian context, the Federal Court is vested with jurisdiction to grant an injunction against a 'carriage service provider' (which similarly encapsulates ISPs) compelling the blocking of infringing websites to which the carriage service provider provides access.[101] As with the Singaporean approach, this could be contrasted with the two EU directives which are narrower in their

98 See Copyright Act 1987, which was amended in 2014 to introduce section 193DDA, authorising the Singapore High Court to order ISPs to block websites that infringe copyright.

99 See Copyright Act 1968 (Cth), which was amended in 2015 in order to introduce section 115A, vesting the Federal High Court with jurisdiction to award injunctions compelling ISPs to block access to websites that infringe copyright.

100 Copyright Act 1987, section 193DDA(1)(a) (emphasis added).

101 Copyright Act 1968 (Cth), section 115A(1)(a).

respective ambits. In fact, the Australian approach is much broader than even its Singaporean counterpart. This is because, unlike under section 193DDA(1) of the Singaporean Copyright Act 1987, which requires a network service provider's services to have been used to access a website *to commit* an infringement, section 115A(1) of the Australian Copyright Act 1968 (Cth) merely requires the website to either infringe, or facilitate an infringement, and not that accessing such a website must lead to the commission of an infringement. Thus, under the Australian approach, it is sufficient to establish that a website sought to be blocked infringes copyright and that the ISP's services are being used to *access* that website, irrespective of whether the act of accessing the website amounts to a copyright infringement.

Thus, it may be posited that the language adopted in the Australian Copyright Act 1968 (Cth) is the broadest, and a direct introduction of that language to the context of the Enforcement Directive would allow for the complete avoidance of the problematic application of Article 11 (third sentence) to the context of injunctions in the field of trade marks. Accordingly, a possible approach is to incorporate a fourth sentence to Article 11 of the Enforcement Directive in the following terms:

Article 11

> **[Proposed fourth sentence]** Member States shall, in addition, ensure that right holders are in a position to apply for an injunction against intermediaries, including information society service providers to which Articles 12, 13 or 14 of the Directive on Electronic Commerce 2000/31/EC apply, whose services are used by a third party to either infringe an intellectual property right or to gain access to an online location comprising content or an activity that infringes an intellectual property right.

The draft provision proposed above, thus, explicitly clarifies that injunctions are available in the online context, and particularly against actors such as ISPs and hosts. It also does not exclude the operation of the provision to navigation providers (such as search engines), as navigation providers could easily be regarded as intermediaries capable of providing *access to* an infringing online location. Most crucially, the proposed fourth sentence will provide a valid legal basis for blocking injunctions against ISPs and navigation providers in the trade mark context, avoiding the need for problematic, and perhaps illogical, extensions of the third sentence of Article 11.

There is, however, one important issue that needs to be addressed. This concerns Article 12 of the E-Commerce Directive, applicable to ISPs. As noted earlier, Article 12(3) permits EU Member States to provide for injunctions to be issued against ISPs compelling them to terminate or prevent an infringement. Article 12(1), however, provides ISPs with complete immunity from all forms of liability, the only exception to this being provided for in Article 12(3). Thus, it would be logical to conclude that any injunction that is directed at an ISP but does not result in the termination or the prevention of the infringement in question cannot be permitted in view of the broad immunity under Article 12(1).

Even if a fourth sentence is added to Article 11 of the Enforcement Directive, to broaden the basis for injunctions against internet intermediaries, it is important to consider whether the injunction contemplated by the proposed fourth sentence would be consistent with Article 12(3) of the E-Commerce Directive. It was argued in the first part of this chapter that a blocking injunction issued against an ISP in the copyright context, for which Article 8(3) of the Info-Soc Directive provides the legal basis, would automatically be compliant with Article 12 of the E-Commerce Directive, because the injunction results in the termination or prevention of infringements. However, this is not the case when ISPs are enjoined to block access to websites infringing trade mark rights.

Therefore, although the proposed fourth sentence to Article 11 of the Enforcement Directive may provide a valid legal basis for blocking injunctions in the trade mark context, such an injunction would still be inconsistent with Article 12(3) of the E-Commerce Directive, because the injunction neither terminates nor prevents an infringement. As such, a corresponding amendment would also have to be made to the E-Commerce Directive to ensure that injunctions contemplated by the Enforcement Directive (incorporating the proposed fourth sentence to Article 11) are consistent with Article 12(3) of the E-Commerce Directive. Accordingly, the following amendment is required to be made to the E-Commerce Directive to reconcile any conflict:

Article 12(3)

> **[Proposed amended provision]** This Article shall not affect the possibility for a court or administrative authority, in accordance with Member States' legal systems, of requiring the service provider to terminate or prevent an infringement or to award an injunction against a service provider as contemplated by Directive 2004/48/EC or Directive 2001/29/EC.

The amendment proposed above expands the scope of injunctions that may be awarded against ISPs, no longer requiring that such injunctions must have the effect of terminating or preventing infringements. In order to ensure uniformity and guard against similar conflicts in respect of the other categories of intermediaries, it may be prudent to incorporate similar amendments to Articles 13(2) and 14(3) of the E-Commerce Directive.

9 Injunctions against intermediaries—*practical considerations*

When internet intermediaries become obligated to remove or disable access to infringing websites, their actions have the effect of regulating the availability of content in the online space. Therefore, it is not surprising that both the Info-Soc Directive[1] and the Enforcement Directive[2] require remedies, including injunctions against intermediaries, to be 'effective, proportionate and dissuasive'.[3] More importantly, the Enforcement Directive provides that remedies must be 'applied in such a manner as to avoid the creation of barriers to legitimate trade and to provide for safeguards against their abuse'.[4] Naturally, these conditions become relevant to EU Member States in providing for injunctions against intermediaries under domestic law.

Insofar as the UK is concerned, although these conditions may not necessarily have a binding effect after Brexit, they may still provide a useful framework for the exercise of the just and equitable jurisdiction of the English High Court in respect of injunctions against intermediaries. In light of this, it is important to consider the extent to which the injunctive remedy, as currently practised, complies with principles of natural justice, safeguards against abuse and tackles circumvention and collateral damage. It is also necessary to consider the costs involved in implementing the technical measures that arise from an injunctive order. Arguably, these considerations will largely determine whether the injunctive remedy, as a whole, is effective and proportionate, and applied in a way that avoids barriers to legitimate trade and safeguards against abuse.

Natural justice

Natural justice, also referred to as due process, procedural fairness or fundamental justice,[5] is supported by twin pillars, which the Romans put into two maxims:

1 Directive 2001/29/EC of the European Parliament and of the Council of 22 May 2001 on the Harmonisation of Certain Aspects of Copyright and Related Rights in the Information Society [2001] OJ L 167/10 (Info-Soc Directive).

2 Directive 2004/48/EC of the European Parliament and of the Council of 29 April 2004 on the Enforcement of Intellectual Property Rights [2004] OJ L 157/16 (Enforcement Directive).

3 Info-Soc Directive, art 8(1) and Enforcement Directive, art 3(2).

4 Enforcement Directive, art 3(2).

5 RA Macdonald, 'Natural Justice' in CB Gray (ed), *The Philosophy of the Law: An Encyclopaedia* (Routledge 1999), 573.

nemo judex in causa sua (no one should be judge in his own cause) and *audi alteram partem* (all parties to a dispute must be heard).[6] For the purposes of this discussion, we shall focus on the latter, which essentially requires a decision maker to provide an opportunity to persons affected by his or her decision to make representations before the decision is ultimately made.[7] This cardinal principle has become enshrined in legal systems across the world since time immemorial.

More specifically in the intellectual property context, Article 42 of the Agreement on the Trade-Related Aspects of Intellectual Property Rights (TRIPS)[8] requires all WTO members to ensure that '[d]efendants shall have the right to written notice which is timely and contains sufficient detail, including the basis of the claims'.[9] The term 'defendants' in Article 42 refers to the alleged infringers of intellectual property rights.[10] In addition, Article 42 (fourth sentence) expressly incorporates the right of all parties to a dispute to be heard before a final decision is made.[11] Thus, Article 42 of TRIPS incorporates the principles of natural justice into the context of intellectual property enforcement. In practical terms, what this means is that any process in place for the resolution of intellectual property disputes must require not only the alleged infringer or infringers to be notified of the impending proceedings, but also that parties to the dispute be given the opportunity to be heard before the court or administrative tribunal makes its final determination. Even though Article 1:1 of TRIPS permits WTO members to afford more extensive protection than what is required under the agreement, such extra protection cannot be granted in a way that is inconsistent with any other provision of TRIPS, including Article 42. Thus, it has been observed:

> Article 42 prescribes that defendants be accorded due process rights in IPR enforcement proceedings. The adoption of more extensive protection that diminishes these due process rights would contravene TRIPS. In this regard, more extensive protection should not include reducing the rights of those asserted to be engaged in infringing acts.[12]

TRIPS has also expressly provided for situations where judicial authorities may make ex parte orders. This is, however, possible only when a ***provisional*** order

6 *Kanda v Government of Malaya* [1962] AC 322, 337.

7 Macdonald, above n5, 574.

8 The text of the agreement is available in Annex 1C of the Marrakesh Agreement Establishing the World Trade Organization 1994.

9 TRIPS, art 42 (second sentence).

10 S Vander, 'Article 42–Fair and Equitable Procedures' in P-T Stoll, J Busche and K Arend (eds), *WTO—Trade-Related Aspects of Intellectual Property Rights* (Martinus Nijhoff 2009), 703:

> On the one hand, Art. 42 is intended to safeguard the effectiveness of the legal enforcement systems in favour of the right holder. On the other hand, it is meant to give the alleged infringers sufficient opportunity to rebut the accusations and to effectively defend themselves.

11 Vander, above n10, 705 ('According to this provision, the parties shall be given an opportunity to substantiate their claims and to present all relevant evidence'). See also A Taubman, H Wager and J Watal (eds), *A Handbook on WTO TRIPS Agreement* (Cambridge University Press 2012), 140–41.

12 UNCTAD-ICTSD, *Resource Book on TRIPS and Development* (Cambridge University Press 2005), 25.

is necessary where a court believes that 'any delay is likely to cause irreparable harm to the right holder, or where there is a demonstrable risk of evidence being destroyed'.[13] However, TRIPS does not contemplate the award of ex parte relief in any other circumstances, especially in respect of final orders.

Arguably, the principles of natural justice as enshrined in TRIPS extend to the context of injunctions as contemplated by the Enforcement and Info-Soc directives. Where a trade mark proprietor seeks out an injunction against an intermediary, as contemplated by Article 11 (third sentence) of the Enforcement Directive, compelling it to remove or disable access to a website on a permanent basis, there are, at least, three categories of rights that have to be considered. The EU Charter[14] recognises the right to property, including intellectual property rights,[15] the freedom to conduct a business[16] and the freedom of speech and information.[17] Thus, compelling an intermediary to disable access to or remove a website, with a view of enforcing trade mark rights, has the potential of interfering with a range of competing rights and interests. For instance, it is possible that the removal or blockade of a website may interfere with the rights of its operators, especially their right to engage in business[18] and free speech.[19] Similarly, there is a possibility that the implementation of technical measures may impact the intermediary's freedom to engage in business.[20]

Importantly, injunctions prescribing technical measures, such as the one awarded in *Cartier v Sky*,[21] signify instances where intermediaries may be called upon to assist in the enforcement process even though they are not themselves liable for infringements. In proceedings where such an injunction is sought against an intermediary, there is really no 'dispute' between the right holder and the intermediary concerned. The dispute, upon which the injunction is granted, is between the right holder and the operators of the website targeted for the purposes of implementing technical measures.

In light of the above, it is clear that when an injunction compelling technical measures is awarded against an intermediary, the ensuing technical measures will inevitably have an effect on the activities of the website in relation to which the injunction was awarded. As such, it may be posited that the process

13 TRIPS, art 50:2. See also Vander, above n10, 743.

14 Charter of Fundamental Rights of the European Union [2000] OJ C364/01 (EU Charter).

15 EU Charter, art 17. IP rights are specifically protected under Article 17(2).

16 EU Charter, art 16.

17 EU Charter, art 11.

18 M Husovec, 'Injunctions against Innocent Third Parties: The Case of Website Blocking' (2012) 4 *Journal of Intellectual Property, Information Technology and Electronic Commerce Law* 116, 123 ('A website operator's right to engage in commercial activities as well as his property rights or other rights as a private individual can be interfered with by such a blockade').

19 C Geiger and E Izyumenko, 'The Role of Human Rights in Copyright Enforcement Online: Elaborating a Legal Framework for Website Blocking' (2016) 32 *American University International Law Review* 43, 54.

20 Geiger and Izyumenko, above n19, 76.

21 *Cartier International AG v British Sky Broadcasting Ltd* [2015] ETMR 1 (*Cartier v Sky*).

that leads to the award of such an injunction should ensure that right holders, at the very least, make a *reasonable attempt* to notify the operators responsible for the website causing the alleged infringements, so that they could intervene in the proceedings, if they so wish, prior to the award of any injunction being made against the intermediary.

However, in the UK, this is far from the case. In every single case in which a blocking injunction was awarded, no attempt was made to notify the operators responsible for the target websites. Nor were they heard. The only parties before court were the right holders and the respective ISPs. This is because, although both the Info-Soc and Enforcement directives provide guidance as to the parties against whom, and the circumstances in which, an injunction may be obtained, they do not provide any guidance on the procedure that must be followed in granting such injunctions. Both directives leave it open to the respective EU Member States to determine the conditions and procedures,[22] or modalities,[23] relating to such injunctions, which has resulted in a divergence in the way the injunctive remedy has been implemented in the various Member States.

In the context of the UK, section 97A of the Copyright Designs and Patents Act 1988 (CDPA), which implements Article 8(3) of the Info-Soc Directive, does not prescribe the procedure that right holders must follow in making an application for an injunction against an intermediary. The following observation of Arnold J in *Dramatico v Sky*[24] clarifies the present legal position:

> [T]here is no jurisdictional requirement to join or serve the operators . . . . Article 8(3) of the Information Society Directive and section 97A of the [CDPA] confer jurisdiction on the Court to grant injunctions against intermediaries whose services are used by a third party to infringe copyright. Neither Article 8(3) nor section 97A requires joinder or service of the third party.[25]

While the above observation was made in the copyright context, it applies equally to injunctions as envisaged by Article 11 (third sentence) of the Enforcement Directive. Thus, when, for the first time, a blocking injunction was awarded in the trade mark context, none of the operators responsible for the target websites were notified, nor were they heard before the injunction was awarded.[26] However, this is by no means ideal, especially in view of the following observation made by Arnold J in *Cartier v Sky*:

22 Info-Soc Directive, Recital (59).

23 Enforcement Directive, Recital (23).

24 *Dramatico Entertainment Ltd v British Sky Broadcasting Ltd* [2012] EWHC 268 (Ch) (*Dramatico v Sky*), [10] (Arnold J).

25 *Dramatico v Sky*, [10] (Arnold J).

26 The issue of joinder and service was not even considered by the English High Court in *Cartier v Sky*.

> It is convenient to note at this stage three points about the cases under section 97A. The first is that neither the ISPs nor the rightholders have appealed against any aspect of the orders made in those cases. . . . The second is that . . . ISPs have not opposed the making of the orders sought by the rightholders. . . . Third, in consequence, most of the orders have been granted after consideration of the applications on paper.[27]

Essentially, what this means is that the court only has sight of the material submitted by the right holder, which often goes uncontested by the relevant intermediary or intermediaries party to the proceedings (this so far being limited to ISPs), leaving the interests of the operators of the target websites completely unrepresented. Accordingly, it may be posited that the manner in which blocking injunctions have been awarded in the UK does not seem to be consistent with the principles of natural justice.[28] It seems that this is a concern even in respect of some of the other EU Member States, as the following extract from a judgment of the District Court of The Hague illustrates:

> The imposing of the claimed order meets the conditions of due process. After all, the measure is imposed after a prior, fair and impartial procedure, i.e. the present proceedings. Contrary to what [the ISPs] argue, it is not required that all its subscribers are parties to the proceedings or are heard. [The relevant Dutch law] provides that 'the person or persons concerned' must be heard. In a case like the present one, in which an order is claimed against intermediaries, such intermediaries can be considered to be the persons concerned in the sense of this provision. Said intermediaries have been heard. Any different interpretation would render the regulation for orders against intermediaries which the European legislator has implemented with the Enforcement Directive meaningless. *It is inherent in such regulation that an order can be imposed upon inter alia internet providers to cease their services in proceedings to which the alleged infringer is not, at least not necessarily a party and so is not heard in it.* One of the reasons for implementing such an

27 *Cartier v Sky*, [4] (Arnold J).

28 Of course, the Civil Procedure Rules 1998 provide that 'a person who wishes to become a party' to any proceedings pending before a court may be permitted to do so with the court's permission (Rule 19.4(2)). Such a party is commonly known as an 'intervener'. In terms of Rule 19.2(2), an intervener must satisfy court that the addition of the new party 'is desirable . . . so that the court can resolve all the matters in dispute in the proceedings' or that 'there is an issue involving the new party and an existing party which is connected to the matters in dispute in the proceedings, and it is desirable to add the new party so that the court can resolve that issue'. When a right holder initiates legal proceedings at the end of which an injunction may be granted against an intermediary prescribing technical measures to be implemented in respect of certain websites, arguably these rules would permit the operators of such websites to intervene and contest the matter. However, it is very likely that such operators may not even be aware of the ongoing proceedings to make an application to intervene. Often, it is only after the injunction is awarded and technical measures are put into place, that the operators of the affected websites come to know that their websites were the subject of proceedings for an injunction.

option is precisely, after all, the situation that the alleged infringer cannot be sued, for instance because his identity is not known.[29]

Of course, this does not mean that the English High Court issued injunctions, pursuant to its discretionary powers, without going into the merits of the dispute and being convinced of the fact that an underlying infringement was taking place. The following UK cases, where blocking injunctions were issued, illustrate this fact. Thus, in *Twentieth C Fox v BT*,[30] the High Court acknowledged and relied on the findings in a previous case,[31] i.e. *Twentieth Century Fox v Newzbin Ltd*,[32] where the same court found the operators of the Newzbin website to be committing large-scale copyright infringements, although the actual perpetrators were not made party to the subsequent action leading to the blocking injunction. Similarly, in *Dramatico v Sky*, although the right holders never filed a separate action against the operators of the infringing website in the UK (although both civil and criminal proceedings were filed in other jurisdictions), the High Court went on to first decide whether the website operators and UK internet users were infringing copyright.[33] This was the approach adopted in *EMI Records v Sky*,[34] *Football Association v Sky*[35] and *Paramount Home Entertainment International Ltd v British Sky Broadcasting Ltd*.[36] In other words, only when there was satisfactory evidence of infringements taking place at a given website was an injunction issued requiring ISPs to block access to that website, even though there is no legal requirement that the operators of the website in question be notified or joined in proceedings. To be fair, in all the cases mentioned above, the websites concerned were patently infringing, and, thus, it would have been disproportionate, if not futile, to expect the right holders to serve notice and join the infringers in the proceedings.

In practical terms, this approach is extremely beneficial to right holders, especially when the identity of the infringers is unknown. However, what must be

29 *BREIN v ZIGGO and XS4ALL* Case 374634/HA ZA 10-3184 (Rechtbank's-Gravenhage, 11 January 2012) (emphasis added). Although The Hague Court of Appeal overturned this judgment (see *Ziggo and XS4ALL v BREIN* Case 200 105 418/01 (Gerechtshof den Haag, 28 January 2014)), that was on the basis that the injunction was ineffective, whereas the Court did not consider issues concerning due process. In any event, the Court of Appeal's judgment was later reversed by the Dutch Supreme Court (see *BREIN v Ziggo and XS4ALL* Case No 14/02399 (Hoge Raad der Nederlanden, 13 November 2015)).

30 *Twentieth Century Fox Film Corp v British Telecom Plc* [2011] EWHC 1981 (Ch) (*Twentieth C Fox v BT*).

31 *Twentieth C Fox v BT*, [2], [48]–[55] and [113] (Arnold J).

32 [2010] EWHC 608 (Ch).

33 *Dramatico v Sky*, [6] (Arnold J).

34 *EMI Records Ltd v British Sky Broadcasting Ltd* [2013] EWHC 379 (Ch) (*EMI Records v Sky*), [42] and [75] (Arnold J).

35 *Football Association Premier League Ltd v British Sky Broadcasting Ltd* [2013] EWHC 2058 (Ch) (*Football Association v Sky*), [47] (Arnold J).

36 *Paramount Home Entertainment International Ltd v British Sky Broadcasting Ltd* [2013] EWHC 3479 (Ch) (*Paramount Entertainment v Sky*), [34]–[38] (Arnold J).

emphasised is that there may be instances where the operators of a website targeted by an injunction have a plausible defence to a claim of intellectual property infringement.[37] In the circumstances where the court is only privy to the pleadings and documentary evidence submitted on behalf of a right holder, the court's discretion may be exercised without due regard to the position of the *alleged* infringers, particularly because the only other party before court (i.e. the internet intermediary) may not necessarily resist an application unless it is in its own interest to do so.[38] The key issue with the manner in which Article 11 (third sentence) of the Enforcement Directive and Article 8(3) of the Info-Soc Directive have been implemented in the UK is that, even in cases where the operators responsible for an alleged infringing website *can* be identified and notified of the impending proceedings, the law does *not* require that to be done *before* an application for an injunction is made. Arguably, such an outcome not only breaches the fundamental principles of natural justice but is also contrary to Article 42 of TRIPS.

In contrast, the regimes providing for injunctions against intermediaries in Singapore, Australia and Chile have expressly incorporated a more proactive notice requirement, albeit limited to the context of copyright enforcement.[39] For instance, section 193DDB(1) of the Singapore Copyright Act 1987 requires every applicant seeking to block a flagrantly infringing online location (such as a website) to:

> send a notice to the owner of the online location that is intended to be the subject of the order (referred to in this section as the relevant online location owner) stating that the online location has been or is being used to commit or facilitate infringement of copyright in the material, and the intention of the owner or the exclusive licensee, as the case may be, to apply for that order if the relevant online location owner does not, within the prescribed period, cease the use of the online location to commit or facilitate infringement of copyright in the material.

In effect, what the Singaporean regime does is to compel right holders to pursue the avenue of notice and takedown as a precondition for a blocking order.

37 Husovec, above n18, 122.

38 Sometimes, when an intermediary does resist an application for a blocking injunction, it may have the effect benefiting the operators of the target website, even if they were engaging in infringing activity. For instance, in *PCCW Media Ltd v M1 Ltd* [2018] SGHC 99, a Singaporean case concerning an application to block access to five websites where copyright infringements were being committed, the ISPs took up the position that the plaintiff had no locus standi to make the application. This was on the basis that the plaintiff was neither the owner nor an *exclusive* licensee of the copyright in the drama and variety shows, which were being unlawfully streamed via the websites in question. The outcome was the dismissal of the application, which, in effect, was to the advantage of the operators of the infringing websites.

39 While both the Singaporean and Australian copyright statutes provide for injunctions against ISPs, the Chilean law targets hosts and navigation providers.

Thus, it is incumbent upon right holders to first notify the operators of the target online location and afford them reasonable time to remove the infringement at its source. Failing that, an order blocking access to the online location may be obtained. Of course, the Copyright Act 1987 of Singapore provides for the possibility where the operators of an online location cannot be traced and therefore notified. Thus, section 193DDB(3) incorporates an exception where the Singapore High Court may dispense with the notice requirement in the event the right holder, 'despite reasonable efforts to do so, is unable to determine the identity or address of the relevant online location owner'. For instance, in *Disney v M1*,[40] the plaintiffs applied to the Singapore High Court for an order compelling the major ISPs in Singapore (such as M1, Singtel and Starhub) to block access to 53 websites, which were being used to commit copyright infringements. Before initiating proceedings, the plaintiffs had sent takedown notices in respect of 41 of the 53 infringing websites, while *reasonable efforts* were taken to send off takedown notices in relation to the remaining 12 websites.[41] In this regard Lee J observed:

> I was satisfied based on the evidence adduced by the plaintiffs that the notice requirements were satisfied in the present case as there *were reasonable efforts* to identify the owners of the 53 online locations.[42]

As such, the general rule is that notice must be served on the operators/owners of the target online location before filing an application for a blocking order, whereas bypassing this requirement is only an exception. Notably, the notice requirement also supplements section 193DDB(4) of the Singapore Copyright Act 1987, which provides that the operators of an online location have a right to be heard on an application for a blocking order and also enjoy the same right of appeal as a party to the application.

The Australian approach bears some similarity to the Singaporean regime. Thus, section 115A(3) of the Copyright Act 1968 (Cth) expressly provides that the operators of an online location which is the subject of a blocking application may apply to court to be joined as a party. In addition, and in order to facilitate that eventuality, section 115A(4) provides that the right holder seeking a blocking order must take *reasonable steps* to notify the operators of the target online location. Moreover, whether the right holder took reasonable steps to notify the operators of the target online location is a factor that the Federal Court must consider in exercising its discretion whether to grant a blocking order.[43] The revised explanatory memorandum on the Copyright Amendment (Online Infringement) Bill 2015 explains this further:

40 *Disney Enterprises Inc v M1 Ltd* [2018] SGHC 206 (*Disney v M1*).
41 *Disney v M1*, [8] (Lee J).
42 *Disney v M1*, [18] (Lee J) (emphasis added).
43 Copyright Act 1968 (Cth), section 115(5)(h).

> In some circumstances, this notification may be difficult, but it is important that the operator of the online location be provided with an opportunity to join the proceedings if desired. The proposed paragraph would require the Court to take into account the copyright owner's efforts in attempting to notify the operator of the online location.[44]

The Singaporean and Australian approaches are comparable to the approach adopted in Chile. The Chilean IP Law[45] was amended not so long ago[46] to enable right holders to apply to court to obtain an order against hosts and search engines (or 'information location tools' as described under the Chilean law) requiring them to remove content infringing copyright or hyperlinks to such content. While the law provides that the proceedings in relation to such applications shall be handled 'briefly and summarily',[47] affording an expeditious remedy, the law also allows the aggrieved content providers/authors to petition court to have the order set aside,[48] ensuring that sufficient checks and balances are in place. Where an aggrieved copyright owner requests the removal, or disabling of access to, infringing content as a preliminary measure (resembling the interlocutory injunction), the court may issue an order against a service provider to adopt reasonable technical measures even without hearing the party responsible for the content, provided that the copyright owner deposits a bond to the satisfaction of the court.[49] However, where such a request is made for the adoption of a permanent measure (or judicial measure, as described in the Chilean law), the court must hear all concerned parties before issuing the order.[50] Therefore, it is clear that the Chilean approach expressly provides for sufficient safeguards that adhere to the basic principles of natural justice.

Although the approaches in Singapore, Australia and Chile with respect to injunctions against intermediaries vary slightly from one another, they all demonstrate a conscious effort to comply with principles of natural justice by expressly incorporating notice requirements. This is in contrast to the manner in which Article 11 (third sentence) of the Enforcement Directive and Article 8(3) of the Info-Soc Directive have been implemented in the UK. Despite the requirement that all remedies under the two directives must safeguard against abuse, the freedom that EU Member States have been given to determine the conditions and procedures,[51] or modalities,[52] relating to the grant of injunctions against intermediaries has resulted in some domestic courts regarding compliance with notice

44 Revised Explanatory Memorandum, Copyright Amendment (Online Infringement) Bill 2015, para 56.
45 Law 17.336 of 28 August 1970 on Intellectual Property (Chilean IP Law).
46 Law 20.430 of 4 May 2010 amending the Law on Intellectual Property.
47 Chilean IP Law, art 85R (fifth paragraph).
48 Chilean IP Law, art 85R (fourth paragraph).
49 Chilean IP Law, art 85R (first paragraph), read with art 85S.
50 Chilean IP Law, art 85R (first paragraph), read with art 85S.
51 Info-Soc Directive, Recital (59).
52 Enforcement Directive, Recital (23).

requirements simply *non-essential* in order to exercise their powers.[53] This is problematic, because, even though the focus of such injunctions is on *intermediaries*, the reality is that the ensuing technical measures have an effect on the activities of *third parties*, such as the operators responsible for websites targeted for blocking by ISPs.

In light of the above, it is submitted that domestic legislation implementing Article 11 (third sentence) of the Enforcement Directive (and Article 8(3) of the Info-Soc Directive) should ideally incorporate sufficient notice requirements as a procedural safeguard. If they presently do not, they should be suitably amended. To that end, the freedom that EU Member States enjoy in determining the modalities, or conditions and procedures, in relation to the grant of injunctions against intermediaries could be made use of to better comply with the principles of natural justice. Insofar as the UK is concerned, any post-Brexit developments concerning the injunctive remedy should take a similar trajectory.

Safeguards against abuse

Article 3(2) of the Enforcement Directive provides that remedies, including injunctions against intermediaries, made available to right holders must safeguard against abuse. In light of this requirement, it is worth noting that blocking injunctions awarded in the UK incorporate certain safeguards aimed at protecting the legitimate activities of third parties. To begin with, the very fact that a court of law makes the initial assessment whether a particular website ought to be blocked owing to an underlying infringement is a significant safeguard against abuse. This is in contrast to the notice and takedown approach, where private intermediaries that host third-party content make this very judgment, subjecting the regime to immense criticism on the basis that it lacks the necessary transparency, accountability and balance that a dispute resolution system geared against abuse must possess.[54] However, the same criticism does not apply to injunctions prescribing technical measures, in view of the judicially supervised process that regulates the remedy.

The blocking injunction, at least in the UK, has evolved over time, adding to the layers of safeguards. Thus, even though in the early stages (e.g. in cases such as *Twentieth C Fox v BT* and *Dramatico v Sky*) there were no specific safeguards in respect of the interests of those operating the target websites, in *Football Association v Sky*, Arnold J laid down the following safeguard that was originally introduced by Mann J in an unreported judgment[55] awarding an injunction blocking access to the 'EZTV' website:

53 See e.g. *Dramatico v Sky*, [10] (where it was made explicitly clear that the English High Court's jurisdiction in the copyright context was not conditional upon the alleged infringers being notified by the applicant seeking an injunction against an intermediary).

54 See discussion in Chapters 6 and 7.

55 See D Meale, 'Premier League 1, Internet Pirates 0: Sports Streaming Website the Latest to Be Blocked' (2013) 8 *Journal of Intellectual Property Law and Practice* 821, 823.

> The operator(s) of the Target Website (as defined in the Schedule to this order) and the operators of any other website who claim to be affected by this Order, are to have permission to apply to vary or discharge this Order insofar as it affects such an applicant, any such application to be on notice to all the parties and to be supported by materials setting out and justifying the grounds of the application. Any such application shall clearly indicate the status of the applicant and indicate clearly (supported by evidence) that it is the operator of the website which is the subject of the application.[56]

By the time the blocking injunction was extended to the trade mark context in *Cartier v Sky*, the following additional layers of safeguards were incorporated aimed at ensuring a greater degree of balance and fairness to minimise abuse:

1 The possibility for 'ISPs to apply to the court to discharge or vary the orders in the event of any material change of circumstances, including in respect of the costs, consequences for the parties and effectiveness of the blocking measures from time to time'.[57]
2 The possibility for the operators of the target online locations to apply to court and have the order varied.[58]
3 The possibility for internet users who are affected by the order to apply to court and have the order varied. Mr Justice Arnold observed, 'future orders should expressly permit affected subscribers to apply to the Court to discharge or vary the orders'.[59]
4 In addition, an ISP must provide internet users with accurate and sufficient information pertaining to the blocking of an online location: 'the page should not merely state that access to the website has been blocked by court order, but also should identify the party or parties which obtained the order and state that affected users have the right to apply to the Court to discharge or vary the order'.[60]
5 The inclusion of a 'sunset clause' in all orders, such that the orders will cease to have effect at the end of a defined period unless either the ISPs consent to the orders being continued or the court orders that they should be continued. According to Arnold J, '[t]his will enable the practical operation of the orders to be reviewed in the light of experience'.[61]

It is worth noting that these safeguards could be suitably adapted in relation to injunctions against navigation providers and hosts, in the event such injunctions are awarded at some point in the future.

56 *Football Association v Sky*, [57] (Arnold J), citing from Mann J's unreported judgment.
57 *Cartier v Sky*, [262] (Arnold J).
58 *Cartier v Sky*, [262] (Arnold J).
59 *Cartier v Sky*, [263] (Arnold J).
60 *Cartier v Sky*, [264] (Arnold J).
61 *Cartier v Sky*, [265] (Arnold J).

Although the above safeguards play an important role in safeguarding against abuse, as well as protecting online speech and the legitimate activities of third parties, the safeguard that permits operators of websites targeted by technical measures to apply to court and have the order varied requires further scrutiny. Although this no doubt is a useful safeguard to have, its effectiveness is to some extent diluted as presently the law does not expressly require operators of websites to be notified before an application for an injunction is made. After all, since injunctions against intermediaries are awarded *solely* based on the pleadings and documents presented to the court by the right holder, in determining the question of infringement, it is possible that the interests of the operators of the target website (e.g. a plausible defence) are overlooked in awarding such injunctions. By the time the operators of a target website apply to have the order varied, much damage may have already ensued. The point is, the interests of the operators of target websites are better served when they are heard *before* an injunction is awarded and not after. The outcome of this is that the injunctive remedy, as implemented in the UK, is not too different from the 'act first, ask questions later' type of approach adopted by intermediaries practising notice and takedown.

Therefore, it is submitted that the safeguard permitting *post-award* intervention by operators of websites targeted by technical measures is only meaningful where such operators cannot be identified and, hence, notified. In contrast, when, in fact, such operators can be identified, their interests are best safeguarded by notifying them and affording them the right of audience *before* the award of an injunction. To that end, the approach adopted in the UK in respect of injunctions against intermediaries remains unsatisfactory.

Circumvention

It must be noted that technical measures implemented by intermediaries are open to circumvention both on the part of ordinary internet users and those responsible for the operation of infringing websites. Circumvention is a key problem, as it impedes the *effectiveness* of technical measures.[62]

Take the following example. Assume that content promoting a trade mark infringement is incorporated in a website and hosted by a web-host in an EU Member State. The aggrieved right holder then may serve the web-host with a notice of infringement. In the event the laws applicable in the EU Member State in which the web-host is located provide for the liability of hosts facilitating

62 Both the Enforcement Directive (Article 3(2)) and Info-Soc Directive (Article 8(1)) require that remedies and sanctions aimed at enforcing intellectual property rights must be effective. In *Cartier v Sky*, despite the risk of circumvention, the English High Court was confident of the effectiveness of the remedy for the enforcement of trade mark rights. The Court arrived at this conclusion based on the experience it had gathered through the grant of copyright-related blocking injunctions (see *Cartier v Sky*, [236] (Arnold J)). On appeal, the Court of Appeal agreed: see *Cartier International AG v British Sky Broadcasting Ltd* [2016] EWCA Civ 658 (*Cartier v Sky* (CA)), [179]–[181] (Kitchin LJ).

infringements, the web-host will have sufficient incentive, and is likely, to remove the infringing content upon notice. As a response to a takedown, the infringers may simply solicit the services of an alternative web-host, in which case the infringing content will become available once again. The aggrieved right holder would have to then go through the same cycle in relation to the new web-host. This cycle could continue ad infinitum. Thus, even though a takedown by the host responsible for hosting the infringing material could terminate the infringement instantaneously, the possibility of the infringers switching hosts, thus effectively circumventing the takedown, remains a problem. In the event the infringers shift the infringing content to a host outside the EU and to a jurisdiction where hosts are not regulated at all, seeking a takedown from such a host might not even be possible. This is perhaps why in *Cartier v Sky* it was contended by the right holders that notice and takedown is less effective, highlighting that the remedy may only result in a short-term disruption of infringement.[63]

Accordingly, in situations where notice and takedown or an injunction compelling a takedown is going to be an ineffective remedy, it is likely that aggrieved right holders will resort to injunctions against domestic ISPs and navigation providers that provide access to infringing websites. However, the English High Court expressly acknowledged that even blocking measures are similarly open to the risk of circumvention both at the end of the target websites and internet users that have subscribed to the access services of the ISPs implementing the technical measures.[64] There is, however, very little that can be done to remedy the latter form of circumvention, especially at the hands of sophisticated internet users who use virtual private networks to bypass technical measures implemented by ISPs.[65] Technical measures that may be implemented by navigation providers (e.g. removal of hyperlinks to infringing websites) could also be circumvented by internet users, either by approaching other navigation providers that have not implemented similar measures or by simply accessing the infringing websites directly by typing the relevant URL[66] in the web browser, effectively bypassing navigation providers completely.[67]

While tackling circumvention on the part of internet users is significantly more challenging, the English High Court has devised methods to deal with circumvention by operators of infringing websites. In order to demonstrate how the

63 *Cartier v Sky*, [201] (Arnold J).

64 *Cartier v Sky*, [26] (Arnold J).

65 Ofcom, *'Site blocking' to Reduce Online Copyright Infringement: A Review of Sections 17 and 18 of the Digital Economy Act* (2010), 5–6 <https://assets.publishing.service.gov.uk/government/uploads/system/uploads/attachment_data/file/78095/Ofcom_Site-Blocking-_report_with_redactions_vs2.pdf> (accessed 31 January 2019).

66 'URL' stands for Unified Resource Locator. An example of a URL is 'www.iwf.org.uk/resources'. In this example, 'iwf.org.uk' is the domain name directing internet users to the relevant resource.

67 Although internet users may not necessary remember URLs as such, since URLs could be shared on various platforms, such as online social media, there is a possibility that users may have the opportunity of accessing infringing websites using the URLs directly without the assistance of search engines to locate the websites.

High Court's judicial innovation operates to dilute the effects of circumvention, it is necessary first to set out how blocking takes place. For this purpose, it is appropriate to refer to the order made in *Cartier v Sky*, which represents the key features of blocking injunctions awarded in the UK against ISPs. The order, in relevant parts, reads as follows:

> In respect of its residential fixed line broadband customers . . . the . . . Defendant [i.e. the ISP] shall within 15 working days in relation to the *initial notification (and thereafter, within 10 working days of receiving any subsequent notification)* adopt the following technical means to block or attempt to block access to the Target Websites, their domains and sub-domains and any other IP address or URL notified to the . . . Defendant whose sole or predominant purpose is to enable or facilitate access to a Target Website. The technology to be adopted is:
>
> (i) IP blocking in respect of *each and every IP address from which each of the Target Websites operate and which is* . . . notified in writing to the . . . Defendant by the Applicants or their agents . . .
> (ii) IP address re-routing in respect of all IP addresses that provide access to *each and every URL available from each of the Target Websites and their domains and sub-domains and which URL is notified in writing* to the . . . Defendant by the Claimants or their agents; and
> (iii) URL blocking in respect of *each and every URL available from each of the Target Websites and their domains and sub-domains and which is notified in writing* to the . . . Defendant by the [Applicants] or their agents.[68]

A reading of the above order reveals that websites may be blocked using both IP addresses or URLs. Any website that is hosted on a server is assigned a unique IP address, such as 92.52.118.124. Since we find IP addresses difficult to remember, they are translated into user-friendly domain names, such as 'www.iwf.org.uk', which corresponds to the above IP address and directs internet users to the website of the Internet Watch Foundation.

All ISPs use a service known as the Domain Name Service (DNS), which contains a database of IP addresses and corresponding domain names. Each time an internet user wishes to access a particular website (associated with a particular domain name), a request is sent to the ISP's DNS so that the domain name is translated to the corresponding IP address in order to make a connection between the user's device (e.g. computer) and the server at which the website is hosted. Thus, a blocking injunction can be implemented using the DNS, 'so that when the ISP's DNS server is asked by a customer's computer for the IP address corresponding to [a domain name], the ISP's system either returns no IP address or points the customer to an IP address defined by the ISP that does not correspond

68 *Cartier v Sky*, [72] (Arnold J) (emphasis added).

to the [domain name sought to be accessed]'.[69] Another approach to achieve a similar result is IP re-routing. Thus, instead of directing the data stream to the IP address of the blocked website, the ISP re-routes the data stream to a pre-defined IP address, thus, redirecting users to a different location on the internet, preventing the blocked website being accessed. These techniques enable blocking, the first using the DNS (DNS blocking) and the second using IP addresses (IP address blocking).[70] Yet another approach is to use URLs to block access to websites (URL blocking). Under this scheme, when a URL is blocked, ISPs monitor data traffic and block *all* data associated with a particular URL.[71]

It is in this technological setting that ISPs have become obligated to block websites. For blocking injunctions to be successful, right holders must provide ISPs with accurate information containing the IP addresses, domain names and URLs of the websites targeted for the blocking measures. Thus, once an action is filed seeking an injunction, and in the event the injunction is awarded, the ISPs subject to the order must implement technical measures to ensure that the target website cannot be accessed by internet users subscribing to the ISPs' services. Doing so would discharge the ISPs' obligations in terms of the injunction.

It is noteworthy that the order (cited above) refers to both an 'initial notification' and a 'subsequent notification'. Initiating legal proceedings seeking the blocking injunction constitutes the *initial* notification. A subsequent notification envisages a point in time that comes *after* an ISP had taken steps to implement blocking measures pursuant to an injunction.

The opportunity a right holder has in serving an ISP with a 'subsequent notification' is important in view of potential circumvention techniques that may be employed by those operating a blocked website to evade the effects of an injunction. The English High Court acknowledged that 'there are circumvention methods which can be used by website operators, *including changing IP addresses and URLs. These can be combated by updating the IP addresses or URLs that are blocked*'.[72] Thus, although the initial blocking of a target website is achieved through a court process, if the perpetrators operating the infringing website change the IP address (akin to changing the location of an illegal operation) or alter its URL (akin to using a different route to access the location), a subsequent notification providing the new IP address or URL would obligate the ISP to update its system so that the target website remains inaccessible. As such, the blocking injunction, by ensuring that right holders could notify ISPs of any future changes in the IP addresses and URLs of infringing websites, creates a system that is capable of efficiently combatting circumvention. Changes in IP addresses and URLs are likely to also circumvent de-linking measures adopted by navigation providers (e.g. search engines). By moving hosts (resulting in a new IP address being assigned) or changing URLs, new paths are made available

69 *Cartier v Sky*, [25] (Arnold J).
70 *Cartier v Sky*, [25] (Arnold J).
71 *Cartier v Sky*, [25] (Arnold J).
72 *Cartier v Sky*, [27] (Arnold J) (emphasis added).

through which the infringing content could be accessed. This in turn creates new links operating as alternatives to links that were disabled by navigation providers. Accordingly, it would be prudent to incorporate a system of 'subsequent notifications' in relation to injunctions against navigation providers, if and when they are issued in future.

It is patently clear that the approach adopted by the English High Court, whereby right holders are permitted to deal with circumvention by issuing 'subsequent notifications', is no doubt a useful judicial innovation.[73] However, this approach, unless implemented with caution, could entail the unwarranted consequence of collateral damage.[74]

Collateral damage

Both the Enforcement and Info-Soc directives provide that remedies and sanctions for the enforcement of intellectual property rights must be proportionate,[75] making the principle of proportionality relevant to the context of injunctions against intermediaries. The fact that such injunctions must be made available only when it is proportionate to do so is a significant safeguard protecting the interests of not just the intermediaries concerned, but also those of third parties engaging in lawful trade and speech. The principle of proportionality becomes relevant when two or more competing rights conflict and it becomes necessary for courts to reach a balanced outcome. As noted earlier on in this chapter, in the discussion concerning natural justice, granting an injunction that effectively removes, or prevents access to, online content in order to protect intellectual property rights, engages two other competing rights, i.e. the right to free speech and the right to

73 The innovative approach adopted by the English High Court was followed recently by the Singaporean High Court in *Disney v M1* in awarding a 'dynamic injunction'. In this regard, Lee J observed (at [50]): 'A dynamic injunction provides a practical means of ensuring the continued effectiveness of the original injunction since it provides an expedited process for the blocking of additional [domain names] which resolve to the same infringing websites, where this is undisputed and unchallenged by the defendants. The defendants and owners of the online locations remain free to challenge the plaintiffs' attempts to block additional [domain names] under the express terms of the order.'

74 For instance, the Federal Court of Australia has preferred to adopt a more conservative approach, which requires the right holder to obtain further orders from the court in order to deal with changes in domain names, URLs and IP addresses. See *Roadshow Films Pty Limited v Telstra Corporation Ltd* [2016] FCA 1503, [137]–[138] (Nicholas J):

> Whether the terms of any injunction should be varied to refer to additional Domain Names, IP Addresses or URLs is a matter for the Court to determine in light of evidence. . . . However, the effect of a notice given by the applicants under their proposed orders will require the respondents to block additional Domain Names, URLs or IP Addresses which might not point to any of the same online locations in relation to which the injunction was originally granted. If the injunction is to apply to new Domain Names, URLs or IP Addresses, then these are matters which should be dealt with by way of further order in the manner proposed by the respondents.

See also *Roadshow Films Pty Limited v Telstra Corporation Limited* [2018] FCA 582, [13] (Nicholas J). It appears that Nicholas J's approach was influenced by his concern for collateral damage and over-blocking.

75 See Enforcement Directive, art 3(2) and Info-Soc Directive, art 8(1).

conduct business. These rights, which are protected under the EU Charter, could only be limited 'if they are necessary and genuinely meet objectives of general interest recognised by the Union or the need to protect the rights and freedoms of others'.[76] Accordingly, Arnold J observed in *Cartier v Sky*:

> As for Article 52(1), what this means is that the rights protected by the Charter can only be restricted where this is necessary to protect other rights protected by the Charter. Where two rights, or sets of rights, are in conflict, then the conflict must be resolved by applying the *principle of proportionality to each and striking a balance between them*. For both reasons, it must be shown that the orders are proportionate.[77]

There is no doubt that if the grant of an injunction amounts to a barrier to lawful trade, including legitimate communications, it is likely to be regarded as disproportionate. In fact, in *Cartier v Sky*, Arnold J observed that the 'impact of [the blocking] measures on lawful users of the internet' is, among other things, a consideration in determining the matter of proportionality.[78] It was for this reason that before the grant of an injunction the court must be satisfied that the technical measures adopted by the ISP are strictly targeted so that they do not affect internet users seeking to gain access to lawful content.[79] These observations are equally applicable to the context of injunctions against navigation providers and hosts.

Implementing an injunction to specifically target only an illegal and infringing website is unproblematic where the entire website is designed to promote the infringement of intellectual property rights, because the removal of, or the prevention of access to, the website at issue forms a strictly targeted measure that does not interfere with legitimate trade or communications. However, where only a part of a website is used to commit infringements, which might be the case with online marketplaces (such as eBay) and social networking sites (such as Facebook), the ability to specifically target the technical measures aimed at terminating or mitigating the infringement *as such* becomes an important consideration. Unless technical measures are capable of being specifically targeted, so that legitimate activities associated with a website remain unhindered, a court is more likely to regard the grant of an injunction as disproportionate.

Although in a slightly different context, *Ahmet Yildirim v Turkey*,[80] a case decided by the European Court of Human Rights, provides some useful insight. This case concerned a measure on the part of the Turkish Telecommunications

76 EU Charter, art 52(1).
77 *Cartier v Sky*, [162] (Arnold J) (emphasis added).
78 *Cartier v Sky*, [189] (Arnold J).
79 *Cartier v Sky*, [182] (Arnold J).
80 *Ahmet Yildirim v Turkey* Case 3111/10 (European Court of Human Rights, 18 December 2012). The full text of the judgment in English is available at http://hudoc.echr.coe.int/sites/eng/pages/search.aspx?i=001-115705 (accessed 31 January 2019).

Directorate (TTD) to block access to the Google Sites service. The move was motivated as a result of a Turkish court ordering the TTD to block access to a particular site hosted by the Google Sites service. However, the TTD convinced the court to extend the scope of the order on the basis that it lacked the technical capacity to block access to a single site hosted by Google Sites. As such, the final outcome was the blocking of the entire Google Sites service, resulting in non-contentious sites also being blocked. When this measure was challenged before the European Court of Human Rights, it was decided that the TTD's action to block access to the *entire* Google Sites service was a contravention of the right of expression.[81] Commenting on *Ahmet Yildirim v Turkey*, it has been suggested:

> Blocking access to an entire platform fails to satisfy the requirement that any restriction on the right to free expression online must be strictly limited. Restrictions on freedom of expression must have a clear legal basis, the interference must pursue a legitimate aim, *and the restrictions must be necessary and proportionate. Blocking access to an entire platform just because of some illegal content is clearly a disproportionate measure.*[82]

The possible impact of injunctions on legitimate internet use was also considered by the CJEU in a series of rulings in relation to blocking injunctions in the copyright context. In *Scarlet Extended v SABAM*,[83] a Belgian court had ordered an ISP to make 'it impossible for its customers to send or receive in any way files containing a musical work in SABAM's repertoire by means of peer-to-peer software, on pain of a periodic penalty'.[84] The CJEU was asked whether an injunction compelling an ISP to introduce a system for filtering all electronic communications, which applies indiscriminately to all its subscribers, exclusively at its own cost and for an unlimited period of time was consistent with the requirements stemming from the protection of fundamental rights under EU law.[85] In respect of a broad injunction such as this, the CJEU cautioned that the 'injunction could potentially undermine freedom of information since that system might not distinguish adequately between unlawful content and lawful content, with the result that its introduction could lead to the blocking of lawful communications'.[86]

81 Article 10 of the European Convention for the Protection of Human Rights and Fundamental Freedoms 1950 guarantees that '[e]veryone has the right to freedom of expression'.

82 ARTICLE 19, *Turkey: Landmark European Court Decision Finds Blanket Google Ban Was a Violation of Freedom of Expression* (2012) <www.article19.org/resources/turkey-landmark-european-court-decision-finds-blanket-google-ban-violation-freedom-expression> (accessed 31 January 2019) (emphasis added). See also G Gürkaynak, I Yılmaz and D Durlu, 'Exploring New Frontiers in the Interface between Free Speech and Access Bans: The European Court of Human Rights' Case of *Ahmet Yıldırım v. Turkey*' (2014) 5(1) *European Journal of Law and Technology* <http://ejlt.org/article/view/282/425> (accessed 31 January 2019).

83 Case C-70/10, *Scarlet Extended SA v Sociétébelge des auteurs, compositeursetéditeurs SCRL (SABAM)* [2011] ECR-I 11959 (*Scarlet Extended v SABAM*).

84 *Scarlet Extended v SABAM*, [23].

85 *Scarlet Extended v SABAM*, [29].

86 *Scarlet Extended v SABAM*, [52].

This position was similarly adopted in a subsequent reference, where the Court made it clear that an injunction compelling an ISP to block access to infringing material would only be compliant with EU law if the technical measures do not 'unnecessarily deprive internet users of the possibility of lawfully accessing the information available'.[87]

In the series of cases decided by Arnold J in the UK, the injunctions awarded were in relation to the blocking of *entire* websites, the sole purpose of which was to infringe intellectual property rights. We are yet to see how blocking injunctions would operate where only parts of a website contain infringing material. Given the CJEU's guidance on the issue of proportionality, unless infringing material contained amidst other legitimate content could be distinctly isolated and identified for the purposes of technical measures, it is likely that a court would find the award of the associated injunction disproportionate, given the danger of collateral damage, i.e. the suppression of legitimate content, communications or activities.

It must be emphasised that, from a technical standpoint, neither ISPs nor navigation providers exercise any control over content giving rise to an infringement, as they merely provide access to such content. On the other hand, hosts exercise direct control over any infringing content they are responsible for storing on their servers. Thus, where only certain parts of a larger website contain the infringing content, measures implemented at the point where the content is hosted entail a much smaller risk of disrupting legitimate communications or activities. In such circumstances, it would be prudent to compel the host on whose servers the infringing content resides to take appropriate action to remove the content associated with the infringement, leaving the other, non-infringing parts of the website unaffected.[88] As such, in any given case, this is a factor that courts must consider in determining whether an injunction sought by a right holder against a particular intermediary is appropriate from the standpoint of collateral damage and proportionality.

Courts must also exercise caution in determining the type of technical measures that they are requested to award, as some measures may be more proportionate than others in a given situation. For instance, in the case of blocking injunctions, the choice between URL, IP address and DNS blocking must be made after considering the circumstances of each case. Where a distinct part (e.g. a single page) within a larger website is the source of infringement, it would be more appropriate to utilise URL blocking, which is the most accurate, although the easiest to circumvent.[89] Where an infringing website shares the same IP address with other 'unlawful' websites, IP address blocking has been regarded as an appropriate measure:

87 Case C-314/12, *UPC Telekabel Wien GmbH v Constantin Film Verleih GmbH* [2014] ECDR 12, [63].

88 For instance, where the content complained of is a product listing on eBay, eBay could easily remove the infringing content.

89 See J Riordan, *The Liability of Internet Intermediaries* (Oxford University Press 2016), 467–68.

> The purpose of [the applicants'] proposal is to ensure that the order is properly targeted, and in particular to ensure that it is as effective as possible while avoiding what counsel for [the applicants] described as 'collateral damage' to other lawful website operators *which share the same IP address. If the websites are not engaged in lawful activity, then the Court need not be concerned about any collateral damage which their operators may suffer.*[90]

Interestingly, the manner in which the issue of collateral damage has been addressed in the context of blocking injunctions has resulted in the remedy having a reach beyond the domain of intellectual property, an outcome that the drafters of the two EU directives on the enforcement of intellectual property rights may not have imagined. On the other hand, where an infringing website shares its IP address with other *legitimate* websites, IP address blocking would not be appropriate, as there is a danger of legitimate content becoming inaccessible to internet users. In such an eventuality, the more appropriate type of blocking would be DNS blocking.[91] However, when DNS blocking is implemented, courts must ensure that blocking takes place at the right level within the domain name structure, depending on the impact on legitimate content sharing the same domain name.[92]

There is no doubt that collateral damage will occupy the minds of judges who are called upon to award injunctions against intermediaries that compel the implementation of technical measures. The choice of technical measure and the type of intermediary implementing it will both be relevant factors in determining whether a court should exercise its jurisdiction in favour of the grant of an injunction.

Costs of implementation

Article 3(1) of the Enforcement Directive provides that remedies and sanctions must not be unnecessarily complicated or costly. This requirement not only applies in relation to the costs of obtaining relief but also to the costs of implementing technical measures consequent to an injunction being awarded. This approach was endorsed by the CJEU in *Scarlet Extended v SABAM* when it made the following observations in respect of the specific circumstances of that case:

> Accordingly, such an injunction would result in a serious infringement of the freedom of the ISP concerned to conduct its business since it would

90 See *Cartier International AG v British Sky Broadcasting Ltd* [2014] EWHC 3765 (Ch), [5] (Arnold J) (emphasis added). During the subsequent appeal, this approach adopted by the English High Court in relation to the issue of collateral damage was approved by the Court of Appeal. See *Cartier v Sky* (CA), [78] (Kitchin LJ).

91 *Cartier v Sky*, [256] (Arnold J).

92 See A Roy and A Marsoof, 'Blocking Injunctions and Collateral Damage' (2017) 39 *European Intellectual Property Review* 74.

> require that ISP to install a complicated, costly, permanent computer system at its own expense, *which would also be contrary to the conditions laid down in Article 3(1) of Directive 2004/48*, which requires that measures to ensure the respect of intellectual-property rights should not be unnecessarily complicated or costly.[93]

It has been the usual practice to consider the matter of costs as part of the proportionality analysis. In the copyright context, Arnold J observed in *EMI Records v Sky* that '[s]o far as the cost of complying with a blocking order is concerned, *this is a factor in the proportionality of the order* as between the Claimants and the Defendants'.[94] This approach was subsequently followed in the trade mark context.[95]

It must be noted that takedown measures (i.e. measures taken by hosts to remove infringing content) are likely to be less costly than the types of measures that ISPs have been required to implement. However, despite the cost-effectiveness of notice and takedown as a remedy, there are likely to be instances where it is less effective, especially when the infringing content is deviously moved from host to host. In such circumstances, despite the costs involved, blocking and de-linking measures may be the only effective means available to tackle infringements.[96]

In the series of cases culminating in the grant of copyright-related blocking injunctions, the English High Court had adopted the stance that it would be appropriate for the ISPs concerned to bear the costs of implementing the ensuing technical measures.[97] In *Cartier v Sky*, this approach was extended by the English High Court to the trade mark context. Thus, in making the order for injunctive relief, the Court was fully conscious about the consequences of compelling the ISPs to bear the costs of implementing technical measures.[98] Mr Justice Arnold observed that the ISPs 'may either absorb these costs themselves, resulting in slightly lower profit margins, or they may pass these costs on to their subscribers in the form of higher subscription charges'.[99] Indeed, ISPs already had in place the technological framework to implement blocking measures, such technology being introduced for other reasons, including to deal with websites that are

93 *Scarlet Extended v SABAM*, [48] (emphasis added).

94 *EMI Records v Sky*, [102] (Arnold J).

95 *Cartier v Sky*, [189] (Arnold J).

96 Injunctions against navigation providers are a useful solution, although ideally both ISPs and navigation providers must work together to provide an effective remedy. The observations made in this chapter in relation to the costs of implementing blocking injunctions are likely to be equally relevant to the technical measures that navigation providers are likely to adopt.

97 See e.g. *Twentieth Century Fox Film Corp v British Telecom Plc* [2011] EWHC 2714 (Ch), [32]–[33]; *EMI Records v Sky*, [107]; *Football Association v Sky, [55]; Paramount Entertainment v Sky*, [42].

98 *Cartier v Sky*, [241] (Arnold J).

99 *Cartier v Sky*, [252] (Arnold J).

recommended for blocking by the Internet Watch Foundation.[100] However, in assessing an ISP's burden of cost, the Court considered it necessary to assess the cumulative cost of implementing *all* website-blocking orders and not just the cost of implementing a single order.[101]

The ISPs in *Cartier v Sky* strongly contended that, when the cost of implementing the court orders made pursuant to section 97A of the CDPA was added to the potential cost of implementing trade mark-related orders, the total implementation costs would undoubtedly skyrocket, given the sheer volume of infringing websites operating at present.[102] However, the Court was not ultimately persuaded that the cost element should stand as an obstacle against the award of an injunction in the specific context of *Cartier v Sky*, although Arnold J made it clear that the cost factor would play a crucial and important role in future cases, especially in circumstances where the cost really does increase by a large scale.[103]

On appeal by the ISPs, the English Court of Appeal approved Arnold J's approach in relation to costs of implementation and dismissed the appeal. In this regard Kitchin LJ (as he then was), with whom Jackson LJ agreed, observed:

> I am satisfied in light of all of these matters that the judge was entitled to require the ISPs to bear the costs of the implementation of the orders in issue. He took proper account of the Enforcement Directive and the other parts of the EU legislative scheme, the guidance given by the Court of Justice, the nature of the orders sought and the circumstances of the case. He has made no error of principle and in my judgment there is no basis upon which this court can interfere with the conclusion to which he came.[104]

However, upon a further appeal being filed by British Telecom, which was one of the defendants in *Cartier v Sky*, the UK Supreme Court took a completely different stance on the issue of implementation costs.[105] Lord Sumption, with whom the other justices agreed, observed that 'the incidence of compliance costs *is a*

100 *Cartier v Sky*, [241] (Arnold J).
101 *Cartier v Sky*, [242] (Arnold J).
102 *Cartier v Sky*, [246]–[249] (Arnold J).
103 *Cartier v Sky*, [253] (Arnold J).
104 *Cartier v Sky* (CA), [150] (Kitchin LJ). Notably, however, Briggs LJ (as he then was) delivered a dissenting judgment on the issue of costs. Applying the principle established in *Bankers Trust v Shapiro* [1980] 3 All ER 353 and *Norwich Pharmacal Co v Customs & Excise Commissioners* [1974] AC 133, Briggs LJ observed (at [202]):

> In both the *Bankers Trust* and *Norwich Pharmacal* types of case, a standard condition or 'modality' for the grant of an injunction requiring the relevant disclosure was that the cost reasonably incurred by the innocent respondent should be reimbursed by the applicant. In both the leading cases, this is treated as an obvious condition, and the reasons for it are not spelt out in detail, beyond the common feature of all such cases, namely that the respondent has not, in becoming mixed up in the relevant wrongdoing, incurred any personal liability to the applicant.

105 *Cartier International AG v British Telecommunications Plc* [2018] UKSC 28 (*Cartier v BT*)

matter for English law'[106] Accordingly, the Supreme Court favoured Briggs LJ's dissenting opinion in the Court of Appeal and observed that:

> The position in relation to website-blocking orders is no different in principle from the established position in domestic law in the case of *Norwich Pharmacal* orders, freezing orders and other injunctions granted to require an innocent party to assist the claimant in the assertion of its rights against a wrongdoer.[107]

Accordingly, the Supreme Court completely reversed the position on implementation costs, among other things, for the following reasons:

> Website-blocking injunctions are sought by rightholders in their own commercial interest. They are wholly directed to the protection of the claimant's legal rights, and the entire benefit of compliance with the order inures to the rightholder. The protection of intellectual property rights is ordinarily and naturally a cost of the business which owns those rights and has the relevant interest in asserting them. It is not ordinarily or naturally a cost of the business of an ISP which has nothing to do with the rights in question but is merely providing a network which has been abused by others. There is therefore no reason why the rightholder should be entitled to look for contribution to the cost of defending his rights to any one other than the infringers.[108]

Lord Sumption did, however, recognise that the allocation of implementation costs must be done within the bounds 'set by the EU principles of effectiveness and equivalence, and the requirement that any remedy should be fair, proportionate and *not unnecessarily costly*'.[109] In this regard, he observed:

> It follows that in principle the rights-holders should indemnify the ISPs against their compliance costs. That is subject to the bounds which EU law sets on the power to grant relief. But there is no reason to believe that these bounds would be exceeded by such an indemnity. *The indemnity must be limited to reasonable compliance costs. The evidence is that the compliance costs resulting from any one order are in fact modest. It is not suggested, nor is there any basis for suggesting that they are excessive, disproportionate or such as to impair the respondents' practical ability to enforce their trade marks.* Nor have any other grounds been proposed for withholding the indemnity on discretionary grounds.[110]

106 *Cartier v BT*, [31] (Lord Sumption) (emphasis added).
107 *Cartier v BT*, [31] (Lord Sumption).
108 *Cartier v BT*, [35] (Lord Sumption).
109 *Cartier v BT*, [31] (Lord Sumption).
110 *Cartier v BT*, [36] (Lord Sumption) (emphasis added).

Arguably, the above passage somewhat tacitly signals the possibility that the allocation of implementation costs could be reconsidered at a later stage, whether in light of EU law principles or the usual discretion that the English courts retain in matters such as this. This is particularly so where implementation costs significantly increase, an eventuality that cannot entirely be ruled out.[111] Ultimately, we might end up with a formula that postulates *cost sharing*, a possibility that Arnold J recognised even at first instance.[112]

Some thoughts for the future

Although injunctions can provide a versatile remedy for the benefit of intellectual property right holders, including trade mark proprietors, it comes with certain challenges that must be addressed. The costs of implementation clearly pose one of the challenges. Based on the recent judgment of the UK Supreme Court, in *Cartier v BT*, on the allocation of implementation costs, one might posit that right holders will exercise greater caution in determining their course of action. In view of the costs of implementation being shifted towards them, it is likely that right holders will pursue the option of notice and takedown as a possible first line of attack, at least in cases where the infringing content is hosted in a country or territory where the law provides hosts with the requisite incentive to remove infringements upon notice. On the other hand, where content giving rise to an infringement is hosted in a country or territory where the legal framework does not incentivise notice and takedown, right holders are likely to pursue injunctions prescribing technical measures against domestic intermediaries, with the hope of preventing internet users from gaining access to such infringements. Notably, the current legal framework in the UK does not provide the necessary inventive to hosts in connection with trade mark-related notice and takedown. The incentive structure will change, however, if the legal reforms proposed in Chapter 5 are brought into effect.

From a cost and efficiency point of view, a more tiered and structured approach must be adopted in respect of the availability of these remedies. In fact, such an approach is reflected in legislation elsewhere, albeit in the copyright context. For instance, section 115A(1) of the Australian Copyright Act 1968 (Cth) provides that copyright owners may obtain a blocking injunction where the website responsible for, or facilitating, an infringement is located *outside* Australia.

111 It must be pointed out that in all the blocking injunction cases that have come up before the English courts so far, *entire* websites were targeted as containing infringing material. We are yet to see a case where the infringing content is contained within a part of a larger website. It is unclear as to how this would impact the issue of implementation costs. Targeting a specific part of a larger website requires precision, and, arguably, that may increase the costs of implementing technical measures. Additionally, it must be noted that to date blocking injunctions have required ISPs to take measures in respect of their *fixed-line residential customers*. However, if mobile and business customers are added to the equation, the costs of implementation could increase even further.

112 *Cartier v Sky*, [240] (Arnold J).

This means that, when infringing websites are *within* the jurisdiction of enforcement, copyright owners must have recourse to other remedies, typically notice and takedown. A similar provision is found in the US Digital Millennium Copyright Act 1998,[113] where blocking injunctions against ISPs are permitted *only* in relation to infringing websites hosted outside of the US, whereas the US safe harbour and substantive copyright law provide the necessary incentive for notice and takedown to operate in respect of locally hosted content.

A similar approach may be adopted in the EU and the UK, where local courts could consider the location of the alleged infringing content in exercising their discretion on whether (or not) to issue an injunction against an intermediary. Such an approach would better meet the standards of proportionality, efficiency and cost-effectiveness.

The need to file *multiple proceedings* is yet another challenge that right holders face, in view of the territoriality of intellectual property rights and the interest right holders have in enforcing rights across jurisdictions. Multiplicity of proceedings is a factor that is usually considered under private international law before a court exercises jurisdiction over a given dispute. Usually, where a claimant has instituted multiple actions against the same defendant concerning the same dispute, a court may, in applying the principle of *forum non conveniens*, stay proceedings before it on the ground of multiplicity of proceedings.[114]

Since, intellectual property rights (and, in particular, trade mark rights) are often protected across multiple jurisdictions, when infringements occur in more than one jurisdiction, right holders are compelled to initiate legal proceedings in every one of those jurisdictions where their rights are infringed. However, in contrast to the conventional understanding of multiplicity of proceedings, in the intellectual property context it is often the case that, although the claimant and the substance of the dispute are the same, the defendant infringers are not.[115] This is a fact that holds true even in relation to injunctions against internet intermediaries.

We know that blocking injunctions target ISPs in order to deal with intellectual property infringements. ISPs operate within the borders of a particular jurisdiction and therefore if all ISPs operating within a jurisdiction are targeted, it is possible to completely block access to an identified infringing website. This outcome is practically achievable because, in any given jurisdiction, there are only a few, if not an identifiable group of, entities that provide internet access. However, what must be borne in mind is that blocking access to an infringing source in one jurisdiction does not mean that the source cannot be accessed

113 17 USC §512(j)(B)(ii).

114 See e.g. FM Manolis, NJ Vermette and RF Hungerford, 'The Doctrine of *Forum Non Conveniens*: Canada and the United States Compared' (2009) 60 *Federation of Defence and Corporate Counsel Quarterly* 3, 8–9 and J Lee, 'Private International Law in the Singaporean Courts' (2005) 9 *Singapore Year Book of International Law* 243, 244.

115 JJ Fawcett and P Torremans, *Intellectual Property and Private International Law* (2nd edn, Oxford University Press 2011), 289.

from other jurisdictions. Since intellectual property rights (especially trade mark rights) could subsist in multiple jurisdictions, the fact that blocking injunctions are always tied to a particular jurisdiction is problematic. In effect, right holders will be compelled to seek out blocking injunctions against ISPs in every single jurisdiction in which they wish to enforce their rights in respect of the identical infringement, leading to a multiplicity of proceedings. This problem could be addressed by introducing a mechanism under which a blocking injunction targeting ISPs in a particular jurisdiction could provide the basis for similar orders against ISPs in other jurisdictions in respect of the *same content* giving rise to the *identical* infringement.

The issue of multiple proceedings is also a concern in respect of injunctions against the other categories of intermediaries (i.e. hosts and navigation providers). This is primarily in view of the problem caused by circumvention. For instance, where a host removes infringing content from its servers, the infringers could simply relocate the content to a new host. In such circumstances, the right holder must identify the new host and serve a fresh notice of infringement to initiate a takedown. In circumstances where the new host does not cooperate, and assuming that it operates in an EU Member State, it should be possible for the right holder to obtain an injunction against that host. Even if it might be assumed that the new host will comply with the injunction, since the injunction only binds the host and not the infringers, the latter could simply relocate the content to another host, continuing the cycle ad infinitum. Assuming further that the new host is also within the EU, the right holder may have to seek out a fresh injunction enjoining that host. This type of tactical manoeuvring on the part of infringers is what makes notice and takedown, and injunctions against hosts, less effective. This problem could be addressed by providing for a mechanism under which an injunction compelling a takedown of identified infringing content could provide the basis for similar orders in the future against hosts whose services are obtained to host the *same content* giving rise to the *identical* infringement.

However, there is currently no conceivable mechanism by which an injunction granted in one jurisdiction could be recognised and enforced in other jurisdictions utilising the standard methods of recognising and enforcing judgments across states. Unfortunately, in the EU, the two key directives on the enforcement of intellectual property rights do not provide for a means of achieving cross-border enforcement of injunctions against intermediaries. Therefore, if the injunctive remedy is to develop into a more versatile one, a framework for the recognition and enforcement of judgments comparable to the Hague Convention on Foreign Judgments in Civil and Commercial Matters 1971 or the Brussels I Regulation (Recast)[116] must be adopted specifically for the

116 Regulation (EU) No 1215/2012 of the European Parliament and of the Council of 12 December 2012 on Jurisdiction and the Recognition and Enforcement of Judgments in Civil and Commercial Matters (Recast), [2012] OJ L 351 (Brussels I Regulation (Recast)), which came into force on 10 January 2015.

intellectual property context, so that the *special enforcement* needs of right holders may be addressed. Ideally, in circumstances where the source and perpetrators of infringement remain the same, an upgraded enforcement regime must allow right holders to enforce an injunction against intermediaries awarded in one jurisdiction against the corresponding intermediaries operating in another jurisdiction, subject to the requirement of establishing rights in the jurisdiction where enforcement is sought.

There are lessons to be learnt from the blocking regimes as currently implemented in Australia and Singapore. In Australia, the competent court may consider 'whether access to the online location has been disabled by orders from any court of another country or territory on the ground of or related to copyright infringement'[117] in exercising its discretion in respect of the grant of a blocking order. The exact provision is also available in Singapore's Copyright Act 1987.[118] Arguably, adopting a similar approach in respect of injunctions in the EU and the UK could significantly increase the efficacy of the remedy as a means of enforcing intellectual property rights.

117 Copyright Act 1968 (Cth), section 115A(5)(d).
118 Copyright Act 1987, section 193DDA(2)(d).

Bibliography

Adler J, 'The Public's Burden in a Digital Age: Pressures on Intermediaries and the Privatization of Internet Censorship' (2011) 20 *Journal of Law and Policy* 231

Ahlert C, C Marsden and C Yung, *How 'Liberty' Disappeared from Cyberspace: The Mystery Shopper Tests Internet Content Self-Regulation* (University of Oxford 2004) <http://pcmlp.socleg.ox.ac.uk/sites/pcmlp.socleg.ox.ac.uk/files/liberty.pdf> (accessed 31 January 2019)

Angelopoulos C, *European Intermediary Liability in Copyright: A Tort-Based Analysis* (Kluwer Law International 2017)

Ardia DS, 'Free Speech Savior or Shield for Scoundrels: An Empirical Study of Intermediary Immunity Under Section 230 of the Communications Decency Act' (2010) 43 *Loyola of Los Angeles Law Review* 373

Arnold R, 'Who Is an Intermediary for the Purposes of Article 11 of the Enforcement Directive?' Speech made at the 1st iCLIC Conference (2015) <https://youtu.be/tpeUyOzI_iw> (accessed 31 January 2019)

ARTICLE 19, *Turkey: Landmark European Court Decision Finds Blanket Google Ban Was a Violation of Freedom of Expression* (2012) <www.article19.org/resources/turkey-landmark-european-court-decision-finds-blanket-google-ban-violation-freedom-expression> (accessed 31 January 2019)

Atiyah PS, *Vicarious Liability in the Law of Torts* (Butterworths 1967)

Bailey S, 'Fighting an Anonymous Enemy: The Uncertainty of Auction Sites in the Face of *Tiffany v eBay* and *LVMH v eBay*' (2009) 40 *California Western International Law Journal* 129

Baily JP and Y Bakos, 'An Exploratory Study of the Emerging Role of Electronic Intermediaries' (1997) 1 *International Journal of Electronic Commerce* 7

Bartholomew M and J Tehranian, 'The Secret Life of Legal Doctrine: The Divergent Evolution of Secondary Liability in Trademark and Copyright Law' (2006) 21 *Berkeley Technology Law Journal* 1363

Bednarz T, 'Keyword Advertising before the French Supreme Court and beyond – Calm at Last after Turbulent Times for Google and Its Advertising Clients?' (2011) 42 *International Review of Intellectual Property and Competition Law (IIC)* 641

Beier F-K, 'Territoriality of Trade Mark Law and International Trade' (1970) 1 *International Review of Intellectual Property and Competition Law (IIC)* 48

Bently L, B Sherman, D Gangjee and P Johnson, *Intellectual Property Law* (5th edn, Oxford University Press 2018)

Blakeney M, *Trade Related Aspects of Intellectual Property Rights: A Concise Guide to the TRIPS Agreement* (Sweet & Maxwell 1996)

Blythe A, 'Trade Marks as Adwords: An Aid to Competition or a Potential Infringement? An Evaluation of the Law in the Light of Recent Decisions' (2015) 37 *European Intellectual Property Review* 225

—— 'A Useful Test for Trade Mark Use: An Analysis of Current CJEU Guidance and the Difference between Defining Use Online and Offline' (2016) *European Intellectual Property Review* 563

Bornkamm J, *Intellectual Property Litigation under the Civil Law Legal System; Experience in Germany* WIPO/ACE/2/3 (4 June 2004)

Bouchoux DE, *Intellectual Property Law* (5th edn, Cengage Learning 2018)

Bradford LR, 'Emotion, Dilution, and Trademark Consumer' (2008) 23 *Berkeley Technology Law Journal* 1227

Brege JR and KA Ovies, 'Taking Down Trademark Bullying: Sketching the Contours of a Trademark Notice and Takedown Statute' (2012) 2 *Wake Forest Journal of Business and Intellectual Property Law* 391

Brown B, 'Fortifying the Safe Harbors: Reevaluating the DMCA in a Web 2.0 World' (2008) 23 *Berkeley Technology Law Journal* 437

Brown, Jr RS, 'Advertising and the Public Interest: Legal Protection of Trade Symbols' (1948) 57 *Yale Law Journal* 1165

Burk DL, 'Cybermarks' (2010) 91 *Minnesota Law Review* 1375

Burrell R and M Handler, *Australian Trade Mark Law* (Oxford University Press 2010)

Burrell R and K Weatherall, 'Before the High Court–Providing Services to Copyright Infringers: *Roadshow Films Pty Ltd v iiNet Ltd*' (2011) 33 *Sydney Law Review* 801

Caddell R, 'Freedom of Commercial Speech and the UK Courts' (2005) 64 *Cambridge Law Journal* 274

Carty H, 'Joint Tortfeasance and Assistance Liability' (1999) 10 *Legal Studies* 489

Calboli I, 'Trademark Exhaustion in the European Union: Community-Wide or International? The Saga Continues' (2002) 6 *Marquette Intellectual Property Law Review* 47

Carpou Z, 'Robots, Pirates, and the Rise of the Automated Takedown Regime: Using the DMCA to Fight Piracy and Protect End-Users' (2016) 39 *Columbia Journal of Law & the Arts* 551

Chang L, 'The Red Flag Test for Apparent Knowledge under the DMCA §512(c) Safe Harbor' (2010) 28 *Cardozo Arts & Entertainment Law Journal* 195

Chaudhry P and A Zimmerman, *Protecting Your Intellectual Property Rights* (Springer 2013)

Cheung ASY and KKH Pun, 'Comparative Study on the Liability for Trade Mark Infringement of Online Auction Providers' (2009) 31 *European Intellectual Property Review* 559

Chikada A and A Gupta, 'Online Brand Protection' in PE Chaudhry (ed), *Handbook of Research on Counterfeiting and Illicit Trade* (Edward Elgar 2017)

Combs NI, 'Civil Aiding and Abetting Liability' (2005) 58 *Vanderbilt Law Review* 241

Cooke J, *Law of Tort* (9th edn, Pearson 2009)

Cooper D, *Secondary Liability for Civil Wrongs* (PhD thesis, Cambridge University 1995)

Cornish W, D Llewelyn and T Aplin, *Intellectual Property: Patents, Copyright, Trade Marks and Allied Rights* (8th edn, Sweet & Maxwell 2013)

Correa CM, *Trade Related Aspects of Intellectual Property Rights: A Commentary on the TRIPS Agreement* (Oxford University Press 2007)

Cross JT, 'Contributory Infringement and Related Theories of Secondary Liability for Trademark Infringement' (1995) 80 *Iowa Law Review* 101

Cross N, *Criminal Law and Criminal Justice: An Introduction* (SAGE Publications 2010)

Curren PD, 'Diluting the Commercial Speech Doctrine: "Noncommercial Use" and the Federal Trademark Dilution Act' (2004) 71 *University of Chicago Law Review* 1077

Davidson A, *The Law of Electronic Commerce* (Cambridge University Press 2009)

Davies PS, 'Accessory Liability for Assisting Torts' (2011) 70 *Cambridge Law Journal* 353

—— 'Accessory Liability: Protecting Intellectual Property Rights' (2011) *Intellectual Property Quarterly* 390

—— *Accessory Liability* (Hart Publishing 2015)

—— 'Accessory Liability in Tort' (2016) 132 *Law Quarterly Review* 15

Davis J, *Intellectual Property Law* (3rd edn, Oxford University Press 2008)

Dawson NM, 'Non-Trade Mark Use' (2012) *Intellectual Property Quarterly* 204

Deaking S, A Johnston and B Markesinis, *Markesinis and Deakin's Tort Law* (7th edn, Oxford University Press 2007)

Debter L, 'Does Etsy Have a Problem with Fake Goods?' *Forbes* (11 May 2015) <www.forbes.com/sites/laurengensler/2015/05/11/does-etsy-have-a-problem-with-fake-goods/#4e89a17a5a88> (accessed 31 January 2019)

de Carvalho NP, *The TRIPS Regime of Trademarks and Designs* (Kluwer Law International 2006)

Diamond SA, 'The Historical Development of Trademarks' (1983) 73 *Trademark Reporter* 222

Dietrich J, 'Accessorial Liability in the Law of Torts' (2011) 31 *Legal Studies* 231

Dinwoodie GB, 'The Demise of Territoriality?' (2009) 57 *William and Mary Law Review* 711

—— 'The Common Law and Trade Marks in an Age of Statutes' in L Bently, C Ng and G D'Agostino (eds), *The Common Law of Intellectual Property Essays in Honour of Professor David Vaver* (Hart Publishing 2010)

—— 'Secondary Liability for Online Trademark Infringement: The International Landscape' (2014) 37 *Columbia Journal of Law and Arts* 463

—— 'A Comparative Analysis of the Secondary Liability of Online Service Providers' in GB Dinwoodie (ed), *Secondary Liability of Internet Service Providers* (Springer 2017)

—— and MD Janis, 'Confusion Over Use: Contextualism in Trademark Law' (2007) 92 *Iowa Law Review* 1597

Dogan SL, 'Trademark Remedies and Online Intermediaries' (2010) 14 *Lewis & Clark Law Review* 467

—— 'Principled Standards vs. Boundless Discretion: A Tale of Two Approaches to Intermediary Trademark Liability Online' (2014) 37 *Columbia Journal of Law & the Arts* 503

Drescher TD, 'The Transformation and Evolution of Trademarks – From Signals to Symbols to Myth' (1992) 82 *Trademark Reporter* 301

EAASM, *The Counterfeit Superhighway* (2008) <www.eaasm.eu/cache/downloads/dqqt3sge9hwssgcgcos440g40/455_EAASM_counterfeiting%20report_020608(1).pdf> (accessed 31 January 2019)

Economides NS, 'The Economics of Trademarks' (1988) 78 *Trademark Reporter* 523

Edwards L, 'Articles 12–15 ECD: ISP Liability' in L Edwards (ed), *The New Legal Framework for E-Commerce in Europe* (Hart Publishing 2005)

Eecke PV and M Truyens, *EU Study on the Legal Analysis of a Single Market for the Information Society–New Rules for a New Age?* SMART 2007/0037 (2009)

Eecke PV, 'Online Service Providers and Liability: A Plea for a Balanced Approach' (2011) 48 *Common Market Law Review* 1455

Electronic Frontier Foundation, *Submission on the Consultation on the EU E-Commerce Directive* (2010) <www.eff.org/files/filenode/international/effeuecommercedirective consultationresponse.pdf> (accessed 31 January 2019)

Elliott C and F Quinn, *Tort Law* (5th edn, Pearson 2005)

European Commission, *Counterfeit and Piracy Watch List* (7 December 2018) <http://trade.ec.europa.eu/doclib/docs/2018/december/tradoc157564.pdf> (accessed 31 January 2019)

European Commission, *Too Good to Be True: The Real Price of Fake Products* MEMO/13/346 (2013) <http://europa.eu/ rapid/press-release_MEMO-13-346_en.htm> (accessed 31 January 2019)

—— *Memorandum of Understanding on the Sale of Counterfeit Goods via the Internet* (21 June 2016) <https://ec.europa.eu/docsroom/documents/30763/attachments/1/translations/en/renditions/native> (accessed 31 January 2019)

—— *Report on EU Customs Enforcement of Intellectual Property Rights–Results at the EU Border 2017* (Publications Office of the European Union 2018)

Europol/EUIPO, 2017 Situation Report on Counterfeiting and Piracy in the European Union (June 2017) <www.europol.europa.eu/sites/default/files/documents/counter feiting_and_piracy_in_the_european_union.pdf> (accessed 31 January 2019)

Farber DA, 'Commercial Speech and the First Amendment Theory' (1979) 74 *Northwestern University Law Review* 372

Fawcett JJ and P Torremans, *Intellectual Property and Private International Law* (2nd edn, Oxford University Press 2011)

Fhima IS, 'Trade Marks and Free Speech' (2013) 44 *International Review of Intellectual Property and Competition Law (IIC)* 293

Fields D and K Shaw, 'UK High Court Considers Extent to Which Retailers May Use Third-Party Trade Marks in Advertisements' (2014) 20 *Computer and Telecommunications Law Review* 113

Fisher H, 'Danger in the DMCA Safe Harbors: The Need to Narrow What Constitutes Red Flag Knowledge' (2015) 49 *University of Richmond Law Review* 643

Fitzgerald B, A Fitzgerald, E Clark, G Middleton and YF Lim, *Internet and E-Commerce Law: Technology, Law and Policy* (Lawbook Co 2011)

Fleming JG, *Law of Torts* (8th edn, Law Book Co 1992)

Fletcher GP, *Rethinking Criminal Law* (Oxford University Press 2000)

Fordham M, 'Breach of Statutory Duty – A Diminishing Tort' (1996) *Singapore Journal of Legal Studies* 362

Fox FS, 'Contributory Trademark Infringement: The Legal Standard After *Inwood Laboratories, Inc. v. Ives Laboratories, Inc.*' (1983) 4 *University of Bridgeport Law Review* 387

Frontier Economics, *The Economic Impacts of Counterfeiting and Piracy* (2017) <www.inta.org/communications/documents/2017_frontier_report.pdf> (accessed 31 January 2019)

Geiger C and E Izyumenko, 'The Role of Human Rights in Copyright Enforcement Online: Elaborating a Legal Framework for Website Blocking' (2016) 32 *American University International Law Review* 43

Gellman R, 'Disintermediation and the Internet' (1996) 13(1) *Government Information Quarterly* 1

Gervais D, *The TRIPS Agreement–Drafting History and Analysis* (3rd edn, Sweet & Maxwell 2008)

Gilles SG, 'Negligence, Strict Liability, and the Cheapest Cost-Avoider' (1992) 78 *Virginia Law Review* 1291

Gilson J, 'Experts in Trademark Cases' (1982) 8 *Litigation* 40

Goldberg JCP and BC Zipursky, 'Tort Law and Responsibility' in J Oberdiek (ed), *Philosophical Foundations of the Law of Torts* (Oxford University Press 2014)

Goold PR, 'Corrective Justice and Copyright Infringement' (2014) *Vanderbilt Journal of Entertainment and Technology Law* 251

—— 'Is Copyright Infringement a Strict Liability Tort?' (2015) 30 *Berkeley Technology Law Journal* 305

Grafton-Green P, 'Brexit Deal Approved by EU Leaders: What Happens Next and When Will Parliament Vote on It?' *The Evening Standard* (25 November 2018) <www.standard.co.uk/news/politics/brexit-news-what-lies-ahead-for-theresa-may-and-her-deal-with-the-eu-a3999501.html> (accessed 31 January 2019)

Greene PJ, 'Keyword Advertising, and Other Invisible Uses of Third Party Trade Marks in Online Advertising: a New Zealand/Australasian Perspective' (2009) 40 *Victoria University of Wellington Law Review* 106

Gürkaynak G, I Yılmaz and D Durlu, 'Exploring New Frontiers in the Interface between Free Speech and Access Bans: The European Court of Human Rights' Case of *Ahmet Yıldırım v. Turkey*' (2014) 5(1) *European Journal of Law and Technology* <http://ejlt.org/article/view/282/425> (accessed 31 January 2019)

Gurr A, 'Accessory Liability and Contribution, Release and Apportionment' (2010) 34 *Melbourne University Law Review* 16

Hamdani A, 'Who's Liable for Cyberwrongs' (2002) 87 *Cornell Law Review* 901

Hamilton L, 'Regulation of the Internet: An impossible task?' (2010) 4 *Galway Student Law Review* 33

Hanak, III FW, 'The Quality Assurance Function of Trademarks' (1975) 65 *Trademark Reporter* 318

Holland HB, 'Section 230 of the CDA: Internet Exceptionalism as a Statutory Construct' in B Szoka and A Marcus (eds), *The Next Digital Decade: Essays on the Future of the Internet* (TechFreedom 2011)

Harbottle G, 'Criminal Remedies for Copyright and Performers' Rights Infringement under the Copyright, Designs and Patents Act 1988' (1994) 5 *Entertainment Law Review* 12

Hartwig H, 'German Court Ruling Cracks Down on Internet Forgeries' (2004) 43 *European Lawyer* 12

Harvey D, *Collisions in the Digital Paradigm: Law and Rule Making in the Internet Age* (Hart Publishing 2017)

Hays T, 'The Free Movement (or Not) of Trademark Protected Goods in Europe' in GB Dinwoodie and MD Janis (eds), *Trademark Law and Theory: A Handbook of Contemporary Research* (Edward Elgar 2008)

Headdon T, 'Beyond Liability: On the Availability and Scope of Injunctions against Online Intermediaries after L'Oréal v eBay' (2012) 34 *European Intellectual Property Review* 137

Hoeren T and S Yankova, 'The Liability of Internet Intermediaries – the German Perspective' (2012) 43 *International Review of Intellectual Property and Competition Law (IIC)* 501

Hohfeld WN, 'Fundamental Legal Conceptions as Applied in Judicial Reasoning' (1913) 23 *Yale Law Journal* 13

Holland HB, 'Section 230 of the CDA: Internet Exceptionalism as a Statutory Construct' in B Szoka and A Marcus (eds), *The Next Digital Decade: Essays on the Future of the Internet* (TechFreedom 2011)

Honoré T, 'The Morality of Tort Law—Questions and Answers' in DG Owen (ed), *Philosophical Foundations of Tort Law* (Oxford University Press 1997)

Horder J, *Ashworth's Principles of Criminal Law* (8th edn, Oxford University Press 2016)

Horsey K and E Rackley, *Tort Law* (4th edn, Oxford University Press 2015)

Hudson E, 'Implementing Fair Use in Copyright Law: Lessons from Australia' (2013) 25 *Intellectual Property Journal* 201

Husovec M and M Peguera 'Much Ado about Little–Privately Litigated Internet Disconnection Injunctions' (2015) 46(1) *International Review of Intellectual Property and Competition Law (IIC)* 10

Husovec M, 'Injunctions against Innocent Third Parties: The Case of Website Blocking' (2012) 4 *Journal of Intellectual Property, Information Technology and Electronic Commerce Law* 116

—— *Injunctions Against Intermediaries in the European Union: Accountable But Not Liable?* (Cambridge University Press 2017)

Hutchinson AC, *Evolution and the Common Law* (Cambridge University Press 2005)

INTA, *Addressing the Sale of Counterfeits on the Internet* (2017) <www.inta.org/Advocacy/Documents/2018/Addressing_the_Sale_of_Counterfeits_on_ the_Internet_021518.pdf> (accessed 31 January 2019)

Jacques S, K Garstka, M Hviid and J Street, 'Automated Anti-piracy Systems as Copyright Enforcement Mechanism: A Need to Consider Cultural Diversity' (2018) 40 *European Intellectual Property Review* 218

Jehoram TC, C van Nispen and T Huydecoper, *European Trademark Law* (Kluwer Law International 2010)

Jones DL, 'Brexit and the Future of English Law' (2018) 49 *Victoria University of Wellington Law Review* 1

Johnson VW and LP Merritt, 'Tiffany v. eBay: A Case of Genuine Disparity in International Court Rulings on Counterfeit Products' (2008) 1 *Landslide* 22

Jones MA, *Textbook on Torts* (8th edn, Oxford University Press 2002)

Jones MA, AM Dugale and M Simpson (eds), *Clerk and Lindsell on Torts* (21st edn, Sweet & Maxwell 2014)

Karl DC, '"Look-Alike" Capsules, Generic Drug Substitution, and the Lanham Act: The Elusive Contributory Infringement Standard of Inwood Laboratories, Inc. v. Ives Laboratories, Inc' (1982) 32 *Catholic University Law Review* 345

Katyal NK, 'Criminal Law in Cyberspace' (2001) 149 *University of Pennsylvania Law Review* 1003

Kentish B, 'MPs Throw Weight behind Fresh Brexit Referendum as Hundreds of Thousands Prepare for Major Demonstration in London' *The Independent* (16 October 2018) <www.independent.co.uk/news/ uk/politics/brexit-referendum-final-say-london-protest-eu-uk-remain-leave-peoples-vote-a8585441.html> (accessed 31 January 2019)

Kessler J, 'Correcting the Standard for Contributory Trademark Liability over the Internet' (2006) 39 *Columbia Journal of Law and Social Problems* 375

Khan S, 'The Potential Impact on Host Intermediaries of Defamatory Remarks Posted following L'Oreal v eBay' (2012) 18 *Computer and Telecommunications Law Review* 204

Kirk A, 'EU Referendum: The Claims That Won It for Brexit, Fact Checked' *The Telegraph* (13 March 2017) <www.telegraph.co.uk/politics/0/eu-referendum-claims-won-brexit-fact-checked> (accessed 31 January 2019)

Kirkland C, 'Brexit Vote Defeat: Theresa May's "Plan B" Options Explained' *The Conversation* (14 January 2019) <https://theconversation.com/brexit-vote-defeat-theresa-mays-plan-b-options-explained-109749> (accessed 31 January 2019)

Koo J, *The Right of Communication to the Public in EU Copyright Law* (Hart Publishing 2019)

Kraakman RH, 'Gatekeepers: The Anatomy of a Third Party Enforcement Strategy' (1986) 2 *Journal of Law, Economics, and Organization* 53

Kuczerawy A, 'The Power of Positive Thinking: Intermediary Liability and the Effective Enjoyment of the Right to Freedom of Expression' (2017) 8 *Journal of Intellectual Property, Information Technology and Electronic Commerce Law* 226

Kur A, 'Secondary Liability for Trademark Infringement on the Internet: The Situation in Germany and Throughout the EU' (2014) 37 *Columbia Journal of Law & the Arts* 525

Kutschke P, 'German Federal Supreme Court: Injunctive Relief May Be Claimed against Online-Auctioneers if Vendors Offer Forgeries on the Internet Platform' (2008) 3 *IP Report* 16

Landes W and RA Posner, *The Economic Structure of Intellectual Property Law* (Harvard University Press 2003)

Landes WM and R Posner, 'Trademark Law: An Economic Perspective' (1987) 30 *Journal of Law and Economics* 265

Landon PA, *Pollock's Law of Torts* (15th edn, Stevens and Sons Ltd 1951)

Law Commission, *Assisting and Encouraging Crime: A Consultation Paper*, Consultation Paper No 131 (1993)

—— *Inchoate Liability for Assisting and Encouraging Crime*, LAW COM No 300 (2006)

Lee J, 'Private International Law in the Singaporean Courts' (2005) 9 *Singapore Year Book of International Law* 243

Lee PW, 'Accessorial Liability in Tort and Equity' (2015) 27 *Singapore Academy of Law Journal* 851

Lehman BA, *Intellectual Property and the National Information Infrastructure: The Report of the Working Group on Intellectual Property Rights* (Information Infrastructure Task Force 1995)

Leval PN, 'Trademark: Champion of Free Speech' (2004) 27 *Columbia Journal of Law and Arts* 187

Levin EK, 'A Safe Harbor for Trademark: Reevaluating Secondary Trademark Liability After Tiffany v. eBay' (2009) 24 *Berkeley Technology Law Journal* 491

Lichtman D and E Posner, 'Holding Internet Service Providers Accountable' (2006) 14 *Supreme Court Economic Review* 221

Lievens D, 'eBay's accessory liability for counterfeiting–why joint tort liability just doesn't cut the mustard' (2011) 42 *International Review of Intellectual Property and Competition Law (IIC)* 506

Lievens D, 'L'Oréal v. eBay – Welcomed in France, Resented in England' (2012) 43 *International Review of Intellectual Property and Competition Law (IIC)* 68

Lindsay D, *International Domain Name Law: ICANN and the UDRP* (Hart Publishing 2007)

Llewelyn D, 'Intellectual Property Liability of Consumers, Facilitators and Intermediaries: Concepts under Common Law' in C Heath and AK Sanders (eds), *Intellectual Property Liability of Consumers, Facilitators and Intermediaries* (Kluwer Law International 2012)

—— 'Assessment of Damages in Intellectual Property Cases: Some Recent Examples of "the Exercise of a Sound Imagination and the Practice of a Broad Axe"?' (2015) 27 *Singapore Academy of Law Journal* 480

—— 'Statutory Damages for Use of a "Counterfeit Trade Mark" and for Copyright Infringement in Singapore: A Radical Remedy in the Law of Intellectual Property or One in Need of a Rethink?' (2016) 28 *Singapore Academy of Law Journal* 61

Loughlan PL, 'Protecting Culturally Significant Uses of Trade Marks (without a First Amendment)' (2000) 22 *European Intellectual Property Review* 328

Macdonald RA, 'Natural Justice' in CB Gray (ed), *The Philosophy of the Law: An Encyclopaedia* (Routledge 1999)

Manolis FM, NJ Vermette and RF Hungerford, 'The Doctrine of *Forum Non Conveniens*: Canada and the United States Compared' (2009) 60 *Federation of Defence and Corporate Counsel Quarterly* 3

McBride NJ and R Bagshaw, *Tort Law* (5th edn, Pearson 2015)

McGregor H, *McGregor on Damages* (20th edn, Sweet & Maxwell 2017)

McKenna MP, 'The Normative Foundations of Trademark Law' (2007) 82 *Notre Dame Law Review* 1856

McKenna MP, 'A Consumer Decision-Making Theory of Trademark Law' (2012) 98 *Virginia Law Review* 67

Meale D, 'Premier League 1, Internet Pirates 0: Sports Streaming Website the Latest to Be Blocked' (2013) 8 *Journal of Intellectual Property Law and Practice* 821

Milchior R, 'eBay Ruling is Good News for Brand Owners – but Evidentiary Burden is Increased' *World Trademark Review Daily* (23 May 2012) <www.granrut.com/IMG/pdf/ WTR_20120724.pdf> (accessed 31 January 2019)

Milmo P and H Rogers (eds), *Gatley on Libel and Slander* (11th edn, Sweet & Maxwell 2008)

Moohr GS, 'The Crime of Copyright Infringement: An Inquiry Based on Morality, Harm and Criminal Theory' (2003) 83 *Boston University Law Review* 731

Moore M, 'Cybersquatting: Prevention Better Than Cure?' (2008) 17 *International Journal of Law and Information Technology* 220

Moore T and R Clayton, 'The Impact of Incentives on Notice and Takedown' in E Johnson (ed), *Managing Information Risk and the Economics of Security* (Springer 2008)

Morcom C, 'Trade Marks and the Internet: Where Are We Now?' (2012) 34 *European Intellectual Property Review* 40

Moreno JM, 'Publisher or Technical Provider? Monitoring as Editorial Control and the "Safe Harbor" of Art.14 E-Commerce Directive' (2013) 49 *Jura Falconis* 663

Mostert FW and MB Schwimmer, 'Notice and Takedown for Trademarks' (2011) 101 *Trademark Reporter* 249

Munro CR, 'The Value of Commercial Speech' (2003) 62 *Cambridge Law Journal* 134

Mylly T, 'A Silhouette of Fortress Europe? International Exhaustion of Trade Mark Rights in the EU' (2000) 7 *Maastricht Journal of European and Comparative Law* 51

Nas S, *The Multatuli Project: ISP Notice & Take Down* (2004) <www-old.bof.nl/docs/ researchpaper SANE.pdf> (accessed 31 January 2019)

Naser MA, 'Trademarks and Freedom of Expression' (2009) 40 *International Review of Intellectual Property and Competition Law (IIC)* 188

Neild D, 'Vicarious Liability and the Employment Rationale' (2013) 44 *Victoria University of Wellington Law Review* 707

Oddi AS, 'Contributory Copyright Infringement: The Tort and Technological Tensions' (1989) 64 *Notre Dame Law Review* 47

OECD, *The Economic Impact of Counterfeiting and Piracy* (OECD Publishing 2008)

—— *Trade in Counterfeit Products and the UK Economy: Fake Goods, Real Losses* (OECD Publishing 2017)

——/EUIPO, *Trade in Counterfeit and Pirated Goods: Mapping the Economic Impact* (OECD Publishing 2016)

Ofcom, *'Site Blocking' to Reduce Online Copyright Infringement: A Review of Sections 17 and 18 of the Digital Economy Act* (2010) <https://assets.publishing.service.gov.uk/government/uploads/system/uploads/attachment_data/file/78095/Ofcom_Site-Blocking-_report_with_redactions_vs2.pdf> (accessed 31 January 2019)

Ormerod D and K Laird, *Smith and Hogan's Criminal Law* (14th edn, Oxford University Press 2015)

Orrick SW, 'Deciphering Rosetta Stone: Why the Least Cost Avoider Principle Unlocks the Code to Contributory Trademark Infringement in Keyword Advertising' (2013) 28 *Berkeley Technology Law Journal* 805

Parsons S, 'Criminal Liability for the Act of Another: Accessorial Liability and the Doctrine of Joint Enterprise' (1998) 62 *Journal of Criminal Law* 352

Paster BG, 'Trademarks – Their Early History' (1969) 59 *Trademark Reporter* 551

Peguera M, '"I Just Know That I (Actually) Know Nothing": Actual Knowledge and Other Problems in ISP Liability Case Law in Spain' (2008) 30 *European Intellectual Property Review* 280

—— 'The DMCA Safe Harbour and Their European Counterparts: A Comparative Analysis of Some Common Problems' (2009) 32 *Columbia Journal of Law & the Arts* 481

—— 'Internet Service Providers' Liability in Spain: Recent Caw Law and Future Perspectives' (2010) 1 *Journal of Intellectual Property, Information Technology and Electronic Commerce Law* 151

Perel M and N Elkin-Koren, 'Accountability in Algorithmic Copyright Enforcement' (2016) 19 *Stanford Technology Law Review* 473

Perrigo B, 'Theresa May's Brexit Deal Was Crushed. What Happens Next?' *TIME* (16 January 2019) <http://time.com/5504210/theresa-may-brexit-deal-defeat> (accessed 31 January 2019)

Powell E and C Turner, '"Fortress Europe": International Exhaustion of Trademark Rights and the EC – The Retailer's Perspective' (2002) 30 *International Business Lawyer* 3

Psaroudakis G, 'In Search of the Trade Mark Functions: Keyword Advertising in European Law' (2012) 34 *European Intellectual Property Review* 33

Ramsey LP, 'Increasing First Amendment Scrutiny of Trademark Law' (2008) 61 *Southern Methodist University Law Review* 381

Rankin J, 'Brexit Transition Could Be Extended to 2022, Says Barnier' *The Guardian* (18 November 2018) <www.theguardian.com/politics/2018/nov/18/brexit-transition-could-be-extended-to-2022-says-barnier> (accessed 31 January 2019)

Rawson S, 'An Emerging Framework for Electronic Commerce: the E.U. Electronic Commerce Directive and Related Developments' (1999) 10 *International Company and Commercial Law Review* 171

Rennie MTM, 'Electronic Commerce: A Review of the European Commission's Proposed Directive' (1999) 5 *Computer and Telecommunications Law Review* 93

Riordan J, *The Liability of Internet Intermediaries* (Oxford University Press 2016)

—— 'Website Blocking Injunctions under United Kingdom and European Law' in GB Dinwoodie (ed), *Secondary Liability of Internet Service Providers* (Springer 2017)

Rogers WVH, *Winfield & Jolowicz on Tort* (18th edn, Sweet & Maxwell 2010)

Ross TP, *Intellectual Property: Damages and Remedies* (Law Journal Press 2005)

Rowland D, U Kohl and A Charlesworth, *Information Technology Law* (4th edn, Routledge 2012)

Roy A and A Marsoof, 'Blocking Injunctions and Collateral Damage' (2017) 39 *European Intellectual Property Review* 74

Rubenstrunk I, 'The Throw Down Over Takedowns: An Analysis of the *Lenz* Interpretation of 17 U.S.C. §512(F)' (2011) 10 *John Marshall Review of Intellectual Property Law* 792

Rue FL, *Report of the Special Rapporteur on the Promotion and Protection of the Right to Freedom of Opinion and Expression* A/HRC/17/27 (2011)

Ruston G, 'On the Origin of Trademarks' (1955) 45 *Trademark Reporter* 127

Ryan C, 'How Disintermediation Is Changing the Rules of Marketing, Sales and Distribution' (2000) 1 *Interactive Marketing* 368

Sales P, 'The Tort of Conspiracy and Civil Secondary Liability' (1990) 49 *Cambridge Law Journal* 491

Sams B, *Neowin's Facebook Page Taken Offline–We're Back! (Again)* (20 April 2011) <www.neowin.net/news/neowin039sfacebook-page-taken-offline-by-bogus-complaint> (accessed 31 December 2018)

Sanders AK and SM Maniatis 'A Consumer Trademark: Protection Based on Origin and Quality' (1993) 11 *European Intellectual Property Review* 406

Sappideen C and P Vines, *Fleming's The Law of Torts* (10th edn, Lawbook Co 2011)

Saunders KM and G Berger-Walliser, 'The Liability of Online Markets for Counterfeit Goods: A Comparative Analysis of Secondary Trademark Infringement in the United States and Europe' (2011) 32 *Northwestern Journal of International Law and Business* 37

Savola P, 'Proportionality of Website Blocking: Internet Connectivity Providers as Copyright Enforcers' (2014) 36 *Journal of Intellectual Property, Information Technology and Electronic Commerce Law* 116

Schechter FI, 'Rational Basis of Trademark Protection' (1927) 40 *Harvard Law Review* 813

Schmidt-Pfitzner JH, 'Article 16–Rights Conferred' in P-T Stoll, J Busche and K Arend (eds), *WTO—Trade-Related Aspects of Intellectual Property Rights* (Martinus Nijhoff 2009)

Segura-Serrano A, 'Internet Regulation and the Role of International Law' in A von Bogdandy and R Wolfrum (eds), *Max Plank Yearbook of United Nations Law, Volume 10* (Koninklijke Brill NV 2006)

Seltzer W, 'Free Speech Unmoored in Copyright's Safe Harbor: Chilling Effects of the DMCA on the First Amendment' (2010) 24 *Harvard Journal of Law & Technology* 171

Senate Report No 105-190 on the Digital Millennium Copyright Act, 105th Congress, 2nd Session (1998)

Senftleben M, 'Overprotection and Protection Overlaps in Intellectual Property Law – The Need for Horizontal Fair Use Defences' in A Kurr and V Mizaras (eds), *The Structure of Intellectual Property Law: Can One Size Fit All?* (Edward Elgar 2011)

Servian M, 'Help! Someone's Squatting on My Brand—Cybersquatting' (2013) 19 *Computer and Telecommunications Law Review* 92

Shanahan D, 'The Trademark Right: Consumer Protection or Monopoly?' (1982) 72 *Trademark Reporter* 233

Shaw D and S Gunnarson, 'Web Hosting Industry Vulnerable to Federal Trademark Liability' (2011) 18 *Westlaw Journal* 3

Smith GHJ, *Internet Law and Regulation* (4th edn, Sweet & Maxwell 2007)

Smithers R, 'Surge in Purchases of Counterfeit Goods', *The Guardian* (2 October 2013) <www.theguardian.com/money/2013/oct/02/counterfeit-goods-surge-uk> (accessed 31 January 2019)

Song SH, *New Challenges of Chinese Copyright Law in the Digital Age: A Comparative Copyright Analysis of ISP Liability, Fair Use and Sports Telecasts* (Kluwer Law International 2011)

Stuart M, 'The Function of Trade Marks and the Free Movement of Goods in the European Economic Community' (1976) 7 *International Review of Intellectual Property and Competition Law (IIC)* 27

Sutter G, 'Online Intermediaries' in C Reed and J Angel (eds), *Computer Law: The Law and Regulation of Information Technology* (6th edn, Oxford University Press 2007)

Takach GS, *Computer Law* (2nd edn, Irwin Law Inc 2003)

Tan A, 'Google AdWords: Trademark Infringer or Trademark Liberalizer?' (2010) 16 *Michigan Telecommunications and Technology Law Review* 273

Taubman A, H Wager and J Watal (eds), *A Handbook on WTO TRIPS Agreement* (Cambridge University Press 2012)

Trimble M, 'Extraterritorial Intellectual Property Enforcement in the European Union' (2011) 18 *Southwestern Journal of International Law* 101

Trimmer B, 'An Increasingly Uneasy Relationship – The English Courts and the European Court of Justice in Trade Mark Disputes' (2008) 30 *European Intellectual Property Review* 87

UNCTAD-ICTSD, *Resource Book on TRIPS and Development* (Cambridge University Press 2005)

Urban JM, J Karaganis and BL Schofield, *Notice and Takedown in Everyday Practice* (BerkeleyLaw/American Assembly 2016)

Urban JM and L Quilter, 'Efficient Process or "Chilling Effects"? Takedown Notices under Section 512 of the Digital Millennium Copyright Act' (2006) 22 *Santa Clara Computer and High-Technology Law Journal* 621

Vander S, 'Article 42–Fair and Equitable Procedures' in P-T Stoll, J Busche and K Arend (eds), *WTO—Trade-Related Aspects of Intellectual Property Rights* (Martinus Nijhoff 2009)

Verbiest T, G Spindler, GM Riccio and A Ven der Perre, *Study on the Liability of Internet Intermediaries* Markt/2006/09/E (2007)

Virgo G, 'Making Sense of Accessorial Liability' (2006) 6 *Archbold News* 6

—— 'The Criminal Law Is Not an Island' (2015) 6 *Archbold Review* 6

Watts J, 'Brexit Deal: Theresa May's Cabinet Approves EU Withdrawal Agreement' *The Independent* (14 November 2018) <www.independent.co.uk/news/uk/politics/brexit-deal-agreed-may-cabinet-uk-eu-withdrawal-negotiation-dup-parliament-support-a8634201.html> (accessed 31 January 2019)

Weatherall K, *Submission to the Joint Standing Committee on Treaties Inquiry into the Anti-Counterfeiting Trade Agreement*, Submission No 3 TT (21 November 2011)

Weckström K, 'Liability for Trademark Infringement for Internet Service Providers' (2012) 16 *Marquette Intellectual Property Law Review* 1

Weinrib EJ, *Corrective Justice* (Oxford University Press 2012)

Williams G, 'The Aims of the Law of Tort' (1951) 4 *Current Legal Problems* 137

—— *Joint Torts and Contributory Negligence* (Stevens & Sons Ltd 1951)

Wilson B, 'Notice, Takedown, and the Good Faith Standard: How to Protect Internet Users from Bad-Faith Removal of Web Content' (2009) 29 *Saint Louis University Public Law Review* 613

WIPO, *Intellectual Property Handbook: Policy, Law and Use* Publication No 489(E) (2008)

—— *Trademarks and the Internet* SCT/24/4 (2010)

—— *Press release of the Seventh Global Congress on Combating Counterfeiting and Piracy* PR/2013/736 (2013) <www.wipo.int/pressroom/en/articles/2013/article_0010.html> (accessed 31 January 2019)

Witting C, *Street on Torts* (14th edn, Oxford University Press 2015)

Wong HC, 'eBay's Liability for Counterfeits: A Transatlantic Comparison' (2010) 5 *Journal of Intellectual Property Law & Practice* 39

Wood D, 'Retribution, Crime Reduction and the Justification for Punishment' (2002) 22 *Oxford Journal of Legal Studies* 301

Index

Names of European Directives are filed under European Union.

'abet', accessory liability 66–67, 75
access to content 126; *see also* notice and takedown
Accessories and Abettors Act 66
accessory liability: actus reus 65–67; as a concept alien to trade mark law 47–53; assisting a tort 70–76; common law 52–63; criminal law 63–70; development of the law 77; hosts 112; joint tortfeasance 55–63; mens rea 65–66
actual knowledge 9–10, 81–83, 88, 90–91, 93, 100–101, 120. 122, 124–126, 129–130, 137, 140, 179–180, 183, 184; *see also* knowledge-based liability
Adam Opel v Autec 39, 40
advertising: commercial communication requirement 41–42; trade marks 13–14
Advocate General: injunctions against intermediaries 190, 192–193; liability under trade mark law 32–36
AdWords 27–29, 31–34
Ahmet Yildirim v Turkey 220–221
'aid', accessory liability 66–68, 74–75
Amazon: commercial communication requirement 44–45; *Cosmetic Warriors v Amazon* 44; as internet intermediary 4
Angelopoulos, Christina 18
anonymity, identifying wrongdoers 6
Anti-Counterfeiting Trade Agreement (ACTA) 47–48
Arsenal v Reed 31, 37–38, 159
Australia, injunctions against intermediaries 201–202, 210–212, 227–228, 230
'awareness', liability 122, 123–124, 137; *see also* knowledge-based liability
Belgium, legal action against hosts 91, 92
BMW v Deenik 161–162
Brein v Ziggo 110–111, 187–188, 191
Brexit 21–24, 46, 122, 177–178, 195–196, 197, 204
British Telecom: *BT v One in a Million* 35–36, 45; cybersquatting 34; injunctions 181; *Twentieth C Fox v BT* 179–181, 209, 213; *Cartier v BT* 195–196, 226–227
Brussels I Regulation (Recast) 229–230
BT v One in a Million 35–36, 45
bulletin boards, copyright cases 132–133
burden of proof 69, 74, 158–159
Business Action to Stop Counterfeiting and Piracy (BASCAP) 15

caching 81–82, 136–137, 140; *see also* system caching
Cartier v BT 195–196, 226–227
Cartier v Sky 5, 21, 177, 181–186, 190, 194–196, 206–208, 214–218, 220, 223–225, 227
Carty, Hazel 72, 74–76
CBS v Amstrad 58–59, 75
cheapest cost avoider 8–9; *see also* lowest cost avoider
Chile, injunctions against intermediaries 210–212
Chilling Effects database 143–146
circumvention 215–219, 229
CJEU: Brexit 22–24; commercial communication requirement 36–46; costs of implementation 223–224; course of trade ruling 36–42; European Union Info-Soc Directive 82; *Google v Louis Vuitton* 31–34; injunctions against intermediaries

185–188, 190–191, 193, 194, 221; navigation providers 109–110; neutrality and liability 125; 'use' on the internet 153–155
collateral damage, injunctions against intermediaries 219–223
commercial communication requirement: accessory liability 50–51; trade mark law 36–46
common design 20, 47, 55–63, 70–71, 74–75
common law: accessory liability 52–63; statutory duty 118–119; tort 52–53
communication: commercial communication requirement 36–46; navigation providers 109–110; trade marks 12–13
Communications Decency Act 134
compensation 7
competition, third-party use of trade marks 155, 161
constructive knowledge 98, 103, 116, 122–124; *see also* knowledge-based liability
contributory infringement: hosts 98–102; *Inwood v Ives* 96–98; Lanham Act 50–51, 95; law reforms proposal 116–117; liability 94–96; United States 50–51, 94–102, 115, 117, 118
control: as a basis for liability 116; direct control and monitoring rule 97–98, 117–118; hosts 112; internet intermediaries 8, 9–10; injunctions against intermediaries 185, 197, 199, 222
copyright: blocking regimes 210–212, 227–228, 230; Digital Millennium Copyright Act 131–138; European Union Directive on Copyright in the Digital Single Market 9, 175; injunctions against intermediaries 178–181; navigation providers 109–111
Copyright Designs and Patents Act (CDPA) 179, 184, 207–209
Cosmetic Warriors v Amazon 44
costs: counterfeit trademark goods 15–16; injunctions against intermediaries 223–227
'counsel', accessory liability 63–67
67
counterfeit trademark goods: contributory infringement 100–102; internet as a source of 14–17; notice and takedown 157–158
counter-notices 146, 156, 170–172, 174–175
Credit Lyonnais v ECGD 57, 58–59
criminal law: accessory liability 63–70, 71–72, 74; actus reus and mens rea elements 65–66
cybermarks 10–11
cyber-security 5–6
cybersquatting 34–36

Davies, Paul S. 70–72, 75–77, 124
defamation, search engines 107–109, 111
deterrence, criminal law 74
Dietrich, Joachim 70, 73–74
digital context *see* internet; online content
Digital Millennium Copyright Act: abuse of 139–146; counter-notices and restoration 170–172; injunctions against intermediaries 228; misrepresentations 172–173; notice and takedown 131, 135–138; safe harbour 131–135, 149–150; similarities with European Union E-Commerce Directive 135–136
direct control and monitoring rule 97–98, 117–118
directories, as internet intermediaries 3–4; *see also* navigation providers
'disable access' 81–82, 126, 137; *see also* notice and takedown
disintermediation 2
Disney v M1 211, 219
DNS blocking 223
domain names: blocking websites 217–219; contributory trade mark infringement 97–98; cybersquatting 34–35
double identity 157–160
Dramatico v Sky 181, 207–209, 213
duty, on hosts 118–119, 129–130

eBay: Belgium 91, 92; commercial communication requirement 43, 44–45; France 85–88, 92; as internet intermediary 2, 4; legitimate resellers 163–164; *Tiffany v eBay* 100–101; 'use' on the internet 154

e-commerce *see* European Union E-Commerce Directive
EMI Records v Sky 181, 209, 224
EMI Records v UPC 188
enforcement *see* European Union Enforcement Directive
EU Intellectual Property Office (EUIPO) 15
Euromarket Designs Inc v Peters 154
European Court of Human Rights 109, 167, 220–221
European Union: Belgium 91; Brexit 21–24; counterfeit trademark goods 17; France 85–88; free speech 167; Germany 88–91; hosts 84–93; legal reforms 126–129, 169–175, 201–203, 213, 215, 227–230; *see also* law reforms proposal; key directives overview 78–84; legal context 20
European Union Directive on Copyright in the Digital Single Market 9, 175
European Union E-Commerce Directive: EU context 79; hosts 82, 84–85, 113–114; injunctions against intermediaries 184, 192, 195–196; legal reforms 126–130, 203; notice and takedown 135–136, 139–140, 149–150, 169–174; remuneration requirement 80–81; safe harbour provisions 20–21, 81, 82–84; search engines 80–81; similarities with Digital Millennium Copyright Act 135–136
European Union Enforcement Directive: costs of implementation 223–225; EU context 79; injunctions against intermediaries 176–177, 183–184, 190–193, 194, 199–200, 210; monetary relief 104; legal reforms 201–203, 212–213, 215, 227–228; proportionality principle 219–220; safeguards against abuse 212–213
European Union Info-Soc Directive: injunctions against intermediaries 176–177, 180, 183, 188, 191, 210; proportionality principle 219–220; safeguards against abuse 212–213
European Union Technical Standards Directive 79–80
European Union Trade Marks Directive: accessory liability 48–49; commercial communication requirement 42–46; double identity 159–160; EU context 79; fair use of descriptive terms 161; international comparison 78; keyword advertising 32, 36; legal reforms 126–129; use requirement 26–27, 33–36, 38
exhaustion doctrine 162–165
expressive use of trade marks 168

fair use, notice and takedown 148
fair use of descriptive terms 161
fault-based liability 106
Fonovisa v CAI 96–98
Football Association v Sky 181, 209, 213–214, 224
France, legal action against hosts 85–88, 92
free speech: collateral damage 219–220; notice and takedown 138–150, 165–169

gateways, internet intermediaries 8
Gatley on Libel and Slander 80
Germany, legal action against hosts 88–91, 92
good faith takedowns 173–174
Google: commercial communication requirement 37, 40–42, 45, contributory infringement 101–102; defamation 107–109; European Union E-Commerce Directive 83; as internet intermediary 4; keyword advertising 27–29, 31–34, 36; notice and takedown 143–146; right of expression 221
Google v Louis Vuitton: commercial communication requirement 40–42, 44–45; double identity 159; keyword advertising 36; liability 19, 31–34; 'use' on the internet 153
Gucci v Hall 98–99

Hague Convention on Foreign Judgments in Civil and Commercial Matters 229–230
Hard Rock v CSI 96–98
health and safety, counterfeit trademark goods 17
Hölterhoff v Freiesleben 38, 40
hosts: cases in the EU 84–93; cases in the United States 98–102; European Union E-Commerce Directive 82, 84–85, 113–114; injunctions against 198–200; as internet intermediaries

2, 3; law reforms proposal 112–120, 121–122, 125–126, 128; notice and takedown 136–138; safe harbour provisions 82–84, 113–115; trade mark infringements 84–85, 112; types of 112, 113
hyperlinks: copyright 109–111; defamation 108–119

immunity, notice and takedown 150
individual infringers, and internet intermediaries 4–10
information, trade marks 12–13
information location tools *see* navigation providers
Info-Soc Directive *see* European Union Info-Soc Directive
infringement *see* trade mark infringements
injunctions against intermediaries: circumvention 215–219, 229; collateral damage 219–223; copyright context 178–181; costs of implementation 223–227; EU level reforms 201–203; future of 227–230; hosts as infringers 199–200; hosts as intermediaries 198–199; legal basis 21, 176–178; natural justice 204–213; practical considerations 204; safeguards 212–215; trade mark context 181–198
injunctive relief 10, 104–105, 198–199, 224
intellectual property rights: accessory liability 47–48; Digital Millennium Copyright Act 134; injunctions against intermediaries 205–206, 210, 228; joint tortfeasance 58–59; *see also* trade mark protection; Trade-Related Aspects of Intellectual Property Rights (TRIPS)
intention, contributory infringement 95
intermediaries *see* internet intermediaries
international comparison: commonalities 103; EU directives overview 78–84; hosts, summary of legal position 92–93; injunctions against intermediaries 201–202, 210–212, 227–228, 230; law reforms proposal 117–118; *see also individually named countries*
international exhaustion 163
International Trademark Association (INTA) 15
internet: definitions 1; greater need for trade mark protection 10–14; impact on contemporary world 1; source of counterfeits 14–17; *see also* online content
Internet Corporation for Assigned Names and Numbers (ICANN) 34
internet intermediaries: accessory liability 52–53; class of intermediaries 105–106; commercial communication requirement 42–46; definitions 2–4; focus on as opposed to individual infringers 4–10; *Inwood v Ives* 96–98; law reforms proposal 121–122; liability 9, 10, 18–20; safe harbour provisions 82–83, 84
internet pests 8
Internet Service Providers (ISPs): circumvention 216, 217–218; contributory infringement 98–100, 102–103; costs of implementation 223–226; injunctions 21, 178, 180, 184–190, 194–195, 201–202, 228–229; as internet intermediaries 2; legal reforms proposal 106–107, 116; neutral and passive intermediaries 93; notice and takedown 136, 139–146; safe harbour provisions 84
Inwood v Ives 94–98, 100, 102, 115–116
IP addresses, blocking websites 217–219, 223

joint tortfeasance 55–63, 70–76
jurisdictions 6–7

keyword advertising 27–33, 36
knowledge-based liability: accessory liability 50–51, 63, 75; actual knowledge 9–10, 81–83, 88, 90–91, 93, 100–101, 120. 122, 124–126, 129–130, 137, 140, 179–180, 183, 184; constructive knowledge 98, 103, 116, 122–124; *see also* red flag knowledge; hosts 112; injunctions against intermediaries 179–180, 184; internet intermediaries 9–10; law reforms proposal 123–126; objective test 123

Lancôme v eBay 91
Lanham Act: accessory liability 50–51; contributory trade mark infringement

50–51, 95; internet intermediaries 93–94, 102–103; *Tiffany v eBay* 100
law reforms proposal: class of intermediaries 105–106; compliance with EU law 126–129; cross-border enforcement 229–230; foreseeable consequences of 129–130; hosts 112–120; injunctions 201–203, 112–213, 215, 227–228; Internet Service Providers (ISPs) 106–107, 116; navigation providers 107–111, 116; notice and takedown 169–175; practical significance of 104–105; trade mark infringement 120–126
legal overview: Brexit 21–24; European Union 20, 78–84; injunctions against intermediaries 176–178; trade mark protection 19; United Kingdom 18–20; United States 20; *see also individually named acts and directives*
legality of content: knowledge-based liability 82–84, 122, 123; notice and takedown 147, 148, 150–151
legitimate resellers 162–164
liability under copyright law 146–150
liability under trade mark law 25; class of intermediaries 105–106; commercial communication requirement 36–46; international comparison 103; internet intermediaries 9, 10, 18–20; keyword advertising cases 27–42; use requirement 25–27, 31, 34; *see also* accessory liability
Liberty Study 138–140, 149–150
Lockheed v NSI 95–99, 115, 122
L'Oréal v eBay: accessory liability 49, 70; commercial communication requirement 43, 44–45; common design 20; injunctions against intermediaries 192–193; joint tortfeasance 59, 61, 62–63; law reforms proposal 125; legitimate resellers 164; safe harbour provisions 88, 92; 'use' on the internet 154
Louis Vuitton: commercial communication requirement 40–42; double identity 159; keyword advertising 36; liability 19, 31–34; right of expression 168; trade mark infringements 85–88, 92; 'use' on the internet 153
Louis Vuitton v Akanoc 99–100
Louis Vuitton v Toea 59–60, 61–62
Lowest cost avoider 4–5, 7; *see also* cheapest cost avoider
Lumen database 143–146
luxury brands, counterfeit trademark goods 16

metatags 42
MIS v Designtechnica 80, 83, 107–108, 126
misrepresentations, notice and takedown 172–173
mixed speech 168
monetary relief, practical significance of 104–105
Multatuli Study 138–139, 140–143, 149–150

natural justice 204–213
navigation providers: circumvention 216; contributory infringement 93, 102–103; copyright 109–111; defamation 107–109, 111; injunctions 196–198; as internet intermediaries 2, 3–4; law reforms proposal 107–111, 116; neutral and passive intermediaries 93; notice and takedown 136–138; safe harbour provisions 83; *see also* search engines
neutral intermediaries 92–93
neutrality, and liability 125
no-fault liability 10, 106
Norwich Pharmacal Co v Customs & Excise Commissioners 21, 182, 194, 225–226
notice and takedown 131; abuse of 138–150; academic commentaries 146–150; clear-cut cases 157–160; context-specific cases 156–157; costs of implementation 224; counter-notices 146, 156, 170–172, 174–175; free speech 138–150, 165–169; frivolous assertions 155–156; implications for the trade mark context 150–151; legitimate third-party uses of trade marks 152; practice of 135–138; restoration 170–172, 174–175; safe harbour provisions 131–135, 149–150; safeguards 169–175; trade mark bullying 160–169; 'use', contextual and complex nature 155; 'use' on the internet 152–155

objective test 123; *see also* knowledge-based liability, constructive knowledge
OCH-Ziff v OCH Capital 43–44
omissions 90
online content: injunctions against intermediaries 178–179; justification for notice and takedown 146–150; trade mark protection 10–14; unlawful content 1
online shopping malls 4
Organisation for Economic Co-operation and Development (OECD) 15
origin function, trade mark protection 12

parallel importation 163–165
passive intermediaries 92–93
Playboy v Frena 132–133
pornographic content 147–148
'procure', accessory liability 67
proportionality principle 219–220, 222, 224, 228

quality, online transactions 12
Quilter, Laura, Urban-Quilter Study 138–139, 143–147

R v Johnstone 38
reasonableness, contributory infringement 95
red flag knowledge 122–123; *see also* constructive knowledge; knowledge-based liability
reform *see* law reforms proposal
regional exhaustion 163
remuneration requirement, European Union E-Commerce Directive 80–81
responsibility theory 7–8
restoration, notice and takedown 170–172, 174–175
retribution, criminal law 74
right of expression 167–169, 221; *see also* free speech
Riordan, Jaani 3–4, 18–19, 115, 182, 222
Roadshow Films v iiNET 106–107
Roger Cleveland v Prince 99
Rosetta Stone v Google 94, 101–102
RTC v Netcom 132–133

safe harbour provisions: Belgium 91; EU legal position summary 92–93; European Union E-Commerce Directive 20–21, 81, 82–84; France 85–88; hosts 82–84, 113–115; law reforms proposal 122, 129–130; notice and takedown 131–135, 149–150
safeguards: injunctions against intermediaries 212–215; notice and takedown 169–175
Scarlet Extended v SABAM 221, 223
Sea Shepherd v Fish & Fish 56–58, 75, 77
search engines: commercial communication requirement 41–42; copyright 109–111; defamation 107–109, 111; European Union E-Commerce Directive 80–81; injunctions 196–198; as internet intermediaries 3–4; keyword advertising cases 27–32; law reforms proposal 107–111; safe harbour provisions 83; *see also* Google; navigation providers
Sega v Maphia 133
Senior Courts Act 18, 177–178, 181–184, 194–198, 200
Singapore, injunctions against intermediaries 201–202, 210–212, 230
Sky: *Cartier v Sky* 5, 21, 177, 181–186, 190, 194–196, 206–208, 214–218, 220, 223–225, 227; *EMI Records v Sky* 181, 209, 224; *Football Association v Sky* 181, 209, 213–214, 224
statutory duty, hosts 118–119, 129–130
subjective/objective test 123; *see also* knowledge-based liability
Svensson v Retriever Sverige 109–110
system caching 135–136, 140; *see also* caching

takedown *see* notice and takedown
Technical Standards Directive *see* European Union Technical Standards Directive
territorial nature of trade mark rights 152–155
third-party use of trade marks: accessory liability 47; notice and takedown 155, 160–164, 165–169; use requirement 32, 33, 39
Tiffany v eBay 100–101
tort: assisting a tort 70–76; common law 52–53; joint tortfeasance 55–63; statutory duty 118–119

trade mark bullying 160–169
trade mark infringements 18–21; Belgium 91; detection of 8; France 85–88; Germany 88–91; hosts 84–85, 112–114; individual infringers 4–10; injunctions against intermediaries 181–198; international comparison 103; internet intermediaries 4–10, 53; joint tortfeasance 59–62; keyword advertising 30–32; law reforms proposal 119–126; safeguards 169; United States 94–96; 'use' on the internet 153–155; *Wilson v Yahoo!* 30–31; *see also* liability under trade mark law
trade mark perspective 10–17
trade mark protection: accessory liability 47–53; commercial communication requirement 36–46; greater need for protection on the internet 10–14; implications of notice and takedown 150–151; keyword advertising 27–33, 36; legal context 19–20; use requirement 25–27
Trade Marks Act: accessory liability 49–51, 64–65, 67–69; injunctions against intermediaries 199–200; international comparison 103; law reforms proposal 113, 119–126; notice and takedown 170
Trade Marks Directive *see* European Union Trade Marks Directive
Trade-Related Aspects of Intellectual Property Rights (TRIPS): accessory liability 47–49; free speech 166; injunctions against intermediaries 205–206; international comparison 78; notice and takedown 158, 160–161; use requirement 25–26
Turkish Telecommunications Directorate (TTD) 221
Twentieth C Fox v BT 179–181, 209, 213

Uniform Domain Name Dispute Resolution Policy (UDRP) 34
United Kingdom: injunctions against intermediaries 177, 179–181, 195–196, 197; legal context 18–20; *see also* Brexit
United States: cases overview 93–98; contributory infringement 94–102, 115, 117, 118; Digital Millennium Copyright Act 1998 131–135; hosts 98–102, 115; ISPs and navigation providers 102–103; keyword advertising 28–29; legal context 20
UPC Telekabel v Constantin Film 186–188, 190–191
Urban, Jenifer, Urban-Quilter Study 138–139, 143–147
URLs, blocking websites 217–219
'use': contextual and complex nature 155; on the internet 152–155; requirement in trade mark law 25–27, 31, 34, 36–42

Vertical Leisure v Poleplus 63

Weatherall, Kimberlee 8, 47–48
web-hosts: circumvention 215–216; as internet intermediaries 3; law reforms proposal 121–122; liability 114–115
website blocking 217–219, 222, 223; *see also* notice and takedown
website operators: liability 115; 'use' on the internet 154–155; *see also* injunctions against intermediaries
Wilson v Yahoo! 30–31, 46
Withdrawal Agreement, Brexit 22, 24
World Intellectual Property Organization (WIPO) 15, 17, 88
World Trade Organization (WTO) 14–15

YouTube: as internet intermediary 2; notice and takedown 146–147, 148–149

For Product Safety Concerns and Information please contact our EU
representative GPSR@taylorandfrancis.com
Taylor & Francis Verlag GmbH, Kaufingerstraße 24, 80331 München, Germany

www.ingramcontent.com/pod-product-compliance
Lightning Source LLC
LaVergne TN
LVHW011122300926
849160LV00008B/483
* 9 7 8 1 0 3 2 2 4 0 9 9 2 *